STRATEGIC
WARNING
INTELLIGENCE

STRATEGIC WARNING INTELLIGENCE

HISTORY, CHALLENGES, AND PROSPECTS

John A. Gentry
and Joseph S. Gordon

Georgetown University Press / Washington, DC

The publisher is not responsible for third-party websites or their content. URL links were active at time of publication.

Library of Congress Cataloging-in-Publication Data

Names: Gentry, John A., 1949- author. | Gordon, Joseph S., author.
Title: Strategic warning intelligence : history, challenges, and prospects /
    John A. Gentry and Joseph S. Gordon.
Description: Washington, DC : Georgetown University Press, 2019. | Includes
    bibliographical references and index.
Identifiers: LCCN 2018018860 (print) | LCCN 2018033681 (ebook) | ISBN 9781626166554 (pbk.
    : alk. paper) | ISBN 9781626166547 (hardcover : alk. paper) | ISBN
    9781626166561 (ebook)
Subjects: LCSH: Intelligence service. | Intelligence service--United States.
    | Military intelligence. | Military intelligence--United States.
Classification: LCC JF1525.I6 (ebook) | LCC JF1525.I6 G46 2019 (print) | DDC
    327.12—dc23
LC record available at https://lccn.loc.gov/2018018860

20 19   9 8 7 6 5 4 3 2   First printing

Cover design by N. Putens.
Cover image by iStockphoto/Getty Images.

To the memory of John Joseph Bird (1937–2017),
a fine man and a fine strategic warning intelligence officer.

Contents

Preface

The genesis of this book was the authors' collaboration in designing and teaching the National Intelligence University's Strategic Warning Analysis Certificate Program. Joe Gordon founded and still teaches with the program. John Gentry was part of the instructional team in 2013–15. As part of course development processes, we discussed desirable readings and lamented that, while Cynthia Grabo's *Handbook of Warning Intelligence* had attained the status of a classic in the intelligence literature, it was completed in 1971 and largely discussed the challenges of warning against Soviet bloc military threats. It therefore was dated. We discussed the possibility of a joint project to write a successor book. In the spring of 2016, after Gentry left NIU, we decided to write a book designed to describe and evaluate the expanded scope of strategic warning intelligence, the global spread of the warning function, the growing history of strategic warning, and the nature and causes of the continued intellectual and institutional challenges of strategic warning, especially in the United States. This book is the result of that effort.

We wrote the book under a division of labor roughly as follows. Gentry initially researched and drafted most of the manuscript. Gordon regularly reviewed and suggested changes in the draft; he focused on specific areas of information gathering and analysis, particularly sections on denial and deception and the warning activities of the North Atlantic Treaty Organization, the Netherlands, and the United Kingdom. Gordon also was our primary continuing contact with people in the US government. In general, both of us discussed warning with people knowledgeable about aspects of strategic warning, although in a few cases each of us alone interviewed experts.

We gratefully recognize many people who contributed to our understanding of strategic warning and to this book. Gentry remembers with fondness and gratitude the insights about warning he received from the then national intelligence officer for warning John J. Bird while working on a warning-related project as a Central Intelligence Agency analyst in 1984–87 and then on Bird's staff in 1987–88. That experience greatly informed this project. Gordon recognizes Robert Kells, now retired from the Defense Intelligence Agency's warning staff, who helped Joe design NIU's Warning Certificate Program, tutoring on warning methodology and sharing an extensive bibliography. Many people helped this book project by providing insights directly, by recommending literature, and by reading portions or all of drafts of this book and a related article. We thank Richard K. Betts, John Bird, Major Christopher Browning (US Army), James Bruce, David Bush, Rory Cormac,

Erik Dahl, Philip H. J. Davies, Commander Rory Dolan (Royal Canadian Navy), Robert Dunfield, B. G. J. (Bob) de Graaff, Thomas Fingar, John C. Gannon, Susan Gentry, Roger George, Kenneth Gerhart, Jay Honigstock, Arthur Hulnick, Robert Jervis, Kenneth Knight, Kevin Logan, Mark Lowenthal, William A. Parquette, Randolph H. Pherson, John Saxe, John Tolson, Gregory F. Treverton, Robert Vickers, James Wirtz, Ronald Woodward, several persons who do not wish to be identified, and two anonymous reviewers.

We acknowledge the students and guest speakers in the courses of NIU's Strategic Warning Analysis Certificate Program and members of the Defense Warning Network of the US Department of Defense who shared with us many insights and informative anecdotes. These people helped prompt us to write this book, and their contributions to our thinking are significant, although we mention few of their names herein.

We are grateful to Georgetown University Press. Donald Jacobs had confidence in our project and helped us get early drafts of this book into decent shape. Kathryn Owens managed the book's production process skillfully. Don McKeon provided copyediting support. Andrew Buss proofread diligently. Virginia Bryant, Nikita D'souza, and Cherylann Pasha provided marketing support. And Jackie Beilhart worked publicity.

∞

Portions of chapters 4 and 11, especially, appear in slightly different ways in John A. Gentry and Joseph S. Gordon, "U.S. Strategic Warning Intelligence: History and Challenges," *International Journal of Intelligence and CounterIntelligence* 31, no. 1 (Spring 2018), pages 19–53, reprinted by permission of Taylor & Francis.

This book was reviewed by security officials of the Defense Intelligence Agency, who approved its public release without change. DIA requires the following disclaimer statement: "All statements of analysis or opinion are those of the authors and interviewees and do not reflect the official policy or position of the Department of Defense or any of its components, or the U.S. Government."

Abbreviations

ADWS	Australian Defence Warning System
AIVD	General Intelligence and Security Service (Netherlands)
AMAN	Agaf HaModi'in (Military Intelligence Directorate of the General Staff) (Israel)
ATb	Counterterrorism Alert System (Netherlands)
B&B	het systeem Bewaken en Beveiligen (Surveillance and Protection System) (Netherlands)
BBC	British Broadcasting Corporation
BND	Bundesnachrichtendienst (German Security Service)
CADTH	Canadian Agency for Drugs and Technologies in Health
CEO	chief executive officer
CEW	competitive early warning
CIA	Central Intelligence Agency
CIC	Cabinet Intelligence Council (Japan)
CIG	Current Intelligence Group (UK)
CIRO	Cabinet Research and Intelligence Office (Japan)
COW	Correlates of War
CT	counterterrorism
CTC	Counterterrorism Center
CTIIC	Cyber Threat Intelligence Integration Center
D&D	denial and deception
DARPA	Defense Advanced Research Projects Agency
DAWS	Defense Automated Warning System
DCI	Director of Cabinet Intelligence (Japan)
DCI	Director of Central Intelligence
DDAC	Denial and Deception Analysis Committee
DHS	Department of Homeland Security
DI	Defence Intelligence (UK)
DI	Directorate of Intelligence (of CIA)
DIA	Defense Intelligence Agency
DIO	Defence Intelligence Organisation (Australia)
DIS	Defence Intelligence Staff (UK)

DIWS	Defense Indications and Warning System
DoD	Department of Defense
DMI	Director of Military Intelligence (Israel)
DNI	Director of National Intelligence
DWN	Defense Warning Network
DWS	Defense Warning System
EAAWA	Every-Analyst-a-Warning-Analyst
EU	European Union
EUCOM	US European Command
FBI	Federal Bureau of Investigation
FCO	Foreign and Commonwealth Office (UK)
FDDC	Foreign Denial and Deception Committee
FUSAG	First US Army Group
GCHQ	Government Communications Headquarters (UK)
GRU	Glavnoye razvedyvatel'noye upravleniye (Main Intelligence Directorate of the General Staff) (USSR)
HPSCI	House Permanent Select Committee on Intelligence
HSAS	Homeland Security Advisory System
HUMINT	human intelligence
I&W	indications and warning
IAC	Intelligence Advisory Committee
IAF	Israeli Air Force
IARPA	Intelligence Advanced Research Projects Activity
IC	Intelligence Community
ICD	Intelligence Community Directive
IDF	Israel Defense Forces
IHL	international humanitarian law
IIF	Intelligence Indications File
IMF	International Monetary Fund
INR	Bureau of Intelligence and Research (Department of State)
INTCEN	Intelligence Analysis Centre (European Union)
JGWE	Joint Global Warning Enterprise
JIB	Joint Intelligence Bureau (UK)
JIC	Joint Intelligence Committee (UK)
JIIC	Joint Intelligence Indications Committee
JIO	Joint Intelligence Organisation (UK)
JIS	Joint Intelligence Staff (UK)
KGB	Komitet gosudarstvennoy bezopasnosti (Committee for State Security) (USSR)
KLA	Kosovo Liberation Army
MAD	mutual assured destruction
MI5	Security Service (UK)
MI6	Secret Intelligence Service (UK)

MIVD	Military Intelligence and Security Service (Netherlands)
MoD	Ministry of Defence (UK)
Mossad	HaMossad leModi'in uleTafkidim Meyuḥadim (Institute for Intelligence and Special Operations) (Israel)
NAC	North Atlantic Council
NATO	North Atlantic Treaty Organization
NCTV	National Coordinator for Security and Counterterrorism (Netherlands)
NGO	nongovernmental organization
NIC	National Indications Center
NIC	National Intelligence Council
NICC	National Infrastructure Coordination Center
NIE	national intelligence estimate
NIM	national intelligence manager
NIO	national intelligence officer
NIO/W	national intelligence officer for warning
NIPF	National Intelligence Priorities Framework
NIU	National Intelligence University
NKGB	People's Commissariat for State Security (USSR)
NIWS	NATO Intelligence Warning System
NSA	National Security Agency
NSC	National Security Council
NTAS	National Terrorism Advisory System
NWS	National Warning Staff
OB	order of battle
OCAM	Organe de coordination pour l'analyse de la menace (Threat Assessment Coordination Unit) (Belgium)
ODNI	Office of the Director of National Intelligence
OKW	Oberkommando der Wehrmacht (High Command of the Armed Forces) (Germany)
ONA	Office of Net Assessment
O/NE	Office of National Estimates
OSS	Office of Strategic Services
OTI	Office of Transnational Issues
PDB	*President's Daily Brief*
R2P	responsibility to protect
RAHS	Risk Assessment and Horizon Scanning (Singapore)
RSHA	Reichssicherheitshauptamt (Reich Security Administration) (Germany)
SAT	structured analytic technique
SAG	Strategic Assessment Group
SD	Sicherheitsdienst (Security Service) (Germany)
SID	Service Intelligence Directorate (UK)
SIGINT	signals intelligence

SNIE special national intelligence estimate
SSCI Senate Select Committee on Intelligence
SWS Strategic Warning Staff
UN United Nations
USGS United States Geological Survey
USIB United States Intelligence Board
USSR Union of Soviet Socialist Republics
WHO World Health Organization
WIMS Worldwide Indications and Warning System
WMD weapons of mass destruction

Introduction

Strategic warning—the process of alerting senior leaders to the emergence of important threats and opportunities that require a policy decision to deter, defend against, or exploit— is a critical intelligence function. It also is frequently misunderstood and unappreciated. The strategic warning function in the United States and elsewhere since World War II has achieved some successes but also many prominent failures. The function has experienced marked cycles in which appreciation was followed by disrespect and decline, then regeneration, largely owing to its perceived successes and failures and the extent to which fluctuating threat situations seemed to warrant national maintenance of a specialized warning intelligence function. Strategic warning in the United States as we write in 2018 is in one of its cyclical troughs.

The purpose of this book is to present a history of the development of the strategic warning function, outline the capabilities of important warning analytic methods, explain why strategic warning analysis is so hard, discuss the special challenges warning has in dealing with senior decision-makers, assess the state of warning generally in the world, evaluate why the United States in recent years largely abandoned strategic warning in favor of a focus on current intelligence, and recommend warning-related structural and procedural improvements in the US intelligence community (IC). By discussing strategic warning intelligence broadly, we aim to partly fill a significant gap in the intelligence studies literature and help strategic warning analysts everywhere. Throughout this book, unless otherwise stated, "warning" refers to strategic warning, not "tactical" warning, which refers generally to notification of an immediately impending military threat.

The Expanding Literature on Warning

This book builds on a modest but growing literature published mainly in the United States, the United Kingdom, and Israel. Warning has, of course, been an issue for soldiers for millennia, and the historical record contains many cases of military surprise attacks—and thus warning failures due to faulty intelligence or the absence of a warning function. But the rigorous study of strategic warning is a post–World War II phenomenon that largely reflects the failure of US military intelligence to warn of the Japanese attack on Pearl Harbor on December 7, 1941, and the surprise Egyptian and Syrian attack on Israel on

October 6, 1973.[1] As the literature expanded and warning failures recurred, scholars evaluated many other surprises, substantially improving understanding of warning processes and the many reasons why warning succeeds and fails.

The initial scholarly treatment of warning arguably was Roberta Wohlstetter's *Pearl Harbor: Warning and Decision*, published in 1962, which was based on reports of the several US government commissions that investigated the attack on Pearl Harbor and on thirty-nine volumes of congressional hearings.[2] While she focused on the single case of Pearl Harbor, Wohlstetter tried to understand broadly the phenomenon of surprise and the general mechanisms of warning intelligence for purposes of anticipating, and thereby preventing, other surprises, including what was in the 1960s a major concern in the United States—the possibility of a surprise Soviet / Warsaw Pact attack on Western Europe and an associated nuclear attack on the United States. In generalizing her understanding of the Pearl Harbor experience, Wohlstetter articulated what quickly became, and remains, the dominant theory of strategic warning.

Wohlstetter argued that fundamental intellectual challenges make effective warning difficult under the best of circumstances and that institutional dysfunctions of US intelligence in 1941 made the task still harder. She judged that in the Pearl Harbor case, and in many other instances, the information available to intelligence personnel usually includes accurate data about the course of future events but also large amounts of partial, irrelevant, misleading, and incorrect information even in the absence of adversaries' deception efforts. The critical task of warning analysts, therefore, is to identify and accurately distinguish the relatively few nuggets of information consistent with what would transpire later, which she called "signals," from the mass of irrelevant or misleading information in which the signals reside, which she called "noise." Because it often is not possible to determine until after the fact which data are in fact signals, misreading the evidence is easy. Such misinterpretations cause warning failures.

Wohlstetter explained why there are not, as US Senator Richard Shelby, then vice chairman of the US Senate Select Committee on Intelligence (SSCI), inaccurately and unhelpfully suggested in 2002 in the context of al-Qaeda's attacks of September 2001, informational "dots" that intelligence analysts "connect," like five-year-olds drawing lines between a few conveniently numbered dots, to derive accurate pictures of forthcoming events.[3] There always are large numbers of dots without helpful numbers, which warning analysts must fashion into accurate images of future events.

Critics of Wohlstetter's views, such as Eliot Cohen and John Gooch, inaccurately assert that because she suggested that warning failures are always to be expected, she presented a "no-fault" school of warning theory in which no one can ever be held accountable for warning failures.[4] Instead, they and Amy Zegart argue that bureaucratic and organizational cultural pathologies are largely responsible for intelligence failures.[5]

Wohlstetter's book does not in fact claim that no one is responsible for warning failures, and analysts who share her views about the difficulty of warning, such as Klaus Knorr and Richard Betts, argue that while warning will never be perfect, it can be improved and the purpose of studying warning performance and improving analytic skills is to boost the "batting average" of intelligence successes.[6] The analogy is that professional baseball players work hard to improve their hitting to help them reduce their strikeouts, hit more line drives, get more hits with runners in scoring position, or hit more home runs—not achieve batting perfection. One variant of this view emphasizes the difficulty of improving warning analysis, while another stresses ways that analysis can be improved but not perfected. Philip Tetlock calls these groups "skeptics" and "meliorists," respectively.[7] Arthur Honig calls the same groups, respectively, the "Orthodox" and "Revisionist" Schools of surprise theory.[8]

One of the goals of this book, consistent with the views of Betts and Knorr, is to help warning analysts improve their performance—to increase their "batting averages"—by helping them to get more warning messages "right" but not to excuse avoidable errors.[9] It is clear to us that while the challenges of strategic warning are daunting, many factors—including organizational structures, institutional processes and incentives, organizational cultures, and the personal traits of analysts—influence the performance of the strategic warning function. Intelligence agencies as organizations and individual intelligence officers can effectively address many of these factors—if they want to do so.

Another, smaller literature holds that warning analysis is not the problem at all. Better collection of information about emerging threats is needed. In this view, clear warning messages spring from excellent collection. David Kahn and Ariel Levite are proponents of this view.[10]

Erik Dahl adopts aspects of both views in focusing largely on tactical-level warning. He argues that successful warning of military attacks depends on two things: good collection of tactical information about an impending attack and receptivity by intelligence consumers—that is, by senior decision-makers who can effectively respond.[11] He says that "the critical factor is the collection of very precise intelligence that convinces and enables a decision maker to take the actions needed to prevent an attack."[12] He defines "*policy-maker receptivity*" as a combination of "*belief in the threat*" and "*trust in intelligence*" (emphasis in original).[13] We devote more attention than Dahl does to the issue of how decision-makers come to trust intelligence and what intelligence personnel can do to foster that trust. And we discuss warning challenges more complicated than identifying the details of conventional military or small-scale terrorist attacks.

In the 1970s and 1980s, an appreciable historical and theoretical literature developed on the nature of surprise military attacks. Prominent writers in this genre include Abraham Ben-Zvi, Richard Betts, Steve Chan, Michael Handel, Ephraim Kam, Klaus Knorr, and Ariel Levite.[14] These analysts note that surprise can come in many ways, including through different types of *behavior* of other actors, the *technical* means by which they act, and the *political* motivations that drive actors, which give meaning to prospective actions and potentially give warning analysts hints about the specifics of future events. This means that warning intelligence must also keep in mind intelligence-focused questions about activities of warning significance: who, what, when, where, and how. We suggest that asking "why" is also important to help understand the political context and motives for surprise attacks, thereby helping decision-makers to deter, defeat, avoid, or exploit them.

The surprise Egyptian and Syrian attack on Israel in 1973, commonly known as the Yom Kippur War, spawned a major extension of the literature on warning-related military surprises. Israeli intelligence failed to warn of this attack, generating much soul-searching in Israel and a major government investigation led by Shimon Agranat, then the chief justice of Israel's Supreme Court. Agranat's report and many other studies, mainly by Israeli analysts, focus on psychological, cognitive, leadership, and institutional aspects of Israel's failures that are also applicable to many other warning issues.[15]

The Egyptians devised an effective deception plan that helped the Israelis fool themselves.[16] The Egyptians borrowed ideas from the Soviet Union, which before World War II developed national-level doctrine for securing their secrets from enemies and for deceiving foes about their capabilities and plans, known as *maskirovka*.[17] Russia retains this doctrine, which is a latter-day version of Sun Tzu's ancient insight: know the enemy and know yourself, deny your enemy that ability, and you will be victorious in battle.[18]

Egypt's successful use of deception in 1973 and the effective (mainly) British effort to deceive Germany about the location of what became the Normandy invasion of June 1944 helped spark a related field of study—"denial and deception" (D&D)—the hiding of relevant information (denial) and misleading adversaries and sometimes friends about the meaning of the information they received in ways designed to achieve an advantage (deception).[19] One way to do so is to exploit Wohlstetter's notion of signals and noise; successful deceivers often mask "signals" they cannot conceal by introducing carefully selected "noise" that victims mistake for signals or divert them from actual signals or both. Michael Handel and others have observed that because deception offers many advantages in achieving surprise attacks, it is a favored technique of materially weak actors; the strong tend instead to rely on mass of material power or technological prowess.[20] Hence, these authors implicitly argue, warning analysts should be especially alert for deception by materially weak actors or those who have embedded deception in national or military doctrines.

Barton Whaley's study of how Germany deceived the Soviet Union about the meaning of the millions of soldiers near its western border who invaded the USSR on June 22, 1941, is a classic in the field.[21] Whaley noted of deception, "The ultimate goal of stratagem is to make the enemy quite certain, very decisive, and wrong."[22] That is, it is to fool the enemy's warning analysts and the decision-makers they support. Virtually all intelligence services and armies know that deception is an important part of military planning and many design deception campaigns to mislead warning analysts.

Recognizing this fact, the IC in 1983 created a center to study D&D, which now resides organizationally in the Office of the Director of National Intelligence's (ODNI's) Foreign Denial and Deception Committee (FDDC). The FDDC has published material useful for all analysts, but especially for warning specialists, and there is a modest academic literature on techniques of counter-deception.[23] The Department of Defense (DoD) in the 1980s also sponsored unclassified studies on D&D, especially on Soviet deception operations.[24] Because warning and deception are intimately related, it is important for warning professionals to know D&D techniques and counter-deception methods. We consider the literature on strategic deception to contain valuable insights about the challenges of strategic warning analysis.[25]

Other writers examine aspects of warning analytical processes, including technical training, desirable types and levels of expertise, desirable mental characteristics, and the ways intelligence organizations and personnel build and maintain the trust of senior decision-makers. Among the most prominent is former Defense Intelligence Agency (DIA) analyst Cynthia Grabo. Beginning her intelligence career during World War II as a civilian intelligence analyst working for the US Army, Grabo transferred to the then new DIA in the 1960s and specialized in strategic warning. She worked on what was then the main concern of US warning analysts: a Warsaw Pact invasion of Western Europe. As a career warning specialist, Grabo saw many young analysts work briefly on warning issues, then move on to other assignments, and noticed how inexperience led to recurrent methodological errors, similar kinds of warning failures, and repeated learning of the same lessons by new, temporary warning analysts. After what she considered to be the weak performance of US intelligence in warning of the Warsaw Pact intervention in Czechoslovakia in August 1968, Grabo decided to record her experiences and insights in a book designed to help new warning analysts learn the specialty, which she wrote at home on her own time.[26] Upon its completion in 1971, DIA security officers classified the entire manuscript, preventing its publication. After much prodding in the late 1990s by Grabo after her retirement and others still working in the IC, DIA declassified the first part of the book, leading to its publication in 2004; DIA released a second tranche in 2010.[27] The complete book was published in 2015, some forty-four years after Grabo finished writing it and a year after she died.[28] Despite its overwhelming focus on large-scale military attacks, now but a small part of the spectrum of strategic warning issues, Grabo's book remains a classic treatment of how warning analysis was done and how parts of the warning function still should be done. It contains valuable lessons for a wide variety of contemporary warning challenges.

In recent years, the warning-related literature expanded considerably in scope and depth. Of substantial significance for this book, analysts applied lessons from psychology to the conduct of intelligence analysis and foreign policy decision-making, helping explain the cognitive limitations and biases of both intelligence analysts and the people they serve. Prominent contributors in this arena include intelligence officer Richards Heuer, political scientists Alexander George, Robert Jervis, and Rose McDermott, and psychologist Philip Tetlock.[29] Other academics who focus mainly on foreign policy decision-making, such as Janice Gross Stein, are less frequently cited in the intelligence literature but make useful observations about cognitive challenges to good decision-making, how misperceptions affect decision-making, and what intelligence professionals call producer-consumer relations.[30] This literature also discusses motivated biases—that is, purposeful ideological, political, or other agendas—which pose challenges for both warning analysis and persuasive intelligence communication with decision-makers.

We believe the literature on intelligence "politicization" is also relevant to strategic warning.[31] Intelligence analysts periodically have warped warning messages to suit perceived decision-maker wants and (less frequently) to try to influence policy decisions, just as they have slanted other forms of intelligence analysis. For example, historian Ernest May notes that French military intelligence in the late 1930s exaggerated German military strength to help the French army lobby for higher budgets, which damaged its warning capacity when Adolf Hitler decided to attack France in 1940.[32]

Evident warning failures prompted a large number of excellent case studies. Some of this literature covers American failures to warn of, for example, the Tet Offensive of 1968 and the overthrow of the shah of Iran in 1979.[33] Other case studies address surprises and warning failures in smaller conflicts involving other countries, revealing some similarities as well as differences across cases.[34] A more recent literature covers al-Qaeda's attacks of September 11, 2001, and counterterrorism (CT) and law enforcement warning problems, which differ appreciably from the challenges Grabo faced.[35] Assessments of failures that identify practices, institutional factors, and personality types both useful for, and damaging to, sound warning provide useful insights about the strategic warning function. Warning has also attracted some attention from analysts with postmodern perspectives.[36]

There also have been accusations of warning failures that have much less merit. We view some of the 9/11 literature, including the 9/11 Commission's report, as being politically motivated and biased.[37] This literature also contributed appreciably to popular and academic misunderstanding of intelligence in general. Examples include Senator Shelby's charge that the IC failed to "connect the dots," the mistaken conflation of strategic and tactical warning, and the idea that the attacks of September 2001 constituted a strategic warning failure.

While the literature is expanding and improving, gaps remain. An obvious characteristic of the literature is its extensive focus on historical warning failures—surprises inflicted on states by other states—most of which were military in nature. The literature correspondingly devotes little attention to identifying and explaining successes and theorizing about steps intelligence services can take to help improve their rates of warning success.[38] The primary reason, we think, is that while the consequences of warning failures are fairly easy to identify and failures generate political pressures to find causes and culprits, warning successes are harder to see, and their causes vary enormously. Moreover, there is less reason for intelligence agencies to study successful practices that seem to work as intended.[39] And discussion about warning of threats claims a far greater share of the literature than does analysis of alerts to policymakers about opportunities they might exploit.

A small literature argues that people with certain personality types are especially good at warning analysis and its chronic adversary—deception. Uri Bar-Joseph, Cynthia Grabo, and Philip Tetlock are among the few who address this issue, which we consider an important topic.[40] We see parallels in this literature to separate discussions of the nature, causes, and consequences of leadership problems in times of national crisis. Armies and businesses devote enormous resources to identifying and grooming future senior leaders, yet they recurrently make mistakes. Personality traits important in good leaders at junior levels often are inadequate or dysfunctional at senior levels, and how people act in crises chronically surprises themselves, their countries, and historians in both good and unfortunate ways.[41] The analogy in warning is that many good current intelligence and research analysts are not good warning analysts. This is a serious contemporary problem for many intelligence services because analysts of current intelligence issues now typically also have significant strategic warning responsibilities.

We address these and other issues, including the strategic warning intelligence–like activities of nongovernmental organizations (NGOs) and businesses. And because strategic warning is evolving in function and scope, we also cover warning by these new actors in new, and in some cases rapidly evolving, contexts.

Plan of the Book

This book primarily addresses the nature, performance, and challenges of the strategic warning function of national-level intelligence services—especially the US intelligence community—while also discussing the evolving nature of strategic warning. We mine history for lessons and identify generalizations that come close to being theories of warning intelligence but do not formally present and test theories. We also provide insights we believe are useful to practitioners and interesting to laypeople.[42]

The book builds on the intelligence literature by addressing warning intelligence as an institution, as a mental process, and as an intelligence sub-discipline. We summarize existing knowledge about processes, successes, and failures, and we describe and assess techniques designed to tackle warning problems directly as well as some methods that are tangentially related to warning intelligence. We use case studies, including postmortems of warning failures, to provide examples of the analytic points we make. We try to fill some of the gaps in the literature and, finally, assess the state of the strategic warning intelligence function.

The first chapter defines warning in detail and introduces concepts we discuss throughout the book. The rest of the book is organized into sections that reflect its subtitle: history, challenges, and prospects. The first part, chapters 2 through 4, discusses the operational and institutional *history* of major intelligence warning entities. A limited history of three major warning failures and one success and discussion of the structural forms that warning organizations frequently take illustrate points to be discussed in the rest of the book. The second section, chapters 5 through 11, discusses operational *challenges*, ways warning intelligence personnel have addressed them, and how warning processes are evolving. Finally, in chapter 12, we assess the current state of strategic warning in its traditional national intelligence service roles and reasons for the varying effectiveness of warning institutions globally. We then speculate about the *prospects* for strategic warning intelligence in coming years. We suggest institutional improvements to enhance the quality of warning intelligence support to national-level decision-making in the United States.

Chapter 2 contains four case studies. Three are warning failures: (1) the inability of Soviet intelligence to persuade Josef Stalin that Germany planned to invade the USSR in 1941, (2) the German failure to warn of Allied plans to invade Western Europe in Normandy in June 1944, and (3) Israel's failure to anticipate the Yom Kippur War. These military cases are especially instructive because we know a great deal about the thinking of both sides, including the deception plans of the attackers, and how the deceptions succeeded. They often for good reasons are cited as classic examples of recurrent patterns of warning-related practices and resultant intelligence performance. We refer to them throughout the book as we present our own ideas about warning intelligence and how to improve it.

The fourth case study discusses a nominal intelligence success: the US IC's prescient warning in October 1990 in a national intelligence estimate (NIE) about the impending collapse of Yugoslavia that did not change the policies of the administration of President George H. W. Bush. We focus on why the Bush administration chose not to act on an accurate warning message that senior leaders fully understood.

Chapter 3 introduces five generic types of warning organizations, thereby providing in essence a theory of warning structures. It describes their characteristics and explains why they matter, using the cases in chapter 2 as examples. These types reappear throughout the book.

In chapter 4, we turn to another form of history—a description and analysis of the ways that the United States, the United Kingdom, the Netherlands, and the North Atlantic Treaty Organization (NATO) have addressed warning problems. These ways reflect definitions and implicit theories of the strategic warning function as well as the influence of distinctive institutions and practices. We track the evolution of organizational missions and structures and show that some have featured more than one of the ideal types discussed in chapter 3.

Chapter 5 begins our discussion of the major methodological issues that challenge the warning function. We focus on issues that explicitly or implicitly influence many warning analytic methods, including the meaning of threat and opportunity, techniques for handling uncertainty, and how concepts of time affect warning in different ways. Issues discussed here recur in later chapters.

Chapter 6 introduces the "indications and warning" (I&W) method of threat warning analysis and assesses its strengths, limitations, and vulnerabilities. We also discuss two variants of the I&W method, showing its applicability to a broader range of warning-related issues by national intelligence services and the private sector.

In chapter 7, we discuss other analytic techniques useful for some kinds of warning problems. While intelligence services developed some of them, non-intelligence parts of governments, NGOs, businesses, and academics also produced important techniques. Methods and approaches that governments use include horizon scanning, "surveillance" and "reconnaissance" techniques, the Global Trends project of the US IC, strategic futures, and so-called anticipatory intelligence. We apply some social science methods to warning, including deterrence theory, prospect theory, political demography, political leadership profiles, and some statistical methods. Because businesses have special warning needs and institutions, we also discuss some of their approaches.

Many observers have noted that intelligence analysis must contend with a variety of cognitive and psychological issues. In chapter 8, we discuss aspects of this literature that pertain to warning analysis. We argue that certain personality types are especially good (and not) at warning analysis and present views of experienced practitioners on character traits that make good warning analysts.

Chapter 9 discusses warning done by actors outside of traditional warning organizations—states' intelligence services—including the non-security parts of national governments. We also discuss nontraditional warning issues such as biological threats and diseases, earthquakes, and tsunamis.

A large literature discusses the challenges of intelligence officers in dealing with senior intelligence consumers. In chapter 10, we address issues especially important for warning and identify steps intelligence officers can take to improve such relationships.

In chapter 11, we focus on the warning function's institutional challenges, including structures, organizational cultures, and the incentive systems they create. We conclude that these are very important, are dysfunctional in the US case, and continue to damage the warning function in the United States.

In chapter 12, we reflect on the history of strategic warning intelligence, assess the efficacy of the warning function, evaluate the current state of warning intelligence in the United States, and speculate about the future of warning. We explain why we believe the warning function in the United States is likely to continue to struggle, and we recommend institutional changes for the US IC that can help mitigate some of the analytic problems that have contributed regularly to warning failures.

Notes

1. Grabo, "Watch Committee."
2. Wohlstetter, *Pearl Harbor*.
3. Gladwell, "Connecting the Dots," 84–85.
4. Cohen and Gooch, *Military Misfortunes*, 41. For a strong critique, see Betts, *Enemies of Intelligence*, 27, 185–86.
5. Zegart, "September 11 and Adaptation Failure"; Zegart, *Spying Blind*.
6. Knorr, "Failures in National Intelligence Estimates," 460; Betts, "Analysis, War, and Decision," 85; Betts, *Enemies of Intelligence*; Gentry, "Assessing Intelligence Performance"; Marrin, "Evaluating Quality of Intelligence Analysis," 902–4.
7. Tetlock, *Expert Political Judgment*, 19.
8. Honig, "New Direction," 699–716.
9. Robert Jervis makes a similar point. See Jervis, "Reports, Politics, and Intelligence Failures," 12.
10. Kahn, "Intelligence Failure at Pearl Harbor"; Levite, *Intelligence and Strategic Surprise*.
11. Dahl, *Intelligence and Surprise Attack*, 3–4.
12. Ibid., 4.
13. Ibid., 23.
14. Ben-Zvi, "Hindsight and Foresight," 381–95; Betts, *Surprise Attack*; Betts, "Surprise Despite Warning," 551–72; Chan, "Intelligence of Stupidity," 171–80; Handel, "Intelligence and Problem of Strategic Surprise," 229–81; Kam, *Surprise Attack*; Levite, *Intelligence and Strategic Surprise*; Knorr and Morgan, *Strategic Military Surprise*.
15. For example, Bar-Joseph, *Watchman Fell Asleep*; Ben-Zvi, "Between Warning and Response," 227–42; Kahana, "Early Warning versus Concept," 81–104; Bar-Joseph, "Lessons Not Learned," 70–83.

16. Handel, *Perception, Deception and Surprise*, 11. For Egyptian accounts, see Sadat, *In Search of Identity*; Badri, Magdoub, and Zohdy, *Ramadan War, 1973*; Asher, *Egyptian Strategy*, 91–92. See also Bell, "Toward a Theory of Deception," 244–79.

17. Heuer, "Soviet Organization and Doctrine," 42–47; Latimer, *Deception in War*, 239–67; Ziegler, "Intelligence Assessments," 1–24.

18. Sun Tzu, *Art of War*, ch. 13.

19. For example, Hesketh, *Fortitude*; Masterman, *Double-Cross System*; Daniel and Herbig, *Strategic Military Deception*; Holt, *Deceivers*.

20. Handel, "Intelligence and Deception," 122–54.

21. Whaley, *Codeword Barbarossa*.

22. Whaley, *Stratagem*, 135.

23. Director of Central Intelligence, "Directive 3/16P"; Whaley, *Textbook of Political-Military Counterdeception*; Whaley, *Turnabout and Deception*; Spielmann, "Strengthening Intelligence Threat Analysis," 19–43; Spielmann, "Using Enhanced Analytic Techniques," 132–55.

24. Daniel and Herbig, *Strategic Military Deception*.

25. Godson and Wirtz, "Strategic Denial and Deception," 424–37; Heuer, "Strategic Deception and Counterdeception," 294–327.

26. Grabo with Goldman, *Handbook of Warning Intelligence*, xiii.

27. The first tranche of declassified material was published as Grabo, *Anticipating Surprise: Analysis for Strategic Warning*. A second release prompted publication of Cynthia Grabo, *Handbook of Warning Intelligence: Assessing the Threat to National Security*, which included the material in *Anticipating Surprise*.

28. Grabo with Goldman, *Handbook of Warning Intelligence*.

29. Heuer, *Psychology of Intelligence Analysis*; Jervis, "Hypotheses on Misperception," 454–79; Tetlock and Gardner, *Superforecasting*; Bar-Joseph and McDermott, *Intelligence Success and Failure*.

30. Stein, *Psychology and Deterrence*; Festinger, *Theory of Cognitive Dissonance*; Janis, *Victims of Groupthink*; Jervis, *Perception and Misperception*; Janis and Mann, *Decision Making*; Kahneman, *Judgment under Uncertainty*.

31. Rovner, *Fixing the Facts*.

32. May, *Strange Victory*, 138, 144–45, 205.

33. Wirtz, *Tet Offensive*; Jervis, *Why Intelligence Fails*.

34. For example, Hopple, "Intelligence and Warning," 339–61; Hoffman, "Anticipation, Disaster, and Victory," 960–79.

35. National Commission on Terrorist Attacks upon the United States, *Final Report*.

36. Cavelty and Mauer, "Postmodern Intelligence," 123–44.

37. For a devastating critique of the 9/11 Commission's report, see Pillar, "Good Literature and Bad History," 1022–44. See also Eiran, "Three Tensions," 598–618.

38. Examples include Bar-Joseph and McDermott, *Intelligence Success and Failure*; and Easter, "Soviet Intelligence and the 1957 Syrian Crisis."

39. The US IC, primarily the Central Intelligence Agency, studies its successes to some extent. To our knowledge, all such studies remain classified. No intelligence agency, to our knowledge, analyzes the failings of its own leaders.

40. Bar-Joseph, *Watchman Fell Asleep*; Grabo, *Handbook of Warning Intelligence*; Tetlock and Gardner, *Superforecasting*.

41. Cohen, *Supreme Command*.

42. Marrin, "Preventing Intelligence Failures," 655–72.

CHAPTER 1

Concepts of Strategic Warning Intelligence

States and intelligence services typically believe that strategic warning—traditionally defined as the process of alerting national leaders to the emergence of grave dangers and convincing them that unpleasant and costly measures may need to be taken in response—is the premier task of intelligence.[1] Israeli officials long saw strategic warning—and the time to mobilize military reservists that warning provides—as key to national survival. In the United States, determination to avoid another warning failure like the Japanese attack on Pearl Harbor in 1941 led to the creation of the Central Intelligence Agency (CIA) in 1947. Intelligence, US law states, can provide no greater service than warning of impending threats to national security.[2] Jack Davis, a longtime CIA analyst, defined strategic warning: "Warning analysis seeks to prevent or limit damage to US national security interests via communication of timely, convincing, and decision-enhancing intelligence assessments that assist policy officials to effect defensive and preemptive measures against future threats and to take action to defend against imminent threats."[3]

As time passed, however, the concept of strategic warning broadened significantly to include concerns about other kinds of threats as well as opportunities to advance national interests. The CIA in 1999 wrote, "Reduced to its simplest terms, intelligence is knowledge and foreknowledge of the world around us—the prelude to decisions and action by U.S. policymakers."[4] Davis similarly wrote, "The central mission of intelligence analysis is to warn US officials about dangers to national security interests and to alert them to perceived openings to advance US policy objectives."[5] The *National Intelligence Strategy of the United States of America* of 2009 said that a core responsibility of intelligence is to "anticipate developments of strategic concern & identify opportunities as well as vulnerabilities for decision-makers."[6] Richard Betts and Thomas Fingar similarly argue that intelligence should help policymakers know as much as possible about both threats and opportunities.[7]

These thoughts in combination yield what we consider to be the primary purpose of strategic warning intelligence: *communication to senior national decision-makers of the potential for, or actually impending, events of major significance to national interests* and *recommendations that leaders consider making policy decisions and/or taking actions to address the situations*. This definition is purposefully vague about what constitutes "major significance" because definitions of national interest vary somewhat across time, by national leader, and for different countries in various situations. Warning intelligence in virtually all countries does not recommend or make specific policy decisions, however. This important point is worth repeating: the warning recommendation is that senior leaders make decisions of their own choosing.

Strategic warning is distinct from tactical warning in that it supports national-level decision-making by senior political and military leaders, not the useful but different purpose of supporting lower-level officials or alerting troops in the field to the likelihood of immediate attacks by hostile forces. Like most intelligence professionals, we do not consider the IC's failure to prevent the attacks of September 11, 2001, which killed many people but did not pose an existential (and thereby strategic) threat to the United States, to be a strategic warning failure.[8] The IC warned repeatedly and persuasively that an al-Qaeda attack on the United States was imminent, but it did not identify specific attack-related activities and plans and therefore was unable to thwart them.[9] The success of the 9/11 attacks therefore represented a tactical US warning failure. We consequently do not discuss the 9/11 attacks in detail in this book. We also do not examine the case because it has been covered extensively elsewhere.[10] And while a nuclear strike would have strategic significance, we do not focus herein on technical means of collection that require little analysis to warn of events that have only two policy options: launch a retaliatory nuclear strike or not.

In contrast, the failure of Israeli intelligence in 1973 to warn of the Egyptian and Syrian attack that became known as the Yom Kippur War badly bloodied Israel's armed forces and appreciably changed the geopolitical situation in the Middle East as a whole. It therefore was both a strategic and a tactical warning failure.

Warning Is a Key Intelligence Analytic Function

Strategic warning is one of the four core functions of intelligence analysis, along with basic research (or strategic) intelligence, current intelligence, and estimative intelligence.[11] (In recent years some agencies have developed a "targeting analyst" discipline to support CT operations; we generally do not discuss this tactical form of intelligence analysis.[12]) These functions overlap, sometimes causing friction within analytic organizations. For example, intelligence in general has a *research* component because it needs to know what is happening in the world.[13] Warning analysts also need to conduct research to acquire the expertise usually required for successful warning. National *estimates*, which typically focus on comprehensive evaluation of a specific international situation, often to support an impending policy decision, also serve a strategic warning function if they alert policymakers to impending, significant threats or opportunities as part of their assessments.[14] *Current intelligence*, which examines the recent past and immediate future—typically measured in small numbers of days—sometimes has a tactical warning element, perhaps including notification that a threat strategic warning analysts long have forecast has finally arrived. This role encourages some intelligence professionals to mistakenly believe that current intelligence analysts also perform the strategic warning function—a point we contest in detail in later chapters. Indeed, we assert that, while current intelligence analysts sometimes provide tactical warning, they cannot give strategic warning.[15]

It is helpful to keep the functions in mind when considering how warning activities have been conducted over the years. Some of the most difficult times for strategic warning have occurred when its practitioners—analysts and managers of analysts—lost track of the differences between the functions, especially when intelligence managers pressured warning officers to write current intelligence articles in response to bureaucratic imperatives to "produce."

Strategic warning is the hardest of the four analytic functions for several reasons.[16] Warning is always about the fairly distant, uncertain future—not a feature of current intelligence. While warning often requires research and expertise, it cannot be simply research; it must assess potential implications. Unlike all other analytic functions, warning requires persuasive communication to key decision-makers, meaning relationships of mutual trust between intelligence producers and senior intelligence consumers are critical. And warning analysts, more than other analysts, face persistent, sometimes aggressive opponents (and sometimes friends) in other states who practice D&D. Deceivers must fool warners if their planned surprise attacks or other deceptive or manipulative activities are to succeed.[17] Warners and deceivers are thus locked chronically in a tightly interactive battle in which, as James Bruce says, "hiders" struggle to defeat "finders."[18] Barton Whaley, a prominent student of military deception, believes deceivers succeed in wartime in an overwhelming majority of deception attempts—an assessment that seems right to us.[19] Warning specialists, more than other analysts, therefore must know how to unmask and to counter deception activities.[20]

Warning Is Often Underappreciated

Despite the sometimes crucial importance of strategic warning, intelligence services do not always value the function. Senior intelligence consumers often ask intelligence to support them as they address important immediate problems, which frequently leads intelligence agencies to defer distant concerns to another day—when they become crises that demand senior leaders' reactive attention and therefore current intelligence coverage. Momentarily pacific international environments sometimes lead consumers, budget hawks, and rivals of a distinct strategic warning function within intelligence services to argue that warning is unnecessary or can be handled by line analytic units, the regional and functional analytic units that perform most intelligence analyses, as part of their normal jobs. Warning's bureaucratic successes are diminished by policymakers' occasional practice of taking credit for warning successes and blaming intelligence personnel for policy failures, and some policymakers tire of warning analysts who only convey bad news in the form of threat warnings. In addition, because the history of strategic warning intelligence contains many failures as well as some important successes, warning does not have a reputation it can rely on for bureaucratic support. These perspectives, often in combination, have led to recurrent fluctuations in the priority that strategic warning receives within intelligence services and sometimes prompted the demise of formal warning structures in the American and British intelligence communities.

Scope of the Strategic Warning Function

The strategic warning function as it developed in the United Kingdom and United States in the immediate post–World War II period focused mainly on interstate military threats—force-on-force conventional and nuclear attacks. Gradually the scope of events deemed threatening expanded, and some intelligence entities came to see alerting policymakers of opportunities to exploit as an important warning function, although many military people, especially, continued to hold the traditional view, leading to divergent definitions of strategic warning. Terrorism-related warning concerns became more pronounced after 9/11, shifting notions of strategic warning toward what once was tactical warning. And because increasing numbers of actors, including businesses and NGOs, see needs to warn about an expanding variety of situations, warning-related activities now occur in arenas very different from the traditional national security parts of national governments.[21] We take the broader perspective on strategic warning in this book.

While strategic warning intelligence analysis includes aspects of all of the functions of intelligence analysis, it is distinctive in two important respects. First, strategic warning intelligence always is about *relatively* distant events—*normally* six months to two years in the future—whose outlines and courses are uncertain but whose implications might be significant. The time horizon for tactical warning is much shorter, typically days or even hours, meaning strategic warning covers events that occur in time periods far beyond the time horizons of both current intelligence reporting and analysis and tactical warning. The time horizons of national estimates often are longer.

Successful strategic warning analysts must identify trends of potential importance and bring them to the attention of decision-makers before the actual course of events is clear—sometimes even to the people who eventually will perform those acts. Warning analysts always, therefore, operate under conditions of fundamental uncertainty. They must alert decision-makers about approaching events in time for the decision-making and policy-implementation mechanisms of government to effectively address impending events before they happen.[22] Because of chronic uncertainties about the future and because the historical record indicates clearly that detailed predictions about the nature, magnitude, and timing of future events are usually wrong, experienced warning professionals rarely make specific predictions.[23] Instead, effective warning identifies worrisome trends or curious anomalies and makes conditional forecasts of future events designed to convince senior leaders to monitor these issues more closely or to encourage them to act incrementally despite substantial uncertainty about the actual trajectory of events. Strategic warning analysts therefore often monitor indicators of possible "low-probability, high-impact" events. Insightful understanding of likely or potential future trends, generated in large part by substantive expertise, enables analysts to generate credible foresight or what some call "foreknowledge."[24] Although intelligence typically tries to make its foresight, forecasts, and analyses as accurate as possible, the uncertainties of the warning function make dubious any claim of possession of "truth."[25]

This process helps improve decision-makers' *understanding* of evolving trends or patterns.[26] This understanding should be as accurate as possible—in this sense it reflects "truth" as it is best understood at any given time—reflecting analysts' insight and wisdom. We use the term "understanding" in the sense of Max Weber's concept of *verstehen*: broad appreciation of the nature and causes of events of significance in the world.[27] This understanding often generates the tacit knowledge, intuition, and associated confidence that help senior leaders to make risky decisions or take costly actions despite considerable uncertainty.

Second, warning analysts must communicate their warning messages *persuasively*. Unlike the other types of intelligence analyses that mainly seek to inform decision-makers who may or may not care about issues noted, warning intelligence aims to convince senior decision-makers to consider making decisions about an emerging trend or event that they might prefer not to make—one that may be costly to their country in terms of treasure and/or blood and to themselves personally in psychological or political terms.[28] Confirmed communication of the warning message from intelligence to decision-maker therefore is essential.

John J. Bird, national intelligence officer for warning (NIO/W) during 1984–88, repeatedly told one of the authors (Gentry) that three core component parts of warning build on each other: adequate collection, sound analysis, and persuasive communication to decision-makers about the significance of the warning message. While each is necessary, Bird maintained that persuasive communication is often the most difficult and the stage where the warning function falters.[29] One of Bird's successors as NIO/W, Mary McCarthy, later made the point similarly in print.[30]

A warning message is persuasive if it enables the receiver of the message to understand its meaning and significance in the context of clearly stated analytical uncertainties. Because it is not a warning officer's role to propose courses of action or try to convince a policymaker to make any specific decision in response to a warning message, persuasiveness does not imply any connection to specific decisions taken.

To warn persuasively, intelligence officers must establish relationships of trust with leaders that are sufficiently strong to give decision-makers confidence that the intelligence they receive is sound, helping them to decide to make sometimes intellectually and emotionally difficult decisions.[31] Trust, therefore, is a critical component of strategic warning. It is composed of several elements. Consumers must have confidence in the quality of warning messages and the people who prepare them. Discretion is an important aspect of this trust; consumers expect that intelligence personnel will not leak their concerns and deliberations to the press to derail policies intelligence people do not like.[32] Thomas Fingar adds that discreet analysts do not share privileged conversations with consumers—even with fellow intelligence people.[33] While mutual trust among intelligence producers and consumers is always good, the consequences of a lack of trust are more pernicious for warning than for the other functions.

Eventual Director of Central Intelligence (DCI) Robert Gates wrote in 1980 about the many reasons presidents were suspicious of CIA analysis—which applies to warning as well.[34] Gates emphasized the importance of trust, of the requirement for intelligence officers to "establish and maintain close personal ties to White House and [National Security Council] officials."[35] To do so, intelligence personnel must develop what Martin Petersen calls a "service mentality."[36] This can be hard to do. Bowman Miller, a career intelligence analyst at the State Department's Bureau of Intelligence and Research (INR), puts the point well:

> Trust is the coin of the realm in relations between intelligence producers and consumers. And trust from the policy and decision levels is always earned, not given. It is built upon a track record of timely, relevant, and useful insights that reward the consumer with advanced warning, informed probabilities about future outcomes, and keys to understanding more fully the problems and situations that decision makers confront. The holy grail for an intelligence agency or analyst is to have one's assessment help shape a decision—better yet is to "be in the room" when key policies and decisions are being debated and made.[37]

Put differently, intelligence officers must, if they are to perform well, deliver knowledge-related services to decision-makers with whom they have established personal relationships.[38] This means meeting "client" needs, including desires for help in identifying opportunities to advance national policies. Former chairman of the National Intelligence Council (NIC) Gregory Treverton also prefers "client" rather than the more commonly used terms "customer" or "consumer" because it conjures an image of equals with different expertise interacting rather than performing a "transaction."[39]

Use of the concept of "client" helps make intelligence more "relevant," even if it modestly increases risks of tainting the objectivity of analysis—a longtime US intelligence concern expressed most prominently by Sherman Kent.[40] Our reading of intelligence history is that politicization of this sort occurs infrequently, however. Politicization is much more likely to occur when intelligence officers try to cater to the perceived wants of policymakers or senior intelligence officers.

To illustrate some of the reasons why effective warning is so difficult, let us imagine ourselves to be national political leaders. We have a political philosophy and an associated program of governance we want to accomplish. We know we have a limited time in office to achieve our goals and to establish our legacies. We have constituencies we want to protect and to favor. We have survived the rough-and-tumble of electoral campaigns to reach high office. We are justifiably self-confident. We also have many sources of information and advice, including trusted advisors who are loyal members of our personal staffs and our personal interactions with world leaders. And then . . . we receive intelligence from nameless, faceless bureaucrats from the intelligence services whom we suspect may secretly be loyal to the opposing major political party, who tell us we need to make decisions that may seriously disrupt our plans and ambitions. If their warnings are accurate, we need to act, but they are not absolutely certain of their judgments, and we are not sure we can trust them. So perhaps it is best to wait until the situation becomes clearer.

Warning Success and Failure Defined

This scenario and John Bird's insights establish our criteria for assessing the performance of strategic warning intelligence. We define warning *success* as the integrated process of (1) managing available collection assets well enough to obtain information adequate to make sound warning-related judgments, (2) assessing the information accurately in ways that may generate a specific prediction but more commonly enable analysis or forecasting of aspects of an emerging situation of concern or opportunity in ways that reduce decision-makers' uncertainty about the situation, and (3) persuasively communicating relevant information and judgments in a timely manner that enables decision-makers to understand the factual and judgmental components of the warning, to make informed decisions about whether to act or not, and to act effectively if they choose to act. Declining to act is also a policy decision. To reiterate an important point, persuasion does not go further. In the United States and most other countries, political cultures firmly prohibit intelligence officers from recommending policy options.

Many historical cases indicate that analysts reached accurate conclusions about the course of future events but did not persuade decision-makers to decide or to act, leading sometimes to "intelligence failures" caused by the refusal of policymakers to accept warning messages.[41] Former senior CIA manager John McLaughlin recalls that a colleague, confronted by charges of intelligence failure, reminded a former secretary of state that she had warned the secretary of an impending war, to which he responded, "You told me, but you didn't persuade me."[42] Similarly, Jimmy Carter administration officials ignored warnings that Nicaragua's President Anastasio Somoza DeBayle was in trouble, then after his overthrow blamed the IC for a lack of warning they clearly had received.[43]

Intelligence people are responsible for ensuring that decision-makers understand their warnings. To achieve this, warnings may have to overcome preconceptions or favorite hypotheses of decision-makers or of those whom policymakers rely on for decision support. Warners should persist until that understanding is reached but not beyond. At that point decision-makers who are, in the final analysis, their own most trusted "intelligence analysts" will decide what to do—or not do.[44] Understanding when full and accurate but not annoyingly repetitive communication is made and withdrawing from discussion in a timely and polite fashion when policy decisions are finalized are key attributes of effective intelligence professionals. The importance of such understanding is another reason why the presence of respect and mutual trust between warning intelligence officers and senior consumers is essential.

Because countries build intelligence services for different purposes and because intelligence agencies function in different political and bureaucratic situations, good warning analysts adjust their communication means and methods of persuasion to meet different consumer needs and desires. This means decision-makers inevitably influence techniques of effective warning, which in turn means that, for yet another reason, warning professionals must know their consumers well.[45]

Like many others, Bird also noted the importance of timeliness: "Warning that comes too late is not warning, it is entertainment."[46] A senior decision-maker who understands and heeds a timely warning message may use any national resource, including diplomatic and military assets, to deter, prevent, avoid, contain, or mitigate a threat; reduce national vulnerabilities; reduce the costs of defense against, or recovery from, threats; enable speedier recovery from an attack; or exploit an opportunity. But the choice of policy or implementing means and the effectiveness of policy actions do not determine the success of the warning intelligence process.

Forecasts of impending events of strategic significance need not be completely accurate so long as they generate timely and effective responses.[47] Hence, successful warning analysts frequently suggest to policymakers that events of concern may occur, specifying degrees of uncertainty in general terms, identifying adversary capacities to conduct threatening behavior, and enabling decision-makers to take partial or preliminary steps that can be amplified or canceled as more information or evolving analytic judgments merit.[48] Such conditional warnings may be successful if policymakers act in ways that discourage other actors from taking the actions they once intended.

Our concept of warning and of measures of warning performance is generally consistent with most definitions of warning, although we more strongly than most analysts emphasize the importance of opportunity analysis as an important component of warning and as a means to achieve the trust and access to decision-makers that help enable more persuasive threat warnings. Opportunity warning is also hard to do because it always requires detailed knowledge of one's own government as well as a foreign intelligence issue. Our definition requires intelligence officers to convey completely and accurately their best assessment of an emerging situation while recognizing that decision-makers, not intelligence people, are selected to make decisions and that many domestic political and international factors virtually always influence statesmen's decisions in addition to intelligence messages. A common misperception of intelligence professionals, sometimes arrogantly stated, is that warning fails if decision-makers do not act in ways directly consistent with their warning messages.[49]

Descriptions of apparent warning failures frequently fall into two general categories: (1) missing an actual threat, which generates the most attention and anxiety, and (2) warning of dire events that do not in fact occur. The first type of failure is usually obvious and may be associated with violence and death—as at Pearl Harbor. The second is a less noticed but more common failing that is costly in many ways, including unnecessary policy decision-making time and effort, unnecessary remedial action that may be financially or diplomatically costly, and damage to the credibility of the warning function. Loss of credibility seriously damages the warning function, although credibility costs sometimes are denigrated as a necessary price of vigilance.[50] Excessive or unwarranted threat warning often is called the "cry wolf syndrome" or, less commonly, the "Chicken Little syndrome."[51]

These types of errors have formal names in academic, especially statistical, usage. Failures to detect actual phenomena are "Type II" errors, or "false negatives."[52] "Type I" errors, or "false positives," identify phenomena that do not in fact exist. Accurate identification of Type I errors is often much harder than seeing Type II errors of the Pearl Harbor sort. The infamous 2002 NIE on Iraqi weapons of mass destruction (WMD), which mistakenly warned that Iraq's WMD programs were robust and threatening, was a false positive.[53]

But more so than for other forms of analysis, it is hard to assess the actual performance of strategic warning. Indeed, warning successes sometimes appear to be intelligence failures. For example, a national leader or leaders may fully understand a warning message but dither in making a policy response or make a dysfunctional policy choice, leading to an unfortunate policy outcome apparently caused by a warning failure.[54] The government agencies a national leader tasks to respond (typically defense and foreign ministries) may act slowly or inadequately, sometimes purposefully, leading to response failures.[55] Or decision-makers may reject sound warning messages because they have other concerns and agendas that lead them to make decisions inconsistent with the intelligence warnings. When senior statesmen do so consciously, they make appropriate decisions even if the policy outcome is suboptimal.

Even apparent failures of warning analysis often are not what they seem to be at first glance. Warning succeeds if it stimulates decision-makers to take remedial action that in turn indicates to some foreign entity that the action it contemplated is no longer viable or desirable and leads to abandonment of the warned-about activity. This kind of success, sometimes known as the "paradox of warning" or the "warning conundrum," or what Michael Handel calls "self-negating prophesy," is hard to identify but is the pinnacle of warning success even though it may generate recriminations about another apparent example of the cry wolf syndrome.[56] Historians (and intelligence services) sometimes identify such successful warning by conducting counterfactual analyses of events, leading them to be reasonably certain that the warning and associated actions led to changes in other actors' plans. For example, when a CIA asset, Polish Army Colonel Ryszard Kukliński, reported in December 1980 that the Soviets were preparing to use military force to thwart liberalization efforts under way in Poland, much like the Soviets had done in Hungary in 1956 and in Czechoslovakia in 1968, President Jimmy Carter warned the Soviets not to invade.[57] Later, President Ronald Reagan threatened Soviet leader Leonid Brezhnev with "the harshest possible economic sanctions" if the Soviets occupied Poland.[58] While we do not know for certain that the Soviets were deterred by Carter's warning and Reagan's more direct threat, there was no overt Soviet military intervention, and lack of Soviet action given their history in similar situations suggests a warning success. James Wirtz argues that even modest preventive steps can achieve such successes in the homeland security arena.[59]

Intelligence collection occasionally yields confirming evidence that warning-induced remedial action thwarted a planned attack or other action. For example, intercepts of German communications in November 1940 led British intelligence to warn the British Army to move antiaircraft units to defend the city of Wolverhampton against a planned German bombing raid, which the army did.[60] The raid did not occur, leading the army to complain about bad intelligence. Later, signals intelligence (SIGINT) indicated that German photo-reconnaissance aircraft discovered the increased air defenses, which led German air force commanders to cancel the raid.[61] Hence, British intelligence in this case produced a tactical-level warning success.

Another case of the "paradox of warning" *might* have happened in December 1941 if US intelligence had been better than it was. The commander of the Japanese naval force tasked with attacking Pearl Harbor was instructed to abort the mission if US forces discovered his ships before the strike commenced.[62] A US reconnaissance aircraft *might* have flown over part of the Japanese fleet, leading the Japanese to believe the Americans probably had mobilized and were fully prepared to defend themselves. The fleet therefore would have turned around, leaving American intelligence officers to wonder what a Japanese naval force was doing so far from home.

Warning analyses also influence policy decisions that indirectly affect national interests. For example, in 1967, American intelligence analysts accurately forecast the Arab-Israeli war and predicted that Israel would attack preemptively. The IC forecast that Israel would win the war quickly and advised senior American leaders to discount appeals for more military assistance by the Israeli government, which argued that Washington's failure to provide more aid would lead to a catastrophic Israeli defeat.[63] This assessment helped save needless expenditure of US military resources.

Opportunity warning sometimes is closely linked to threat warning. While encouraging leaders to act to address a threat, warning also can identify exploitable vulnerabilities in the actors that intended to surprise them.[64] Opportunity alerts are also useful to warning professionals as ways to help keep their consumers interested in seeing them; a steady flow of bad news, especially when coupled with chronically dire and frequently mistaken warnings of the cry wolf syndrome, wears out the welcome of warning analysts and desensitizes decision-makers to warning messages. The common rationale of practitioners for avoiding opportunity warning is that it allegedly crosses the line into policy advocacy. Former senior US policy official James Steinberg summarizes the problem:

> Policymakers look to the intelligence community to uncover facts that will help them achieve their goals. Contrary to the views of some critics, most policymakers do not resist bad news if it is reliable and timely, because they know they cannot succeed by sticking their heads in the sand and pretending that adverse developments will go away if they simply ignore or dismiss them. But often policymakers feel that the intelligence

community views its mission as solely being the bearer of bad news or "warning"—that is, telling the policy community about all the obstacles to achieving their objectives, rather than *identifying opportunities and how to make the best of the situation to achieve them* [emphasis added]. Yet for many analysts such a role is tantamount to "supporting" the policy and thus violates the most sacred canon of analytical objectivity and policy neutrality.[65]

We argue, like Steinberg, that such analyst views are mistaken and dysfunctional.[66]

Despite such widespread opposition to opportunity warning, the IC and other intelligence services provide it periodically. Mark Lowenthal offers an example of successful opportunity warning, evidently from a line analytic unit: intelligence support gave President George W. Bush insights that led him to negotiate in 2003 with Libyan leader Muammar el-Qaddafi the end of Libya's WMD programs.[67] In another case, US intelligence recognition that India and Pakistan were headed for war in 1990 led President George H. W. Bush to dispatch the then deputy national security advisor, Robert Gates, to help defuse the crisis.[68]

The history of warning intelligence therefore generates a continuum of different kinds of performance, not a dichotomous record of complete successes or total failures. Richard Betts similarly argues that warning failures rarely are total and that surprise attacks correspondingly are rarely complete.[69]

The historical record of the performance of warning intelligence also is fundamentally unbalanced. Failures to warn of threats that materialize are obvious and much studied, but successes either are not apparent owing to the "paradox of warning" or morph into policy successes that rarely or modestly credit intelligence. And missed-opportunity warning chances may be invisible. It is impossible to know how many chances for effective opportunity warnings were missed—or their significance. Moreover, because the mechanisms leading to warning successes of all sorts are harder to identify and generate much less scrutiny, even by intelligence services, the literature on warning intelligence successes is tiny compared to that on failures.

Strategic Warning Is about Mysteries, Not Puzzles

Strategic warning is about divining the meaning of important mysteries of international affairs. At least as far back as the 1980s, NIC chairman Fritz Ermarth observed that there are three components of intelligence: *secrets*, *puzzles*, and *mysteries*. Another chairman of the NIC, Joseph Nye, later popularized the characterization.[70] In Ermarth's scheme, spies try to steal *secrets*—not a warning analyst's job.

But many intelligence analysts, particularly specialized analysts such as imagery and counterterrorism analysts, try to solve *puzzles*, which are intelligence problems for which there are knowable, although often difficult to discern, answers. For example, it may be hard to figure the accuracy, defined quantitatively as the circular error probable, of a new missile system deployed by a potential adversary because the puzzle has many pieces missing and many other pieces are discolored or damaged, perhaps purposefully. It also is hard to track the movements of a terrorist planning an attack. Analysts may not be able to solve any given puzzle, but such puzzles can be solved. Tactical warning issues, we believe, generally concern puzzles. Strategic warning analysts sometimes also address puzzles.

The most difficult analytic challenges that chronically concern strategic warning analysts are *mysteries*, which are analytic questions for which there are not yet objective answers.[71] Relevant actors may not yet have been appointed or made key decisions. They need to work with bureaucratic and political actors who have not decided to help or oppose a policy or action. As Gregory Treverton notes, mysteries usually are about people and their actions, not physical things; they have no definitive answers, and forecasts about them are always contingent on later decisions by the actors.[72] Paul Pillar notes that mysteries are unknowable if decision-makers have not yet decided about a course of action or because relevant decision-making processes are "too complex to fathom."[73] Unforeseen events, including lack of adequate preparations or bad weather or cold feet by allies, can alter the timing or the realization of what once seemed to be firm plans. A modern term for the cause of this kind of situational uncertainty is "complex systems."[74] Treverton argues that the purpose of strategic warning analysis—especially the indications and warning analytic method discussed in chapter 6—is to identify ways to turn intractable mysteries into solvable puzzles.[75]

Mysteries have long concerned intelligence analysts, and the intelligence literature recounts how analysts addressed them: sometimes well, sometimes not. For example, a considerable literature describes how US analysts debated whether the Soviets would use force in Afghanistan in 1979.[76] The communist government in Kabul had been in considerable turmoil for two years or so previously, and the IC monitored Soviet troop movements, public rhetoric, and other data to try to figure whether, and if so how, Moscow would react to what was, from the Soviet perspective, a bad and deteriorating situation. An invasion might improve the political situation in Afghanistan but would appreciably damage East-West relations. Analysts debated extensively among themselves about whether Moscow would make a big military move to resolve the situation but did not reach consensus about what the Soviets would do. The IC therefore did not make a formal "call" that an invasion was likely before the actual invasion on December 24, 1979, even though it reported relevant events steadily in current intelligence publications and issued three "Alert Memorandums," the IC's warning art form of the time, regarding Afghanistan in 1979.[77] Hence, in many eyes, there was an appreciable warning failure.

Arguably there was a failure, but what kind was it? Was it a failure to collect *secret* Soviet plans? Or did analysts fail to solve a *puzzle* by misidentifying indicators of the impending use of force? We know now that senior Soviet leaders debated for months about what to do, and the communist party politburo decided to launch the invasion on December 12, 1979—less than two weeks before the invasion.[78] The IC's intelligence question for most of 1979 therefore was a *mystery* until the politburo made its final decision to intervene, at which point the political decision and associated military plans became secrets that might have been discovered and Soviet military preparations were a puzzle that might have been solved. Hence, to give their leaders warning of the invasion before early December, US intelligence analysts would have had to accurately forecast the outcome of apparently intense debates within the politburo, something that politburo members themselves may not have been able to do, and interpret Soviet military preparations, masked by deception operations, that were parts of contingency-planning processes subject to a final political decision.[79]

A definitive warning judgment had to go well beyond the reporting of ongoing major events and the modest levels of analysis normally contained in current intelligence publications to assess the collective state of mind of politburo members and their likely final decision(s). The analysts did not do so, and senior consumers understandably expressed surprise when the Soviets quickly put several divisions of troops into Afghanistan—a large expansion of their role in the country but a small part of Soviet armed forces as a whole and too small a force to pacify the country. Moreover, many analysts thought the Soviets would be foolish to invade with such a small force for exactly the reasons that eventually drove them out nearly a decade later. Douglas MacEachin, who participated in this work as director of the Strategic Warning Staff in 1979, later wrote that analysts among themselves assessed their failure with more colorful words than his sanitized "the analysts got it right, and it was the Soviets who got it wrong."[80] IC analysts thus relearned an enduring lesson: the leaders of major states often make mistakes, thereby failing to do what is best for their countries and for themselves.

Viewing things somewhat differently, Richard Betts, writing in 1998, divided warning challenges into two categories, which he defined as follows:

- *Factual-Technical* Warning. This is generally straightforward and scientific in character, and depends essentially on *collection* of information. The main problem is detecting what the intelligence target is doing.
- *Contingent-Political* Warning. This is more subjective, artful, and uncertain, and depends essentially on *analysis* of data. The main problem is figuring out where, why, and when a crisis of interest to the United States might occur.[81]

We suggest that Betts's contingent-political warning is similar to evaluating mysteries. Betts concluded that in the post–Cold War world,

> with many moderate and murky threats rather than one big and clear one . . . it will become harder to view as many warning objectives in terms of the Cuban missile crisis or [the Battle of] Midway [factual-technical] models. What were always the tougher challenges for warning, but could be considered secondary in wartime or the Cold War, are the contingent-political eruptions in all sorts of small countries. The simplest inferences from this are that the United States needs to cultivate more expertise on the new trouble spots, and to put more effort into human intelligence.[82]

Similarly, in 1964, Sherman Kent identified two kinds of what he called uncertainty: "things that are knowable but happen to be unknown to us, and . . . things which are not known to anyone at all."[83]

Identification of relevant background conditions, political cultures, key character traits of important personalities, and other variables can help analysts make educated if tentative judgments about mysteries. Policymakers crave informed intelligence assessments of this sort because they often involve issues of pressing importance. Such questions today might include: will the Chinese Communist Party be able to retain political control while liberalizing the economy in 2025? Or will North Korean leader Kim Jong-un actualize his threats to use nuclear weapons against his neighbors or the United States? Producing consistently accurate judgments about such mysteries is very hard, but it is the consistent goal of strategic warning analysis.

Notes

1. Betts, "Intelligence Warning," 26; Davis, "Watchman for All Seasons," 37; Patton, "Monitoring of War Indicators," 55; Davis, "Strategic Warning: Intelligence Support," 174; Hilsman, *Strategic Intelligence and National Decisions*, 46–51; Goodman and Berkowitz, "Intelligence without the Cold War."

2. For example, the 1992 Intelligence Authorization Act says, "The Intelligence Community's highest priority is warning of threats to US interests worldwide." See US Congress, House, Permanent Select Committee on Intelligence, Intelligence Authorization Act: Fiscal Year 1992, 102nd Cong., 1st Sess., 1991, H. Rep. 102–65, pt. I. See also Hilsman, "Intelligence and Policy-Making," 2.

3. Davis, "Strategic Warning: Intelligence Support," 179.

4. Central Intelligence Agency, *A Consumer's Guide to Intelligence* (Washington, DC: Office of Public Affairs, 1999), vii.

5. Davis, "Strategic Warning: If Surprise Is Inevitable," 3.

6. As cited in Lowenthal, "Strategic Early Warning?," 8. For many more references to intelligence-provided opportunities, see Director of National Intelligence, *The National Intelligence Strategy of the United States of America*, August 2009.

7. Betts, *Enemies of Intelligence*, 1; Fingar, "Intelligence and Grand Strategy," 124–25.

8. Marrin, "9/11 Terrorist Attacks," 182–202.

9. Byman, "Intelligence War on Terrorism," 842.

10. For example, National Commission on Terrorist Attacks upon the United States, *Final Report*.

11. Stack, "Competitive Intelligence," 197; Bodnar, *Warning Analysis for Information Age*; Hulnick, "The Intelligence Producer–Policy Consumer Linkage," 223–24.

12. Byman, "Intelligence War on Terrorism," 848–49.

13. Kent, *Strategic Intelligence*, xx, 8, 11–29, 39–65.

14. Ford, *Estimative Intelligence*, viii, 26, 44, 47.

15. Davis, "Strategic Warning: Intelligence Support," 179.

16. Mark Lowenthal concurs with the judgment that warning is the most difficult intelligence analytic task. Authors' discussion with Lowenthal, July 17, 2017.

17. Calhoun, "Musketeer's Cloak," 47–58; Handel, *Perception, Deception and Surprise*, 16.

18. Bruce, "Countering Denial and Deception," 19.

19. Whaley, *Stratagem*.

20. Bennett and Waltz, *Counterdeception Principles*; Bennett and Waltz, "Toward a Counterdeception Tradecraft," 77–86. For an example of such an analysis, see Grabo, "Soviet Deception in the Czechoslovak Crisis," 19–34.

21. Gentry, "Toward a Theory," 465–89.

22. Gentry, "Intelligence Failure Reframed," 247–70.

23. For a good summary of the role of prediction in intelligence, see Jensen, "Intelligence Failures," 267–70. See also Tetlock and Gardner, *Superforecasting*; Gazit, "Estimates and Fortune-Telling," 36–56; Jervis, "What's Wrong with Intelligence Process?," 28–41; and Pillar, "Predictive Intelligence," 25–35.

24. Fingar, *Reducing Uncertainty*; George and Bruce, "Intelligence Analysis," 2; Davis, "Strategic Warning: Intelligence Support," 178; Davis, "Paul Wolfowitz," 35–42.

25. Inlaid in the foyer of CIA headquarters are the biblical words "And ye shall know the truth, and the truth shall make you free." John 8:32, King James Version.

26. Treverton, *Intelligence for an Age of Terror*, 11, 54.

27. For a good intelligence-focused discussion of this concept, see Petersen, "What I Learned," 17–18. See also Handel, "Intelligence and Problem of Strategic Surprise," 250.

28. For a discussion of why decision-makers sometimes avoid making tough decisions, see Posner, "Thinking about Catastrophe," 7–19; and Belden, "Indications, Warning, and Crisis Options," 182.

29. Former chairman of the NIC Joseph S. Nye Jr. made the point similarly in "Peering into the Future," 91.

30. McCarthy, "Mission to Warn," 23.

31. For examples, McDermott and Bar-Joseph, "Pearl Harbor and Midway," 949–62; Priess, *President's Book of Secrets*, 42, 45, 62, 66, 74, 87, 193–94, 201, 225–26, 271, 281, 289.

32. Davis, "Policymaker's Perspective," 9, 11.

33. Fingar, *Reducing Uncertainty*, 43–44.

34. Gates, "Opportunity Unfulfilled," 17–26.

35. Ibid., 23.

36. Petersen, "What I Learned," 16–17.

37. Miller, "U.S. Strategic Intelligence Forecasting," 690.

38. Kerbel and Alcott, "Synthesizing with Clients," 11–27; Davis, "Strategic Warning: Intelligence Support," 174.

39. Treverton email communication to Gentry, June 23, 2017.

40. Kent, *Strategic Intelligence*.

41. Gentry, "Intelligence Failure Reframed."

42. McLaughlin, "Serving the National Policymaker," 91.

43. Hulnick, "Indications and Warning," 597.

44. Marrin, "Why Strategic Intelligence."

45. Petersen, "What I Learned," 13–16.

46. Gentry telephone discussion with John Bird, February 17, 2017.

47. Saffo, "Six Rules for Effective Forecasting," 122–31.

48. Davis, "Strategic Warning: Intelligence Support," 175.

49. For examples, see Pillar, "Intelligence, Policy," 15–27; and Miscik, "Intelligence and the Presidency," 57–64.

50. Donovan, "Escaping New Wilderness," 737; Lowenthal, *Intelligence*, 166.

51. The cry wolf syndrome appears frequently in the intelligence literature. The Chicken Little syndrome refers to false warnings that "the sky is falling" by fairy tale character Chicken Little. For discussions of the damage false alarms do to the warning function, see Vickers, "State of Warning Today," 10–11; Betts, *Surprise Attack*, 95–101; and Kam, *Surprise Attack*, 186–89.

52. For use of these concepts in an intelligence context, see Jones and Silberzahn, *Constructing Cassandra*, 34–35; Betts, "Fixing Intelligence," 57.

53. Chang and Tetlock, "Rethinking Training of Intelligence Analysts," 910.

54. Gentry, "Intelligence Failure Reframed," 254.

55. Ibid., 255.

56. Handel, *Perception, Deception and Surprise*, 55; George and Wirtz, "Warning in an Age of Uncertainty," 218–19; Marrin, "Evaluating the Quality of Intelligence Analysis," 898–900.

57. Weiser, *Secret Life*, 194–228, esp. 217.

58. Andrew, *For the President's Eyes Only*, 462. See also MacEachin, *U.S. Intelligence*, 2, 6, 48, 50, 61, 98, 134–35.

59. Wirtz, "Indications and Warning," 550–62.

60. Jones, *Wizard War*, 153.

61. Ibid.

62. Morgan, "Examples of Strategic Surprise," 53.

63. Grabo, "Watch Committee," 378–79.

64. Breakspear, "New Definition of Intelligence," 678–93.

65. Steinberg, "Policymaker's Perspective," 95. For similar views of Robert Blackwill, see Davis, "Policymaker's Perspective," 11. See also Miller, "U.S. Strategic Intelligence Forecasting," 688; Rice, "Rethinking the National Interest," 2.

66. For similar perspectives, see McLaughlin, "Serving the National Policymaker," 83–84, 88; Kringen, "Serving the Senior Military Consumer," 113; and Davis, "Kent-Kendall Debate," 100.

67. Lowenthal, *Intelligence*, 6th ed., 181.

68. Davis, "Strategic Warning: Intelligence Support," 180; Hersh, "On the Nuclear Edge."

69. Betts, *Enemies of Intelligence*, 19; Betts, *Surprise Attack*, 88–92.

70. Nye, "Peering into the Future." For another view, see Jones and Silberzahn, *Constructing Cassandra*, 29–30.

71. Ford, "US Government's Experience."

72. Treverton, *Intelligence for an Age of Terror*, 3, 18–19.

73. Pillar, *Intelligence and U.S. Foreign Policy*, 7.

74. Kerbel, "Thinking Straight," 27–35; Jervis, *System Effects*.

75. Authors' discussion with Gregory Treverton, April 6, 2017.

76. MacEachin, "Predicting the Soviet Invasion."

77. For a description of the Alert Memorandum, see Anonymous, "National Warning Intelligence," 13–15.

78. MacEachin, "Predicting the Soviet Invasion," 27.

79. Dailey and Parker, *Soviet Strategic Deception*.

80. Ibid., 30.

81. Betts, "Intelligence Warning," 26–35.

82. Ibid.

83. Kent, "Crucial Estimate Relived," 113.

CHAPTER 2

Four Classic Warning Cases

This chapter presents four case studies that illustrate many of the important aspects of strategic warning. The first three cases are failures to warn of major military attacks. The German invasion of the USSR in 1941 and the Normandy invasion of 1944 posed existential threats to the states that failed to accurately assess threats or accept warning messages. Israel's failure to anticipate the Yom Kippur War of 1973 shocked Israel and fundamentally altered the politics of the Middle East. In each case, the historical record presents fairly clearly the flaws of intelligence services and senior-level decision-making, as well as the deception campaigns of attackers who understood their adversaries' intelligence organizations and leaders and effectively exploited both groups' biases and vulnerabilities. Hence, we can track the motives and actions of the major belligerents' intelligence organizations in dynamic interaction, making these relatively complete as well as important cases. Barton Whaley believes the two World War II cases of strategic deception were the biggest in size and degree of comprehensiveness of some seventy cases of general wars between 1914 and 1968 that he studied.[1]

The fourth case, the US IC's warning in October 1990 that Yugoslavia was on the verge of collapse, was excellent strategic-level intelligence analysis that had no effect on policy. At first glance, this case presents a conundrum: conventional wisdom holds that sound intelligence analysis should improve policy decision-making. In this case, we know why President George H. W. Bush and his administration did not act in response to an unwelcome message. Because senior administration officials understood and accepted what intelligence told them, we count this case as a warning success. Because this was a political warning, and a nominal success, our analysis of its accomplishments, challenges, and problems is quite different than our discussion of the cases of military warning failures.

Together, these cases illustrate many of the challenges that confront warning specialists and the decision-makers they support, which we address in detail in later chapters. These include cognitive and motivated biases, problems of separating relevant signals from noise, the impact of intelligence structures on analysis and decision-making, and reasons why even accurate warning messages sometimes are not persuasive.

Plan Barbarossa, 1941

One of the costliest warning failures in history became apparent early in the morning of June 22, 1941, when some three million German and allied soldiers invaded the Soviet Union. It barely avoided total defeat, dismemberment, and the absorption of European Russia into a new German empire. Although it survived, much of the USSR was devastated, and some twenty-seven million Soviet citizens died in the war. Numerous accurate warning messages reached Soviet leader Josef Stalin, who chose, for all practical purposes, to ignore them even after strong evidence mounted in June 1941 of German Chancellor Adolf Hitler's hostile intentions, German attack plans, and German military preparations. Germany effectively deceived and confused Stalin, helping him to make bad decisions.[2] Hence, the Soviet army was surprised by, and largely unprepared for, the attack.

Hitler long had despised Soviet communism and saw, as he wrote in *Mein Kampf*, first published in 1925, the Eurasian land mass of the Soviet Union as possessing natural resources Germany needed to grow and thrive. Upon assuming power in 1933, Hitler abandoned many of the cooperative agreements Germany and Soviet Russia, then international pariah states, had reached in the 1920s. In August 1939, Hitler and Stalin nevertheless concluded another pact, known as the Molotov-Ribbentrop Accord after the foreign ministers who arranged it, which divided Poland between them, gave the Baltic states and Bessarabia to the USSR, and enabled Hitler to launch his invasion of Poland on September 1, 1939, without fear of Soviet opposition.[3] France and the United Kingdom declared war on Germany in response but did not fight much in 1939 as they frantically sought to rearm and to find a peaceful way to address Hitler's ambitions.[4] Germany ended the "Phony War" with decisive victories over Denmark, Norway, the Netherlands, Belgium, and France in the spring of 1940 and forced British armies on the Continent to retreat to their home islands, where new Prime Minister Winston Churchill vowed to fight on.

Despite the 1939 agreement to divide spoils of conquest and Soviet agreement to provide Germany with large volumes of foodstuffs and other raw materials, Soviet-German tensions remained high. Stalin understood the weakness of his armed forces, intelligence services, and diplomatic corps, which he decimated in purges in 1937–38 that killed thousands of senior military officers, diplomats, and intelligence operatives. Therefore, he hoped to avoid antagonizing Germany until the USSR could rebuild its military strength sufficiently to defend itself. Stalin told Soviet officials to meet the terms of contracts for commodity deliveries to Germany assiduously and ordered his soldiers to ignore German reconnaissance flights over Soviet territory in 1940 and 1941.[5] He worried that an annoyed Hitler might demand more deliveries of materials or better terms or make other demands on Moscow.

Meanwhile, German efforts to subdue Britain militarily foundered in setbacks during the aerial Battle of Britain in the summer and fall of 1940, wrecking plans for an invasion of the British Isles, which the Germans called Operation Sea Lion. Despite Germany's inability to defeat Britain or entice London to quit the war, Hitler on December 18, 1940, issued Directive No. 21, which ordered German armed forces to prepare to invade the Soviet Union in 1941 under Plan Barbarossa.[6] Despite the fact that he understood intelligence well, Hitler never, before issuing this directive, consulted German intelligence about prospects for success of the war he planned; he used intelligence only to provide tactical- and operational-level planning support for German military operations.[7] Only later did German economic analysts conclude that Hitler's plan to stop at the Urals, leaving a rump USSR in Siberia that he intended to control, could not destroy Soviet war-making capacities and that the Soviets would continue to fight even if Hitler achieved all of his initial territorial goals.[8] Such a realization in early 1941 might have led Hitler to alter his view of the attractiveness of war against the Soviet Union.

To assess lessons of this warning failure, three main issues must be addressed: (1) what did Soviet intelligence know of German plans to attack the Soviet Union, and what did it tell Stalin?; (2) why did Stalin not listen to his intelligence officers, analyze correctly, or act wisely?; and (3) how did German deception facilitate Soviet intelligence analytic and policy errors?

First, Soviet intelligence knew a lot about German war plans.[9] In the late 1930s, the foreign intelligence services of the USSR collected much relevant information. The military's Fourth Directorate, renamed in 1942 the Main Intelligence Directorate of the General Staff (GRU), and the foreign operations of the civilian People's Commissariat for State Security (NKGB), a predecessor of the better-known Committee for State Security (KGB), collected relevant material. The Soviets had spies in the Communist International (Comintern) and the communist parties in many countries, including in Germany until Hitler largely destroyed the German communist party, and in the United Kingdom, which dutifully reported intelligence information to Moscow. The GRU had a superbly placed agent in Tokyo, Richard Sorge, who provided excellent information acquired from his contacts in the German embassy there.[10] A joint GRU/NKGB network in several countries in Western Europe (what German intelligence called the Rote Kapelle, or Red Orchestra) and a military network based in Switzerland provided accurate information, much of it from anti-Nazi German military and civilian government officials.[11] The NKGB had sources in several parts of the British government, including the "Cambridge Five," who reported British assessments of German intentions and British policies toward Germany and the USSR.[12] The Soviets had a signals intelligence service, received reports from their embassies abroad, and got assessments and threat warnings from many countries, including neutral countries such as the United States, whose embassy in Berlin received much good intelligence information from anti-Nazi German officials.[13] Moreover, Soviet intelligence knew that weak German internal security enabled many anti-Nazi Germans to report aspects of Hitler's plans to the Soviets and to representatives of other governments that in turn warned Moscow.

The British government repeatedly warned Stalin about Hitler's intentions. In a letter dated June 25, 1940, for example, Prime Minister Churchill advised Stalin that Hitler's insatiable thirst for power threatened both the British and the Soviets.[14] Churchill's warning was based on his personal assessment of Hitler's character, not intelligence reports. Indeed, for months thereafter, the British Joint Intelligence Committee (JIC) doubted that Hitler intended to attack the USSR; because Soviet spies in the British government acquired JIC documents, Stalin saw Churchill's warnings as part of a plot to coax the Soviet Union into a war with Germany.[15] In 1941, however, British intelligence issued a series of increasingly specific warnings, many of which were based on sensitive intercepts of German communications known as Ultra, about German intentions and eventually came to agree with Churchill's assessment. The JIC formally warned the British government of the impending German attack on the Soviet Union on June 12, 1941—ten days before the attack.[16] This degree of foresight amounts to a strategic warning success. Ten days of preparations presumably would have significantly improved Soviet defenses, reducing the cost of the German attack, had Stalin then accepted the warnings he received.

Barton Whaley in 1973 documented eighty-four separate cases in which clear warning messages reached Stalin from a wide variety of sources, including those noted above.[17] In 1990, historian of intelligence Christopher Andrew and KGB defector Oleg Gordievsky argued that material that became publicly available after 1973 meant the real number of warnings was "over a hundred."[18] Stalin never accepted any of them. He also denied most of the relevant collection to senior Soviet military officers, including Marshal Georgy Zhukov, chief of the General Staff, who in any case were denied powers to raise alert postures of their forces without Stalin's explicit permission.[19] Although the somewhat more autonomous navy raised its alert status just before the invasion, the much more important army and its leaders were surprised by the German attack.

The Germans realized they could not keep secret the posting of several million men along the Soviet border from Finland to the Black Sea. They therefore devised a deception plan to entice Stalin to misinterpret German troop movements and to discredit and exploit the accurate information the Germans knew was leaking.[20] Whaley argues that there were four complementary German deception themes, some of which, like other German strategic deceptions, Hitler personally devised:

1. The German buildup in Eastern Europe was part of the preparations for the invasion of Britain, Operation Sea Lion. Deployments far from Britain kept troops safe from British bombers and reconnaissance aircraft. The German military high command (OKW) made sure the troops were not initially organized for attack, making them look like they were operating in a rear area. Propaganda Minister Joseph Goebbels contributed supporting materials to the press.
2. The buildup was designed to defend against a Soviet attack the Germans feared.
3. The troops were to invade the Balkans. The actual invasion of the Balkans by Italian and German troops in April and May 1941 supported the notion that other troops in the east had the same mission.

4. The buildup was to back an ultimatum to Moscow to redress unspecified griev-
   ances.[21]

The Germans conveyed deceptive messages in many ways, including rumors. Government-sponsored rumors included purposefully accurate accounts of German plans to attack the USSR as well as wholly inaccurate, sometimes fantastic reports such as the alleged signing in May 1941 of a Soviet-German military alliance.[22] The internal Security Service—the Sicherheitsdienst (SD)—produced many of the rumors. The large number of inaccurate rumors led many foreign observers to discredit accurate reporting from well-placed sources, including anti-Nazi German officials.

In aggregate, Germany generated three types of rumors: accurate information disguised as unverified rumor, disinformation, and informed speculation. The rumors therefore produced a lot of what Roberta Wohlstetter later called "noise," which Germany designed to hide "signals" of actual German plans that, as is often the case, became readily identifiable only after the invasion. Donald Daniel and Katherine Herbig call this kind of deception "ambiguity increasing," or "A-type" deception.[23]

Barton Whaley argues that a capable intelligence analyst in 1941 before the invasion and without the advantages of hindsight, who was aware of most of the intelligence information Whaley later assembled, could reasonably have identified five plausible hypotheses about Hitler's intentions:

1. *Unilateral war hypothesis*—Hitler intends to attack Russia, regardless of Russia's diplomatic or military anticipations.
2. *Ultimatum hypothesis*—Hitler intends to attack, *if* Russia does not meet conditions of a forthcoming ultimatum.
3. *Bluff hypothesis*—Hitler does not intend war, but will use military demonstration as a bluff to obtain further Soviet concessions.
4. *Contingency hypothesis*—Hitler does not intend war, merely protects [the eastern] frontier while pursuing Operation Sea Lion.
5. *Preventive war hypothesis*—Hitler, expecting a Soviet attack, intends to strike first.[24]

Stalin believed hypothesis 2. In fact, hypothesis 1 was correct. German deception operations partly explain why Stalin erred so badly. But he was not alone. Most knowledgeable analysts globally also misjudged Hitler; for example, the astute US ambassador to Moscow, Laurence Steinhardt, and reporters of the *New York Times* shared Stalin's view.[25] Indeed, the evidence widely available in early 1941 fit the ultimatum hypothesis fairly well, meaning Stalin's assessment was plausible. At least some of those who correctly forecast German actions, most prominently Churchill, based their analyses on their assessments of Hitler's character, built over years, not intelligence data directly focused on German invasion plans and preparations. Senior British diplomat Robert Vansittart, who shared Churchill's views, described the difference between the bureaucracies' view of Hitler and his own: "Prophesy is largely a matter of insight. I do not think the Service

Departments have enough. On the other hand they might say that I have too much. The answer is that I know the Germans better."[26]

Stalin had personal biases and fears that hindered an accurate assessment of Hitler's intentions, which the Germans noticed and built into their deception operations.[27] These amounted to what later theorists of intelligence would call his "mindset" and cognitive biases.[28] For example, Stalin believed in conspiracy theories and, according to Christopher Andrew and Oleg Gordievsky, was captivated by three: (1) a belief, based on his Marxist-Leninist upbringing, that emphasized the ineluctable conflict between capitalism and communism, that British warnings were designed to entice him into a war with Germany that would destroy Soviet socialism; (2) Hitler planned to deliver an ultimatum; and (3) German generals, "intoxicated" by their battlefield successes in 1939 and 1940, were determined to mount a provocation on their own.[29] Whaley believes the Germans may not have originally planned to spread the Hitler ultimatum rumor but did so when they perceived Stalin to be vulnerable to it.[30]

Stalin was handicapped by other emotional and institutional problems, most of which he created. He distrusted virtually everyone, including his own intelligence operatives, and the foreign intelligence services he decimated in the purges of 1937–38 had not recovered by 1941.[31] While he is widely viewed to have been paranoid, not all of his fears were irrational; Stalin had enemies, but his fears were excessive and his penchant for executing people for the smallest infractions and unfounded suspicions clearly was dysfunctional.[32] He distrusted his intelligence services' German sources, whose names and backgrounds he knew, and he often verbally abused and threatened intelligence officers and sources who reported information he did not like.[33] Just before war began, Stalin informed Pavel Mikhailovich Fitin, chief of the NKVD's foreign intelligence operations, that "there are no Germans who can be trusted, except Wilhelm Pieck"—who was a communist he liked; Fitin dutifully agreed.[34] Stalin was biased to disbelieve news that Germany might attack before the Soviets could rebuild their strength, which he believed would happen by 1943. Christopher Andrew and Vasili Mitrokhin argue that Stalin trusted Hitler more than Churchill and, like Whaley, believe the Germans were aware of Stalin's fears and exploited his suspicions of Churchill by planting information designed to enhance those suspicions.[35]

Stalin similarly did not trust anyone other than himself to analyze the information his collection agencies gathered.[36] Military intelligence had an analysis unit until 1932, when Stalin ordered it discontinued because he disdained its quarterly assessments of foreign events.[37] Thereafter, Stalin himself was the only national-level intelligence analyst in the Soviet Union. In July 1940, he chose Lieutenant General Filip Ivanovich Golikov to run the GRU for reasons of political reliability, not competence as an intelligence officer; Golikov was a combat soldier, not an intelligence professional, and he dutifully gave Stalin what he wanted to hear. Golikov later said he lied to Stalin because he feared the dictator's penchant for killing subordinates who were not totally compliant.[38] More generally, Stalin instituted a culture of sycophancy, paranoia, and political orthodoxy that led Soviet intelligence services to suppress important but unpleasant information and assessments, which crippled Soviet intelligence support to Stalin and all other Soviet leaders until the end of the USSR in 1991.[39]

Operation Overlord, 1944

In 1943, German intelligence and Hitler, who like Stalin was his own chief strategic intelligence analyst, faced a major warning challenge. The Western Allies long had promised to open a second front to relieve pressure on the USSR, and by 1943 it was clear that British, American, and Canadian military strength in the British Isles was growing. German intelligence and Hitler understood the importance of divining Allied plans for invading northwestern Europe and worked the issue extensively. German intelligence agencies included the Abwehr—the umbrella military collection-and-analysis organization for which army, navy, and air force intelligence organizations worked—and the Reich Security Administration (Reichssicherheitshauptamt, or RSHA), which eventually ran government police organizations including the Gestapo secret police organization and the Nazi Party's SD.[40] All had foreign intelligence responsibilities.

Key political and military leaders included Hitler, who as armed forces commander (in addition to his other positions) made most major military decisions, and senior generals including Field Marshal Wilhelm Keitel and Field Marshal Alfred Jodl of the OKW; Field Marshal Gerd von Rundstedt, commander in the West; and Field Marshal Erwin Rommel, commander of Army Group B, which consisted of the Fifteenth Army in northern France and Belgium and the Seventh Army in northwestern France, including Normandy. They were supported by military intelligence analytic organizations, including the strategic-level intelligence operation of the army called Fremde Heere West (Foreign Armies West), located at Zossen, just south of Berlin and headed by Colonel Alexis Freiherr von Rönne, and the intelligence arm of the OKW, headed by Colonel Friedrich-Adolph Krummacher.[41]

In late 1943, Germany's leaders knew a lot about intelligence matters. Rundstedt and Rommel were experienced troop commanders, and Hitler had used intelligence wisely on many previous occasions.[42] Hitler devoured the news his intelligence collection agencies brought to him, and several intelligence analytic organizations competed to give him assessments he liked.[43] German leaders understood the importance of surprise, had studied their enemies' past actions, and knew the Allies previously had successfully used deception against them in support of military operations, including the invasion of Sicily. They anticipated another Allied attempt at surprise. Said Admiral Karl Dönitz, the enemy was "endeavoring to conceal his real main object and to make full use of the element of surprise."[44] Hence, the intelligence mission was to work through Allied security and deception techniques to identify the Allies' actual plans and to alert senior commanders in time to prepare effective fixed defenses and to place units of the strategic reserve to enable them to rapidly defeat the initial Allied invasion force before it could consolidate positions on the Continent. It was a strategic warning problem given the size and importance of the invasion:

successful Allied opening of a second front would be devastating for Germany, while the loss of an invasion force crushed on the beaches would be a major blow to the Allies. The key intelligence questions were where, when, and in what strength would the invasion or invasions come?[45]

To figure Allied intentions, Germany used the full range of its intelligence collection means: human assets located in enemy countries and important neutral countries such as Portugal, Switzerland, and Sweden; SIGINT, including a naval SIGINT service that had broken and read encrypted Royal Navy communications since 1935; diplomatic collection at embassies abroad; aerial reconnaissance over the United Kingdom, especially southeastern England; liaison relationships with its allies Italy and Japan; monitoring of open sources including newspapers and British Broadcasting Corporation (BBC) broadcasts; and domestic collection, including interrogation of Resistance fighters captured in northern France, who the Germans knew were cooperating with Allied special operations forces.[46]

By the spring of 1944, German intelligence accurately assessed that Allied invasion preparations were nearly complete. Intelligence alerted senior leaders that the Allies could strike at any time and that there would be little warning of the actual launching of the invasion.[47] Order-of-battle (OB) estimates indicated a force in England large enough to make two landings, which the Germans expected to be, first, a diversionary attack to draw reserve German divisions away from the location of the main attack and then the major assault. German intelligence and Germany's leaders felt the invasion would be on the coast of northwestern Europe—France, Belgium, or the Netherlands—because that area would be easier to support logistically from the United Kingdom than more distant locations and because air forces based in southeastern England could support the offensive. But the Germans still were not sure exactly where or when the attack would occur.

The "where" question puzzled intelligence officers until Hitler decided that the Allies planned to attack Pas-de-Calais—the coastal region of northern France and Belgium near the city of Calais that is nearest to England. Hitler's Directive No. 51 of November 3, 1943, ordered the military to prepare defenses with that expectation in mind.[48] Hitler believed the force-generation advantages of a location close to England overwhelmed Allied concerns about strong German defenses there. He thought the Allies preferred to minimize the open-water distance their troops would have to travel. Aircraft flight times from southeastern England would be shorter than to other possible landing sites, station times correspondingly would be increased, and turnaround times would be shorter. Therefore, Allied air forces could deliver more ordnance on German targets. German generals thought similarly. Hence, senior political and military leaders conducted their own intelligence analyses and came to the same judgment, which intelligence officers came to share much later.

As the early months of 1944 passed, Hitler seemed to have estimated correctly. Germany's human agents in Britain and SIGINT identified a large new Allied formation—the First US Army Group, or FUSAG—in southeastern England, whose reported mission was to land at Pas-de-Calais as the primary Allied invasion force. A smaller force would depart first from ports in southern England for Normandy as a diversion. Aerial reconnaissance, newspaper reports, and radio broadcasts were consistent with SIGINT and clandestine human intelligence (HUMINT) collection. In addition, the Germans studied Allied reconnaissance activities and the patterns of their air attacks. The large volume of air attacks on targets in, and rail lines leading to, the Pas-de-Calais region confirmed what the Germans increasingly believed must surely be the main target; they did not believe the Allies would devote so much military power to a feint.[49] Moreover, Hitler reasoned, the German V-1 cruise missiles the British knew would soon be striking England would be fired from Pas-de-Calais, and they must want to stop those attacks. In May and early June 1944, intelligence officers began to agree with Hitler; the evidence from many apparently independent sources all pointed in that direction. Rönne declared soon after the Normandy landings started, on June 6, that he believed there would be a second invasion.[50]

The Germans were aware that even a diversionary attack could be dangerous, and immediately after the Allied landings Rundstedt ordered two infantry divisions of his strategic reserve to support the Seventh Army in Normandy. But Hitler refused Rundstedt's request to order a panzer division to Normandy and kept all of the Fifteenth Army and most of the strategic reserve focused on defending Pas-de-Calais against the impending main attack.

But there never was a second landing at Pas-de-Calais—or anywhere else. It was part of the Allied deception plan.[51] It was so effective that some Germans worried about the actually nonexistent FUSAG into the autumn of 1944 even after its notional commander, Lieutenant General George Patton, reportedly was "fired" in a bureaucratic squabble with his military superiors and was "demoted" to lead the US Third Army in Normandy. Given Hitler's wishes, the Germans only began to release divisions dedicated to the defense of Pas-de-Calais for use in Normandy in late July.[52] As their landing force grew in size, the Allies eventually broke out of the Normandy beachhead and moved toward Germany. The deception is widely thought to have given the Allies the extra margin of safety for the initial landing that helped secure the beachhead and ensure the success of the invasion, which eventually helped produce victory in the war.

Hence, a core question is, how could Germany's professional intelligence officers and its experienced political and military leaders have been fooled so completely? How did they fail to discern details of a deception they clearly anticipated?

Let us look first at German intelligence capabilities. German intelligence was at least moderately competent.[53] Hitler understood intelligence principles well and, as we have seen, earlier was imaginative in designing successful deceptions against the USSR.[54] Integration of German intelligence and operational planning was excellent in 1940, contributing prominently to the German conquests of France and Norway.[55] German intelligence had a range of collection assets and intelligence personnel who understood the importance of careful analysis of independent sources—that is, they understood principles of analytic "tradecraft." They knew the Allies had tried to deceive them in the past and recognized that these deception efforts sometimes had succeeded—as in Sicily. They identified elements of deception in Allied preparations for Normandy. For example, they correctly assessed some Allied radio communications as deceptive, and they did not fall for the Allies' ruse that the British Fourth Army based in Scotland (which was in fact wholly imaginary) was poised to attack Norway.[56] They also reasoned correctly that the Allies would enlist the support of Resistance fighters on the Continent and used SD assets to identify coded messages broadcast by the BBC that signaled the start of the invasion, but when German SIGINT units heard the messages and informed a local commander in Normandy just before the invasion, the commander declined to alert his troops.[57]

But in the end German intelligence, and the leaders it supported, made some fairly common analytic mistakes as well as errors reflecting Germany's unique leadership and institutional context. First among the problems was that Hitler, like Stalin, was his own chief intelligence analyst. Hitler made clear that he wanted intelligence reporting and assessments consistent with his beliefs, leading subordinates to give him what he wanted.[58] Unlike Stalin, who executed even slightly wayward subordinates, Hitler merely verbally abused or transferred them, but he made clear what he wanted and generally got it. He engaged in "mirror imaging"—imagining what he would do if he were in the Allies' position—and based his analytic judgments on those biases.[59] He paid close attention to the assignments of Allied generals *he* respected, believing the Allies surely must think similarly. In addition, Colonel von Rönne made an appreciable estimative error purposefully. He knew Hitler earlier had reduced military intelligence estimates of Soviet strength on Germany's eastern front and erroneously expected him to do so again in the west; therefore, when he received reports that parts of Canadian and American units had arrived in Britain and new British formations had been built, he rounded their estimated troop strengths up, thereby inflating German estimates of the Allied OB sufficiently to make two major landings on the Continent seem possible.[60] There were bureaucratic rivalries and tensions too; the Abwehr was absorbed into its bitter rival RSHA on June 1, 1944, just before the invasion.

The Germans received an unusually large amount of help in making their analytic errors from Allied, especially British, deception operations. The history of intelligence rightly gives a special place to the unusually successful deception that misled German intelligence, and Hitler, into thinking the main Allied invasion of Western Europe would occur in the Pas-de-Calais area. By keeping the Germans believing into September that the Normandy landing was a feint, the Allies aimed to freeze many German divisions some 160 miles northeast of the main landing area and a panzer division in the Bordeaux region in southwestern France—thereby helping their troops consolidate their foothold in Normandy. They successfully fooled German warning professionals and German commanders in only one respect—the location of the main attack—but it was enough to make the deception, and the invasion, highly successful. This kind of deception is sometimes described as an example of the "misleading variety," or M-type, deception.[61]

How did the British achieve such a feat? And what led German intelligence officers to so badly fail to accurately assess the information they had? The answers are linked in a fascinating story based on good British accounts of their activities, Ultra intercepts that told the British how German intelligence officers and commanders reacted to material the British planted, extensive German documentary records, and interviews with captured German commanders and intelligence officers after the war.[62]

The deception success in 1944 began years earlier in British counterintelligence activities. German agents operated in Britain before the war, leading the Security Service (MI5) and, after war broke out, other government agencies that soon organized into what was known as the Twenty Committee (also known as the XX Committee or the Double Cross Committee) to attack German HUMINT networks. By 1942, it was clear to the British government that this effort had eliminated all active German agents on British soil and had doubled many of them.[63] As British intelligence officers recognized their accomplishment, they realized they had an unusual opportunity to conduct deception operations against Germany, especially in offensive operations. Senior British officials therefore waited until 1943, when the tide of the war had turned, before authorizing the Twenty Committee to focus on one deception in support of a major offensive Allied operation—the invasion of northwestern Europe. The Twenty Committee then worked with the newly established London Controlling Section, the Allied organization charged with managing strategic deception.

Meanwhile, in November 1943, Prime Minister Churchill told Stalin at the Tehran Conference that "in wartime, truth is so precious that she should always be attended by a bodyguard of lies."[64] Britain's global deception effort thereby became Operation Bodyguard. By mid-1944, Operation Bodyguard had spawned a number of deception campaigns, including deceptions that supported other Allied military operations, many in the Mediterranean.[65] But Operation Bodyguard's greatest success was the deception in support of the invasion of Europe at Normandy—a deception known as Operation Fortitude South.

The British were unusually successful owing to the skill of their intelligence officers, possession of Ultra, some help from their allies, and appreciable good fortune. While the record of German intelligence performance showed some mistakes, the British always assumed German intelligence organizations were competent; some believed German intelligence generally was good, with some exceptions such as the Abwehr.[66] The British therefore did not underestimate their opponents, an error they recognized could be potentially fatal to deception operations. This meant the Twenty Committee and later the London Controlling Station designed their deception campaigns to take advantage of the intelligence analytic tradecraft practices known to competent intelligence analytic organizations—which the British knew German intelligence also knew.

The British studied their targets carefully. Later Oxford University professor Hugh Trevor-Roper and others studied the intelligence and operational organizations and specific personnel they intended to attack—including senior intelligence analyst Adolf Hitler.[67] The British designed their deception to exploit the personality characteristics, policy preferences, and intelligence analytical "mindsets and biases" they perceived in their targets.[68] For example, in designing the notional FUSAG and British Fourth Army, which were key elements of the effort to lead the Germans to conclude that there would be invasions in the Pas-de-Calais region and Norway, respectively, they assigned notional commanders they knew Hitler respected—Patton for his reputation as a fighter and British Army Lieutenant General F. A. N. Thorne, whom Hitler knew personally when Thorne was the

United Kingdom's defense attaché in Berlin.[69] Said Ewen Montagu, one of the Twenty Committee's operatives, about how the British matched their messages to the personal and collective character of their German targets:

> It occupied a great deal of time and energy but it was fascinating work. In a way it was like a mixture of constructing a crossword puzzle and sawing a jig-saw puzzle and then waiting to see whether the recipient could and would solve the clues and place the bits together successfully, except that it was we who would get the prize if the recipient succeeded. We had no illusions about the efficiency of the German Abwehr, so we had to make sure that the puzzle was not too difficult for them to solve.[70]

Knowing German intelligence skills and practices, the British planted bits of information that hinted at the conclusions they wanted the Germans to reach, knowing both normal intelligence analytic methods and the fact that the agents the Germans thought they controlled were told to answer the questions they were asked, not freelance by offering personal opinions.[71] They carefully studied how the Germans regarded "their" HUMINT assets' reporting, to a large degree by monitoring German communications via the Ultra program that broke the codes that most German government entities, including the intelligence services, used on their Enigma cypher machines. The deceivers integrated the reporting of apparently independent sources by feeding bits of apparently relevant information via agents they knew the Germans thought were reliable. Ultra enabled the British to refine their deception messages based on how the Germans appreciated reports each agent sent in the context of German intelligence collection assets as a whole, most of which the British did not control.

The Allied deception operation fed data through the entire range of intelligence sources that analysts rely on: deceptive information scattered in the generally truthful reports their controlled human agents provided, communications between nonexistent military formations provided by military communicators using military radio gear, dummy aircraft and naval landing craft deployed for the benefit of German photoreconnaissance aircraft, stories planted in the British and international press, and fake shoulder patches of nonexistent US Army divisions and the imaginary FUSAG, which troops wore in England and in the United States. These seemingly independent reports provided the authoritative sourcing that competent intelligence analysts hope to receive but often do not get. The British presumed the Germans would be able to deduce desired messages from bits of information and thought the Germans would have more confidence in analytic judgments they reached themselves than by receiving ostensible Allied plans in a clear message.[72]

Later the British learned that German analysts did not recognize some of the clues the British gave them, while Germans put much faith in other messages the Twenty Committee considered less important.[73] Still, Ultra, postwar interviews with German prisoners of war, and captured documents indicate that German analysts usually evaluated the deceptive messages they received roughly as the British intended, leading the Germans to reach the single incorrect conclusion the British wanted: a mistaken judgment about the location of the invasion.[74]

The deceivers were a remarkable set of organizations and men. The relatively small number of British women were mainly support personnel; some women were double agents. Few of the successful deceivers were professional intelligence officers or other career government employees. Brought into government service under the extraordinary circumstances of an existential national threat, an eclectic group of academics, lawyers, poets, and amateur magicians gave the Twenty Committee and the London Controlling Section intellectual power and creative imagination that produced considerable competence and earned the confidence of the Allied chiefs of staff and of political leaders, especially Prime Minister Churchill.[75] They acted very differently than did most government employees. We will return in chapter 8 to the characteristics of successful strategic warning intelligence officers—and of those who try to deceive them.

Operation Badr: The War of Ramadan, or the Yom Kippur War

On October 6, 1973, the armed forces of Egypt and Syria attacked Israel, surprising and shocking Israelis who depended on, and previously were highly confident in, the ability of their intelligence services to provide accurate and timely strategic warning. Even though they lost the war in narrowly military terms, the Arabs bloodied Israel badly and altered the political climate in the Middle East, enabling Egypt to reengage Israel diplomatically and eventually to achieve its political/military goals in the Egypt-Israel Peace Treaty of 1979. How did Israel's warning failure occur? How did Egyptian deception help the Israelis make their warning mistakes? And what are its lessons for warning more generally?

The origin of this war was Israel's June 1967 defeat of the armies of Egypt, Syria, and Jordan and of smaller contingents from other Arab states, as well as the capture by the Israel Defense Forces (IDF) of the Sinai Peninsula from Egypt, the Golan Heights from Syria, and East Jerusalem and the west bank of the Jordan River from Jordan.[76] The decisive victory emboldened Israel and posed for the Arab states, especially for Egypt, daunting challenges: how could Egypt restore its national self-respect after a crushing defeat, rebuild the self-confidence of its armed forces, and reclaim lost land when its military might was substantially diminished and the newly confident Israelis were unwilling to negotiate the return of its territory, which gave Israel some welcome strategic depth? Egypt fought its War of Attrition against Israel in 1969–70, which mainly involved exchanges of artillery and air strikes across the Suez Canal and got Egypt nowhere.[77] Then, on September 28, 1970, President Gamal Abdel Nasser, whose aggressiveness had precipitated the 1967 war, died suddenly.

New President Anwar el-Sadat, a former military officer who initially had a modest political base and was therefore politically insecure, inherited a major challenge.[78] By 1972, he was under increasing pressure domestically—politically for failing to regain the Sinai and economically for slow growth caused in part by loss of revenues from the closed Suez Canal and the lost oil fields in the Sinai—and from Egypt's Arab benefactors, who were tired of the continuing political logjam and of paying seemingly endless subsidies to Egypt. To break the impasse, Sadat on October 28, 1972, informed his senior military leaders that he had decided to go to war with Israel.[79] Recognizing the unattractive realities of his situation, Sadat saw two options: return to the approach of the War of Attrition or launch a limited war to break the Egypt-Israel diplomatic stalemate and establish conditions for negotiations with Israel about the return of captured Arab territories.[80] The costly ineffectiveness of the War of Attrition quickly ruled out that option. Recognizing Israel's military strengths and Egypt's many military weaknesses and limitations, Sadat and the new military leaders he installed to operationalize his scheme sought to exploit Israeli weaknesses with Egypt's few strengths while minimizing Egyptian exposure to the IDF's considerable strengths.[81] He then enlisted Syrian involvement in a supporting role.

A first task was to identify Israeli strengths and exploitable *national*, not just military, vulnerabilities. General (later Field Marshal) Ahmed Ismail Ali, whom Sadat charged with making military plans, recognized major Israeli strengths in airpower and access to immediate, substantial aid from the United States, but he saw four strategically important vulnerabilities he planned to exploit in his war and deception plans:

1. long lines of communication (supply lines) from Israel proper to the banks of the Suez Canal—a *military* consideration;
2. inability to withstand a long war—primarily a national *economic* factor given Israel's heavy reliance on mobilized reservists who normally were workers;
3. unwillingness to withstand large losses of Israeli lives—a national *political* factor;
4. and, most important, "wanton Israeli conceit"—a *cognitive, emotional,* and *cultural* affliction derived largely from the ease of Israeli victory in 1967, which led most Israeli political leaders and the IDF to seriously underestimate Egyptian capabilities in 1973.[82]

Egypt built its political/military strategy in the context of an Israeli national security strategy and beliefs about its capabilities that were publicly well known. First, the Israelis aimed to be stronger than the combined conventional armed forces of their prospective Arab enemies. Second, they threatened massive retaliation for any Arab attack, thereby producing a deterrent effect, they hoped. Third, they relied on what they considered to be—and generally had been to that time—an excellent intelligence capacity to provide them with enough warning time to mobilize their largely reserve armed forces. Given the IDF's force structure, the country's small size, mobilization procedures, and likely Arab threats, Israel believed it needed forty-eight to seventy-two hours' warning to adequately prepare to quickly and effectively repulse a major Arab attack from any direction. Israeli failures in these arenas, Sadat believed, would lead Israel to alter its diplomatic positions, thereby influencing the political aftermath of the war—his major objective.

Sadat's limited war strategy aimed to achieve his goals by exploiting Israeli vulnerabilities with limited Egyptian military assets. The Soviet Union refused to replace the air force Egypt lost in 1967 and before October 1973 gave Egypt only a few long-range Scud missiles, meaning the Egyptians could not attack Israeli air bases, which Egypt long believed was necessary to successfully fight the capable Israeli Air Force (IAF). Without a deep-strike capability, the Egyptians decided to launch a surprise attack to take the forts the IDF had built along the Suez Canal since 1967—the so-called Bar Lev Line, named after former IDF Chief of Staff Lieutenant General Haim Bar Lev—advance into the Sinai eight to ten kilometers, dig in, and then defend against IDF counterattacks.[83] The forces east of the canal would rely on two weapon types the Soviets provided after the 1967 war: man-portable AT-3 Sagger antitank guided missiles to destroy Israeli tanks and air-defense missile systems (SA-2, SA-3, and SA-6 missiles), whose launchers would remain on the western side of the canal but protect troops in their shallow penetration of the Sinai. With these new weapons, Egypt planned to bloody Israeli air and ground forces and prolong the fight—thereby exploiting two major Israeli national vulnerabilities. A successful defense would set the stage for the negotiations that would return the Sinai to Egypt. And a successful crossing of the canal—a technical challenge given the canal's depth, strong current, and steep sides, in addition to Israeli defenses—and then a determined defense against Israeli counterattacks would restore Egyptian national self-respect and dispel Israeli disdain for Arabs as fighters.

Sadat characterized this scheme as "an all-out war of limited proportions."[84] In essence, Sadat planned to use nominally tactically "defensive" weapons in an offensive way to achieve a strategically important goal. It was an imaginative approach that escaped Israeli military intelligence officers and political leaders who had come to think of Arab-Israel conflicts in terms of the big tank battles of the 1956 and 1967 wars.

The Egyptians' deception strategy used a variant of a standard deception technique that is hard to guard against—creating a "new normalcy" in Israel's perceptions of the level and tempo of Egyptian military activity to dull Israeli sensitivities to what would, eventually, be final preparations for the actual attack.[85] Egypt conducted a series of exercises and partial mobilizations—some twenty-two mobilizations in 1973 alone, according to an Egyptian general involved with war planning.[86] The final "exercise" that began in late September in fact completed Egyptian preparations for war. The Egyptians used a modified version of the USSR's *maskirovka* D&D doctrine, which includes use of exercises as cover for surprise attacks.[87] Because Egypt's deception plan was sound and well executed, the Israelis were surprised.[88] Like the Germans with Plan Barbarossa, the Egyptians employed what Donald Daniel and Katherine Herbig call an "ambiguity increasing," or "A-type," deception.[89]

In the Israeli intelligence scheme, the intelligence directorate of the IDF General Staff, known by its Hebrew acronym AMAN, was a collection agency as well as the primary intelligence analysis organization of the Israeli government as a whole.[90] Mossad, the civilian-run external intelligence service, was primarily a collection agency. The Foreign Ministry had no analysis unit. The analysis arm of AMAN, its Research Department, therefore provided warning of military threats to senior IDF commanders and national political leaders in conjunction with the intelligence arms of the military services, especially the air force. In 1973, the Research Department had over 400 staff, including 185 in officer positions, consisting of about 100 career army officers, 50 officers in compulsory service, and 30 civilian IDF employees.[91]

AMAN monitored Egyptian and Syrian activities, including the Egyptian exercises, and issued at least eleven warnings of strategic threats in 1973—that is, of Arab military activities not designed for training or defensive purposes.[92] When Israeli intelligence warned of Egyptian and Syrian military activities in April and May 1973 and the IDF mobilized for the third time in 1973 but no attack occurred, the cry wolf syndrome emerged to discourage later warnings and to reduce political leaders' receptivity to such warning.[93] On October 5, 1973, the day before the attack, Major General Eli Zeira, the IDF's Director of Military Intelligence (DMI), told Prime Minister Golda Meir that observations of mounting Arab military activity in late September and early October probably reflected defensive preparations driven by fear of the IDF, not an offensive threat, and that a serious attack was unlikely because of the Arabs' inferior air forces.[94]

Zeira was unconcerned about an Arab attack for several reasons. First, Israel's excellent HUMINT sources in Egypt had not warned of war, and Zeira felt confident that Israeli intelligence assets again would provide adequate warning to enable Israeli mobilization. One of Mossad's best sources, later identified as former President Nasser's son-in-law Ashraf Marwan, finally did so on October 5, the day before the war began.[95] Zeira also had confidence in a "special means of collection," apparently a tap of a sensitive Egyptian communication means the Israelis developed in early 1973 that they believed would provide certain warning of war, which could be "turned on" if AMAN thought a war was possible.[96]

Second, Israel's intelligence sources earlier had provided AMAN with copies of the war plans Egypt developed immediately after its 1967 drubbing, which remained Egypt's war plans until Sadat changed them in late 1972. These plans called for a conventional conquest of the Sinai that reflected conventional soldiers' ideas about how to defeat Israel and depended on replacement by the Soviets of the airpower lost in 1967. Because the Israelis saw Egypt's post-1967 war plan as wholly unrealistic given Soviet refusal to replace Egypt's air force and its limited delivery of Scud missiles and (accurately) thought the Egyptians did too, they anticipated no appreciable strategic threat to Israel for several years to come. DMI Zeira did not accept Marwan's reports, beginning in late 1972, that Egypt's war plans had changed.[97]

The logical analysis of late 1967 that Egypt lacked viable options for conducting a major war without deep-strike capabilities that only the Soviets could provide solidified over time into a rigid, conventional wisdom within AMAN that because the Soviets had not rebuilt Egypt's air forces, no major Egyptian military operations of any sort against Israel were feasible. Former IDF intelligence officer Dani Asher believes the idea reified from reliable intelligence reporting and sound analysis soon after the 1967 war into an unchallenged assumption by 1971.[98] This view came to be known as "the Concept" or "the Conception." (American intelligence analysts sometimes call this process "layering."[99]) Zeira and like-minded officers thus developed a "mindset" that saw Egypt as militarily weak and incapable of winning a full-scale conventional war to reconquer the Sinai—the only kind of war they considered to pose a threat to core Israeli interests. (The IDF saw occasional

Egyptian and Syrian cross-border raids as nuisances that posed no existential threat to Israel.) Hence, because the Egyptians knew their limitations, there would be no war.

The Conception thus became a heuristic, a theory or model or core belief that its adherents in AMAN used to process new information. The two core beliefs that guided Conception's influence on AMAN's thinking became (1) Egypt would not go to war with Israel until it had gained an ability to conduct deep strikes into Israel to nullify Israeli air superiority and (2) Syria would not launch a large-scale attack without Egyptian participation.[100] Therefore, when AMAN picked up signs of Egyptian and Syrian preparations in the weeks before October 6, under Zeira's guidance IDF analysts dismissed their significance by viewing them as either normal activity or as parts of an ostensibly routine exercise the Egyptians called "Tahrir 41." Because, in Israel's political/military/intelligence organizational scheme, Zeira as the DMI was chief of Israeli national intelligence estimates, including warnings of war, his views prevailed.

But as sure as Zeira and Lieutenant Colonel Yona Bandman, who was chief of Branch 6 (Egypt, Sudan, and North Africa) and thus was AMAN's chief analyst of Egyptian military intentions, were about the absence of a threat from Egypt, other senior Israeli intelligence, military, and political leaders were worried.[101] In April 1973, Mossad received warnings of Egyptian and Syrian preparations for war from several sources, including Marwan and King Hussein of Jordan.[102] In a meeting with Prime Minister Meir on April 18, Mossad chief Zvi Zamir and IDF Chief of Staff Lieutenant General David Elazar expressed concern, Defense Minister Moshe Dayan flatly predicted war, and Meir also was worried, leading the cabinet to authorize war preparations.[103] In April and May, the IDF heightened its alert status, senior Israeli leaders publicly threatened Egypt about its military moves, and Israel spent some seventy million Israeli pounds (then about US$10 million) to partially mobilize and to enhance its war readiness.[104] But nothing happened, leading skeptics to claim that intelligence had failed—that there had been another example of the cry wolf syndrome. In fact, Sadat appears to have wanted to attack on May 19 but was dissuaded at the last minute by Syrian protests that Syrian preparations were incomplete and by Israeli preparations and public comments.[105]

Hence, Israeli intelligence warnings that produced effective remedial action evidently were at least partly successful in discouraging an Egyptian attack, but Israeli officials did not recognize the warning success—a classic case of the "paradox of warning."[106] The episode also desensitized the Israelis to Egyptian preparations for the attack in October.[107] Some of Israel's human intelligence sources may also have been affected by this incident. King Hussein, who regularly talked with Arab leaders and the Israelis, was more constrained in late September than in April.[108] And, we know now, Egyptian and Syrian leaders did not finally agree on a start time for the war until October 3—only three days before the war began—giving Israel's intelligence sources, including Marwan, little time to learn and to report the war's start date before the war started.[109]

The periodic warnings of events that did not seem to materialize—especially in April and May and warnings that the start of the Tahrir 41 exercise in late September was actually the beginning of a real war, not just preparations or an exercise alone—led some Israelis, including Zeira and Bandman, to dismiss new warnings in early October.[110] They minimized growing evidence of serious preparations in September and October, citing earlier cry wolf syndrome episodes and the Conception heuristic, thereby illustrating the dysfunctions of what psychologists call "confirmation bias." Zeira was so unconcerned that he did not activate the "special means of collection" because he did not want to risk compromising the system.[111] To make matters worse, he misled senior officials into thinking the special means of collection had been activated.[112]

People less committed to the Conception, such as Chief of Staff Elazar and Defense Minister Dayan, who had been so concerned in April and May, by September concluded that they had been wrong.[113] They were desensitized by apparent cry wolf events and Egyptian efforts to create a new normalcy that seemed to be benign—the phenomenon known as "creeping normalcy." The result was that Zeira and the Israeli government as a whole, despite dissents by "alarmists" in AMAN who saw Egyptian moves as more threatening, did not recognize that war was likely until the morning of October 6, 1973—the day that Egypt and Syria attacked and too late to give the IDF and political leaders the warning time they believed they needed to adequately mobilize for war.

As a result, while Elazar raised the alert status of the regular armed forces on October 5, the IDF was only partly prepared for war, contributing to high Israeli casualties (2,689 fatalities), heavy losses of aircraft and tanks, initial loss of territory, a delayed counteroffensive, and a longer and much more costly war than Israel expected.[114] The war ended after the IDF drove back the Syrian and Egyptian armies, inflicting another tactical military defeat on both. But the shock of the warning failure, initial military reverses, and the human and material costs of the war led to a political crisis in Israel that generated the changed international political environment that Sadat hoped to achieve. Israel decided to negotiate with Egypt. In September 1978, at Camp David, Maryland, as President Jimmy Carter's guests, Sadat and Israeli Prime Minister Menachem Begin agreed on steps that led to a formal peace treaty in 1979 and the return to Egypt of the Sinai Peninsula and national self-respect.

Hence, the narrowly military focus of Zeira and Bandman, like many military-oriented warning analysts in other situations before and since, led them to fundamentally misread Sadat's domestic political situation, his political reasons for going to war, his political/military goals, and hence his strategy.[115] Captured by inapplicable military doctrine and inappropriate lessons of recent history, they failed to ask themselves relevant questions and did not imagine or evaluate scenarios of plausible Egyptian actions given Sadat's political/military environment and his resource constraints. They thereby failed to meet their warning responsibilities.

This case illustrates, too, the impact of organizational structure and other institutional arrangements on the effectiveness of strategic warning. DMI Zeira was the widely accepted maker of Israel national intelligence estimates including strategic warning, but he was, as we have seen, both brash in his judgments and wrong. Uri Bar-Joseph and Rose McDermott believe he displayed an unusually high need for cognitive closure—a firm decision about the likely course of events.[116] He was supported by a small group within AMAN, including Research Department Director Brigadier General Aryeh Shalev and Lieutenant Colonel Bandman. They quashed the concerns of many within AMAN that there was enough evidence of a likely Egyptian attack to warrant a significant Israeli preparatory response through restrictions on communication with people outside AMAN and by admonishments to AMAN officers who nevertheless spoke of their concerns to intelligence officers of other military organizations. Put differently, they used their bureaucratic power in a hierarchical military organization to suppress alternative views, which prevailed because AMAN then was the only producer of intelligence analysis in the Israeli government.[117] We know now that the chiefs of the Research Department's Branch 2 (Egyptian political affairs), Lieutenant Colonel Zusia Kaniazher, and Branch 5 (Syria), Lieutenant Colonel Avi Yaari, thought war was likely.[118] So did some AMAN collectors, including the chief of its SIGINT element, Unit 848.[119] After Yaari reported his concerns to the intelligence officer of Northern Command, Lieutenant Colonel Hagai Mann, and said AMAN had not issued a warning, Mann convinced Northern Command chief Major General Yitzhak Hofi to mobilize some of his reservists. When Zeira learned of the set of events, he told Shalev to rebuke Yaari, which he did.[120] The reprimand evidently was widely known within AMAN, discouraging other intelligence and operational personnel from other efforts to warn.

Other Israelis also foresaw the war but were not in decision-making positions or were marginalized. For example, Israeli naval intelligence officers saw signs they believed to be threatening, but they had no role in mobilization decisions.[121] And, more famously, a junior intelligence officer at Southern Command headquarters, Lieutenant Binyamin Siman-Tov, using less information than was available to AMAN analysts, penned a short memo on October 1 arguing that Egyptian activities amounted to deceptions designed to cover war preparations and citing eight indicators of impending hostilities. His boss, Lieutenant Colonel David Gdalia, who apparently shared Zeira's and Bandman's faith in the Conception, dismissed his concerns and quashed the report, preventing it from reaching AMAN analysts in Tel Aviv.[122]

Uri Bar-Joseph, an Israeli student of intelligence who is well connected with Israeli government officials, argues that there were five clusters of problems that afflicted only parts of Israel's intelligence system but did so in ways that effectively caused the system as a whole to fail:

- *First, obstacles unique to the warning-response process.*[123] Bar-Joseph argues that Egyptian deception activities, especially the repeated exercises and mobilizations, created a cry wolf syndrome that desensitized Israeli intelligence people and policymakers to signs of preparations for the real attack. The Israelis were overconfident in their collection and analytic capabilities, and they compartmented sensitive information too closely. The Israeli political establishment was worried that mobilizing when it was not certain that the Arabs' actions were hostile would seem provocative abroad and generate undesirable diplomatic tensions with the United States and other countries. And an Israel election campaign was under way; the incumbent Labor Party was running, in part, on a claim that it had helped make Israel more secure than ever. Mobilization would undercut that claim.

- *Second, bureaucratic obstacles.*[124] AMAN was riven by internal disputes and had a bureaucratic rival in Mossad, leading Zeira to exclude Mossad chief Zvi Zamir from important discussions with senior political leaders about Arab intentions. Because AMAN had a national monopoly on the warning function as a matter of government policy, other actors who might have contributed, including Mossad and foreign ministry officials, were largely excluded from intelligence analytic discussions. Zeira's and like-minded deputies' efforts to quash dissent within AMAN and to limit the distribution of alternative views of some AMAN officers generated an external appearance of unanimity of analyst judgment within AMAN that did not in fact exist.
- *Third, "groupthink."*[125] Irving Janis's original notion of "groupthink" as a small group phenomenon seems to have occurred infrequently in this case but may have affected the small group of adherents of the Conception as they fought criticism from skeptics.[126] Zeira, Bandman, and a few others were insular and strongly resisted the criticism of others.[127]
- *Fourth, individual psychological issues.*[128] Zeira and Bandman surely displayed confirmation bias, the tendency to see new information through the lens of existing beliefs, and used heuristic reasoning—the Conception. We will return to these and other psychological pathologies in chapter 8.
- *Fifth, the "human factor."*[129] The major actors in this warning saga displayed a variety of personal characteristics that sometimes are useful but in this case helped generate a major warning failure. These traits were amplified in the organizational context of Israeli military intelligence and in how intelligence served senior national decision-makers. Most prominently, Zeira's overconfidence, unwillingness to accept a degree of uncertainty about Arab intentions, and suppression of alternative views within AMAN contributed significantly to the IDF's warning failure. The Agranat Commission, the panel headed by then chief justice of Israel's Supreme Court Shimon Agranat tasked with investigating the failures that preceded the Yom Kippur War, in its postmortem report named Zeira as a primary cause of the disaster.[130]

Others have reached similar conclusions.[131] Variations on Bar-Joseph's insights recur and are the subject of discussion in later chapters.[132]

The Israeli institutional context for warning—a focus on military threat warning functions reported through a single, hierarchical military chain of command—may work when organizational and leadership judgments are sound and/or when commanders allow minority views of junior personnel to percolate up. Neither occurred in the Israeli case in 1973—a situation, as we discuss later, that elsewhere has repeatedly caused other warning failures and is a continuing, prominent feature of military intelligence organizations especially.

National Intelligence Estimate 15–90, *Yugoslavia Transformed*

Yugoslavia gradually fractured during the 1980s. Economic and political problems multiplied after Josip Broz Tito, who controlled centripetal forces during his long tenure as leader, died in 1980. The IC watched Yugoslavia closely for decades owing to its importance as a leader of the "Third World" and its position between East and West, both geographically and politically. By October 1990, the IC was concerned enough about growing problems to publish another NIE on Yugoslavia—this time called *Yugoslavia Transformed*—which was prepared primarily by CIA, DIA, the National Security Agency (NSA), and State/INR.[133] Like many other NIEs, this one performed a strategic warning function.

The estimate forecast the collapse of Yugoslavia and the outbreak of violence, yet it prompted essentially no reaction by the administration of President George H. W. Bush.[134] Why? Did the IC fail to convey its message or persuade senior leaders of the importance of the events it foresaw? The answer to both questions appears to be no, meaning the NIE was a warning success by our definition. Senior US officials understood the message but chose to do relatively little in response to the warning. This case study focuses on why senior officials made that decision.

The NIE's analysis and forecast of future events was unusually good. The forecast of large-scale violence in Bosnia was clearly accurate; the civil war of 1992–95 is variously estimated to have taken 100,000 to 200,000 lives. The prediction that Kosovo would erupt in violence was premature but not by much. The estimate's authors demonstrated deep knowledge and keen insights about the future of Yugoslavia. They converted expertise into accurate analytic judgments.

Senior officials of the Bush administration did not quarrel with the NIE's judgments about the significance of events in Yugoslavia, but the NIE had no appreciable effect on US foreign policies for several reasons. First, President Bush and Secretary of State James Baker were focused on other things. In the fall of 1990, Bush was working to secure domestic political and international military support for his eventually successful United Nations (UN)–sanctioned liberation of Kuwait from Iraqi control. Second, the Soviet Union was in disarray, and Bush and Baker were trying to keep separatist leaders of several republics within the USSR from seceding, which they worried would have negative consequences for regional stability. Third, Bush and Baker saw responsibility for handling the Yugoslav crisis as mainly residing in Europe. Baker, a Texan, famously invoked Texas slang to say "we have no dog in this fight."[135]

In addition, the NIE told policymaking officials that the United States and other external powers could do little to prevent the dissolution of Yugoslavia and that Washington would be pulled in different directions, potentially creating a politically unattractive situation. Because the IC judged the problem to be intractable, with no opportunity for a constructive US role, it was reasonable for an official who respected the IC's views to decide not to invest effort in what seemed likely to be a major diplomatic effort with modest prospects of a meaningful payoff.[136] Hence, while the IC refrains from offering specific policy advice, in this case its judgment that US policy could not affect the course of events was an implicit recommendation to ignore the deepening crisis.

Independent of the NIE, some commentators at the time suggested that dissolution of Yugoslavia was a good outcome and that the international community could help by facilitating the dissolution, not trying to prevent it. But this idea, too, was unattractive to administration officials, who then were trying to quash centripetal forces in the USSR. They worried that US support for national self-determination in Yugoslavia would inevitably lead to demands for the same in Soviet republics, with resulting negative implications for regional stability and the control of nuclear weapons based in several non-Russian republics—a concern about nuclear proliferation that did not materialize, partly owing to US efforts.

Hence, the NIE generated little policy response, leading some American intelligence officials to see the estimate as a failure. We disagree for three reasons. First, much of the disappointment intelligence people voiced centered on the notion that policymakers should have acted in some way because the IC warned. This reflects mistaken arrogance on the part of intelligence officers who knew that a core part of the political culture of the United States was and is that intelligence informs policymakers but does not make policy or recommend any specific policy decisions. Decision-makers make policy decisions; intelligence does not.

Second, administration foreign policy at the time clearly reflected other factors, including tensions with European allies concerning their handling of the Yugoslav crisis, including refugee flows into their countries, and a domestic US political climate opposed to any significant American involvement in Yugoslavia—especially a military troop role that might generate US military casualties in a conflict that appeared irrelevant to core US national interests. These factors suggested to Bush and Baker that a heightened US role in Yugoslavia was politically unattractive.

Third, the NIE said US diplomatic initiatives were unlikely to have much effect. As we have noted, policymakers appreciate intelligence that suggests avenues they can take to advance national and personal interests—which the estimate ruled out. Even threat warnings sometimes contain implicit suggestions for effective remedial action. Recognizing the impotence of US foreign policy in this case evidently was sound intelligence analysis. But, as Gregory F. Treverton and Renanah Miles note, the NIE did not assess implications for the United States. It thereby missed a chance to identify opportunities for US diplomatic action.[137]

A postscript: the United States gradually became more involved in the breakup of Yugoslavia. The number of Yugoslav refugees entering Western Europe rose dramatically, posing problems for America's European allies, and President Bill Clinton proposed a "lift and strike" policy that favored Bosnian Muslims by lifting the UN arms embargo on belligerents and launching air strikes on Bosnian Serb Army units. In late 1995, the United States hosted "peace" talks at Dayton, Ohio, and in December 1995 deployed some 20,000 troops to a large NATO peacekeeping mission in Bosnia. Hence, the crisis eventually affected US interests in important ways.

Summary Lessons of the Case Studies

We believe these case studies illustrate some important aspects of warning intelligence that we will discuss in greater detail in chapters to follow.

Individual psychological factors are important. The limits of the human brain and tendencies psychologists have identified as substantial obstacles to clear thinking recurred in these cases. IDF intelligence analysts developed, and became wedded to, a "Conception" of Arab war potential that resisted new information. The Israelis and Stalin experienced the dysfunctions of confirmation bias. More generally, analysts show different capacities to ask relevant questions, to learn, and to accept new information.

Leaders' points-of-view matter. Leaders have, in addition to the cognitive issues all humans have, perspectives and biases that make them differentially receptive to intelligence information. Stalin's and Hitler's biases hindered responses to adversary actions in 1941 and 1944, respectively, while Churchill's political understanding of Hitler enabled him to anticipate the German attack on the USSR before British intelligence officers did. But Churchill also made many errors, and Hitler accurately forecast Western responses to his aggression in 1939 and 1940. Leaders' prescience varies dramatically from case to case for reasons that are often unclear—but are well worth understanding.

Leaders' entire situations matter. Stalin knew the USSR needed time to rebuild its defense capabilities after the purges he initiated, leading him to want to delay a fight with Germany. President Bush was concerned with many things and saw NIE 15–90 as minimally helpful for managing his diplomatic and domestic political challenges. The lesson for intelligence: always keep in mind that intelligence is but one of many inputs to leaders who face many complicated problems. Be humble, but also try to understand leaders' needs in order to make warning and other intelligence as useful as possible.

Expertise is important. In all three military cases, deceivers studied and became expert on the institutions, personalities, perceptions, and technical expertise of their intended victims. In all four cases, the expertise of intelligence professionals conducting warning/estimative analyses was crucial. The NIE drafters knew Yugoslavia well. AMAN's analysts on the Egypt political desk discerned Sadat's plan in enough time to warn effectively but were over-ruled by others with different and analytically flawed perspectives.

Intelligence institutions matter. The organization of intelligence services helps or hinders the creativity that often is essential to creation of a seamless collection-analysis-warning-policy decision-action process. The personality-centric institutional structure that Hitler, and especially Stalin, created works well when leaders are insightful but very poorly when leaders err, as they inevitably do. The IDF's hierarchical intelligence analytic structure in 1973 made the Conception effectively analytic policy and quashed alternative perspectives that were more accurate, but the Twenty Committee gave an eclectic group of amateur intelligence officers opportunities to excel.

The quality of intelligence personnel matters. Very bright people make good intelligence officers. People of middling ability learn to do intelligence work in predictable ways and are subject to deception. The unusually high-quality personnel of the Twenty Committee, the product of a national emergency that actually brought the "best and the brightest" into wartime service, managed to deceive German intelligence officers who were merely able.

Deceivers have learned all of these lessons—and more. That is why we discuss them in this book.

Notes

1. Whaley, *Codeword Barbarossa*, 224.
2. Ibid., 170–87.
3. Ibid., 12–15.
4. May, *Strange Victory*.
5. Whaley, *Codeword Barbarossa*, 32; Bar-Joseph and McDermott, *Intelligence Success and Failure*, 68, 81.
6. Kahn, *Hitler's Spies*, 445.
7. Ibid.
8. Ibid., 456–57.
9. Dvoinykh and Tarkhova, "What Military Intelligence Reported," 76–93.
10. Andrew and Gordievsky, *KGB*, 175–78, 239–40, 264–65.
11. Andrew and Mitrokhin, *Sword and Shield*, 102.
12. These agents included Kim Philby in the Secret Intelligence Service (MI6), Donald Maclean and Guy Burgess in the Foreign Office, Anthony Blunt in the Security Service (MI5), and John Cairncross of the Cabinet Office and Foreign Office.
13. Dippel, "Jumping to the Right Conclusion," 213–27.
14. Whaley, *Codeword Barbarossa*, 24.
15. Levite, *Intelligence and Strategic Surprise*, 144.
16. Ford, *Estimative Intelligence*, 49.
17. Whaley, *Codeword Barbarossa*.
18. Andrew and Gordievsky, *KGB*, 260.
19. Volkogonov, *Stalin*, 372–402.
20. Stolfi, "Barbarossa," 195–223; Latimer, *Deception in War*, 71, 132–44; Barros and Gregor, *Double Deception*; Bar-Joseph and McDermott, *Intelligence Success and Failure*, 69–70.
21. Whaley, *Codeword Barbarossa*, 170–75.
22. Ibid., 180–87.
23. Latimer, *Deception in War*, 71.
24. Whaley, *Codeword Barbarossa*, 223.
25. Ibid., 180.
26. Quoted in Watt, "British Intelligence," 268.
27. Bar-Joseph and McDermott, *Intelligence Success and Failure*, 74–83.
28. Heuer, *Psychology of Intelligence Analysis*.
29. Andrew and Gordievsky, *KGB*, 267–69.
30. Whaley, *Codeword Barbarossa*, 180.
31. Haslam, *Near and Distant Neighbors*, 85–88.
32. Ibid., 84; Bar-Joseph and McDermott, *Intelligence Success and Failure*, 88–90.
33. Andrew and Mitrokhin, *Sword and Shield*, 93.
34. Andrew and Gordievsky, *KGB*, 265.
35. Andrew and Mitrokhin, *Sword and Shield*, 91, 93.
36. Ibid., 93; Garthoff, *Soviet Leaders and Intelligence*, 12.

37. Haslam, *Near and Distant Neighbors*, 67.

38. Bar-Joseph and Levy, "Conscious Action and Intelligence Failure," 481; Murphy, *What Stalin Knew*, 249.

39. Andrew and Mitrokhin, *Sword and Shield*, 94–95. For a discussion of the consequences of fear on intelligence professionals, see Gentry, "Intelligence of Fear," 9–25.

40. Kahn, *Hitler's Spies*, 6. For a brief history of the early development of the Abwehr, see Whaley, "Covert Rearmament in Germany," 3–39.

41. Kahn, *Hitler's Spies*, 486–87.

42. Ibid., 537–38; Whaley, *Codeword Barbarossa*; Whaley, "Covert Rearmament in Germany."

43. Geyer, "National Socialist Germany," 310–46.

44. Kahn, *Hitler's Spies*, 488.

45. Hughes-Wilson, *Military Intelligence Blunders*, 16–37.

46. Kahn, *Hitler's Spies*, 507.

47. Ibid., 506, 508–10.

48. Ibid., 489.

49. Ibid., 497–98.

50. Ibid., 514–15.

51. Smith, "*Overlord/Bodyguard*," 550–68.

52. Kahn, *Hitler's Spies*, 517.

53. Cubbage, "German Misapprehensions."

54. Ibid., 494, 537–38; Hesketh, *Fortitude*, 10.

55. May, *Strange Victory*, 348, 368–70, 456–58; Claasen, "German Invasion of Norway," 114–35.

56. Kahn, *Hitler's Spies*, 501–2, 504–5, 510.

57. Ibid., 513.

58. Ibid., 538.

59. Ibid., 506.

60. Ibid., 495–96. Kahn's account of Rönne's OB inflation is much lower than reported in Hughes-Wilson, *Military Intelligence Blunders*, 31.

61. Latimer, *Deception in War*, 71; Daniel and Herbig, *Strategic Military Deception*, 5–7.

62. For example, Bell, "'Die deutsche Spionage ist auf Zack,'" 49–59.

63. Masterman, *Double-Cross System*; Hesketh, *Fortitude*.

64. As cited in McIntyre, *Double Cross*, 3.

65. McIntyre, *Operation Mincemeat*.

66. Hesketh, *Fortitude*, 10; Masterman, *Double-Cross System*, 109, 112, 146, 187–89.

67. Hesketh, *Fortitude*, 4; Kahn, *Hitler's Spies*, 486.

68. For a discussion of deception and counter-deception principles, see Bennett and Waltz, "Toward a Counterdeception Tradecraft."

69. Hesketh, *Fortitude*, 72–74; Hughes-Wilson, *Military Intelligence Blunders*, 25.

70. Montagu, *Beyond Top Secret U*, 60.

71. Masterman, *Double-Cross System*, 112.

72. Handel, *Military Deception*, 25.

73. Bell, "Toward a Theory of Deception," 244–79.

74. Hesketh, *Fortitude*, 174–90, 351–60; Masterman, *Double-Cross System*; 83–84.

75. Hughes-Wilson, *Military Intelligence Blunders*, 18.

76. Bar-Joseph and McDermott, *Intelligence Success and Failure*, 188–91.

77. Adamsky and Bar-Joseph, "'Russians Are Not Coming,'" 1–25.

78. Sadat, *In Search of Identity*.

79. Heikal, *Road to Ramadan*, 208–10; Asher, *Egyptian Strategy*, 51–52.

80. Badri, Magdoub, and Zohdy, *Ramadan War, 1973*, 17.

81. Ibid., 15–22.

82. Ibid., 19. For other examples, see Shalev, *Israel's Intelligence Assessment*, 26, 32, 54–55.

83. Bar-Joseph, *Angel*, 155.

84. Asher, *Egyptian Strategy*, 10.

85. Sheffy, "Overcoming Strategic Weakness," 809–28.

86. Asher, *Egyptian Strategy*, 92–93; Shazly, *Crossing of the Suez*, 206–7.

87. For an extensive discussion of Egyptian adaptation of Soviet doctrine in 1973, see Asher, *Egyptian Strategy*.

88. For complementary Israeli assessments, see ibid. and Handel, *Perception, Deception and Surprise*.

89. Latimer, *Deception in War*, 71.

90. For a description of the Israeli intelligence system at this time, see Shalev, *Israel's Intelligence Assessment*, 1–13; Doron, "Israeli Intelligence," 305–19; Kahana, "Early Warning versus Concept," 81; Hershkovitz, "'Three-Story Building,'" 765–84.

91. Shalev, *Israel's Intelligence Assessment*, 5–6.

92. Bar-Joseph, "Israel's 1973 Intelligence Failure," 12.

93. Betts, *Enemies of Intelligence*, 36.

94. Bar-Joseph, "Israel's 1973 Intelligence Failure," 12.

95. Bar-Joseph, "Question of Loyalty," 667–85.

96. Bar-Joseph, "'Special Means of Collection,'" 531–46.

97. Bar-Joseph, *Angel*, 58–162.

98. Asher, *Egyptian Strategy*, 48–50.

99. Lowenthal, *Intelligence*, 6th ed., 163.

100. Shlaim, "Failures in National Intelligence Estimates," 352; Asher, *Egyptian Strategy*, 48–50.

101. Bar-Joseph, *Watchman Fell Asleep*, 48, 64; Sheffy, "Early Warning," 420–37.

102. Bar-Joseph and McDermott, *Intelligence Success and Failure*, 191; Bar-Joseph, *Angel*, 165–69.

103. Bar-Joseph, *Watchman Fell Asleep*, 66–73.

104. Handel, *Perception, Deception and Surprise*, 30, 42. Ephraim Kahana reports costs of $13 million to $18 million. See Kahana, "Early Warning versus Concept," 86.

105. Bar-Joseph, *Watchman Fell Asleep*, 34; Bar-Joseph, *Angel*, 169.

106. Stein, "Military Deception, Strategic Surprise," 99.

107. Doron, "Israeli Intelligence," 314.

108. Bar-Joseph, *Watchman Fell Asleep*, 237.

109. Handel, *Perception, Deception and Surprise*, 12; Bar-Joseph, *Angel*, 194–205.

110. Bar-Joseph, *Watchman Fell Asleep*, 111.

111. Bar-Joseph and McDermott, *Intelligence Success and Failure*, 192–93, 202–3, 210–11.

112. Bar-Joseph, *Angel*, 205–7.

113. Ibid., 94; Gelber, "Collapse of Israeli Intelligence's Conception," 520–46.

114. Bar-Joseph and McDermott, *Intelligence Success and Failure*, 185.

115. Shalev, *Israel's Intelligence Assessment*, 73.

116. Bar-Joseph and McDermott, *Intelligence Success and Failure*, 212.

117. Handel, *Perception, Deception and Surprise*, 55.

118. Bar-Joseph, *Watchman Fell Asleep*, 91–92.

119. Bar-Joseph and McDermott, *Intelligence Success and Failure*, 199.

120. Ibid., 105.

121. Ibid., 99–100.

122. Ibid., 135; Hughes-Wilson, *Military Intelligence Blunders*, 246–47.

123. Bar-Joseph, *Watchman Fell Asleep*, 236–40.

124. Ibid., 240–42.

125. Ibid., 243–48.

126. Janis, *Victims of Groupthink*.

127. See also Handel, *Perception, Deception and Surprise*, 56.

128. Bar-Joseph, *Watchman Fell Asleep*, 236–40.

129. Ibid., 248–51.

130. Agranat Commission, "What Went Wrong on October 6?"

131. Asher, *Egyptian Strategy*, 52–55. See also Stein, "Military Deception, Strategic Surprise," 107–18.

132. For this discussion, see Bar-Joseph, *Watchman Fell Asleep*, 235–51. For a different perspective, see Shalev, *Israel's Intelligence Assessment*.

133. Director of Central Intelligence, *Yugoslavia Transformed*.

134. Treverton, *Intelligence for an Age of Terror*, 137; Treverton and Miles, "Unheeded Warning of War," 506–22.

135. Holbrooke, *To End a War*, 26–27.

136. Treverton and Miles, "Unheeded Warning of War," 4.

137. For a similar assessment involving the European Union and the Arab Spring, see Arcos and Palacios, "Impact of Intelligence."

CHAPTER 3

Types of Government
Warning Institutions

The case studies of chapter 2 refer to several types of institutional arrangements that states have used to conduct strategic warning. Some of these institutional arrangements worked well. Others facilitated intelligence failures. States have appreciably different warning organizations and other arrangements and change them periodically, sometimes for good reasons, sometimes not.

We assert in this chapter that structures and related institutional arrangements recur and their characteristics appreciably affect the performance of warning intelligence. No organizational arrangement is ideal. All have advantages and disadvantages. Warning institutions evolve for substantive and bureaucratic reasons as leaders struggle to devise ways to make the warning function work or to achieve other goals. While some people argue that almost any intelligence organizational structure can perform well if it is run well by good leaders, and we accept that this may be true if leaders are exceptionally good, we are also sure that leaders of intelligence organizations are not consistently excellent.

While they overlap in some respects, we identify five general types of governmental warning structures: (1) leaders as principal warning analysts; (2) organizations in which every analyst has warning analysis as an additional duty, which we call the Every-Analyst-a-Warning-Analyst (EAAWA) model; (3) dedicated, specialized warning organizations; (4) hybrid organizations that combine elements of types 2 and 3, with the warning function coordinated by a dedicated, senior-level warning specialist; and (5) a whole-of-government effort conducted by government agencies generally, meaning that warning is not solely an intelligence function. We describe how variants of these ideal types have actually functioned in the institutional case studies in chapter 4.

National Leaders as Warning Analysts

Some national leaders choose to be their own warning analysts. Chapter 2 recounts how Stalin was the only strategic-level intelligence analyst in the Soviet Union in the late 1930s and early 1940s and how Hitler, while devouring raw information and using the analytical components of his intelligence services for some purposes, was his own chief analyst. All leaders perform some "intelligence analysis" when they decide to accept or reject the information and assessments intelligence provides, but we refer here to situations in which leaders perform what usually are duties of professional intelligence analysts. This practice has some strengths but also significant drawbacks.

On the positive side, senior political decision-makers functioning as their own primary intelligence analysts do not experience the trust issues that recurrently bedevil "producer-consumer relations" in some countries, especially the United States. Leaders make decisions based on their own trusted analytic judgments. Sometimes smart and experienced leaders do in fact reach better judgments more quickly than do professional intelligence officers. Hitler sometimes did so.[1]

But important disadvantages outweigh the advantages. Leaders by definition have many more responsibilities than intelligence analysis and rarely are expert in more than a few regional or functional issues. Leaders tend to have strong opinions, and autocratic leaders, in particular, have few checks on their flawed analytic judgments, cognitive biases, and prejudices. The literature on foreign policy decision-making makes clear that national leaders recurrently use historical analogies poorly because they misunderstand history and apply lessons inappropriately to new situations.[2] Moreover, leaders, like all people, have "mindsets and biases" that, as we saw in the German and Soviet cases in chapter 2, are identifiable and enable adversaries to devise ways to deceive them in order to defeat them militarily or to manipulate them in other ways.[3]

The obvious leader-as-analyst role in the Soviet and German instances is less clear in most other cases, but all leaders decide whether to accept warning messages and how to use them. These decisions are based on analytic judgments about the completeness, validity, and persuasiveness of intelligence reporting and whether the analyst(s) and messenger(s) are trustworthy, with trust defined in many ways. Strong leaders of democracies sometimes wisely conduct their own analyses of the intelligence assessments they receive. Other leaders reject intelligence as biased or inept. Still other leaders are more accepting of professional intelligence judgments. As we saw in chapter 2, Prime Minister Churchill beat the JIC to the accurate judgment that Hitler was likely to attack the USSR, and he played an active role in British intelligence matters throughout World War II.[4] Churchill said to his staff in 1941, "I had not been content with this form of collective wisdom [the JIC assessments] and preferred to see the originals [messages] myself . . . thus forming my own opinion sometimes at much earlier dates."[5]

A clear implication of the checkered history of leaders acting as their own intelligence analysts is that intelligence analysis that effectively serves national leaders must account for the interests, preferences, expertise, and biases of senior leaders as decision-makers and de facto intelligence analysts. Failure to do so usually damages the persuasion part of the warning task, dooming it to failure however good intelligence collection and analysis may be.

All Analysts Are Warning Analysts

A common intelligence organizational scheme is to assign the warning function to all analysts.[6] In the EAAWA model, all analysts who see threatening activities or opportunities during the course of their research, estimative, or current intelligence responsibilities report them through normal channels. This system exists in national systems in which there is a single major analytic agency—as in AMAN in 1973—and in structures with multiple agencies, as in the United States.[7] The British JIC internally uses a variant of the EAAWA model.[8] The German military intelligence system in 1943 and 1944 appears to have been similar. This also is effectively the system adopted by many small states with modest intelligence services that do not have significant warning needs and formal warning institutions or simply do not have the resources to have dedicated warning persons or organizations.

Two versions of this model exist. The first, which we call the "moderate" version, has long been the CIA model; it gives all analysts warning responsibilities while recognizing and accepting a role for dedicated warning organizations.[9] This view is consistent with what we call the "hybrid" model, discussed below. The second, or what we call the "strong" version, holds that all analysts' warning responsibilities make a dedicated warning organization both unnecessary and undesirable. This more extreme view is now dominant in the IC and is not consistent with the hybrid model.

The strength of both variants of the EAAWA model is that an agency's "warning analysts" cover every issue the intelligence entity deems to be important enough to monitor. Each analyst also, presumably, has at least some knowledge of his or her subject of responsibility. In principle, therefore, all organizational and individual expertise is available to address warning issues. Analysts and/or their managers also (presumably) interact regularly with their most important consumers, fostering producer-consumer trust and thence enhancing the persuasiveness of warning messages. Some knowledgeable intelligence professionals believe this structure adequately performs the strategic warning function.

But there are major problems with the strong version of this system. First, analysts usually are so consumed with their day-to-day assignments—a research paper or current intelligence piece, for example—that they do not have the time or inclination to dive deeply into warning-related aspects of their account. Deadlines and the rush to produce may preclude the research and reflection that often is essential to identifying emerging issues before they become common knowledge. Similarly, if current intelligence is the main organizational priority, warning issues with longer time horizons than the short-term focus of current intelligence pieces may be deemed irrelevant—and so not reported. Robert Jervis argues similarly that the focus on current intelligence may have contributed to the errors of the Iraqi WMD NIE of 2002; he suggests that its emphasis on current intelligence may have meant the IC "lacked the time, as well as incentives, to step back, re-examine central assumptions, explore alternatives, and be more self-conscious about how it was drawing its conclusions."[10]

Second, any warning message analysts draft must work its way through regular review (by management) and coordination (with other organizations with a stake in the issue) processes, which may be time-consuming. Especially if the message is controversial, it may be watered down in either or both processes, muddying the clarity of message needed to adequately focus consumers' thoughts and perhaps damaging the credibility of the warning message. If warning is a low priority or the bureaucratic rewards for producing warning are modest (which may amount to the same thing), the review and publication of warning messages may be delayed or warning messages may be killed. Cynthia Grabo wrote decades ago that the "most accurate warning judgments often are made by a minority of individuals."[11] Coordination processes, however, are designed to ensure that outlying, minority views do not prevail—even if they are prescient.

Third, a warning message placed in an article in a current intelligence serial publication or in a research piece may get "lost." That is, it may not appear to readers to be new or important. If the warning is placed in a serial publication, it will reach many recipients who may not care about, or have responsibility for, the issue, and it may not reach or be focused on the needs of the senior decision-makers who could use intelligence support to make specific decisions. Moreover, most analytic formats have no institutional feedback mechanisms; analytic organizations may not know if they have reached appropriate senior officials persuasively or at all. Hence, if organizations do not take the extra step of bringing warning messages directly to appropriate consumers persuasively, warning may not reach important audiences. An exception to this generalization is the *President's Daily Brief* (PDB), which is tightly targeted on presidential desires and has strong feedback mechanisms.[12]

Fourth, and relatedly, because they largely depend on the presence of relationships of mutual trust, warning messages by potentially any analyst or analytic organization, especially if the messages' primary authors are not identified in products—as is normally the case in the IC now—will not have the credibility that, experience clearly shows, makes warning messages persuasive. Intelligence agencies nevertheless implicitly, and sometimes explicitly, claim that association with an agency "brand" is enough to produce credibility—a judgment we believe is incorrect. As Bowman Miller notes, the challenge for intelligence *people* is to be "in the room" when policies are made—something institutions can never do.[13]

Fifth, because major warning events occur rarely, it is easy for managers to ignore warning or to make it a low institutional priority, meaning they are unlikely to emphasize the use of analytic techniques especially useful for warning analysis. Hence, even if analysts receive elementary training on warning principles during their initial training courses, they may not appreciate or use warning analytic methods or communication techniques. Moreover, because organizational priorities shape institutional incentive structures, a low priority for warning means managers are less likely to authorize the study that experience

has shown is important to enable analysts to generate the expertise and confidence necessary to produce persuasive warning messages. Time spent researching is time not spent
"producing." For analysts and managers alike, activities that produce modest rewards
intermittently tend to be ignored.

Sixth, analytic offices and analysts' accounts virtually always are specialized, meaning analysts are unlikely to have the expertise, breadth of view, and curiosity that are
important in warning analysts. Furthermore, they will not be free to follow leads to areas
outside their designated areas of responsibility for bureaucratic reasons. This is a serious
problem in large organizations that strongly specialize and remind their people to stay in
their "lanes" for reasons of bureaucratic "turf" protection—such as the American IC. This
system thereby tends to generate mediocre warning analysts and, correspondingly, mediocre warning messages.

This problem is exacerbated by the tendency of most US intelligence agencies to
follow the "hot" topics of the day, meaning that agency managers purposefully leave gaps
in coverage, contributing appreciably to future crises. We call this phenomenon the "five-
year-olds'-soccer-game syndrome"—the propensity of some agencies, like young children
playing soccer, to chase the ball and not play their positions. The similar propensity of
collection agencies to focus on the same hot issues is known in the IC as collection "swarm-
ball."[14] The gaps that a focus on hot topics generates help make future intelligence failures.
CIA and INR tend to "play position" better than some other agencies.

Seventh, warning within line organizations means some office bureaucratically "owns"
the warning issue; if the office strongly holds a position on a warning issue or, in an opposite
case such as Lieutenant Colonel Bandman's AMAN Branch 6 in 1973, rejects a developing
warning situation that other analysts see, it can block alternative views by using bureaucratic
rules—or delay a collective decision about a warning issue or dilute analytical messages to
the point of irrelevance. Similarly in 1950, US intelligence analysts who followed China
"owned" the assessment of whether China might intervene in the Korean War; because they
judged an attack on Taiwan more likely, they downplayed reports of Chinese troop movements in and near Korea and thwarted warning by analysts who were more concerned about
an intervention in Korea.[15]

Separate Warning Organizations

A diametrically opposite approach is to assign warning to a dedicated warning organization, which "owns" warning bureaucratically. Several major national military systems have
had aspects of it, including the Watch Committee of the United States during the 1950s and
1960s (discussed in chapter 4), the US Defense Warning Network (DWN), the Australian
Defence Warning System (ADWS), and the Canadian Armed Forces Intelligence Command.[16] The warning apparatus of Britain's Defence Intelligence (DI) also seems to be an
internally focused Ministry of Defence entity but does not contribute to the warning analyses eventually released by the JIC (chapter 4).

The ADWS is an organization within Australia's military intelligence agency, the Defence Intelligence Organisation (DIO). According to one of the DIO's brochures, the mission of the ADWS is "to provide timely, relevant, and predictive warning of situations that could have an adverse influence on Australia's national interests. The ADWS intent is to be estimative and provide the earliest possible indications of changes to specific warning problems that could adversely affect Australia's national interests rather than assessments of current events."[17]

In contrast, distinct Belgian and Dutch warning systems are outside defense ministries and emphasize counterterrorist intelligence. Belgian law—the Act Governing the Analysis of Threats of July 10, 2006—created the Organe de coordination pour l'analyse de la menace (OCAM, or Threat Assessment Coordination Unit) and requires specific Belgian government agencies—including the two intelligence services, the finance and foreign ministries, the customs service, and police—to provide relevant raw information to OCAM within specific time frames to enable timely threat assessments.[18] The law's Article 14 mandates modest criminal penalties for intelligence personnel who fail to share relevant information with OCAM.[19]

In a different organizational form, the European Union's (EU's) Intelligence Analysis Centre (INTCEN), formed in 1999 as the Joint Situation Centre and renamed in 2012, has responsibilities for "intelligence analyses, early warning, and situational awareness."[20] It has a small staff that since 2002 has compiled and analyzed intelligence reporting contributed by member states, including an "insiders club" of France, Germany, Italy, the Netherlands, Spain, Sweden, and the United Kingdom.[21] It provides its assessments to leaders of the EU and member states. INTCEN became part of the European External Action Service in 2010.

Like the other organizational options, this structure has advantages and disadvantages. Its main advantage is that it is dedicated to the warning mission. It can attract and train people who believe in and want to specialize in warning—not a common feature of intelligence analysts as a whole, in our experience or in the intelligence literature. It has an established bureaucratic existence, which may give it some clout for specifying collection priorities, and it has means to establish personal and institutional arrangements with key intelligence consumers, which are significant virtues.

Its disadvantages, though, are several. First, analysts may not have requisite expertise, especially on enduring warning problems they monitor regularly. They also need enough experience and wisdom to identify curious anomalies and appreciate analytic insights. The separate warning organization structure requires that most of the knowledge, understanding, and wisdom needed to effectively warn must reside in the organization because it cannot much tap the expertise of line analytic units. This is a tough challenge for any small organization; it has existed sporadically in US intelligence history when senior intelligence leaders wanted to strengthen the warning or estimative functions. The Dutch and Belgian variants address this problem by legally mandating information sharing by the main intelligence services.

Second, agencies skeptical about warning can easily marginalize the warning function by ignoring specialized warning units and denying them the cooperation and expertise warning officers often need. This is easy to do if warning unit managers or analysts are abrasive. Maladroit American warning personnel have sometimes needlessly offended line organizations by, for example, claiming as warning issues topics that line analytic units believed rightly "belonged" to them. This problem may increase if warning personnel assigned to one agency disagree with line units of other analytic agencies. Unless personalities are congenial, this system risks generating personal and organizational conflicts that damage the warning function. While such conflict is not inevitable, there is a greater risk of strife over warning issues that appear infrequently, are controversial, or are significant than when line units regularly interact with warning, including work in interagency groups and via coordination of each other's analyses. Some warning officers have tried to be prescient if lonely Cassandras, sometimes seeming to enjoy their loneliness.[22]

Third, a specialized warning organization may only report to a segment of national consumers, leaving the rest ignorant of the warning message and effectively relying on consumers to adequately communicate among themselves. This situation appears to characterize the ADWS, which, according to its public information, is designed to serve "strategic and operational level commanders, other senior Defence decision makers and their staff"—a narrow slice of the Australian security establishment.[23] It also has been a recurrent characteristic of defense-focused warning organizations of the United States, which provide threat warning intelligence primarily to military organizations—including the secretary of defense and senior officers such as the chairman of the Joint Chiefs of Staff—but not to warn civilian agencies about threats or opportunities.[24] Perhaps worse, focus on the needs and wants of some consumers may limit the scope of warning problems considered, inviting surprise elsewhere. This appears to be primarily a problem for military warning entities, which in many countries still focus narrowly on military threat warning issues.

Fourth, because serious issues that merit warning messages arise relatively infrequently and at unpredictable intervals, important warning messages are also likely to be infrequent, meaning for appreciable periods warning organizations may not "produce" many intelligence "products," making them appear to be laggards in organizations that establish the volume of "production" as a core measure of performance. Individuals and organizations that are laggards in the intelligence equivalent of the "publish or perish" race, especially in intelligence organizations that strongly value current intelligence and reward analysts and managers who produce a lot, may feel strong pressures to morph their warning outfit into yet another current intelligence production office that produces "warnings" on regular schedules, which historically in the United States and United Kingdom have often been weekly. This makes sense when consumers know of enduring warning problems and want status reports occasionally, but the practice of making "warning" routine or converting the warning office into another current intelligence unit is virtually certain to eventually damage the credibility of the warning office. Indeed, such warning offices typically lack the focused expertise of line units, hampering their ability to produce competitive current intelligence. And, eventually, the competence of "warning" officers who write only current intelligence is also likely to damage the ability to generate insightful strategic warning messages, thereby making the warning entity generally less able and making it a candidate for elimination. We believe this process largely explains the fate of the Watch Committee of the 1960s (see chapter 4). More recently, it appears also to be affecting the relatively new warning office of Joint Staff J-2 (the intelligence directorate) in the Pentagon—the hub of the DWN.

Hybrid Warning Intelligence Systems

The hybrid model combines the best of the moderate version of the EAAWA model with dedicated warning officers—topical expertise combined with a specialized focus on warning issues and analytic methods, respectively—while minimizing the weaknesses of each. This model features a small, specialized warning office that is the focal point for warning issues but interacts regularly and extensively with line analytic units. The central office acquires substantive expertise from line units as needed, communicates questions and warning concerns to analytic units, and prods line units to analyze warning-like issues. The central office coordinates with line units that issue warning messages or issues warnings itself. The central office's chief is a senior intelligence analyst who is responsible for managing the warning "system," including warning-related research and development of warning-focused analytic methods. Authority for warning enables the central office authority to levy warning-related collection requirements, and its senior specialists are institutionally positioned to develop enduring relationships of trust with key decision-makers. These powerful advantages lead us to believe that this model, while not guaranteeing success, is most likely to consistently perform well.

The primary weakness of this system is its vulnerability to the personality quirks of the chief warning officer. This incumbent (and his or her staff) must have the strengths of a good warning analyst and manager while being able to interact constructively with many line analytic units that may not be wholly receptive to warning concerns. The history of US warning (see chapter 4) illustrates examples of both characteristics in NIO/Ws. There are many potential variants of the hybrid warning model.

The tenure of NIO/W John Bird demonstrates how the hybrid model's organizational structure works when it works well. Bird was a career CIA analyst who was NIO/W from 1984 to 1988. His staff was small. He had in his permanent office at CIA headquarters an assistant NIO/W, who was an NSA careerist, and two analysts (including author Gentry). Several military and DoD civilian analysts of the National Warning Staff (NWS) worked at the Pentagon. Bird knew he did not have the personnel or collective knowledge to cover all important intelligence issues. He therefore gave the DoD people on his staff primary responsibility for military-related issues and gave the three officers working directly for him responsibility for scanning the world for issues of potential interest, doing their own research and, importantly, keeping in close touch with capable people working relevant issues throughout the NIC and the IC. When they found an issue of interest and alerted Bird, he investigated it himself. When he believed an issue merited a warning, he normally encouraged the relevant NIO or line analytic office to issue a warning message; when they did so, Bird used his considerable network of contacts to help spread the word to relevant senior consumers. Sometimes Bird decided to issue a warning himself. He always followed up with personal communications, by telephone or a personal visit in the days before email. His unassuming personal style and willingness to let others take the credit for a good warning message meant the office had few of the interoffice tensions some other NIO/Ws had. Bird was well respected, and senior consumers frequently sought his insights. When he spoke, people listened—the hallmark of an effective warning officer. Other NIO/Ws were not as effective—due largely to different personal characteristics.

The Japanese intelligence warning system also appears to be a hybrid system. While for many years Japan had no formal strategic warning entity, it effectively created such an organization in recent years.[25] In 2008, in response to North Korean missile launches over Japanese territory, Prime Minister Shinzō Abe reorganized and strengthened Japanese intelligence.[26] The new system has five core intelligence agencies, including elements of the Ministries of Defense and Foreign Affairs, the Public Security Intelligence Agency, the National Police Agency, and the Cabinet Research and Intelligence Office (CIRO), which is part of the Cabinet Secretariat and is headed by the Director of Cabinet Intelligence (DCI).[27] The CIRO deals regularly with the Cabinet Intelligence Council (CIC), which is composed of senior officials of policymaking departments and the intelligence services. The CIC determines intelligence priorities and disseminates them to the intelligence agencies. The DCI meets regularly (about twice a week) with the prime minister, providing briefings that apparently are roughly equivalent to the American *PDB*.

The CIRO has significant analytic capabilities and is responsible for producing intelligence estimative reports, which are similar to US NIEs. Abe's 2008 directive strengthened the CIRO by giving it senior, experienced analysts; giving it additional responsibilities, including the task of conducting all-source analyses under the direction of the DCI; and improving links between the Japanese Intelligence Community and policymakers by designating the DCI and CIC as "hubs" for intelligence producer-consumer interaction.[28] As of 2012, one Japanese estimate put CIRO's personnel strength at about 170.[29] By providing current and estimative intelligence through the DCI to the prime minister, CIRO can also provide warning intelligence. While we do not discount CIRO's capacity to provide opportunity warning, the Abe reforms were stimulated by threats; we therefore expect that CIRO focuses mainly on threat warning.[30]

Whole-of-Government Systems

The whole-of-government model is characterized by the involvement of many government bureaus, not just intelligence agencies, in identifying warning situations and then responding to them. There are no distinctive intelligence producer or consumer roles. All participating agencies identify issues that warrant attention by senior leaders and potentially are part of effective responses. The advantage of this kind of system is that more collection assets and kinds of expertise are employed to identify issues of warning importance. It prospectively is capable of better identifying a wider range of threats and opportunities than traditional national security-focused intelligence services.

This kind of model depends on the existence of close working relationships among government agencies, meaning it relies on collegial bureaucratic and perhaps national cultures. It therefore is likely to be a viable model for smaller countries with more closely knit bureaucracies. Given the need for close working relationships between ministries and other agencies, it is unsurprising that only a few countries integrate warning intelligence with operations at a national level. These include the United Kingdom and, to a greater extent, Singapore. Each variant of the model seems to work well.

The British JIC system is the oldest of this kind and best known. The JIC combines collection and assessments of British intelligence agencies, along with the views of policy agencies, into coordinated assessments that reflect the views of intelligence, policy agencies, and the Cabinet Office—that is, the security-focused part of the British government as a whole. These national-level assessments include warning issues. While this system is in flux (see chapter 4), it still seems to retain the function of integrating intelligence and operational offices of the British government to reach consensus national positions.[31] Hence, the British system purposefully does not maintain the separation of intelligence from policy offices that is a prominent feature of the American system.

Singapore in recent years has developed a different whole-of-government model that is centered on an analytic approach the Singaporeans call Risk Assessment and Horizon Scanning (RAHS), which we discuss in more detail in chapter 7.[32] This effort has its origins in two big surprises for the government of Singapore: arrests in December 2001 of members of the Jemaah Islamiyah terrorist group and a perceived threat from the SARS (Severe Acute Respiratory Syndrome), which led the government in March 2003 to quarantine infected persons.[33] In response, the government adopted a process, not a specific program or organization, that shares information and insights to help the government identify and effectively respond to threats.

RAHS is characterized by a network of analysts who monitor emerging events imaginatively and share their insights. The Singaporeans see RAHS as a whole-of-government, and even a whole-of-society, process designed to enable the state to identify and manage risks better.[34] This effort relies on encouraging imaginative consideration of new events and sharing insights—or what is known elsewhere as "collaboration." By networking people with diverse "thought patterns," Singapore hopes to be able to overcome the "stove pipes" that the 9/11 Commission in the United States concluded was a cause of the failure of the US IC to prevent the 9/11 attacks.

Some characteristics of this process merit discussion. First, this is a threat-focused process. It focuses on identifying and solving analytic puzzles, not mysteries. In this respect, it is like most military warning systems. Second, RAHS is explicitly a government-wide process, conceived and adopted by government leaders—not an intelligence program. The Singaporeans see the broader perspective as essential. This system, like the British system, thereby minimizes the distinction between intelligence "producers" and "consumers" and seems to do so without endangering the objectivity of intelligence analysis—the core reason US intelligence maintains distance from its consumers. Third, it depends on the cooperation of disparate agencies, including ones not normally considered in other states to be part of the national security establishment. We speculate that this approach is a feature of the relatively small size of Singapore and its government and the political culture of Singapore. This model may be hard to replicate elsewhere, especially in much larger governments with agencies that strongly value their bureaucratic independence.

No Warning System—No Effective Intelligence

Some states seem not to have warning functions because their intelligence services are small, weak, poorly regarded, or simply ineffective. The intelligence literature does not much address reasons that states have minimal intelligence capacities, but some studies of national intelligence services provide glimpses of institutional reasons why effective warning sometimes does not occur. For example, Stéphane Lefebvre reports that some Polish officials believed in the 1990s that Poland, when it was still recovering from its experience with communism, had an intelligence apparatus that had not convinced senior political leaders that it had anything to offer, including strategic warning.[35]

Summary

While the five models of strategic warning are established variants of warning structures of national intelligence agencies, other institutional arrangements are possible. Indeed, since 9/11, intelligence agencies globally have emphasized CT more than they previously did, and "strategic" intelligence increasingly means information and analysis that saves modest numbers of lives from "terrorist" attacks. Hence, strategic warning already means (and may more so in the future) what heretofore has been tactical warning and involves more actors, including law enforcement agencies, domestic intelligence agencies, and the unfocused US Department of Homeland Security (DHS). In the United States, "fusion centers" that often contain representatives of federal, state, and local government organizations share and integrate information designed mainly to conduct CT-focused intelligence work. Hence, the variety of warning-related organizational models is increasing and evolving.

Notes

1. May, *Strange Victory*.
2. Khong, *Analogies at War*; Miller, "Graveyard of Analogies," 446–76; Neustadt and May, *Thinking in Time*, 34–57.
3. Gentry, "Warning Analysis," 64–88.
4. For example, Jones, *Wizard War*, 100–102, 124.
5. Ibid., 205.

6. This view is quite old. See Hilsman, *Strategic Intelligence and National Decisions*, 100–108.

7. Davis, "Strategic Warning: If Surprise Is Inevitable," 1, 7; Davis, "Strategic Warning: Intelligence Support," 174–75, 179; Shalev, *Israel's Intelligence Assessment*, 4–10.

8. Goodman, "Learning to Walk," 40–56; Davies, "Twilight of Britain's Joint Intelligence Committee?," 427–46.

9. McLaughlin, "Serving the National Policymaker," 87; Petersen, "What I Learned," 16.

10. Jervis, "Reports, Politics, and Intelligence Failures," 45–46.

11. Grabo, *Handbook of Warning Intelligence*, 423.

12. Priess, *President's Book of Secrets*.

13. Miller, "U.S. Strategic Intelligence Forecasting," 690.

14. Lowenthal, *Intelligence*, 6th ed., 95.

15. Grabo, "Watch Committee," 367.

16. Canada's warning doctrine, *Canadian Forces Joint Publication 2*, is not publicly available.

17. Undated, publicly released Australian Ministry of Defence paper pamphlet *Australian Defence Warning System: Providing Strategic Warning*, published by the DIO, received by authors in August 2016.

18. Lefebvre, "'Belgians Just Aren't Up to It,'" 8–9; Lasoen, "Indications and Warning in Belgium."

19. Lefebvre, "'Belgians Just Aren't Up to It,'" 8.

20. Jones, "Secrecy Reigns."

21. Ibid., 1.

22. In Greek mythology, Cassandra, daughter of the king of Troy, foresaw and warned of the Greeks' use of the Trojan horse and the fall of Troy but was ignored.

23. *Australian Defence Warning System*.

24. Landers, "Defense Warning System," 21–31.

25. Oros, "Japanese Foreign Intelligence-Related Activities," 241.

26. Kobayashi, "Assessing Reform," 717–33.

27. Ibid., 718.

28. Ibid., 723–25.

29. Ibid., 718.

30. Ibid., 722, 730.

31. Goodman, "Learning to Walk"; Davies, "Twilight of Britain's Joint Intelligence Committee?"

32. For details, see Quiggin, *Seeing the Invisible*; and Tan Kwan Chong et al., "Risk Assessment."

33. Quiggin, *Seeing the Invisible*, 199.

34. Ibid.

35. Lefebvre, "Poland's Attempts to Develop," 481.

CHAPTER 4

The Evolution of US, British, Dutch, and NATO Warning Institutions

Literature on the history of warning organizations is sparse. Most public information is on the American and British warning structures, but to our knowledge there is no definitive history of either.[1] In this chapter, we recount major aspects of the development of the US and British warning systems and assess their performance characteristics in the context of the taxonomy discussed in chapter 3. We present an overview of the primarily terrorism-focused warning system the Netherlands developed in recent years. And we discuss the military threat-oriented warning system that NATO uses. While NATO borrows analytic methods from the US Defense warning system, it is structurally different from all national warning organizations—a function of the politics of an alliance of sovereign states.

US Warning Systems

The history of US warning-focused organizations reflects evolving structures and procedures, sharply different levels of performance, and a cyclical pattern of emphasis on strategic warning, including strong emphasis on warning in periods of major perceived threats (especially during the 1950s) and de-emphasis on warning and the periodic demise of warning organizations when warning was seen as unnecessary or ineffective (during the early 1970s and 2010s). This cyclical process is characterized by perceived need, prosperity, decay, crisis, failure, and regeneration when new needs are identified. This history illustrates how intellectually and institutionally difficult warning analysis is: how structures and the degree of emphasis on warning by senior intelligence leaders influence the performance of the warning function, how internal bureaucratic pressures kill dedicated warning organizations, how administrations struggled to create structures and broader institutions (including procedures, policies, and organizational incentives) that effectively perform the warning function, and why lessons learned half a century ago continue to be relearned. We integrate in this case study three aspects of US warning: formal, dedicated warning structures of the IC; warning aspects of NIEs produced by the Office of National Estimates (O/NE); and practice of the EAAWA philosophy. The first two overlapped at times in varying degrees, reflecting both the national priority of strategic warning during the Cold War, especially, and the personal desires of leaders.

The Early Years

The intelligence debacle of Pearl Harbor led to the creation of the CIA in 1947 and to improved US intelligence capabilities in general, but the rise of Cold War tensions in the late 1940s led to the first formal structures focused specifically on strategic warning.[2] In 1948, three CIA analysts, with assistance from British intelligence, began to compile a list of "indicators" of possible hostile actions by adversary states.[3] The idea that one could identify signatures of military mobilization that indicated enemy intentions as well as capabilities appealed to the analysts. In time, this group invited personnel from other agencies to join them, thereby expanding the group, which became known as the Watch Committee. Intelligence officers scrutinized incoming intelligence reports for indications that the Soviets planned an imminent attack on the United States or American interests more broadly, including attacks on allies and friends. This method eventually became the "indications and warning" analytic method still in use (see chapter 6). Early in the postwar period, the United States also developed warning intelligence relationships with some allies, many of which continue to this day.[4]

In January 1949, the US Army's intelligence directorate (G-2) began a similar effort housed in a section devoted to Soviet military activities, which was called the Intelligence Indications File (IIF). In April 1950, CIA and IIF analysts became concerned about North Korean intentions toward South Korea. The US Army wrote, buried in the body of an assessment, "The outbreak of hostilities may occur at any time in Korea."[5] Senior decision-makers unsurprisingly ignored the message—an early lesson on the importance of direct, persuasive communication between warning officers and senior decision-makers.[6] The Watch Committee on June 15, 1950, listed Korea as the fifth most dangerous global source of conflict with the Soviet Union.[7] Neither the IIF nor the Watch Committee forecast the North Korean invasion of June 25, 1950.[8]

The invasion of South Korea triggered greater US government interest in what Cynthia Grabo called "the indications business."[9] In August 1950, the DoD expanded the IIF to include intelligence personnel from other military services; invited CIA, Federal Bureau of Investigation (FBI), and State Department people to join the effort; and renamed the organization the Joint Intelligence Indications Committee (JIIC). As before, a US Army brigadier general chaired its weekly meetings, and its reports were widely circulated in the government.[10] The expanded organization failed to warn early of the meaning of the large Chinese military buildup in Manchuria that led to China's massive intervention in the

Korean conflict in the fall of 1950.[11] Grabo explained why—an explanation that using slightly different words continues to characterize many warning failures:

> These two stumbling blocks to the issuance of timely warning—the reluctance to change preconceived opinion in the face of new evidence, and the underestimating of enemy military strength and capabilities because of rigid OB criteria—were to be encountered again and again. What seemed at the time to be mere stubbornness and flawed analysis by a few researchers (a one-time problem) would prove to be far more widespread and pervasive in the future. Indications analysts had also learned, as they would time and again, that the vigorous support of higher authority would be necessary for their views to be even considered, let alone prevail over those of the entrenched bureaucracy.[12]

The JIIC eventually warned of a major Chinese attack in October, about ten days before the event, but its warning was overshadowed by more sanguine views of General Douglas MacArthur and the intelligence assessments of his Far East Command headquarters in Tokyo, which carried more weight in Washington.[13]

Soon after the Chinese attack, the Intelligence Advisory Committee (IAC), the senior national-level intelligence board and predecessor of the current US National Intelligence Board, decided it did not need two warning committees. The IAC kept the JIIC but renamed it the Watch Committee in January 1951.[14] The new Watch Committee remained under army chairmanship for four more years. Throughout the Korean War, the Watch Committee focused on that war, largely duplicating the current intelligence activities of other intelligence entities while ignoring other issues—a practice that would recur.

In 1954, at the urging of the US Air Force, the IAC augmented the warning function by creating the National Indications Center (NIC), which supported the Watch Committee and was located in the Pentagon. The Watch Committee's charter, and therefore the NIC's mission, was to warn of military threats to the United States and its allies and situations that communist countries could exploit.[15] At the same time, the chair of the Watch Committee became a senior CIA officer or the deputy DCI, who often in the 1950s was a senior military officer. The Watch Committee had no mandate to do opportunity warning—alerting policymakers of opportunities to act to advance US interests—but had an implicit directive to identify exploitable US and Western vulnerabilities. It encountered resistance, however, from the Defense Department, which declined to share US information, and therefore abandoned as bureaucratically impossible the mission of providing net assessments of the relative positions of friendly and potential adversary nations. In 1973, the Office of Net Assessment, a part of the Office of the Secretary of Defense headed by Andrew Marshall, assumed this aspect of the warning function.[16] Marshall's biographers say his office "sought to provide the secretary of defense and other senior defense officials with early warning of emerging strategic problems or opportunities to gain competitive advantage over rivals."[17]

The NIC and Watch Committee monitored crisis situations in the 1950s, including the French war in Vietnam, the Chinese attacks on Quemoy and Matsu, the Warsaw Pact intervention in Hungary in 1956, and the turmoil in Lebanon that led to US military intervention in 1958. The Watch Committee in October 1956 warned of the British-French-Israeli attack on Suez about thirty-six hours before the attack.[18] President Dwight Eisenhower quickly responded forcefully in diplomatic terms, dealing a stinging rebuke to the American allies. The Watch Committee also monitored troubles with the Soviets over the status of Berlin. The NIC established a committee to monitor events in Berlin in 1958 but discontinued it before construction of the Berlin Wall in August 1961. The NIC tracked these crises along with current intelligence analysts throughout the IC.

Grabo argues that the NIC successfully monitored and warned of Soviet actions during the Cuban Missile Crisis and believes this performance was "probably the high tide of the Watch Committee and the NIC."[19] Grabo's perspective differs considerably from most assessments of the performance of intelligence regarding Cuba in 1962, which emphasize the failures of the estimative process and the belated success of tactical collection in the form of aerial photography, not tactical military warning.

The Watch Committee in the late 1950s and early 1960s remained a senior-level organization. Its chair was a two- or three-star military officer or civilian equivalent, and its members included CIA, State, DIA after it was created in 1961, NSA, and the FBI. DIA represented the military services, which assigned observers to the committee. The NIC had fairly senior military and civilian analysts who, Grabo recalled, never numbered more than "about 13."[20] Support staff raised the total number of NIC personnel to about thirty.[21] The NIC developed a twenty-four-hour-per-day "watch center" that monitored traffic for signs of activity in the arenas highlighted by its indications lists; some analysts also researched existing and potentially emerging warning issues.[22]

The focus of warning in this era was fairly narrow. Analysts looked for indications of military attack. Studies of surprise attack indicated that it was often accompanied by efforts at D&D of critical information, such as intent (that is, whether an attack was planned), time of attack, place of attack, strength of the attacking force, and "style" of attack (that is, how the attack would be conducted).[23] Warning analysts therefore worked to develop ways to better identify these factors.

The Watch Committee and the NIC developed a routine and issued "warning" reports periodically, normally weekly, just as current intelligence was published.[24] They further developed the I&W method.[25] As the I&W method and warning function became institutionalized, each major military command built a variant of the NIC in its intelligence directorate. These centers mainly supported their own commanders but also interacted with the broader Defense warning establishment.

The Watch Committee enjoyed considerable status within the US government as a whole and could, in a crisis situation, make autonomous analytic decisions—that is, without a requirement to coordinate messages with the rest of the IC—and get a warning message to the White House within one hour.[26] Its work was featured in the President's Intelligence Checklist, President John Kennedy's version of the current *PDB*.[27] DCI John McCone called on the Watch Committee immediately after Kennedy's death on November 22, 1963, to look for indications of a conspiracy to kill the president.[28]

The 1960s saw a diffusion of global threats to US interests, leading to debates within the Watch Committee and NIC about issues to follow that were consistent with what warning personnel informally called the "beartrap" clause of their charter: their mandate to focus on Soviet-related threats. In addition to monitoring the USSR, China, Cuba, and other communist countries, in these years the Watch Committee followed events in Laos, Korea, parts of the Middle East, South Vietnam, and Thailand, and it monitored the Sino-Indian conflict of 1962.[29] The NIC in the late 1960s spent most of its time following events in Southeast Asia. Again, it largely competed with line analytic units producing current intelligence.

US intelligence generally gets poor reviews of its performance on Vietnam during both the French and American periods.[30] For example, US Army civilian (and later CIA) analyst George Allen wrote that the Watch Committee's chairman rejected his assessment in early 1954 that the Viet Minh planned, and had the ability, to trap the French military garrison at Dien Bien Phu, leading the committee to refuse to warn of an impending French disaster.[31] During the American period, most intelligence work addressed traditional, tactical-level military issues. Intelligence units that used the I&W method sometimes were surprised. Nevertheless, in the view of a panel formed to review the Tet Offensive of January 1968, strategic warning was moderately effective.[32] Some units were well prepared to meet the offensive based on their own collection and analytic resources. Threat warning success during Tet also produced an "opportunity" intelligence success: the Fourth Infantry Division's awareness of enemy plans enabled it to effectively attack enemy forces in the Central Highlands, especially near Pleiku.[33]

Still, the review panel noted appreciable inadequacies in both intelligence and the responsiveness of the military in general, providing much fodder for critics of US intelligence. Grabo identified obstacles to effective and timely warning analysis during the Vietnam period—all of which have recurred in other situations:

- overreliance on order of battle "proof" to assess mobilization and deployments of units.
- slowness to reallocate analytic resources in new situations (in this case, failure to assign analysts specifically to examine mobilization, not just order of battle).
- reluctance to accept readily available unclassified information as too "low grade."
- overreliance on classified sources even when they are not productive.
- *excessive preoccupation with current data at the expense of longer term basic research* [emphasis added].
- dismissal of foreign public statements and decrees as "mere propaganda."
- reluctance of current and military "experts" to consider the alternative views of indications specialists.
- reluctance to alarm senior officials with unpleasant information, particularly when it was not yet proven.[34]

The IC did much better in 1967, warning of a likely war between Israel and its Arab neighbors and accurately forecasting its outcome. The IC still revels in this success.

But the Watch Committee stumbled again in 1968 over the Soviet-led Warsaw Pact intervention in Czechoslovakia, which unfolded over several months as the "Prague Spring" generated worries in Moscow and Eastern Europe that Czechoslovakia might abandon communism.[35] The Watch Committee watched intently as Department D of the KGB's First Chief Directorate worked with the Soviet military to plan deception aspects of the operation, but it did not formally warn of the invasion.[36] Grabo characterizes the analytic errors of this failure as

- a widespread belief that the Soviet Union had "matured" since the suppression of the Hungarian revolt twelve years before and would not do such a thing again.
- a failure to perceive how seriously the Soviet leaders viewed the situation in Czechoslovakia and how committed they were to restoring orthodox control by any means.
- a prevalent view that the importance of detente with the United States would deter Soviet leaders from taking overt military action to assert control in Czechoslovakia.
- inadequate attention to a host of crucial details (small but highly significant indications), particularly in the military preparations, which were lost in the tremendous volume of information received.
- *an excessive emphasis on current reporting rather than in-depth analysis of cumulative indications* (emphasis added).
- the inadequate integration of military and political developments, which would have provided clearer insight into the Soviet decision-making process.
- the repetition in current intelligence reporting of Soviet announcements that their military actions were "exercises," without considering that these announcements could be cover for bona fide military preparations.
- a relaxation of vigilance and weakening of warning judgments during the seeming delay in Soviet action in the three weeks prior to the invasion.[37]

Grabo noted that a few analysts accurately interpreted Soviet actions and anticipated the intervention, but they, like George Allen in 1954, were unable to convince the majority who established the Watch Committee / NIC analytic position. We know now that the Soviet communist party politburo did not finally decide to intervene until just before the August 20 intervention, meaning analysts for months debated the likely outcome of a mystery, not the solution to a puzzle.[38] Disagreements about the meaning of Warsaw Pact actions led to compromise language that fell short of clear warning messages. These analytic mistakes were similar to errors Grabo saw often in the 1950s and 1960s, which prompted her to write her book.[39]

By the early 1970s, Grabo argued, the once-vibrant National Indications Center and the Watch Committee had become ineffective for several reasons.[40] The NIC's once-considerable freedom to draft and quickly disseminate crisp warning reports disappeared when the Watch Committee decided, at a time apparently lost, to review and edit its work before disseminating warning messages. In 1963, the United States Intelligence Board (USIB), which replaced the IAC, decreed that warning reports had to be fully coordinated

professor, OSS veteran, and author of the then recently published and today still influential *Strategic Intelligence for American World Policy*, initially was Langer's deputy.[52] Kent succeeded Langer and O/NE's chief from 1952 to 1967, when he retired. Ray Cline, who later led CIA's analysis directorate and headed State/INR, was O/NE's first chief of staff. Other staff members included retired military flag officers, retired ambassadors, and senior civilian intelligence analysts, many of whom were known to, and trusted by, senior US policymakers. Former senior analyst Harold Ford, who spent much of his CIA career on the O/NE staff, assesses the high caliber and political connectedness of these people to have been among the chief strengths of O/NE in its early years.[53]

Although O/NE was housed within CIA, it worked for the DCI. O/NE analysts regularly interacted with analysts throughout the IC and with consumers, and they subjected their judgments to review by an outside board of experts—a practice resumed in recent years and claimed as an innovation, a reflection of the weak institutional memory of the IC.[54] O/NE's culture strongly valued objective analyses. Because O/NE had some organizational independence, it initially submitted its products for review only to the IAC and its successor, the USIB, which helped to maintain its objectivity and avoid the lowest-common-denominator syndrome that was a common feature of later interagency coordination processes. For these reasons, most observers assess its performance in the 1950s on major issues involving the USSR, China, and the Sino-Soviet split to have been good.[55]

O/NE famously missed, however, Soviet efforts to place nuclear missiles in Cuba in 1962—a strategically important warning issue. Aware of growing Soviet activity in Cuba, O/NE issued four estimates on Cuba in 1962. The last, Special National Intelligence Estimate (SNIE) 85–3-62, published on September 19, 1962, about a month before the Cuban Missile Crisis broke, discussed many possibilities but concluded that the Soviet buildup was designed to defend the new communist regime against American attacks—an understandable Soviet motive given the numerous American attempts to kill Fidel Castro, the Bay of Pigs invasion, and other ongoing John F. Kennedy administration efforts to destabilize the Castro regime.[56] The SNIE judged that while the Soviets could derive benefits from placing nuclear missiles or a submarine base on Cuba, "the establishment on Cuban soil of Soviet nuclear striking forces which could be used against the U.S. would be incompatible with Soviet policy as we presently estimate it."[57] Photographs taken by US reconnaissance aircraft soon thereafter revealed the presence of nuclear missiles. The photos did not show O/NE's judgment to be wrong but indicated that the Soviets had done something out of character that the SNIE did not forecast. Hence, because the discovery of the missiles was a surprise, SNIE 85–3-62 is widely seen as a significant warning failure.

In a rare event for an intelligence agency, Sherman Kent published an initially classified article in the CIA's internal journal *Studies in Intelligence* that explained the misjudgments he and his colleagues made.[58] It is an excellent discussion, devoid of the self-defensive dissembling that characterizes some internal postmortems of intelligence failures and the hindsight bias of most investigatory commissions.[59] Kent's argument is summarized in the oft-quoted sentence "We missed the Soviet decision to put missiles into Cuba because we did not believe that Khrushchev could make such a mistake."[60] Kent also concluded that the inherent difficulty of such analyses makes some estimative, and hence also warning, errors all but certain. He agreed with Roberta Wohlstetter's then recent assessment of the Pearl Harbor failure and anticipated Richard Betts's assessment in 1978 that some intelligence failures are inevitable.[61]

But despite the difficulty of the call and the fact that the IC redeemed itself soon thereafter by acquiring aerial photos confirming the deployment of Soviet strategic missiles in Cuba and then effectively supporting President Kennedy's dealings with the Soviets, the SNIE cost the O/NE a considerable amount of credibility. In the 1960s, many other factors caused the status and performance of O/NE to decline further, including diminished quality of O/NE staffers, reflecting senior management decisions about personnel appointments; diminished contact between O/NE people and their main consumers; less able O/NE bureaucratic in-fighting skills; increased resentment of O/NE within the IC as a CIA, not a community, entity; perceptions that newly imposed interagency coordination processes reduced the clarity and quality of estimative messages; and perceptions that NIEs' "batting average" was declining, prominently including the SNIE of September 1962.[62] In addition, President Richard Nixon was unhappy with the quality of the intelligence support he received in general.[63] In 1973, DCI William Colby abolished O/NE.[64]

To redress the perceived problems of O/NE, Colby in October 1973 established a group of national intelligence officers (NIOs), usually about fifteen in number, who were senior analysts responsible for specific regions of the world and an evolving set of functional issues. The NIOs were to interact closely with key intelligence consumers, becoming trusted advisors of their clients. The NIOs had warning as well as estimative duties within their areas of responsibility, detracting further from the decaying Watch Committee.

In 1975, both houses of Congress established committees to investigate allegations of inappropriate actions by IC agencies, which led soon thereafter to the creation of the current intelligence oversight committees. The subcommittee on evaluation of the new House Permanent Select Committee on Intelligence (HPSCI) issued a report on warning intelligence in August 1978 that recommended improving the function by creating an NIO/W and an interagency, national warning staff.[65]

DCI Stansfield Turner in 1979 established the National Intelligence Council (NIC), whose chair and vice chair coordinated the activities of individual NIOs more closely. The NIC structure added institutional formality, a mechanism for coordinating the activities of the NIOs, and some additional seniority—all of which helped the NIC perform better.

The National Intelligence Officers for Warning

Also in 1979, in the wake of the HPSCI report on warning and another warning failure—the surprise overthrow of the shah of Iran[66]—DCI Turner issued DCI Directive 1/5, which created a new National Intelligence Warning system that built on earlier methods and created the position of NIO/W.[67] The directive gave the NIO/W specific responsibilities, including coordination of the warning activities of the regional and other functional NIOs, and provided some definitions that remain valid:

a. *Warning* as used herein encompasses those measures taken, and the intelligence information produced, by the Intelligence Community to avoid surprise to the President, the NSC [National Security Council], and the Armed Forces of the United States by foreign events of major importance to the security of the United States. It includes strategic, but not tactical warning.

b. *Strategic Warning* is intelligence information or intelligence regarding the threat of the initiation of hostilities against the US or in which US forces may become involved; it may be received at any time prior to the initiation of hostilities. It does not include tactical warning.

c. *Tactical warning* is notification that the enemy has initiated hostilities. Such warning may be received at any time from the launching of the attack until it reaches its target.[68]

Note that "warning" is defined as avoidance of "surprise" about "events of major importance" to senior civilian and military leaders. This meant, in practice, that NIO/Ws and much of the NIC at this time provided both threat and opportunity warning, with primary but not exclusive focus on the needs of senior civilian policymakers. The old "beartrap" restrictions thereby were lifted. Defense warning, which operated largely independently, remained focused on military threats.

The new warning system was soon tested as the IC monitored increasing Soviet unhappiness with chaotic events in Afghanistan involving rival communist groups within the Afghan national government. The IC wondered how Moscow would redress what was, in the Soviet view, a deteriorating political situation. While current intelligence reporting in 1979 on Soviet activity was extensive, the IC did not specifically warn of the Soviet invasion of December 1979. In response to an NSC request to assess intelligence on the invasion from a warning perspective, the IC in October 1980 published a seventy-three-page report that concluded that the "Indications and Warning System" the IC used had generally worked well, enabling issuance of three "Alert Memorandums"—one in September 1979 and two in December, including one on December 19, 1979, a week before the invasion.[69] The report concluded that the I&W method generally enabled and reflected good understanding of Soviet military practices. The official responsible for this "warning problem," which is a formal process for warning on a specific area (see chapter 6), was the NIO for General Purpose Forces—not the new NIO/W.[70]

Successive NIO/Ws had generally the following assets and responsibilities. They had small personal staffs of analysts who conducted their own analyses and interacted with experts in line analytic units and the other NIOs and were free to issue warning messages to the DCI and senior policymakers as they considered appropriate. NIO/Ws shared warning-related concerns with other NIOs and helped them communicate warning messages they developed within their own areas of responsibility. NIO/Ws also worked to increase the priority of warning-related collection. While each NIO/W operated differently, they all used variants of the "hybrid" structural model of strategic warning analysis—a small central warning office interacting regularly with analysts who primarily worked current intelligence issues. Early NIO/Ws also worked closely with the Strategic Warning Staff, still located at the Pentagon. The CIA's Douglas MacEachin headed the SWS in the late 1970s, including the period of the Soviet invasion of Afghanistan, while the CIA's John Bird was director in 1980–82.[71] The SWS later was renamed the National Warning Staff (NWS) and became largely a DIA/ military organization; unlike the J-2, it did not focus mainly on current intelligence. Both groups issued warning messages to an overlapping set of consumers and challenged line organizations to be more alert to warning issues. The NWS focused on military threats, while the NIO/W interacted closely with senior consumers of intelligence throughout the government on a wide variety of military and civilian issues, including threats and opportunities.[72]

The first NIO/W was Richard Lehman, a career CIA officer who also was chairman of the NIC. Lehman had a reputation for caution and issued relatively few warning messages.[73] He preferred to wait until evolving issues became relatively clear before warning, thereby sometimes defeating the purpose of warning by not giving senior decision-makers adequate reaction time. He sometimes disagreed with members of the SWS, who preferred to warn more aggressively and developed their own informal contacts with key decision-makers.[74] Later NIO/W John Bird succinctly assessed the cost of Lehman's approach: "To never be wrong is also to be never right."[75] Bird attributed the lack of a formal warning message in 1979 about prospects for the Soviet invasion of Afghanistan largely to Lehman's conservative approach to warning.[76]

The second NIO/W was NSA careerist David McManus (1981–84). We know little about his tenure. In 1984, he reportedly was involved in a controversial NIE over Soviet reaction to NATO's Able Archer exercise of 1983, which we discuss in chapter 6.

John Bird, who succeeded McManus, was NIO/W in 1984–88. Bird practiced a form of the hybrid warning model that we consider to be especially effective. His view was that warning is a group activity that is successful when many organizations are involved.[77] He therefore interacted with other NIOs—both regional and functional NIOs—and line units in many ways. First, he himself dealt regularly with the NIOs, suggesting that they, not his office, issue warning messages because he believed they would have to deal with consumers on warning issues on a continuing basis and should therefore originate warning messages. Second, he and his staff interacted regularly with line analysts and their managers to get insights and expertise when needed and to communicate that the NIO/W was interested in an issue, thereby eliminating surprise warning messages and consequent unhappiness by line unit managers. Bird knew that warning was sometimes hard for line analytic units— especially when issues were contentious and data controversial. Giving others credit for warning successes, he also was willing to make warning calls too hot for line units. If he was mistaken, all could say it was just the dumb warning guys being wrong again, thereby protecting the line units.

Bird's approach repeatedly revealed differences in analytic perspective within the IC but was designed to keep disagreements professional, not personal.[78] He was keenly aware that his function was to alert people to situations the line analytic units were covering inadequately in some way, and he kept prominently in mind "whose ox was being gored."[79] He tried to keep the wounds shallow and easily healed—and usually succeeded. Bird used his understanding of basic human psychology and bureaucratic politics to perform his job.

He also realized the importance of wisely supervising subordinates. It was important to let them learn by making mistakes, giving them cover and support while making sure the mistakes were not big. He saw strategic warning as a skill to be developed through practice—a view other experienced warning officers have adopted.

Bird covered a wide variety of issues, not just military threat warning. He considered one of his greatest warning successes to have been alerting the Department of the Treasury and other civilian agencies about an impending financial crisis in a country of importance to the United States, which Washington was able to help effectively.[80] Another success was warning of an impending conflict between two countries; Washington intervened diplomatically to help defuse the situation.

McManus and Bird reported directly to DCI William Casey, who had an unusually great appreciation of the warning function, bypassing chairmen of the NIC who were NIO/Ws' nominal supervisors.[81] Casey periodically called Bird to his office to discuss issues. When he thought a warning issue was sufficiently important, Casey called on President Ronald Reagan, sometimes generating presidential responses.[82] Other NIOs sometimes complained about the warners to Casey, who replied that if warning professionals did not occasionally irritate other analysts, they were not doing their jobs—thereby usually backing McManus and Bird. Casey was, however, a cause of what Bird considered his greatest warning failure—an inability to convince Casey to alert President Reagan about a developing foreign environmental threat of importance. Casey instead accepted the views of a CIA analytic office, whose sanguine view was later disproved by clear scientific evidence.[83]

Charles E. (Charlie) Allen replaced Bird as NIO/W in mid-1988. Allen considered Bird to have been effective but "low key" and believed the office of the NIO/W atrophied during Bird's tenure in that Bird's staff was too small.[84] Allen increased the size of his office in collaboration with John F. McCreary, a longtime DIA warning specialist on the NWS, who also worked for Bird. Allen and McCreary eventually assembled a staff of some ten to twelve analysts at the Pentagon, some detailed by agencies that supposedly wanted to get rid of them, and generated some opposition from the sitting Joint Staff J-2, who resisted giving Allen's staff more office space.[85]

Allen operated differently than did Bird. He considered himself a contrarian who "got into trouble for his independence" but "did not care" if he "upset people."[86] Allen recalled, "We didn't play by the rules."[87] Allen regularly encountered opposition, including from a chairman of the NIC who frequently "wanted to quash" his papers and from others whom he worked around.[88] He did, however, maintain what he considered to be good relations with US military personnel, who helped him keep abreast of friendly military activity. In retrospect, Allen said he did not regret his unconventional ways and said they were effective, but he regretted that a US Navy lieutenant commander on his staff once gave a memo about Russia's threats to Lithuania directly to the then Undersecretary of Defense Paul Wolfowitz prematurely, which produced a "bad effect."[89] Like some warning officers since, Allen published a weekly warning report but was not sure many people read it. As a contrarian, he used red team and devil's advocate techniques now firmly established in the IC as structured analytic techniques (SATs), which are designed to help analysts avoid common analytical mistakes.

Allen focused mainly on military threats, although he conducted some opportunity warning analyses. His time horizons tended to be short, although he also looked out to the periods addressed in NIEs: three to five years.[90] Allen counted among his successes warning about Iraq's threat to Kuwait in 1990, which his staff studied extensively before he issued his warning of the Iraqi attack and warning about tensions between India and Pakistan, which led to effective US diplomatic action.[91]

Warning about Iraq's invasion of Kuwait provoked some controversy. US intelligence—including Allen and the Joint Staff J-2—monitored the Iraqi military buildup that preceded its invasion of Kuwait in 1990 and issued warnings to US military commanders, but senior civilians in the administration of President George H. W. Bush apparently were surprised.[92] Allen publicly claimed in his defense that he and his staff had done their job by issuing warnings, but he did not cite any policy officials with whom he communicated (although in his discussion with Joseph Gordon he mentioned Richard Haass, who was then on the NSC staff, as a regular interlocutor).[93] Former DoD warning officer Daniel Landers agrees with Allen, saying the system worked because the military combatant commands were alerted and US Central Command raised its alert status, or what US military people call a "Watch Condition" or "WATCHCON."[94] However, Allen's assistant NIO/W at the time, Mary McCarthy, says there was a warning failure in that senior leaders were not notified.[95] Later Haass wrote that he received warnings from Allen but did not believe him until just before the invasion.[96]

Whatever the facts of the matter, this case illustrates the critical importance of communicating warning messages persuasively to all relevant senior decision-makers, not just military leaders. The "outreach" function long has been a core responsibility of NIOs. It requires them to establish close personal relationships with important civilian as well as military decision-makers.[97] The then former vice chairman of the NIC (and later chairman) Gregory Treverton, who oversaw production of NIEs in 1993–95, wrote in 2009 that he saw the main "product" of the council as its NIOs, whose relationships with senior consumers were more valuable than its NIEs.[98] Such relationships are especially important for senior warning officers given the costs that warning messages often implicitly ask policy-makers to bear.

Treverton believes the warning establishment performed two especially useful functions in the 1990s. First, warning provided "an institutional second view" about issues the other NIOs and line analytic units assessed.[99] While the latter often did not appreciate having someone "look over their shoulder," Treverton liked the additional perspective and different data or methodological approaches to analyses that warning officers usually offered. Second, NIO/Ws were a focal point for warning analyses and were "cheerleaders" for the warning function. These are core characteristics of the hybrid warning structure.

Meanwhile, the Defense Department's warning system again changed. Now called the Defense Warning System (DWS), it cooperated with NIO/Ws to varying degrees over time through the NWS at the Pentagon.[100] For example, while NIO/W Bird had a moderately close working relationship with the NWS in the late 1980s, in the early 1990s NIO/W Allen chaired weekly meetings of a newly established Warning Committee that included the DWS. The DWS consisted of DIA personnel assigned to the Joint Staff J-2, the military services, the intelligence arms of the unified and specified commands (now called combatant commands), US Forces Korea (owing to chronic concerns that North Korea might again attack South Korea), and some foreign military intelligence services.[101] The focus of the DWS remained exclusively on military threats. The primary consumers of its warning messages were the commanders of the military combatant commands.

Warning declined in priority after the demise of the Soviet Union in 1991.[102] The formerly bipolar, deeply competitive world suddenly became unipolar. The United States seemed to be its unchallenged hegemon, with no existential threat to itself in any direction. The DoD boasted in its *Joint Vision 2020* strategic vision document, published in 2000, that it would achieve "full spectrum dominance" over all military rivals.[103]

Aware of the changing world and the controversy over warning of the invasion of Kuwait, DCI Robert Gates in 1992 commissioned a Task Force on Improving Intelligence Warning to study the strategic warning function.[104] A distinguished panel concluded that warning was not performing adequately and that the causes were systemic. It recommended changes. It concluded, in the judgment of former NIO/W Mary McCarthy, that "with the exception of Defense, all intelligence agencies had treated *warning intelligence assessments as by-products of their routine analytical activities, an approach that had proven inadequate*; that there had been little accountability; and, most disturbingly, that the system previously in place had been largely notional [emphasis added]."[105] In essence, the panel sharply criticized what we call the strong variant of the EAAWA model of strategic warning.

To correct these problems, Gates's panel designed what McCarthy called a comprehensive system to integrate regional and functional experts with professional warning specialists headed by the NIO/W, who would remain the principal advisor to the DCI on warning issues.[106] Previously, the panel assessed, NIO/Ws and line analytic units had operated excessively independently and in parallel. In essence, the panel saw what we call the hybrid model as not hybrid enough and sought to strengthen NIO/Ws, including by making the NIO/W a vice chair of the NIC—or a VC/NIC/W—a recommendation that was not enacted.[107] Jack Davis argues that this effort little affected the priorities of line analytic units.[108] We see little evidence that it had much effect of any sort.

In the 1990s, in the wake of the collapse of the USSR, Congress reduced the IC's budget sharply and correspondingly cut its number of intelligence analysts. At the same time, largely at Gates's directive to produce more "actionable" intelligence, CIA refocused its analysis toward current intelligence and, correspondingly, away from research or strategic analysis—and warning.[109] Analytic units thereby diminished their repositories of organizational expertise, largely by reducing their attention to the long-term trends whose monitoring also produces sound strategic warning.[110]

Although many in the IC considered warning to be a relic of the Cold War, the DWS broadened its mission concept somewhat and monitored low-intensity conflicts such as the fighting in Bosnia after 1992 and more generalized threats to stability such as government collapse, civil war, the deterioration of some states' control of strategic weapons, weapons proliferation, terrorism, and drug trafficking.[111]

But the DWS held to its threat warning focus and chose not to suggest opportunities for policymakers to advance US interests in its formal products, which NIO/Ws, other NIOs, and some IC analytic components did regularly.[112] Many in the IC, primarily but not exclusively in Defense intelligence, continued to maintain incorrectly that *any* opportunity warning effort was incompatible with the long-standing US political cultural standard that intelligence avoids direct involvement in policymaking. The DWS thereby, in an important sense, chose to become less relevant to senior civilian consumers.

NIO/W Mary McCarthy (1994–96), who replaced Allen, reportedly was a dedicated user of the I&W method. She thereby worked known, primarily threat warning issues and issued some Alert Memoranda. McCarthy warned accurately of the Mexican financial crisis of 1995, but she was unable to convince some US government agencies of impending trouble until the crisis broke.[113] More like Bird than Allen, McCarthy worked closely with other NIOs, often asking other analytic entities to look into issues and acting as a facilitator rather than publishing warnings on her own.[114] In 1996, she became the intelligence representative on the NSC staff, where she worked as an intelligence consumer of the work of her successor as NIO/W, Robert Vickers.

McCarthy and the DCI's Counterterrorism Center (CTC) concluded a formal written agreement that the CTC would handle CT-related warning issues, which are generally tactical in nature.[115] Thereafter, the CTC's analytic unit published numerous papers on terrorism-related issues, including reports on al-Qaeda and Osama bin Laden, and interacted regularly with the Counterterrorism Security Group, a unit of the NSC staff.[116] Its chief, Richard Clarke, regularly interacted with Presidents Bill Clinton and George W. Bush. Given that CTC worked counterterrorism extensively from collection, analysis, and operational perspectives, we think the shift in warning responsibilities made sense, and we do not see the lack of an NIO/W role as contributing to the 9/11 tactical warning failure. The 9/11 Commission Report did criticize the CTC's lack of use of warning analytic methods.[117] The Joint Staff J-2 similarly ceded CT responsibilities to other elements of the department. Today, the National Counterterrorism Center has primary IC responsibilities for CT issues.

Robert Vickers was NIO/W from 1996 to 2004, the longest tenure of any NIO/W. He and his small staff of analysts, mainly from the CIA, produced a series of warning products, usually in association with other NIOs—an example of collegiality that seems to have paid dividends in producing respect for the warning function and generally good warning performance. Vickers published a monthly warning document, assembled in coordination with other NIOs, which looked in depth at indicators associated with key warning issues.[118] He also published a weekly one-page "Watch List" of the major issues of concern. He compiled these reports after consulting via teleconference with representatives of CIA, DIA, NSA, State/INR, and the National Photographic Interpretation Center.[119] This group was called the National Warning Committee. Vickers normally issued warning messages after a majority of the agencies voted to do so.[120] Beginning in 1999, Vickers published his *Atrocities Watchlist* quarterly.[121]

Vickers also initiated an annual warning document that identified items he expected to be of concern over the next year; this publication was widely distributed within the US government and to a few US allies.[122] His staff prepared more detailed warning-related assessments of relatively few issues of unusually significant concern, which were published as formal NIC analytic products at levels lower than NIEs. These mainly concerned what later would be called "enduring" warning problems, such as the long-running situation on the Korean Peninsula. On one occasion another NIO objected to such a study as interference in his area of responsibility; the eventual resolution allowed Vickers to complete and publish the paper.[123] Vickers also issued a few "Alert Memoranda," which was still the formal warning message format of the IC as a whole.

Vickers saw interaction with other NIOs as an essential part of his mission, consistent with the Gates task force's recommendations of 1993; he regularly reviewed drafts of NIEs prepared under the auspices of other NIOs for warning issues.[124] He attended National Foreign Intelligence Board meetings on NIEs that contained warning issues. His staff also coordinated warning messages with relevant line analytic units. Although his procedures were similar to those of NIO/W John Bird, Vickers provided threat warnings only; opportunity warning was too close to policy prescription for his taste.[125] Instead, Vickers believed line units should provide "opportunity analysis" as a normal part of their duties.[126]

The IC as a whole had a small cadre of warning officers in the late 1990s. CIA's analytic arm, the Directorate of Intelligence (DI, now the Directorate of Analysis), had a single analyst dedicated (part-time) to the warning function. This analyst attended National Warning Committee meetings, but his primary job was to ensure that warning messages produced by DI units reached the staff preparing two major current intelligence publications, the *Senior Executive Intelligence Bulletin* and the *PDB*.[127] Similarly, in 1998 the only dedicated warning personnel at State/INR and the National Imagery and Mapping Agency were representatives to the National Warning Committee; only DIA and NSA had more than one dedicated warning officer, and DIA's contingent of warners was much smaller than in earlier years.[128]

Disenchantment with warning grew more pronounced after al-Qaeda's attacks on the United States in September 2001 increased concerns about terrorism, which traditional warning offices seemed ill equipped to handle. Many people erroneously considered the 9/11 attacks to be a strategic warning failure even though the IC had warned extensively that bin Laden and his people planned to attack targets within the United States and CT intelligence work is generally tactical in nature.[129]

In 2003, Vickers commissioned a survey of senior consumers of his warning reports. They responded that they did not need coverage of "hot" topics contained in his weekly Watch List because they already followed them; rather, they wanted alerts about issues they did not then know might become significant.[130] Vickers believed the military combatant commands were the most avid consumers of his Watch List.[131]

John Gannon, who was chairman of the NIC during 1997–2001, like many senior policymakers often did not read Vickers's weekly updates even though he described Vickers as a "terrific" NIO/W and approached Vickers frequently about warning issues.[132] Vickers's staff provided Gannon a briefing on warning issues on most Monday mornings.[133] Gannon found Vickers's skills as an analyst and as a prod to line units helpful when line units developed collective analytic perspectives they refused to revisit. In Gannon's view, Vickers helped to challenge their sometimes misplaced conventional wisdom.[134]

Vickers says he believes two warning failures occurred on his watch: the 1998 India nuclear test and the 9/11 attacks. The CTC-McCarthy agreement excluding the NIC from responsibility for terrorism warning gave him considerable cover for the tactical warning failure of 9/11, but DCI George Tenet told Vickers to expect to take blame for the nuclear test, and Gannon confirms that line analytic units that had been convinced the Indians would not test tried to blame Vickers.[135] Vickers survived both failures, however, and his long tenure indicates that the warning function can succeed in challenging times if it is performed well.

In 2004, senior IC leaders asked newly appointed NIO/W Kenneth Knight (2004–10) to reassess the warning function. Knight's review included an extensive survey of classified and open-source literature on warning, detailed interviews with current and former senior intelligence and policymaking officials, a series of workshops with an advisory panel composed of veteran government officials and academic experts on intelligence issues, and discussions with outsiders engaged in "warning-like" activities, including pension fund managers, risk consultancies, and insurance executives.[136] The review generated recommendations for improving the national warning system, such as updating directives that governed warning, reinvigorating the warning community's interactions with policymakers, modernizing warning tradecraft, moving away from the emphasis on shorter-term crisis monitoring and current intelligence, and expanding the scope of warning to better address new and emerging threats and challenges. These and other recommendations were encapsulated in Intelligence Community Directive (ICD) 201, which the first director of national intelligence (DNI), John Negroponte, signed in June 2006.[137] As of April 2006, the National Warning System consisted of an NIO/W, a Strategic Warning Staff, and a Strategic Warning Committee.[138] Evidently more so than his predecessors, Knight addressed longer-term issues while working with staff of the NIC's then new Strategic Futures staff. He wanted warning analysts to use futures-like methods to improve their warning techniques. However, like other NIO/Ws, he mainly focused on short-term issues.[139]

Knight, like Bird and Vickers, tried to work with experts in the IC and with other NIOs.[140] He preferred to write warning products in conjunction with other NIOs and sometimes offered members of his staff to work with other NIOs during crisis situations. On rare occasions when he did not agree with other NIOs, he communicated directly with DNIs and NSC staffers. He also looked to the private sector for practices applicable to government warning and held quarterly meetings with IC agency representatives.

analysis—in their specific areas of responsibility as they as individuals saw fit.[159] ICD 900 states, "This integrated approach [the NIM structure] shall also be applied to the production of current and strategic intelligence, and to processes and activities that support warning."[160] These warning responsibilities were, and remain, imprecise.[161] Clapper's decision left most warning to line units using a strong version of the EAAWA philosophy of warning analysis.

At about the same time, the ODNI reduced the size and effort of IC-level efforts to counter adversary deception. The US government long has been aware of the importance of D&D. In the 1970s, DoD created an organization to analyze foreign deception activities while the military services independently addressed D&D issues.[162] In 1983, President Reagan, who then was negotiating with the Soviet Union, asked the IC two questions: (1) are the Soviets telling us the truth, or are they deceiving us, and (2) how do we know?[163] In response, the CIA took several steps. It convened a large-scale conference, established a course to train analysts about deception and how to deal with it, and it created the Denial and Deception Analysis Committee (DDAC) to address D&D at the national level.[164] The DDAC's main focus was adversary knowledge of US intelligence collection and ways foreign intelligence services could deceive US analysts and policymakers. Immediately after the collapse of the Soviet Union, the DDAC was abolished but was reconstituted in 1992 under the same name.[165] In 1995, the DDAC was renamed the Foreign Denial and Deception Committee (FDDC). Also in 1995, the NIO for science and technology, Lawrence Gershwin, became chairman of the FDDC. Gershwin remained chairman until 2014, when he also was NIM for science and technical intelligence.[166]

James Bruce, a longtime D&D specialist and a former vice chair of the FDDC, reports that the IC's D&D effort and effectiveness improved in the 1990s and early 2000s.[167] DCI James Woolsey strongly supported an effort to revive D&D. The FDDC's mission was, and remains, to lead research, collection, analysis and publication, and training on methods of countering foreign D&D.[168] It challenges conventional wisdom about D&D in IC analyses, including NIEs, and it fosters education and training on D&D methods. It is the IC's hub for collaboration and integration of the counter-deception mission.[169]

Bruce estimates that the IC's D&D capacities peaked around 2005 and declined markedly thereafter. The committee was sharply reduced in size, ostensibly to free resources for other purposes. The FDDC was reduced in size and status again in about 2012, leaving what in 2018 is a small staff.[170] The position of FDDC chair lost its NIO-level status, and resources devoted to D&D declined across the IC; by 2015, Bruce reports that there were no D&D assets at the CIA, the DIA, or the NSA.[171] Hence, as Clapper splintered the warning "finder" mission, his ODNI also damaged the IC's capacity to understand how deceptive "hiders" operate.

Clapper commissioned a review of the warning function in 2014, co-chaired by a member of the ODNI and the Joint Staff's J-2 warning office. Evidently after considerable debate about many options, the IC's review group on warning, which ODNI called a "tiger team," could not agree on specific recommendations in its formal report. But in early 2017, it published internally a short paper on strategic warning written by RAND Corporation analysts, which is mainly historical and proposes little that is new.[172] The review did not convince Clapper to revive a variant of the hybrid warning structure—dedicated warning professionals headed by a re-created NIO/W or a warning-focused NIM who would interact closely with specialists in the NIC and in line analytic units.

Under Clapper, formal IC policy continued, however, to embrace "anticipatory intelligence," which is now one of seven core IC mission objectives for analysts in general.[173] The 2014 *National Intelligence Strategy of the United States* says that threat and opportunity warning continue to be core IC responsibilities within the context of "anticipatory intelligence." The ODNI published several internal documents thereafter outlining how "anticipatory intelligence" is part of the package of "tradecraft" skills all analysts use.[174] The Intelligence Advanced Research Projects Activity, a part of the ODNI, somewhat differently describes anticipatory intelligence as production of "timely and accurate forecasts"—which we consider to be only part of the warning mission.[175]

Clapper's decision to downgrade warning had international repercussions. At least one US ally soon thereafter terminated its warning program, and another one downgraded the warning function's priority. Both since have resurrected strategic warning to some extent—including their dedicated warning organizations. Both retain the term "warning" and have not adopted the "anticipatory intelligence" term.

Meanwhile, soon after General Martin Dempsey became chairman of the Joint Chiefs of Staff in October 2011, he asked, literally brandishing Grabo's warning book, where his warning element was, prompting DoD to form a committee to restore the strategic warning function.[176] The committee's report led the Office of the Secretary of Defense and director of the DIA Lieutenant General Ronald Burgess in 2012 to issue directives that reestablished a warning office in the J-2 of the Joint Staff at the Pentagon and assigned other DoD organizations' warning-related responsibilities.[177] The new J-2 sub-organization, a division designated J27, was led by a senior executive—a reflection of appreciable appreciation for the warning function.

The new DoD warning system adopted established I&W and other warning analytic methods, but it also developed some new warning doctrine.[178] J27 administered a structure known as the Defense Warning Network (DWN), which then and now includes the intelligence-related components of the DoD, has modest involvement with the rest of the IC, and interacts with some allied military intelligence services. The DWN's senior decision-making body is the Defense Warning Council, which is composed of representatives of DWN member organizations and is chaired by the J-2. The DWN tracks "enduring" warning problems—issues that are bureaucratically established as issues US defense intelligence should continue to monitor—and looks for "emerging" warning issues that may be intelligence and policy challenges in the future.[179] It recognizes opportunity warning in principle and discusses possibilities in "communities of interest" roundtable sessions.[180] According to its 2014 manual, the DWN mainly addresses four general categories of enduring military threat warning problems:

increased in 1945 and again during the early Cold War, when it began to support all major British foreign policy decisions. The JIC headed the national-level Joint Intelligence Organisation (JIO), which included all intelligence services. In 1957, responsibility for the JIC and its machinery was transferred from the Chiefs of Staff to the Cabinet Office. The Foreign Office provided the JIC chairman, while the Ministry of Defence (MoD) provided the "alternate," later the deputy, chairman to reflect a balance between the two most powerful departments on the JIC.[187] Although the Foreign Office continued to provide the chairman for much of the twentieth century, other departments and agencies (in recent years the Secret Intelligence Service, the MoD, and the Home Office) have also filled the post.

The military members of, and main contributors to, the JIC before, during, and after World War II were the three single-Service Intelligence Directorates (SIDs) of the Royal Navy, the British Army, and the Royal Air Force. They were joined in 1946 by the Joint Intelligence Bureau (JIB), which assumed the responsibilities of several wartime agencies concerned with economic, geographic, and logistics intelligence.[188] A scientific and technical division was added in 1952. In 1964, as part of consolidation of the previously independent military services into the MoD, the service intelligence arms and the JIB were amalgamated into the Defence Intelligence Staff (DIS). Unlike the SIDs, the JIB served consumers across government; the JIB accounted for about one-third of the budget of the fledgling DIS.[189] The DIS was responsible for the study of the full spectrum of defense capabilities and intentions of countries worldwide. This study ranged from assessments of national economic and defense economic problems and prospects through research, development, production, export, and deployment of weapon systems and platforms, to evaluations of all elements of military effectiveness, particularly OB and capability analyses.[190] Some British students of intelligence saw DIS as more similar to the CIA's broadly focused analysis arm, the Directorate of Intelligence (now Directorate of Analysis), than to the more narrowly military-focused DIA.[191]

In 2009, the DIS was renamed Defence Intelligence (DI) but continued to support military and MoD needs as well as the national-level JIC process.[192] The DI is the United Kingdom's largest intelligence analytical organization, responsible for studying foreign defense and security matters. Since the early 1990s, the then DIS expanded from an organization of around 500 people to incorporate the Joint Air Reconnaissance Intelligence Centre (JARIC), the Directorate General of Military Survey, all civilian and military intelligence training units, and a number of smaller defense intelligence elements. In 2017, its total strength was more than 4,000.[193] These entities are integrated under Commander Joint Forces Intelligence Group (JFIG).

The JIC is part of the Cabinet Office, reporting to the secretary of the cabinet.[194] The JIC is composed of representatives of the intelligence-producing and -consuming departments of the British government, including the JIC chairman; the JIC "coordinator," who supervises the collection agencies; the chief of the Secret Intelligence Service (SIS, also known as MI6); the director general of the Security Service (MI5); the director of Government Communications Headquarters (GCHQ); the chief of DI; the deputy undersecretary of the Foreign and Commonwealth Office (FCO) responsible for defense and security matters; the director of policy of the MoD; senior officials of the Treasury, the Department of Trade and Industry, and the Home Office; the chief of the JIC Assessments Staff, the analytic part of the JIC; and the JIC secretary, whose administrative functions help keep the JIC running smoothly.[195] Representatives of the CIA, the Australian Office of National Assessments, and the Canadian Intelligence Assessment Secretariat also attend some JIC meetings.[196] The JIC in turn reports to the most senior group of security/intelligence officials in Britain, a committee of ministers known under Conservative and Labour governments as the Committee on Intelligence and Security (CIS) and the Committee on Security and Intelligence (CSI), respectively.[197]

The JIC has several responsibilities, including providing early warning of the development of direct or indirect foreign threats to British political, military, and economic interests.[198] The JIC assembles the collection priorities of government departments (including the FCO, the Treasury, and the Home Office, for example), prioritizes them, and publishes them annually in a so-called National Intelligence Requirement and Priorities Paper, which is binding on the collection agencies.[199] Issues of prospective warning significance are identified as a part of this annual process by the JIO as a whole.[200]

The JIC's Assessments Staff, which for decades had about twenty desk officers, or analysts, drawn from JIO member departments, drafts assessments, including warning assessments as appropriate. Assessments Staff personnel work closely with counterparts in the departments as drafts are prepared. The JIC validates the analyses of the Assessments Staff and other elements of the JIO, especially Defence Intelligence and the Foreign Office, that submit material to it for review, perhaps modification, and eventual approval for national distribution as intelligence that in US terminology includes current, estimative, and warning intelligence.[201] In this respect it performs a role similar to that of the US National Intelligence Board, although the chief of the Assessments Staff is authorized to issue some urgent or uncontentious reports.[202]

The JIC's core products, drafted mainly by the Assessments Staff, long have included two weekly reports—the *Weekly Survey of Intelligence*, or "Red Book," containing sensitive material that is distributed to very senior officials only, and the *Weekly Review of Current Intelligence*, or "Grey Book," which contains less sensitive material and is more widely disseminated.[203] The JIC also produced in the 1960s a *Weekly Situation Review* for NATO commands.[204] Ad hoc reports, including some warning messages, are issued as "Immediate Assessments." In recent years a less formal JIC production process also has provided short briefing notes and advice to prime ministers.

JIC assessments are based on a "consensus rule," which means that the assessments reflect the judgments of the entire JIC membership. Hence, there are no "footnotes"—statements of disagreement with a position other organizations hold, as is common in the US national estimative process.[205] The consensus rule does not, however, mean unanimity of views reflecting "lowest common denominator" language that often results from the coordination process in the United States. Instead, assessments reflect the range of judgments and uncertainties held by JIC members and drafters.

Like most intelligence organizations, the JIC evolved over time, but until recent years it did so in relatively minor ways compared to some other national intelligence services. In 1968, for example, its Joint Intelligence Staff became the Assessments Staff, which produced analyses in direct support of the JIC rather than brokering the divergent views of the departments. The Assessments Staff drew analysts from departments throughout Whitehall, typically on two-to-three-year rotational assignments; the Assessments Staff variously has been divided into three to five groups, totaling in 2017 about sixty staff.[206] Current Intelligence Groups (CIGs), which were created in 1964, are small groups of floating memberships of substantive experts from throughout government organized along regional and functional lines that review the work of the Assessments Staff; they do not have dedicated warning personnel.[207] In the mid-1980s, CIGs were organized around the following regions and functional issues: the Middle East, the Far East, Western Europe, Northern Ireland, South and Central America, sub-Saharan Africa, the Soviet bloc, terrorism, proliferation, and economic issues.[208]

The CIGs also evolved. They all have a core membership of the CIG chairman, who is a deputy chief of the Assessments Staff, and the Assessments Staff drafter of the paper under review. In addition, representatives of the FCO, the MoD (always the DI but perhaps also one of the policy divisions), the SIS, the Security Service, and the GCHQ participate as necessary. Hence, Assessments Staff analysts and deputy chiefs of the Assessments Staff are at the center of the JIC's analytic machinery.

In the 1980s, the JIC had a watch function known as the JIC Watch Room, which was staffed continuously by a total of only five retired military officers known as duty intelligence officers, evidently one person on duty at a time.[209] The primary mission of the Watch Room was to monitor events and report emerging events of warning significance, particularly military threats from communist countries.[210] It also collated incoming reports to ensure that analysts received interesting reports promptly. The Watch Room function was discontinued in the early 1990s after the Soviet threat disappeared but was reconstituted after September 2001. Defence Intelligence's watch center sometimes disagrees with the JIC; for example, the DIS warning cell became concerned about Argentine intentions regarding the Falklands before the JIC did.

Prior to creation of the DIS in 1964, the MoD's warning mechanism was communication of warning messages through the single-Service Intelligence Directorates to their respective Chiefs of Staff and into the national warning process through the JIC machinery. Warning similarly became a priority task for the new DIS. Although the Scientific and Technical and Economic Intelligence Directorates made significant inputs, from mid-1965 the newly established Directorate of Service Intelligence (DS Int), which replaced the three SIDs, took the lead in warning because it was responsible for all political-military intelligence production.

Provision of timely and accurate warning of military action by a potential adversary or of significant changes in a foreign country's defense capability continued to be among the most challenging tasks faced by intelligence analysts in the DIS and their supporting collection assets. In the 1960s and 1970s, responsibility for warning lay exclusively with the units studying a particular region or capability. They reported up the DIS command chain, alerting senior staff, who then determined which consumers within the defense establishment, the wider intelligence community (notably the JIC), and across government needed to be informed and how this should be accomplished. There was no warning team or set of dedicated warning products.

In the late 1970s, the DIS formally adopted a systematic approach to warning and allocated analytic resources separately from the line units, which were organized regionally or functionally. This approach used a variant of the American I&W method that later became, misleadingly, synonymous with the concept of giving "warning." Its purpose was to improve the DIS's ability to fulfill its primary function to warn of an increased threat from the Warsaw Pact, principally the Soviet Union.

Since the Japanese attack on Pearl Harbor, successive UK defense intelligence organizations had observed the work of, and cooperated with, US intelligence in the search for better techniques for providing strategic warning. This continued to be so throughout the latter half of the twentieth century as numerous strategic surprises occurred. The British also monitored the evolution of US warning institutions, including establishment of the National Indications Center, the position of National Intelligence Officer (NIO) for Warning, and the National Warning Staff, which in the early 1980s, following the failure to foresee the fall of the shah of Iran, invited the UK intelligence community to join in developing strategic indicators. The DIS learned from all these efforts of the US intelligence community as well as its own successes and failures, helping to improve its performance.[211]

The DIS therefore drew on US experience to introduce, belatedly in the view of some DIS managers and analysts, a structured warning methodology of its own. Among the lead coordinators for this effort was Lieutenant Colonel Derek Stirling, who became the driving force behind development of the United Kingdom's I&W system and a legend in his own lifetime. The successor to the warning system he developed is now known as Project Stirling. Coverage continued to focus on the Warsaw Pact through the early 1990s. The DIS's I&W team then was increased by one analyst tasked with developing and maintaining I&W systems for warning of threats to British interests from selected "Rest of the World" countries, including threats to the Falkland Islands (from Argentina), British bases on Cyprus (from Turkey), Gibraltar (from Spain), and Hong Kong (from China). An I&W list for Yugoslavia in existence since the death of Josip Broz Tito in 1980 proved invaluable for giving warning of events as the country fell apart in the 1980s and as Slobodan Milošević rose to power in 1987.

The 1990s were difficult years for British intelligence in general. In the United Kingdom, as in the United States, there was near-irresistible demand for a "peace dividend." Reductions in DIS staffing levels produced pressure to reduce even the handful of analysts devoted to monitoring a few warning problems (Russia, Argentina, Gibraltar, Honduras/ Belize). Increasingly, the regional analysts alone were expected to deliver warning without benefit of the rigor of the long-term analysis of capabilities and/or activities the I&W method recommends. During the 1990s, DIS priorities moved from strategic intelligence to current intelligence in support of the United Kingdom's contribution to coalition operations, first in Iraq and later in the former Yugoslavia.

By the late 1990s, the DIS's independent warning capability had been reduced to one analyst. Products became more broad-brush, and detailed, methodologically sound analyses of warning problems were rare, with high-profile, usually sensitive exceptions. In these cases, warning responsibility fell to the appropriate regional or functional team, with the single I&W specialist providing help and guidance on the application of the method. By 2006, this single position had been cut and responsibility for I&W was transferred to the DIS's current intelligence reporting team. Concurrently, a semi-automated indicator-based warning system hosted on the DIS site of MoD's main classified information-technology network, named Project Stirling, was introduced. The current intelligence team's main routine task was to review and update the warning pages in consultation with analytical teams. This period was the nadir of the DIS's resourcing and use of the I&W method; it generated difficulties for effective burden sharing on warning issues with "Five Eyes" partners and with NATO.[212]

Since 2010, the DI has worked to reestablish core warning capabilities. This has involved use of temporary staff available part-time or those between permanent jobs and the exploitation of newer structured analytic techniques that complement "Indicator-based Warning." Some British observers believe the process has benefited considerably from the timely availability of training on strategic warning matters made available to partners by the United States.[213] There is in 2017, once again, a full-time "warning" post in the DI.

Despite the domestic difficulties of the warning function over the years, the DIS continued to contribute significantly to NATO warning intelligence. Routinely this involved taking a significant share of the work on enduring warning problems in support of the relevant intelligence working group and contributing to efforts to develop and modernize NATO's analytic methods (to identify "emerging warning problems," for example), procedures, and ability to serve NATO consumers. The DIS also exploited its physical proximity to NATO headquarters in Brussels to provide short-notice personal briefs and intelligence advice to NATO seniors and staffs on urgent warning and other issues. A particular milestone in this arena was the level of service provided before and during NATO-led operations against Yugoslavia in 1999.

The issue of how best to organize for "Warning" has often been controversial throughout the history of the DIS/DI. Much like in the United States, proponents of the application of "I&W" argue that such a measured, methodical approach is essential if the risk of strategic surprise is to be minimized. In contrast, regional analysts assert that as specialists they understand their countries best and therefore can provide the timeliest warning of significant changes. Some regard the mechanistic approach of I&W as insufficiently flexible to give due weight to intangibles such as cultural or local political factors that a leader or leadership group might take into account in a decision to go to war. At best, I&W is an insurance against incompetence and/or a helpful guide for a new analyst in post. The issue has become murkier for the DI as new SATs relevant to provision of warning have emerged. SATs complicate DI endeavors to explain what it means by "Warning" its consumers. Such is the ingrained habit of using "I&W" as shorthand for "Warning" that it is difficult to explain that I&W is just one analytical tool, a variant within the category of "Indicator-based Warning," and is not the only useful technique available.

Since the 1990s, Prime Ministers Tony Blair, Gordon Brown, and David Cameron made several structural and procedural changes to British intelligence whose full implications are not yet clear. A new National Security Council, created in 2010, considers threats identified by intelligence information.[214] Philip Davies, a knowledgeable observer of British intelligence, believes recent reforms have appreciably affected the processes of the JIC and the broader JIO community.[215] Many observers believe the changes have been positive.[216]

Given its structure and functions, the JIC system would handle a new warning issue roughly as follows. The emergence of an event as identified by DI analysts, or the Watch Room, or personnel from any other element of the JIO would be assigned to the relevant analytic team of the Assessments Staff, probably to a single desk officer. After consulting relevant experts in government, the Assessments Staff analyst would produce a "Preliminary Draft" assessment that would be given to the relevant CIG for review and comment. The CIG would be chaired by the substantively appropriate deputy chief of the Assessments Staff.[217] After what the US IC calls review and coordination processes, the revised draft would be approved by the chief of the Assessments Staff and then submitted to the full JIC membership. Upon the JIC's approval, a warning message would be issued, perhaps as an item in the Red Book, perhaps as the stand-alone message of an "Immediate Assessment."[218] The warning would reflect the best judgment of the government as a whole about an emerging threat situation, reflecting the uncertainties voiced during the review and coordination processes. The DI would communicate the warning to the military, within the MoD, and to relevant allies, who in many cases would include traditional Australian, Canadian, US, and NATO allies.[219]

Like other national governments, the British government periodically studies the performance of its intelligence organizations, especially after major perceived failures, and publicly releases reports of some findings. The JIC was the subject of a major study in 1951. Career intelligence officer Douglas Nicoll prepared another, known as the Nicoll Report, which the JIC approved in March 1982, just before the start of the Falklands War. Other major inquiries followed the Falklands War and the invasion of Iraq in 2003 and are known respectively as the Franks and Butler Reports, after the peers who oversaw them.[220] The Franks Report detailed publicly the workings of the JIC for the first time. Official histories, declassified government documents, and other studies provide additional information about British warning. These records reveal British intelligence priorities, modest resources allocated to warning, and a history of warning analyses that contains some successes and some appreciable failures, as well as lessons British officials drew from failures.

Like their American counterparts, the British failed to anticipate North Korea's invasion of South Korea in 1950, the Yom Kippur War of 1973, the Warsaw Pact incursion into Czechoslovakia in 1968, and the Argentine invasion of the Falkland Islands in 1982—the

latter an especially big failure given that British territory was attacked. But the JIC performed well in its assessment of the Suez Crisis of 1956, and British academics think the
JIC fairly accurately forecast the Cuban Missile Crisis of 1962—not generally considered
an American intelligence success.[221] British students of intelligence typically attribute
British failures to problems somewhat differently from those on which Americans tend to
focus.

The partially declassified Nicoll Report critiques the JIC and makes specific recommendations for improvement. It offers in slightly different ways some of the best insights
on the warning function of other analysts, such as Cynthia Grabo. It therefore is worth
discussing at length, especially since the basics of the JIC system Nicoll assessed remain
in operation.

Nicoll argued that warning of hostile action by the USSR was the JIC's highest priority.[222] He therefore primarily focused on the military aspects of threat warning, not
opportunities.

Judging that British collection and analysis were good, Nicoll concluded that faulty
procedures were major causes of the JIC's intelligence failures. He criticized the structure
and format of JIC assessments as not being conducive to warning of emerging threats.
Reports about emerging warning issues got buried in the "Weekly Surveys" that, as current
intelligence publications, did not adequately generate what Nicoll called the "cumulative
collation" needed to adequately apprise consumers of developments that eventually
appeared as crisis warnings in "immediate assessments."[223] Nicoll judged that warning
messages were best received within the existing product mix when they featured current
reporting of new developments accompanied by relevant analysis.

Nicoll implicitly observed that the JIC had no dedicated warning analysts by suggesting that when evidence of the emergence of potentially troubling events occurred, an
analyst—that is, one person—should be assigned to dig deeply into the issue and focus on
"detailed collation of relevant political and military activities" of the potential aggres-
sor.[224] He did not believe the JIC then was staffed adequately to enable this kind and level
of work.[225] We think this language amounts to advocacy of ad hoc development of
warning-related expertise, a practice that dedicated warning entities of the more richly
resourced US IC sometimes have done. His proposal also indicated that the JIC effectively
took the EAAWA approach *within* the Assessments Staff by leaving the identification of a
potential warning issue, and its development, to a dedicated desk officer.

Nicoll observed six types of analytic and analysis-related errors that he believed
recurrently plagued British efforts to avoid surprise. These differ slightly in some cases
from similar American concepts:

1. *Mirror imaging*—the assumption that factors constraining the British government
   would equally constrain leaders of one-party states. In particular, Nicoll argued
   British intelligence inappropriately assessed that foreign actors would be constrained by the same forces of international opinion that constrain British use of
   force.

2. *Transferred judgment*—the assumption that foreign actors would make the same judgments about military balances, and thus about prospects for success, as did British analysts. This is not the same thing as mirror imaging but is similar. It reflects an inability to fully "empathize" with foreign actors' situations, even when one consciously recognizes that they see things differently.

3. *Perseveration*—the belief that judgments made early in the development of a crisis would remain valid. Nicoll argued that it is important to keep an open mind and alter judgments as appropriate in the face of new information. (The term is roughly equivalent to what the intelligence literature usually calls confirmation bias.)

4. *War as a deliberate act*—failure to recognize that because wars are deliberate acts that often take a long time to prepare, it is possible to identify emerging threat situations as they are prepared, not just when forces are deployed, thereby increasing warning times. (Cynthia Grabo made this point strongly about US warning failures.[226])

5. *Coverage*—The Assessments Staff found it hard to warn about events in low-priority areas, which reflected weak collection and sometimes meant less collection and analyst attention in the future.

6. *Deception*—Nicoll recognized that aggressors virtually always devote considerable effort to deception, meaning analysts must constantly keep in mind that foreign actors are trying to deceive them.[227]

In sum, the British warning system, like the American system, has had successes and failures and organizational ups and downs over the years. The DIS/DI had a dedicated warning function occasionally, working mainly military warning issues, but consistently injected warning messages to the JIC. The JIC's Assessments Staff, however, always has operated under an EAAWA model. Hence, we believe the British warning system amounts to a variant of a hybrid model even as the JIC system as a whole is a variant of the whole-of-government model.

The Dutch Threat Warning System

Surrounded by political and military allies, the Netherlands has little need for an independent military threat warning system, but it developed a complex system to assess domestic threats, which government agencies communicate to many consumers, including senior government leaders and the general public.[228] The National Coordinator for Security and Counterterrorism (NCTV), which was established in 2004 as a primarily terrorism-focused entity and was formerly called the National Coordinator for Counterterrorism (NCTb), is the key actor. In 2012, the National Crisis Centre became part of the NCTV's office, making the NCTV responsible for warning of all types of threats. The Government Computer Emergency Response Team also became part of the NCTV in 2012, bringing its total staffing level to about 300 people.[229] The primary mission of the NCTV then became keeping the Netherlands safe and stable by preventing or minimizing social disruption and strengthening resilience to disruptions. The National Coordinator, currently H. W. M. (Dick) Schoof, appears frequently in public. The coordinator and NCTV therefore have considerably broader responsibilities than the traditional military threat warning systems of foreign intelligence services—including some policymaking and policy implementing functions.

The NCTV is responsible to the minister for security and justice, but it operates autonomously in issuing warnings. It has no intelligence-collection assets, but its analysis component evaluates the information NCTV receives from many sources. This independent analytical capacity has been a bone of contention with the two Dutch intelligence services: the civilian General Intelligence and Security Service (AIVD), which mainly addresses internal threats, and the Military Intelligence and Security Service (MIVD), which focuses on external ones. The NCTV is not subject to Dutch intelligence oversight laws.

The NCTV and the minister for security and justice are primarily responsible for four threat warning systems that address different issues, have considerably different audiences, and use different sets of standardized terms to communicate threat levels:

1. The Surveillance and Protection System (het systeem Bewaken en Beveiligen, or B&B system) is the core government system used to protect services, facilities, and important persons. It was established in 2002 after the murder of Dutch politician Pim Fortuyn. The system identifies threats and assigns responsibilities for ameliorating them. Protection priorities include members of the royal family, government officials (including members of parliament), ambassadors, foreign embassies in the Netherlands, and some international organizations (including military organizations). Responsibility for protecting these individuals and organizations rests with several authorities, including the Surveillance and Protection Department of the NCTV, civilian and military police, and the Royalty and Diplomatic Protection Department (DKDB), an organization similar to the US Secret Service. Five alert categories are: not severe, moderate, average, severe, and very severe.

2. The Terrorist Threat Assessment (or Dreigingsbeeld Terrorisme Nederland [DTN]) is the best-known Dutch warning alert system. It communicates perceived threat levels in the Netherlands proper and to Dutch interests abroad, normally every three months. Its audience is the public at large. The DTN appeared in 2005, just before the terrorist attacks in London and several months after the killing of Dutch screenwriter and columnist Theo van Gogh. DTN reports are all-source assessments, embedding information and analyses of the AIVD and the MIVD, the police, and assessments from foreign agencies focused on terrorism, including Britain's Joint Terrorism Analysis Centre. A secret-level version that goes to Dutch government agencies, legislators, and national leaders is an important basis of national counterterrorism policy. A confidential-level version goes to law enforcement officials and national and local officials charged with implementing CT policies. An English translation of the confidential version is shared with European partners involved in CT. Reports typically are six pages in length or longer. Since

its inception, the DTN has had four levels of threats: minimal, limited, substantial, and critical.

3. The Counterterrorism Alert System (ATb), established in June 2005, communicates threat levels to fifteen vital economic sectors, including utilities, transportation, finance, industry, and flood defenses. The minister of security and justice sets alert levels. Raising the alert level encourages representatives of the sectors and relevant public officials to take appropriate measures, as defined by the alert levels. There currently are four alert levels: standard, low, moderate, and high threat.

4. The Aviation Security System is run by the Surveillance, Protection, and Civil Aviation Security Department of the NCTV. It interacts with several other elements of the Dutch government and airlines to warn of, and respond to, aviation-related threats.

The B&B and ATb systems use a unique risk-assessment method that incorporates both the likelihood of any specific threat and the severity of impact if each threat materializes. Analysts of the NCTV generate separate tables for the likelihood and severity of events, which each are three-by-five matrices that have five severity levels for three categories of targets: persons, physical targets or objects, and society as a whole. The overall threat rating reflects subjective judgment about the degree of threat and the relative importance of likely targets. The rough probability of an attack is judged on the basis of an actor's expected intent and potential to conduct an attack and the evidence that an actual attack is planned. The NCTV has developed fairly specific indicators for each threat level, linking this approach loosely to the standard I&W method.[230]

Dutch warning therefore is judgmental and has a strategic element. It assesses trends, not just immediate tactical threats, although many individual threats and remedial actions are tactical in nature. According to one NCTV analyst, the NCTV's analyses are "probability reasonings without mathematically defined outcomes."[231] The Dutch system's national audience reflects the rise of CT-focused warning globally, including the blending of what traditionally were distinctly strategic and tactical warning issues consistent with small threats thought to be strategically important—to politicians' careers, at least—as the political salience of terrorism grows. The Dutch public seems to consider the system to be effective, and it has had fewer of the credibility problems that plagued similar threat levels established by the US Department of Homeland Security in its early years especially.

The NATO Warning System

Alliances need many of the kinds of information and assessments that states require, but different structures and organizational purposes of international organizations shape their needs for, and abilities to conduct, warning intelligence. The North Atlantic Treaty Organization is constrained appreciably by its institutional arrangements, and it designed ways to both share enough intelligence to be helpful and to protect sensitive national sources and methods of intelligence collection. NATO has addressed warning consistently since its early years in ways that reflect the political structure of the alliance and its original purpose—concern about attacks by the Soviet Union and its allies.[232] Since the demise of the USSR and the Warsaw Pact, NATO warning, like US Defense warning, has broadened the scope of its interests and analyses.

NATO's warning mechanism largely reflects the US I&W system discussed in chapter 6.[233] During the Cold War, NATO intelligence focused on providing early warning of strategic attack by the Warsaw Pact and tracking developments that might indicate that an attack was imminent. The analytical focus on war was reflected in the various names of the NATO warning committees: Indications of Attack (1952–79), Indications and Warning (1979–84), and NATO Indications & Warning System (1984–2000). With the end of the Cold War and the major alliance intervention in Bosnia and Kosovo beginning in 1995, NATO adjusted again by establishing the NATO Intelligence Warning System (NIWS) (2000–present).[234] NATO now has "out-of-area" and crisis-management missions that may also prompt warning concerns.

The NIWS provides primarily threat warning to NATO decision-makers and to the political and military leaders of member nations. The warning committee (designated MC 0166) meets on a rotating basis in member capitals once a year to discuss and formally establish warning problems and related policy issues, which like many issues in NATO must be approved by consensus (that is, unanimously). While some observers contend that this process is too slow, the nations can deliberate at NATO headquarters between annual meetings to address new issues as necessary.[235] In addition, member states can adopt and begin to monitor warning problems on national bases as they desire, then ask for alliance-wide recognition later.

The focal point of warning analysis is located at NATO headquarters in the office of the deputy chief of staff for intelligence (DSCINT), a two-star chief of one of the five divisions of the International Military Staff. Supported by a small team that manages the NIWS, the DCSINT communicates warning messages to the chairman of the Military Committee, NATO's senior military authority; the secretary-general; and the North Atlantic Council (NAC), NATO's senior political decision-making body, as appropriate. However, this process may eventually change as the secretary-general appointed in October 2016 a German diplomat and former vice president of the Bundesnachrichtendienst (BND, Germany's foreign intelligence service), Arndt Freytag von Loringhoven, to be the first assistant secretary-general for intelligence and security, popularly called the first chief of NATO intelligence.[236] His mandate is to set up a new intelligence and security division at NATO headquarters, merging the civilian International Staff and the International Military Staff. The NAC called for this reform at the Warsaw meeting of NATO heads of state and government in July 2016 to strengthen intelligence within NATO by improving intelligence cooperation, which was expected to increase early warning, force protection, and the general resilience of the alliance. The new intelligence organization will support the NAC and the Military Committee and advise the secretary-general.

Because NATO bureaucracy usually moves slowly, the impact on NATO warning is not yet clear.[237]

Currently warning problems are divided into two categories of threats: conventional and transnational. Conventional threats focus on a nation or region (such as internal stability or interstate conflict). Transnational threats are divided into three categories: terrorism, WMD, and "computer network operations" or cyber threats. The MC 0166 committee crafts the definition of each warning problem, to which committee members agree by consensus. Once the committee approves warning problems, it asks for volunteer nations to monitor and report on them.[238] Volunteers typically have special national interests in problems they agree to work. States responsible for warning problems are required to submit monthly updates on their warning problems, including new information and assessments, to the warning staff at NATO headquarters, using the NATO Intelligence Warning Software.[239]

We have argued that an essential and difficult challenge for any warning entity is convincing decision-makers of the importance of an issue and the need to consider action. This problem is magnified by a factor of twenty-nine, given NATO's need to convince all member states of the need to act before any alliance action can occur. John Kriendler cautions in this context, "No matter how well structured an early-warning system . . . its success depends, above all, on the judgement and vision of political authorities."[240] Such judgment and vision has long been a challenge for NATO. The NATO warning system aids this process, however, by specifying a senior military warning officer who has established communications links with senior military and civilian leaders. Relying on the analysts of the member nations for many substantive judgments, this officer and his small staff of warning specialists head a variant of the hybrid warning structure.

Warning also plays a critical role in the NATO Crisis Response System. If member states unite in concern about an issue, the first step of the response process—alerting leaders of a possible problem—triggers a long process of assessment, developing response options, planning, execution, and return to stability. The object of this system is to "deploy diplomats instead of soldiers" through diplomatic pressure, economic sanctions, threats of military force, or actual military force as the alliance deems appropriate.[241]

Aware of the challenges of producing effective warning and the need for member nations to be able to communicate warning issues among themselves clearly, NATO trains warning analysts at the NATO School in Oberammergau, Germany, which currently offers three one-week warning courses per year. The course, which is similar to the warning course the US DIA teaches, exposes students to the basic I&W analytic method as well as NATO-specific organizational, process, and substantive issues. We believe this course usefully introduces staff to strategic warning. But competence in warning analysis requires substantive expertise and experience that the course does not have time to deliver to students. NATO's warning analysts, like those within national intelligence systems, vary greatly in their abilities and background—a serious issue because most NATO member countries treat intelligence as a secondary career specialty.

Comparing the Systems

The three national systems and the NATO system discussed in this chapter are appreciably different. The British and American warning systems reflect significant differences in government structures and organizational cultures, but the two countries have worked closely together since World War II. The Dutch system is much newer and focuses more on domestic and "tactical"-level issues than do the American and British systems. The NATO warning system addresses its military-focused needs in ways that reflect the special political characteristics of the alliance. Each has evolved to reflect new mission needs, to remedy institutional deficiencies, and to account for changing world situations.

These four warning communities reflect aspects of several of the five ideal types of warning systems discussed in chapter 3. The Netherlands has a dedicated warning office and senior analyst in the Coordinator; the Dutch mitigate the risk that dedicated warners may not be adequately expert by creating a large warning organization and forcing national intelligence services to provide input. NATO's small dedicated warning office relies on input from the nations, making it clearly a hybrid system. The JIC handles UK warning along with other analytic messages from various agencies, giving it hybrid characteristics. The US system has at times featured something close to a dedicated warning office (the Watch Committee with its National Indications Center) and variants of the hybrid system (the different NIO/Ws used). In none of the cases except current American practice has anything close to a strong version of the EAAWA model existed.

Notes

Portions of this chapter previously appeared in John A. Gentry and Joseph S. Gordon, "U.S. Strategic Warning Intelligence: History and Challenges," *International Journal of Intelligence and CounterIntelligence* 31, no. 1 (Spring 2018): 19–53, reprinted by permission of Taylor & Francis.

1. There is no definitive, published history of US warning. A part-time project to do a classified history is under way as this book is being written.

2. This section draws heavily on Grabo, "Watch Committee." Cynthia Grabo worked for the Watch Committee for its entire existence (1950–75).

3. For some history on British assistance, see "Nightwatch: A Brief History of Indicators Analysis," October 12, 2012, Public Intelligence Blog, http://www.phibetaiota.net/2012/10/nightwatch-a-brief-history-of-indicators-analysis/.

4. Landers, "Defense Warning System"; authors' discussions with warning specialists.

5. Grabo, "Watch Committee," 366.

6. George and Wirtz, "Warning in Age of Uncertainty," 216; Voskian and Pherson, *Analytic Production Guide*, 22–25.

7. Andrew, *For the President's Eyes Only*, 187.

8. Ford, "US Government's Experience," 45.

9. Grabo, "Watch Committee," 366.

10. Ibid., 366–67.

11. Unsinger, "Three Intelligence Blunders in Korea," 549–61; Mobley, "North Korea's Surprise Attack," 490–514.

12. Grabo, "Watch Committee," 367–68.

13. Ibid., 368; Bar-Joseph and McDermott, *Intelligence Success and Failure*, 143–83.

14. Grabo, "Watch Committee," 369–70.

15. Ibid., 368.

16. Krepinevich and Watts, *Last Warrior*.

17. Ibid., 247.

18. Grabo, "Watch Committee," 370.

19. Ibid., 376.

20. Ibid., 373.

21. Patton, "Monitoring of War Indicators," 57.

22. Ramsey and Boerner, "Study in Indications Methodology," 75–76.

23. Davis and Grabo, "Strategic Warning and Deception," 32.

24. Patton, "Monitoring of War Indicators," 55–68.

25. Ramsey and Boerner, "Study in Indications Methodology."

26. Patton, "Monitoring of War Indicators," 58.

27. Priess, *President's Book of Secrets*, 26.

28. Andrew, *For the President's Eyes Only*, 308.

29. Grabo, "Watch Committee," 376; Davis, "Watchman for All Seasons," 38.

30. Ford, *CIA and the Vietnam Policymakers*.

31. Allen, *None So Blind*, 60–61.

32. Director of Central Intelligence, "Intelligence Warning of the Tet Offensive." For another view, see Moyar, "Hanoi's Strategic Surprise," 155–70.

33. Director of Central Intelligence, "Intelligence Warning of the Tet Offensive," 6.

34. Grabo, "Watch Committee," 377.

35. Valenta, *Soviet Intervention in Czechoslovakia*.

36. Latimer, *Deception in War*, 262–64; Grabo, "Soviet Deception in the Czechoslovak Crisis." Created in 1959, Department D later became Service A of the First Chief Directorate. See Heuer, "Soviet Organization and Doctrine," 28.

37. Grabo, "Watch Committee," 379–80.

38. Loch K. Johnson says the decision was made on August 20; see Johnson, "Glimpses into the Gems," 356. Jiri Valenta reports the decision was made on August 17; see Valenta, *Soviet Intervention in Czechoslovakia*, 145.

39. Grabo with Goldman, *Handbook of Warning Intelligence*.

40. Grabo, "Watch Committee," 381–85.

41. Betts, *Enemies of Intelligence*, 49–50; Anonymous, "National Warning Intelligence."

42. Information in this paragraph was provided by Robert Dunfield, who worked warning issues from 1987 to 1993 at the Joint Staff J-2 as a US Army officer.

43. Authors' multiple discussions with several DoD warning people in 2014–2018.

44. Authors' discussion with Robert Dunfield, May 13, 2017.

45. Ibid.

46. Richelson, *US Intelligence Community*, 415.

47. Martin, "Measurement of International Military Commitments," 151–80; Andriole and Young, "Development of an Integrated Crisis Warning System," 107–50.

48. Martin, "Measurement of International Military Commitments."

49. Andriole and Young, "Development of an Integrated Crisis Warning System."

50. Ibid., 182–83.

51. Ford, *Estimative Intelligence*, 26, 44.

52. Kent, *Strategic Intelligence*.

53. Ford, *Estimative Intelligence*, 83–84.

54. Ibid., 85.

55. Ibid., 85–87.

56. Andrew, *For the President's Eyes Only*, 251, 253–57, 275, 286; Horelick, "Cuban Missile Crisis," 363–89.

57. Special National Intelligence Estimate 85–3-62, "The Soviet Military Buildup in Cuba." In *CIA Documents on the Cuban Missile Crisis*, 91–95, at https://www.cia.gov/library/center-for-the-study-of-intelligence/csi-publications/books-and-monographs/Cuban%20Missile%20Crisis1962.pdf.

58. Kent, "Crucial Estimate Relived." See also Wohlstetter, "Cuba and Pearl Harbor."

59. For example, see Allen, "Warning and Iraq's Invasion," 33–44.

60. Kent, "Crucial Estimate Relived," 118.

61. Wohlstetter, *Pearl Harbor*; Betts, "Analysis, War, and Decision."

62. Ford, *Estimative Intelligence*, 97–104; Betts, *Enemies of Intelligence*, 41; Johnson, "Glimpses into the Gems," 341–54.

63. Andrew, *For the President's Eyes Only*, 350–96.

64. Ford, *Estimative Intelligence*, 82.

65. McCarthy, "National Warning System," 5–19; Snider, *Agency and Hill*, 203–4.

66. Jervis, *Why Intelligence Fails*, 15–122; Bar-Joseph, "Forecasting a Hurricane," 718–42.

67. Available at http://fas.org/irp/offdocs/dcid1–5.html.

68. Ibid.

69. Director of Central Intelligence, "Soviet Invasion of Afghanistan."

70. Ibid., 1.

71. For details on its functioning, see DIA memo S-0656/DIA/DN-1A, "Overview of the Strategic Warning Staff," December 8, 1978, at https://www.cia.gov/library/readingroom/docs/CIA-RDP83B01027R000300140009–4.pdf.

72. In 1987 and 1988, John Gentry used this system while working on the staff of NIO/W John Bird, whose small office had a deputy and two analysts.

73. As reported by a former senior warning official to Gentry, February 2017.

74. Ibid.

75. Gentry telephone conversation with John Bird, February 17, 2017.

76. Ibid.

77. Ibid.

78. Ibid.

79. Ibid.

80. Ibid.

81. Ibid.

82. Ibid.

83. Ibid.

84. Gordon discussion with Charlie Allen, March 17, 2017.

85. Ibid.

86. Ibid.

87. Ibid.

88. Ibid.

89. Ibid.

90. Ibid.

91. Ibid.

92. Authors' discussion with Robert Dunfield, May 13, 2017; Russell, "CIA's Strategic Intelligence in Iraq," 194–97.

93. Allen, "Warning and Iraq's Invasion."

94. Landers, "Defense Warning System," 25.

95. McCarthy, "Mission to Warn," 19.

96. Haass, *War of Necessity*, 1, 59.

97. Davis, "Sherman Kent's Final Thoughts," 1.

98. Treverton, *Intelligence for an Age of Terror*, 11.

99. Authors' discussion with Gregory Treverton, April 6, 2017.

100. Landers, "Defense Warning System."

101. Ibid., 21–23.

102. Goodman and Berkowitz, "Intelligence without the Cold War."

103. Chairman of the Joint Chiefs of Staff, *Joint Vision 2020*.

104. McCarthy, "National Warning System," 5–19; Director of Central Intelligence, "DCI Task Force Report."

105. McCarthy, "National Warning System."

106. Ibid.

107. Director of Central Intelligence, "DCI Task Force Report," 10.

108. Davis, "Strategic Warning: Intelligence Support," 175.

109. Vickers, "State of Warning Today," 12.

110. Davis, "Strategic Warning: Intelligence Support," 179.

111. Landers, "Defense Warning System," 25–26; authors' discussion with Robert Dunfield, May 13, 2017.

112. Multiple authors' discussions with DoD warning analysts.

113. Authors' discussion with Gregory Treverton, April 6, 2017.

114. Authors' telephone discussion with Ron Woodward, June 11, 2017.

115. Authors' discussion with Robert Vickers, February 8, 2017.

116. Pillar, "Good Literature and Bad History," 1027–29.

117. National Commission on Terrorist Attacks upon the United States, *Final Report*, 346–48.

118. Authors' discussion with Robert Vickers, February 8, 2017.

119. On October 1, 1996, the NPIC became part of the National Imagery and Mapping Agency, which was renamed the National Geospatial-Intelligence Agency in 2003.

120. Source: a member of the National Warning Committee in this period.

121. Albright and Cohen, *Preventing Genocide*, 24–25.

122. Ibid.

123. Authors' discussion with Robert Vickers, February 8, 2017.

124. Ibid. See also National Commission on Terrorist Attacks upon the United States, *Final Report*, 346–48.

125. Ibid.; Gentry experience on Bird's staff.

126. Gentry telephone conversation with Robert Vickers, July 3, 2017.

127. Authors' discussion with Robert Vickers, February 8, 2017; Gentry experience on Bird's staff.

128. Vickers, "State of Warning Today," 12.

129. Davis, "Strategic Warning: If Surprise Is Inevitable," 6; Sirseloudi, "How to Predict," 369–85; Aid, "All Glory Is Fleeting," 72–120; Marrin, "9/11 Terrorist Attacks." For a view that the failure was strategic, see Parker and Stern, "Bolt from the Blue," 301–31.

130. Authors' discussion with an agency warning official.

131. Authors' discussions with Robert Vickers and John Gannon, February 8, 2017, and March 16, 2017, respectively.

132. Authors' discussion with John Gannon, March 16, 2017.

133. Gentry telephone conversation with Robert Vickers, July 3, 2017.

134. Ibid.

135. Authors' discussions with Robert Vickers and John Gannon, February 8, 2017, and March 16, 2017, respectively.

136. Authors' discussion with Ken Knight, November 30, 2016.

137. ICD 201, "National Foreign Intelligence Warning System."

138. Davis, "Strategic Warning: Intelligence Support," 175.

139. Gordon discussion with a former warning official, July 2017.

140. Authors' discussions with Ken Knight, a member of his staff, and another intelligence official, at various times.

141. The DIA reestablished its Military Capabilities Analysis Course in 2010.

142. Gentry email communication with Thomas Fingar, December 21, 2016; George and Wirtz, "Warning in Age of Uncertainty," 222–23.

143. ICD 207, "National Intelligence Council."

144. ICD 203, "Analytic Standards," June 21, 2007. A revised version was published in January 2015 at https://www.dni.gov/files/documents/ICD/ICD%20203%20Analytic%20Standards.pdf.

145. Authors' discussion with Ken Knight, November 30, 2016.

146. Ibid.

147. Gordon England, Department of Defense Directive 5105.21, "Defense Intelligence Agency," March 18, 2008, para. 6.3.5, http://www.esd.whs.mil/Portals/54/Documents/DD/issuances/dodd/5105 21p.pdf.

148. Ibid., para. 6.1.12.

149. Gentry email communication with Thomas Fingar, December 21, 2016. Other former senior intelligence officials report similar sentiments in this period.

150. Authors' discussion with John Gannon, March 16, 2017.

151. George and Wirtz, "Warning in Age of Uncertainty," 223.

152. Thomas Fingar email to Gentry, December 21, 2016. Other former senior intelligence officials report similar sentiments in this period.

153. Thomas Fingar email to Gentry, December 21, 2016.

154. Ibid.

155. Authors' discussion with a former national intelligence officer, April 2017.

156. Gordon telephone discussion with Ron Woodward, June 11, 2017.

157. Authors' discussions with several current and former officials at various times.

158. Source: a former senior intelligence official familiar with the decision.

159. ICD 900, "Integrated Mission Management," at https://fas.org/irp/dni/icd/icd-900.pdf.

160. Ibid.

161. Ibid. See also George and Wirtz, "Warning in Age of Uncertainty," 223–24.

162. Source: an IC officer, July 2017.

163. Heuer, *Rethinking Intelligence*, 30.

164. Ibid., 30–31; Bruce and Bennett, "Foreign Denial and Deception."

165. Director of Central Intelligence, "Directive 3/16P."

166. Bruce, "Countering Denial and Deception," 22.

167. Ibid., 22–23.

168. For examples of government-sponsored counter-deception studies, see Daniel and Herbig, *Strategic Military Deception*; and Dailey and Parker, *Soviet Strategic Deception*.

169. Gordon discussion with IC official, May 15, 2017.

170. Bruce, "Countering Denial and Deception."

171. Ibid., 23.

172. George and Wirtz, "Warning in Age of Uncertainty," 226; Cozad and Parachini, "(U) Strategic Warning."

173. Director of National Intelligence, *National Intelligence Strategy, 2014*, 7.

174. Joseph Gordon has seen these documents.

175. Intelligence Advanced Research Projects Activity website, accessed February 18, 2017, https://www.iarpa.gov/index.php/about-iarpa.

176. Source: a J-2 official.

177. Joseph Gordon served on this committee. One result was DIA Instruction 3000.001, "Defense Warning (U)," July 16, 2012. This instruction is not publicly available.

178. Joint Chiefs of Staff, Joint Staff J2, Defense Warning Staff, J2 Warning, *(U) Defense Warning Network Handbook*; George and Wirtz, "Warning in Age of Uncertainty," 225.

179. Treverton, *Intelligence for an Age of Terror*, 145.

180. Authors' discussions with numerous DoD warning personnel in 2014–18. See also Joint Chiefs of Staff, Defense Warning Staff, J2 Warning, *(U) Defense Warning Network Handbook*, 43.

181. Joint Chiefs of Staff, Defense Warning Staff, J2 Warning, *(U) Defense Warning Network Handbook*, 48.

182. Authors' multiple discussions with J27 personnel, 2015–17.

183. George and Wirtz, "Warning in Age of Uncertainty," 215.

184. Personal experience of Gentry and authors' communications with NIOs and others who worked with such people.

185. The UK section of this chapter was helped considerably by review, suggestions, and several written paragraphs provided via personal communication by John Tolson, a retired British intelligence officer, on September 1, 2017.

186. Davies, *Intelligence and Government*, 13.

187. Davies, "Twilight of Britain's Joint Intelligence Committee?," 429.

188. See "Defence Intelligence," UK Ministry of Defence website, https://www.gov.uk/guidance/defence-intelligence; Dylan, *Defence Intelligence and the Cold War*.

189. Davies, "Estimating Soviet Power," 818–19; United Kingdom Government, *National Intelligence Machinery*, 11; John Tolson, personal communication with Joseph Gordon, September 1, 2017.

190. John Tolson, personal communication with Gordon, September 1, 2017.

191. Freedman, *Official History of Falklands Campaign*, 155; Davies, "Estimating Soviet Power," 819, 835.

192. Davies, *Intelligence and Government*, 25–26; Davies, "Problem of Defence Intelligence," 797–809.

193. Source: John Tolson, personal communication.

194. United Kingdom Government, *National Intelligence Machinery*, 15.

195. Davies, *Intelligence and Government*, 35–36.

196. Ibid., 36.

197. Davies, "Twilight of Britain's Joint Intelligence Committee?," 429.

198. Davies, *Intelligence and Government*, 38–39; Aldrich, "British Intelligence during the Cold War," 152.

199. Davies, "Twilight of Britain's Joint Intelligence Committee?," 430.

200. Goodman, "Creating Machinery for Joint Intelligence," 66–84.

201. Goodman, "Avoiding Surprise," 265–92; Mobley, "Gauging the Iraqi Threat," 19–31.

202. Source: John Tolson.

203. Davies, *Intelligence and Government*, 176.

204. Joint Intelligence Committee, "JIC Watch Manual," INT 42(74)1, unpublished draft document, January 31, 1974, 2. For additional detail, see Davies, *Intelligence and Government*.

205. Ibid., 45.

206. Aldrich, Cormac, and Goodman, *Spying on the World*, 295.

207. Freedman, *Official History of Falklands Campaign*, 154–56; Davies, *Intelligence and Government*, 25–26.

208. Davies, *Intelligence and Government*, 41.

209. Ibid., 48–49.

210. Joint Intelligence Committee, *J.I.C. Watch Manual*, 1962, 3.

211. John Tolson, communication with Joseph Gordon, September 1, 2017.

212. The "Five Eyes" are Australia, Canada, New Zealand, the United Kingdom, and the United States.

213. John Tolson, communication with Gordon, September 1, 2017.

214. "National Security Council," UK government website, https://www.gov.uk/government/groups/national-security-council.

215. Davies, "Twilight of Britain's Joint Intelligence Committee?"

216. Devanney and Harris, *National Security Council*; Bangham and Shah, *National Security Council and the Prime Minister*, http://thewilberforcesociety.co.uk/wp-content/uploads/2012/04/TWS-National-Security-and-the-Prime-Minister-George-Bangham-Sarang-Shah.pdf.

217. Davies, *Intelligence and Government*, 41.

218. Goodman, "Avoiding Surprise," 285–86.

219. Ibid.

220. Lord Franks chaired the committee of six privy counselors that produced the *Falkland Islands Review* (or the Franks Report of 1983), while Lord Butler's *Review of Intelligence on Weapons of Mass Destruction* was published in 2004.

221. Aldrich, Cormac, and Goodman, *Spying on the World*, 4.

222. Goodman, "Avoiding Surprise," 278.

223. Ibid., 285–86.

224. Ibid., 286, 291.

225. Ibid., 286.

226. Grabo, *Handbook of Warning Intelligence*, 266–79.

227. Goodman, "Avoiding Surprise," 272–74.

228. This section relies heavily on information provided by B. G. J. (Bob) de Graaff of the University of Utrecht, the Netherlands.

229. Bob de Graaff, PowerPoint presentation, "Terrorist Threat Levels in the Netherlands and Risk Communication to the Public," June 7, 2016.

230. Ibid.

231. Abels, "Dreigingsbeeld terrorisme Nederland," 539.

232. Gordon, "NATO Intelligence Fusion Centre," 645–50.

233. NATO's warning doctrine is a variant of DoD doctrine. Its current doctrinal manual is based on the US *Defense Warning Network Handbook*.

234. Background information on NATO warning milestones provided by the director of the NIWS course, NATO School Oberammergau, Germany.

235. Kriendler, "Anticipating Crises."

236. Atlantic Council, "NATO Selects German Diplomat as New Chief of Intelligence," *NATO Source*, October 21, 2016, http://www.atlanticcouncil.org/blogs/natosource/nato-selects-german-diplomat-as-new-chief-of-intelligence. See also Julian Barnes, "NATO Appoints Its First Intelligence Chief," *Wall Street Journal*, October 21, 2016.

237. Ballast, "Trust (in) NATO."

238. For basic information on NIFC, see "NATO Intelligence Fusion Centre (NIFC)," http://web.ifc.bices.org/index.htm.

239. Lecture notes, "Introduction to NIWS," 2015, provided by NATO School Oberammergau.

240. Kriendler, "NATO Intelligence and Early Warning."

241. Lecture notes, "Introduction to NIWS." See also NATO, "Crisis Management," http://www.nato.int/cps/en/natohq/topics_49192.htm, updated February 27, 2018.

CHAPTER 5

Warning Methodological Issues

Our discussion thus far covers many aspects of warning, but we have not systematically addressed issues that recurrently bedevil practitioners and are important for students of warning to appreciate. Understanding these concepts and figuring ways to embed them in both warning analyses and strategic deceptions are key to operational success. Just as surely, failure to understand them virtually guarantees operational failure. These issues appear frequently in the history of strategic warning. They also affect analytic techniques, including the I&W method, which intelligence practitioners developed. We discuss these techniques in following chapters.

What to Follow? What to Warn About?

Definitions of strategic warning traditionally focus on tangible threats—usually major, overt, conventional military threats one state (or states) pose(s) to other states. For a long time, this definition made good sense. Interstate wars were common. In pre-Westphalian days, conquerors consumed their victims—the ultimate existential threat. In the immediate post–World War II era, memories of two major interstate wars were fresh. World War II began in both the European and Pacific theaters with surprise attacks. And after 1945, the division of much of the world into opposing ideological camps kept the threat of conventional, and then nuclear, war a major concern. As noted, Roberta Wohlstetter's study of the Pearl Harbor warning failure was motivated not just by an interest in history or social science theorizing but also by a quest for lessons that could help prevent a surprise attack on the United States by nuclear-armed enemies.

Stalin saw the conflict between capitalism and socialism ending in war.[1] Revisionist historiography notwithstanding, it was evident to most reasonably objective observers in the early Cold War period that Soviet leaders, even after Stalin's death in 1953, saw the East-West competition in stark terms. The Soviets might attack if they thought the war's outcome was likely to be favorable at acceptable cost. While later Soviet leaders were less hostile than Stalin, they probed Western defenses chronically. Hence, Western strategic warning professionals understandably focused initially on the threats that Moscow, its Warsaw Pact allies, and its apparently close communist friends in China, Vietnam, and elsewhere seemed to pose. The rough East-West parity of the 1970s and 1980s did not alter US concerns that the Soviets might be tempted to use force if they thought the cost-benefit trade-off was acceptable or, more likely, engage in varieties of lower-level conflicts globally, perhaps through proxies.

Influenced by successful Soviet deception efforts enabled by a sophisticated D&D doctrine known as *maskirovka* that hid its weaknesses in the 1950s and 1960s, Western intelligence incorrectly saw rapidly growing Soviet might far exceeding that necessary for defense alone.[2] The same *maskirovka* doctrine helped mask Soviet strengths and intentions thereafter, leading to some Western underestimates of Soviet strength in the 1970s.[3] In different ways, Soviet D&D practices for decades produced some Western misunderstanding of the Soviet threat.

But recognition of a Soviet threat and devotion of intelligence resources to watching the USSR and its allies were not enough. The IC recruited, developed internally, and hired as consultants first-class experts on the communist world in the early Cold War era and developed many methods that improved its collection on, and analysis of, communist states. Robert Jervis believes that the CIA in this period had (but no longer has) experts who could match the best specialists in academia.[4] Expertise and demonstrable analytic rigor helped the IC to persuasively communicate its warning messages to senior decision-makers. This expertise also helped refine strategic warning analytical processes.

Although the Soviets clearly posed a military threat, other actors and situations also worried US intelligence. Warning doctrine, intelligence people reasoned, should be able to handle these situations too. A major, ongoing question thus became: what other issues should warning intelligence address? If a senior executive requested an assessment of the status of Soviet threats, the early Watch Committee could respond without hesitation.[5] But not all potential warning issues were so clear, and they became less clear as the once-seemingly monolithic, Moscow-led communist world split and noncommunist actors such as revolutionary Iran after 1979 gave the West difficult policy choices and intelligence challenges. The identification and formal establishment of warning problems in the US IC therefore often were matters of considerable debate. Hence, criteria for identifying warning issues evolved over time but never were codified definitively, which probably was wise given the history of recurrent surprises. But it complicated warning analysis and relationships of warning officers with line analytic units.

Definitions of warning problems were important for establishing "lanes" of responsibility or "ownership" within warning organizations because, once established, warning problems often developed independent institutional lives. Hence, warning officers faced another set of questions: when, how, and why should a "warning problem" die? When does an issue "go away" sufficiently for line analytic units to cover it adequately in both long-term research-focused and current intelligence production? The termination of a warning problem that no longer is relevant is essential. Otherwise, as happened frequently in the history of US warning, a warning office simply becomes another current intelligence shop monitoring growing numbers of yesterday's big issues while ignoring tomorrow's challenges. The threat of another North Korean invasion of the Republic of Korea has been a legitimate warning concern since 1953 given chronic North Korean belligerence. But transient warning problems hang on far longer than appropriate if owning entities cling to them for bureaucratic reasons or warning analysts do so for reasons of personal preference even after underlying issues dissolve, policymakers are well aware of situations, or line analytic offices have issues well in hand. One potential solution to this problem is "sunset" provisions on warning problems: they expire after a set period of time unless formally renewed by a process akin to the initial establishment of a problem.[6] The IC has done this at times.

What Is a Threat?

Warning chronically focuses on threats, but definitions of "threat" vary. Choosing a relevant definition may enable a successful warning or doom a warning analysis to failure. Gregory Treverton observes that threats come in two varieties: "threats that come with threateners" and "threats without threateners."[7] The strategic warning offices of the Western world arose during the Cold War with a dominant focus on a clearly, purposefully threatening Soviet bloc, but that is no longer the case. Political, economic, health, and environment threats are more diffuse and impersonal. While warning has adapted and continues to adapt to a changing world, the scope of strategic threat warning remains unclear.

If there is any truism in military intelligence, it is that threats are composed of "capabilities" and hostile intentions—or what was once called "political warning."[8] Military intelligence people, especially, accurately note that it usually is much harder to assess intentions than capabilities defined in material terms such as large weapons that are hard to hide. But many intelligence personnel err in claiming that intelligence should focus only, or primarily, on capabilities—or what some once called "military warning."[9] They mistakenly argue that it is essential to focus on "worst-case" situations because they can hurt most, that because military people typically are not skilled at political or psychological analyses they should not try to assess intentions, and that the costs of over-warning are negligible. The last error is especially pernicious for warning because it damages the credibility that effective warning requires.

Because military "capabilities" are typically defined as products of existing military forces, warning intelligence at its inception became enthralled with assessments of force structures, or what military people call order-of-battle (OB, OOB, or ORBAT) estimates.[10] Traditionally, OB data include numbers and types of units, major pieces of equipment, and military bases—all of which are discrete and can, at least potentially, be identified, counted, and assessed. They usually are intelligence secrets and puzzles—not mysteries. OB databases often also contain less firm information on other factors relevant for understanding military forces' capabilities, including leadership characteristics, current military doctrine, the status of unit and individual troop training, unit readiness, and troop morale, which OB analysts typically think they can assess fairly objectively. Besides, it is thought, the intangible factors are less important than material military assets. While intelligence services normally do not conduct net assessments—their own colleagues typically refuse to share important friendly data with them—military analysts generally understand the structures of their own forces and roughly estimate force balances with foreign countries or alliances.

The belief that "threats" can be accurately described or measured by traditional OB tables is, however, seriously mistaken. As we saw in the Normandy case study in chapter 2, British deceivers misled German OB analysts into thinking Allied strength was much greater than it actually was. And AMAN nearly perfectly knew the Egyptian OB in 1973 but did not understand how Egypt planned to use its new antiaircraft and antitank missiles, a significant cause of Israel's intelligence failure.[11]

More generally, there is no reliable formula for measuring military or any other variety of national "capabilities." The abilities of any one person or military force or national government depend on three variables that are *always* relevant: (1) the mission of the armed force; (2) the actions of adversaries and relevant third parties including belligerents' allies and the UN; and (3) the operational environments, including physical terrain and weather, which soldiers understand well, but also including local populations and the presence of NGO personnel and the press. Any given force may succeed or fail badly, depending on the details of the three variables. Therefore, any "capabilities" assessment that does not address all three factors is almost certainly faulty. For example, as described in chapter 2, Egypt imaginatively used air defense missiles to produce effective military power in 1973 near the Suez Canal in support of an unusual political military goal. Use of the same ground force for another purpose—conquest of the Sinai Peninsula away from the protective air defense shield—probably would have ended catastrophically for Egypt. Stephen Biddle similarly argues that operational success, for a given mission, depends on a combination of factors, including physical assets, troop skills, and technology.[12]

The error of focusing on the material aspects of military force is widespread. Beginning in 1963, political scientist J. David Singer, soon joined by historian Melvin Small, studied war in what became known as the Correlates of War (COW) Project.[13] The project focused initially on interstate wars after the complicated set of Napoleonic wars ended in 1815 and later extended to address internal wars. The project developed what its contributors believed to be objective, quantitative measures of national power, including military spending, national and urban population, military manpower, iron and steel production, and energy production. The COW Project also developed a series of data sets that are available to scholars on the Internet, thereby making some of the most widely cited data in academic international relations scholarship and intelligence analysis. COW measures ignore all three variables noted above.

Because military analysts and national leaders often fail to consider relevant aspects of bilateral (or dyadic) military power relationships, they often make strategically important mistakes, which sometimes lead to war and defeat. Australian scholar Geoffrey Blainey observed similarly that "wars usually begin when two nations disagree on their relative strength, and wars usually cease when the fighting nations agree on their relative strength. . . . When nations prepare to fight one another, they have contradictory expectations of the likely duration and outcome of the war."[14] Like many participants in the COW Project, Blainey erroneously suggests that the quantity of "power" of prospective adversaries is objectively measurable but often initially is misidentified or misinterpreted, only later to be seen accurately by all belligerent parties.

Yet, as examples in chapter 2 illustrate, states regularly try to alter the relative power applicable in a given situation by, among other things, conducting surprise attacks, which effectively alter missions, enemy actions, and the operational environment. And intelligence people, as AMAN analysts did in 1973, regularly misunderstand enemies' objectives—thereby fundamentally mistaking their capacities to achieve their goals.

Hence, threat warning analysts must, if they are to avoid such errors, understand the flexible and contingent nature of military power in the context of specific mission goals—a challenging task when effective warning messages usually must be made under conditions of deception-enhanced uncertainty about actors' intentions. Analysts addressing military warning problems must effectively analyze the details of likely conflict situations and assess how belligerent adversaries may do the same; errors in either analysis may change warning messages, or their accuracy, considerably. Because diplomatic and economic instruments of national power are useful in different situations, threat and opportunity warning analyses should also account for asymmetries in these arenas. Michael Handel notes that while the Western (and Israeli until 1973) military tradition usually holds that success in war is achieved through battlefield victories, that is not the case elsewhere.[15] Warning analysts need to understand other cultural perspectives.

Good analysts account for such different perspectives by examining a broad range of factors. Andrew Marshall, who directed the Pentagon's Office of Net Assessment (ONA) from 1973 to 2015, used a variant of this approach to help his analysts make better judgments than are possible using the basic OB comparison approach. He instructed his analysts to evaluate balances of forces of major weapon systems within national armed forces establishments. For example, rather than simply count comparable Soviet and US strategic bomber fleets—which would never fight each other directly—Marshall examined whether Soviet air defenses would be able to stop American bombers' penetrations of Soviet airspace. Finding that US stealth technology was good and Soviet attempts to defend its long borders would be futile and expensive, he suggested in 1976 that the United States buy more B-1 bombers to exploit America's comparative advantage—an idea President Jimmy Carter rejected in 1977 but President Ronald Reagan later accepted.[16] In such ways, Marshall developed net assessment into an analytic discipline in which analysts look for exploitable asymmetries in specific dyadic contexts— not their stocks of military assets.

We think Marshall's method for conducting net assessment is directly applicable to warning.[17] History demonstrates that states and non-state actors look regularly for exploitable vulnerabilities in their opponents and sometimes their "friends."[18] Net assessment of potential adversaries in dynamic interaction is essential. Because actors have different risk perceptions and tolerances, net assessment requires understanding different national and small-group political cultures as well as capacities for learning and adaptation. Marshall emphasized the psychological and political aspects of net assessment and, like Albert Einstein, often said, "Not everything that can be counted counts; and not everything that counts can be counted."[19]

Interestingly, Soviet intelligence, which suffered mightily under Stalin, did not make this mistake. After 1945, Stalin ordered his intelligence apparatus to focus on the intentions and plans of Western powers, not their material "capabilities." In response, Soviet collection services acquired many documents from Western states and NATO, including detailed war plans.[20]

The Purpose of Warning: Uncertainty Reduction or Prediction?

The purposes asserted for strategic warning commonly include accurate prediction, or forecasting, of events of importance—especially major military threats. Intelligence should, the standard critique goes, have predicted the Japanese attack on Pearl Harbor and the specifics of the 9/11 attacks and warned accordingly. But capable intelligence professionals know that predicting specific events is very hard and that attempts to do so usually fail, leading to criticism of faulty analysis. As the famous intelligence analyst Yogi Berra once said, "It's tough to make predictions, especially about the future."[21]

Instead, warning analysts usually try to do what Thomas Fingar, Mark Lowenthal, and others suggest: provide information and analyses that help reduce decision-makers' uncertainties about unfolding events.[22] Their logic is based on recognition that decision-makers in most cases do not need crystal clarity about what will happen; they need general understanding about how events are unfolding to act to prevent, deter, defend against, or exploit them. The IC sometimes refers to this concept as "foresight." Decisions based on such warning can be partial or preliminary by, for example, increasing vigilance or taking measured steps to partially prepare for possible events. Subsequent analysis leading to greater confidence that warned-about events are developing can lead to gradually increased preparations, diplomatic action, or a decision to stand down if events turn out not to be worrisome or if preliminary actions precipitate a change in other actors' plans—indicating a warning success. Hence, accurate predictions of specific events may be unnecessary for strategic warning, so long as warning professionals accurately detect anomalies and fairly accurately assess the range of meanings they may have.[23] This process may require iterative interactions between warning analysts and decision-makers about the evolution of a warning issue.

Intelligence can help policymakers in other ways. Former Secretary of State Dean Acheson once said the best service intelligence can perform is to boost the confidence of decision-makers.[24] This makes sense if uncertainty has had the debilitating effect of reducing senior leaders' confidence in their decision-making capabilities. We see the latter problem rarely, however. Robert Jervis notes the occasional importance of the opposite function—to increase leaders' doubts when they are excessively confident—especially when intelligence information is weak and analysts' confidence in their judgment correspondingly is low. Jervis argues that this role would have been appropriate for analysts assessing Iraqi WMD capabilities in the late 1990s and early 2000s.[25]

Nevertheless, prediction of future events in general terms, or forecasting, is an important part—although only a part—of intelligence analysis generally and of strategic warning. In recent years the US IC has conducted studies, including experiments, designed to both generate better predictions and to figure out how the IC as a whole can predict better.[26] Among them, in 2011 the Intelligence Advanced Research Projects Activity (IARPA), a part of the ODNI that mainly conducts technology-focused research, sponsored a tournament scheduled to last four years, in which five teams answered discrete questions whose answers could readily be assessed for accuracy.[27] The team assembled by psychologist Philip Tetlock beat the experiment's control group by 60 percent in the first year of the experiment and by 78 percent in the second year. Thereafter, IARPA ended the tournament and focused on why Tetlock's group did so well. Tetlock then created a team of star forecasters, in what he called his Good Judgment Project, and studied their forecasting traits.[28]

Tetlock's project is indirectly applicable to warning in the sense that forecasting specific events—developing discrete answers to narrow questions like those IARPA asked—is not usually characteristic of strategic warning cases, which typically involve mysteries that often unfold over extended periods of time in ways that do not become clear until well after warning ceases to be relevant. The IC does not normally measure predictive accuracy of its assessments for several reasons, including the fact that "accuracy" is only evident over extended periods of time and can be partial; agencies also dislike having their performance measured because they might look bad in absolute terms and in comparison to their bureaucratic rivals.[29] But Tetlock's study of forecasters, especially his identification of characteristics that make the best ones very good at addressing complex analytic challenges, is relevant to the issue of whether there are types of people, training, or education that make warning analysts particularly good or poor. We return to this issue, and Tetlock's judgments about important traits in intelligence analysts, in chapter 8.

Uncertainty Shifting

Intelligence officers often, as Thomas Fingar writes, try to understand situations and communicate that understanding to senior decision-makers, thereby reducing their uncertainties and, other things equal, improving the quality of decision-making.[30] Martin Petersen similarly argues that the purpose of intelligence analysis is "bounding uncertainty" of policymakers, thereby "helping make my guy smarter than their guy whether . . . across a conference table or across a battlefield and enabling our policymakers to make the best decisions possible given the time and information available."[31] High-quality intelligence support thereby helps provide what the IC calls "decision advantage," which variously means making US decisions wiser or giving US decision-makers a relative advantage over other leaders.[32] Michael Warner adds that a common purpose of intelligence support is to shift relative uncertainties from one's own decision-makers to others they face in dynamic relationships, thereby similarly producing favorable "decision advantage."[33]

States can alter the relative balance of leaders' uncertainty by keeping their own key activities and decisions secret and by using deception against adversaries to create in them uncertainty in some situations, certain but erroneous judgment in others, or both. In each case, the point of deception is to generate faulty decisions in target actors. Under this understanding of the purpose of intelligence, warning serves to identify unfavorable asymmetries in one's own policymakers and suggest (if indirectly in the US case) ways to ameliorate unfavorable situations in threat warnings, identify favorable asymmetries that are exploitable, and identify ways to create favorable uncertainty asymmetries that might be exploitable.

Communicating Warning: Risk versus Uncertainty

We have argued that persuasive communication in warning is as important as good analytic judgment. A key element in that communication is an accurate conveyance of the degree of uncertainty analysts have about an unfolding situation. As recalled, strategic warning virtually by definition requires analytic judgment in the face of substantial uncertainty. However, while some indication of confidence levels is important to convey, the use of probabilistic language appropriate for descriptions of risk may be misleading if it communicates a false sense of certainty about an assessment.[34] For example, most people readily grasp that the chance of "heads" when flipping a coin is about the same as "tails," and the likelihood of a coin settling on edge is near zero. The probability, or "risk," of a flip of "heads" is therefore about 50 percent. But far more common in strategic warning is the assessment of trends or possible events whose likelihood, eventual details, and consequences are unknown. The challenges of forecasting the policies (and their implications) of leaders who have not yet been selected and the views of leaders that are both evolving and subject to change in the rough-and-tumble of domestic politics reflect uncertainties, not risks. In these cases, risk is an inappropriate concept and use of its terminology is similarly inappropriate.

Hence, many strategic intelligence analysts long have held the view of Frank Knight, a prominent early twentieth-century economist, who argued that uncertainties, unlike risk situations, should not be discussed in probabilistic terms.[35] Nassim Taleb makes the same point more dramatically in his discussion of "black swan" events.[36] These analysts opposed the perspective of Sherman Kent, who argued in the 1950s and 1960s for use of probabilistic language in analytic messages, including NIEs.[37] Kent accurately recognized that consumers often want confidence statements using quantitative language more appropriate to discussions of risk than uncertainty. Cynthia Grabo also favored use of probabilistic language in warning messages, presumably also reflecting her understanding of consumers' wants.[38]

The perceived lessons of the 9/11 attacks changed the course of this debate in the United States. Many intelligence consumers, some producers, and some academic observers in the decade after 9/11 supported Kent's view for reasons that are not completely clear or are mistaken.[39] Failure to stop the 9/11 attackers had little to do with miscommunication about risk or uncertainty. Nevertheless, to help address a long-standing and more legitimate complaint about the clarity of analytic messages, some argued that greater use of probabilistic language would help. Some within the IC, responding to the national mood to "do something" to prevent another 9/11, helped push the IC finally to adopt specific terms to express degrees of analytic confidence in ICD 203, "Analytic Standards," as revised in January 2015.[40] Some intelligence entities, including DIA and the Joint Staff J-2, adopted similar policies. The policy mandates use of specific adjectives that match numerical percentages of risk that an event seems likely to entail (see table 5.1). Hence, the IC now publishes definitions of probabilistic language in all major intelligence products, including NIEs. To the extent that warning messages are formal, national-level intelligence products, the new policy applies to warning analyses as well.

Also in 2015, NATO adopted similar standards in the form of NATO Allied Joint Doctrine for Intelligence Procedures AJP 2.1. Several NATO countries, including Canada, Denmark, the Netherlands, Norway, and the United Kingdom, have similar national-level communication doctrine for their military intelligence services.

Whether this will help decision-makers make better decisions remains to be seen. We doubt there will be much effect. Help, if there is any, lies in the communication of assessments only; there is no effect on the quality of analyses that leads analysts to issue warning messages. We accept that consumers who do not carefully distinguish risk from uncertainty may be comfortable with probabilistic language, but we also expect this fashion to change again over time. We continue to agree with John Maynard Keynes, who was in Knight's camp and more wisely than ICD 203 once said, "It is better to be roughly right than precisely wrong."[41] Former senior policymaker James Steinberg concurs: "I am somewhat skeptical of what I believe is a false sense of concreteness implied in assigning numerical

Table 5.1. ICD 203–Mandated Probabilistic Language

almost no chance	very unlikely	unlikely	roughly even chance	likely	very likely	almost certain(ly)
remote	highly improbable	improbable (improbably)	roughly even odds	probable (probably)	highly likely	nearly certain
1%–5%	5%–20%	20%–45%	45%–55%	55%–80%	80%–95%	95%–99%

Note: The terms in the two top rows are synonyms for the numeric likelihoods in the third row immediately below them.

Source: Office of the Director of National Intelligence, Intelligence Community Directive 203, "Analytic Standards," January 2015, 3.

probabilities to individual events, particularly contingent outcomes that depend on choices others have yet to make."[42]

Furthermore, the influence of probabilities on policy decisions varies considerably, making it essential for warning analysts to understand their consumers' attitudes and concerns. A comparison of the perspectives of two prominent, senior intelligence consumers illustrates this point dramatically. In mid-1991, soon after the successful conclusion of the Gulf War, the then chairman of the Joint Chiefs of Staff, General Colin Powell, opened a conference of military warning officers at the Pentagon by recounting how intelligence effectively warned him in the first half of 1990 of Iraqi military preparations that could lead to an invasion of Kuwait.[43] He reminded his audience that he was hard to persuade about emerging threats but that they should keep trying to do so if they felt strongly about an issue, and he said the threshold for him to take action was "point seven" (70 percent) confidence that something "bad" would happen.[44] Certainty was undesirable because he would not have enough time to take effective counter- or defensive measures, and a lower estimate of likelihood would not convince him to act. Hence, the task for warning officers was to persuade Powell that the event they worried about warranted *Powell's* assignment of a 70-percent confidence level.

In sharp contrast, in the immediate aftermath of the 9/11 attacks, a much lower likelihood of a threatening action was needed to induce Vice President Richard Cheney to act to prevent another such attack. Given the trauma the country suffered on 9/11, Cheney told his staff the United States would act if there was even a 1-percent chance that Pakistani scientists would provide al-Qaeda with a nuclear-weapon means for another major attack.[45] This "one percent doctrine" became part of the George W. Bush administration's justification for the invasion of Iraq in 2003 after some (later revealed to be inaccurate) reports suggested that Saddam Hussein might provide chemical weapons to al-Qaeda.

Clearly Powell and Cheney, experienced decision-makers who understood intelligence well, had different perspectives. For warning professionals, the importance of knowing consumer sensitivities is apparent: "70 percent" and "1 percent" are very different numbers. Another warning that would have been unpersuasive to Powell might have led Cheney to view intelligence support as unsatisfactory because it was too conservative and, probably, too late.

Other people have different probability thresholds for taking action. Former NIO/W Robert Vickers generally warned when he believed the likelihood of a significant event's occurrence was about 50 percent—an implicit judgment about the probability thresholds of effective warning messages.[46]

The Mistake of Assessing the Wrong Question

Warning analysts repeatedly err by assessing situations as threatening (or benign) based on flawed understanding of the problems, challenges, or goals their analytic targets perceive. Intelligence professionals too frequently, in our experience and our reading of the literature, see their intelligence targets' situations in fairly conventional terms. These may reflect organizationally acceptable ways to address intellectual challenges, organizational "best practices" that become doctrinaire, intelligence "requirements" that reflect mirror imaging by prominent consumers, or simply issues of importance to consumers, not those important to intelligence targets. In other words, analysts do not "ask the right question" that might identify strategies and tactics necessary to achieve a target's nonstandard goals under conditions of (often) substantial constraint. Surprise can come in many forms— including technical and doctrinal innovation—meaning warning analysts should be alert to many aspects of each warning problem.[47] German intelligence analysts in 1940 asked themselves important questions about how the French and British governments made major political-military decisions and used their answers to help develop war plans that enabled Germany to defeat France.[48] Analysts who ask themselves irrelevant or self-misleading questions unsurprisingly often develop incorrect or, perhaps worse, accurate but irrelevant "answers."

We saw in the Yom Kippur War case in chapter 2 that AMAN's leader and its chief Egyptian analyst assessed the likelihood of Egypt initiating a war as low because they saw no way Egypt could defeat the IDF and reconquer the Sinai Peninsula in a high-intensity conventional war. Instead, as is clear in retrospect, President Sadat intended a limited military action designed to alter political conditions in ways that would lead to diplomatic recovery of the Sinai, not to defeat Israel militarily—something Israeli military intelligence officers using normal military analytic practices did not anticipate. Hence, the Israelis misidentified Sadat's situation and goals and did not ask themselves a "right" question: given Egyptian military weaknesses, how might Sadat try to achieve his political-military goals in nonstandard ways that effectively used Egypt's limited abilities and minimized its vulnerabilities to Israeli strengths? Instead, they restricted themselves to a narrower and less relevant question: can the Egyptians defeat Israel militarily in a large-scale war to conquer the Sinai? Their probably accurate conclusion of no led to a major warning failure given Sadat's alternative strategy.

AMAN's analysts did not ask *the* wrong question. They asked one of many potentially irrelevant or misleading questions. Thereby, at the beginning of their analysis, independent of quality of reporting and cognitive or other blinders, AMAN's leaders headed in a direction likely to lead to an analytic error because they missed the unusual nature of Sadat's situation, his character, his logic, his goals, his possible actions, and their meaning. They should not have put themselves in Sadat's shoes, committing the mirror-imaging error, but they could have used their expertise on Egypt to empathize with Sadat in his situation.

Similarly, retired CIA analyst George Allen, who earlier worked for the US Army and DIA and who assessed the French and then American wars in Vietnam for nearly twenty years, notes that American military intelligence, especially, chronically focused on tactical aspects of the US war in Vietnam rather that the critical strategic-level questions relating to communist intentions, strategies, and prospects for success.[49] By focusing on tactical issues, US intelligence consistently during the 1950s and 1960s failed to assess the long-term

- In 1967 and early 1968, few American analysts foresaw the unusually large size and timing of the offensive that North Vietnam launched on January 30, 1968. Those who did so accurately foresaw a military defeat for the Viet Cong.[61] However, most analysts did not perceive that North Vietnam also hoped to achieve the strategic political objective of shocking the American public in a presidential election year, and they did not understand their country's vulnerability to such a shock.[62] Hence, they did not anticipate the striking strategic political success of the offensive, its military cost notwithstanding. American intelligence analysts did not recall that the communists, unlike most Americans, considered military activities subordinate to strategically important political goals. NSA failed to anticipate the full extent of the Tet Offensive because it focused its reporting on the Khe Sanh area in the far north because commanding General William Westmoreland was concerned about it—in large part owing to the success of North Vietnam's deception operations.[63] Analysts also failed in part because of their cultural prohibition on avoiding analysis of the US government or Americans as people, which precluded their understanding of North Vietnamese perceptions of US political vulnerabilities that were critical to Hanoi's decision to launch the offensive.[64] After the war, General Vo Nguyen Giap said in a conversation with US Navy Admiral Elmo Zumwalt that the war was won in the United States and that the antiwar movement in the United States was very useful to him.[65]
- In 1979, American intelligence analysts assessed that the Soviet military would have trouble in Afghanistan and that Moscow therefore would not order an invasion. They got the part about the difficulty of fighting in Afghanistan right—but not the politburo's belief that it needed to preserve the achievements of Soviet-backed socialism in Afghanistan, a view that also led the Soviets to intervene militarily in East Germany in 1953, Hungary in 1956, and Czechoslovakia in 1968.
- In 1983, worried by what it perceived to be the aggressiveness of President Reagan, the Soviet Union saw in a NATO exercise named Able Archer US preparations for a nuclear first strike on the USSR. American intelligence personnel accurately understood that NATO leaders intended no such thing, but Western intelligence did not detect the Soviet misperception until considerably later, leading to a warning failure that fortunately did not have serious practical consequences.[66] Intelligence was not briefed about the exercise in advance—a standard and not infrequently debilitating practice that keeps US analysts from knowing what their intelligence targets study closely and sometimes know well.

Ways Time Is Important

Strategic warning has important but vague time dimensions. Time can be important to the strategic warning function in several ways, sometimes simultaneously. A background condition is that analysts have time constraints. Large volumes of incoming traffic and deadlines may lead to hasty judgments.

To be effective, strategic warning must be provided in time for decision-making processes to reach a policy decision and for policy-implementing organizations to effectively prepare for and implement policies.[67] The chronological time needed for each of those steps varies according to the nature of the warned-about event, the organization of government decision-making, the decisiveness of decision-makers, and the speed and effectiveness of responding government bureaucracies, each of which may be influenced by the clarity and persuasiveness of the warning message. While most intelligence analysts understand that there can be no single, general statement of chronical time that is "enough" for adequate warning, other aspects of time get less attention and often are misunderstood.

A first principle is that the time leaders can spend on intelligence is limited. Experienced CIA analyst Martin Petersen argues that time is more precious to senior leaders than information.[68] Analysts therefore have short windows to get their messages to senior leaders even if they have established close working relationships. Hence, warning messages, like other forms of intelligence, generally should be succinct. This is a major cause of the "make the call" mantra once common in US analytic units, which tends to lead analytic organizations to write messages without nuance. Producing succinct warning messages that include relevant alternative views and degrees of uncertainty is much harder.

The sequencing of warning indicators before an important event varies, and the logic that indicators should become more apparent with proximity to a major event may not hold. Cynthia Grabo notes that attack preparations often are completed well before attacks begin, resulting in a lull in activity and correspondingly fewer, not more and better, indicators immediately before an attack.[69] That is why warning analysts sometimes report to consumers that an attack can come at any time without additional warning—as US intelligence did just before Iraq invaded Kuwait in 1990, as German intelligence did in June 1944 before the Normandy invasion, and as Israeli intelligence did in early October 1973 before the Yom Kippur War. Yet there are always possible reasons for delays, ranging from bad weather to leaders' cold feet to the unpreparedness of allies, the latter apparently being a reason why Sadat delayed his attack on Israel from May 1973 to October. Hitler postponed his attack on France repeatedly in late 1939 and early 1940 for a wide variety of reasons, including logistical shortcomings, internal debates over war plans, bad winter weather, and security compromises.[70] Anti-Nazi German Army Colonel Hans Oster repeatedly warned Western governments accurately about Hitler's plans and reasons for their delays, but what seemed to be repeated false alarms eventually led Western leaders to largely ignore him.[71] The weak record of accurate warning about specific timing of attacks led Grabo to suggest that analysts not should forecast attacks but rather should warn that preparations are sufficiently complete to make attacks possible—which is how military warnings often are couched.[72]

Warning about nonmilitary issues and military-related technological developments may involve considerably longer time horizons, but warning should not be very long-term in nature. Senior decision-makers typically are busy people who have many concerns, and notification of a distant event is easy to set aside for later in the face of more pressing issues. Robert Jervis argues persuasively that policymakers have windows of time in which they are receptive to intelligence, implicitly including warning analyses.[73] Such windows can be narrow. Decision-makers tend not to be receptive to intelligence on an issue before it becomes important to them, want intelligence input when they understand the issue and are looking for help in addressing it, but tend to reject intelligence after making policy decisions and initiating government action.

Once committed, leaders typically do not want to know that they may be making a mistake. An example from World War II illustrates this point. Just before the September 1944 initiation of Operation Market Garden, an Allied operation designed to capture bridges across the Rhine River in the Netherlands, thereby facilitating the Allied invasion of Germany, intelligence identified a strong German armored force near where the British First Airborne Division was to land. British commanders rejected the information, however, saying it was too late to change the operational plan.[74] As a result, as intelligence forecast, the paratrooper force was mauled and the operation failed.

Ariel Levite makes Jervis's point less clearly. He theorizes that the initial reaction of policymakers to warning is based on three factors: (1) aspects of the warning message, (2) "possession of other pertinent information on the issue at hand," and (3) the political and personality traits of policymakers.[75] Levite argues that factor 2 can be a result of the "logic of the situation" or lessons the policymaker learned from the past, which we equate to Jervis's window. In Levite's view, policymaker traits relate to vague characteristics of leaders as people. We prefer Jervis's more succinct observation that policy closure after a decision has been made leads decision-makers to be unwilling to revisit their decisions when additional, "inconvenient warning" intelligence develops.[76]

Similarly, leaders work in what Stephen Skowronek calls "political time," which some intelligence people call the "climate of the times."[77] Skowronek argues that historians can usefully assess US presidential administrations in the context of the general circumstances in which they governed. This perspective, like Jervis's, helps identify windows in which leaders may be receptive (or not) to warning messages for political or emotional reasons.

The political times concept also is useful for thinking about the targets of intelligence analysis. All leaders face constraints, and recognition by warning intelligence analysts of the possibilities and constraints of foreign leaders in their distinct political time can help analysts frame more accurate warning assessments of both potential foreign actions and their time frames. In the Soviet case discussed in chapter 2, Stalin was unreceptive in 1941 to messages warning of German plans to attack because he focused on a future—evidently about two years hence—when economic development and recovery of Soviet security institutions from the ravages of the purges he instigated in 1937 would enable the Soviet Union to defend itself better. In 1973, Israeli military and civilian leaders thought the IDF so superior to Arab armies that warning lost importance; the active forces of the IDF alone could handle an initial Arab attack.[78]

How far into the future is warning potentially effective? Most policymakers long have liked current intelligence. Many American, Australian, and British observers of intelligence believe senior government decision-makers' preoccupation with the immediate is becoming more pronounced, leading to what many have called the "tyranny of current intelligence."[79] Jervis's windows of receptivity therefore may be short and close to warned-about events. Gregory Treverton, for example, wrote in 2009 that the US IC had a "bias toward current intelligence and . . . over-warning."[80]

Chronological time preferences for warning messages usually are unstated, but the intelligence literature provides some hints. Strategic warning can be effective as little as forty-eight to seventy-two hours before warned-about events occur—the time Israel once believed it needed to adequately mobilize to successfully defend against a large-scale attack by the conventional forces of neighboring Arab states. This short time was strategic in the Israeli context because Israel designed its national decision-making process for rapid decisions and the IDF built its reserve forces to enable rapid mobilization.

In other situations the time needed to make and implement strategically important policy may be chronologically much longer. For example, the literature on US NIEs, which has tracked the planned time horizons of estimates from their inception in 1950, indicates that NIEs traditionally address the next five years unless explicitly otherwise stated. In the 1970s, for example, the annual NIE 11–3/8 series on the Soviet strategic military situation had a ten-year time horizon, while NIE 15–90, *Yugoslavia Transformed*, discussed in chapter 3, had a two-year time horizon that presumably reflected the IC's expectation of significant near-term change.[81] And NIE 93–2 is titled *Haiti over the Next Few Months*—a short time horizon for an NIE.[82] The latest in the NIC's Global Trends series, titled *Global Trends: Paradox of Progress* and issued in January 2017, looks ahead to 2035 but has a separate five-year analytic horizon designed to meet the needs of the then incoming Donald Trump administration.[83]

Mark Lowenthal suggests that the optimal time horizon for senior American decision-makers is no more than three years, which is most of a presidential term.[84] Lowenthal argues that administrations focus primarily on issues they expect to address during their term in office and give little attention to issues relevant after they leave office. Martin Petersen similarly believes the maximum time horizon of any American presidential administration is four years.[85] Four years may actually be much longer than the horizons of departmental assistant secretaries and other political appointees who make and implement many policies. In the mid-1980s, for example, Robert Gates told CIA analysts that the average tenure of deputy assistant secretaries and more senior political appointees then was twenty-three months; in 2009, Gregory Treverton reported that the average tenure of assistant secretaries was just over a year.[86]

The authors, as retired US Army Reserve officers, repeatedly have seen the same logic in military affairs. Commanders tend to be much more concerned about what will happen during their time in command than after they rotate to new assignments. Military command tours tend to be considerably shorter than four years, enhancing the tendency of military personnel to have short time horizons.

Dedicated warning officers have tended to focus on relatively short time horizons. The Watch Committee in 1950 forecast dangers of conflict with the Soviet Union "in the near future," which it defined as six months to a year.[87] NIO/W Mary McCarthy wrote in

1994 that "the National Warning System usually concentrates on threats judged to be about six months away or less."[88] At various times DIA has published serial publications with specific warning time horizons. For example, the *Weekly Warning Forecast* looked out two weeks, while the *Quarterly Warning Forecast* examined issues about a year in the future.[89] As a combat support agency, DIA has both tactical and strategic warning responsibilities.

NIO/W Robert Vickers's "Watch List" contained events that could be significant in the next six months.[90] In association with other NIOs, Vickers also compiled each January a list of warning issues he considered likely to be salient for the rest of the calendar year—implicitly a twelve-month time horizon.[91] More recently, US defense and NATO warning professionals have argued that two years is the longest period warning professionals should focus on, and the six-month period McCarthy noted still is commonly cited as a reasonable time horizon.

Assessments produced by the UK's JIC now generally have a six-month outlook as a matter of policy.[92] Former Australian intelligence practitioner Patrick Walsh said in 2016 that he saw strategic warning as typically having one-to-five-year time horizons; Walsh's survey work in English-speaking Five Eyes countries indicated that the foreign and domestic intelligence agencies that use strategic intelligence—down a priority rung or two from senior national leaders as key decision-makers—usually look out one to two years,[93] and law enforcement agencies concerned with strategic-level evolution in major organized crime groups, for example, had similar one-to-two-year horizons.[94] The Dutch *Terrorist Threat Assessment* (DTN) is published every three months.

We think six-month to two-year time horizons make sense as a general rule for dedicated strategic warning officers, subject of course to the specifics of individual warning issues. They are within the political horizon of civilian leaders most of the time, longer than most tactical warning issues, and short enough to attract decision-makers' attention. They thus are likely to be in the window of receptivity Jervis notes.

But there are exceptions to the general trend toward shorter warning messages and time horizons. For example, Andrew Marshall's ONA wrote long documents with long time horizons specifically for very senior decision-makers: secretaries of defense. According to Andrew Krepinevich and Barry Watts, no secretary of defense over the forty-two-year period Marshall produced net assessments rejected his approach even though some were more enthusiastic readers of his assessments than others.[95]

Bureaucratic time is sometimes important because bureaucracies support senior-level decision-making and implement policy decisions at speeds they largely determine. Bureaucracies also work to legislative/budgetary cycles, and they have their internal clocks for research programs and other decision-making processes. Decisions about personnel and financial resources devoted to the warning mission also are subject to this concept of time. In the United States, budgetary planning processes are complex, but annual congressional appropriations cycles and related annual ODNI and agency/department decision processes are especially important. Intelligence priorities are revised more frequently. Hence, numerous twelve-month and shorter cycles are important for all parts of US intelligence, including warning. And, of course, any perceived intelligence failure normally can also be considered a warning failure, meaning retribution can come swiftly for those perceived to be responsible.

Business intelligence theorist Ben Gilad believes that "competitive early warning" analyses should generally push senior executives to make decisions "several months to several years" before those decisions otherwise would have been made in response to an evolving business environment.[96] Alfred Rolington says strategic outlooks should be for one to five years, with more frequent in-process reviews.[97]

Given that terrorist attacks are becoming a greater focus of intelligence services and, as we argue elsewhere, CT activities are increasingly "strategic" if only to politicians' career prospects, the time horizons relevant for what once were tactical attacks are much shorter. They may be a day or less in many cases, given police forces' abilities to rapidly arrest recently identified terrorists and/or protect anticipated targets.

How is a warning analyst to know the "right" time horizon to target? Once again, knowing key consumers' needs and preferences is important to help focus intelligence support and to avoid presentational mistakes. The variation in consumer concerns is considerable, and the typically longer focus of staffers and nongovernmental consumers than senior government executives makes attractive the long-term focus of the Global Trends project described in chapter 8. Nevertheless, we believe key national security–focused government executives generally prefer short time horizons for intelligence as they deal with recurrent crises du jour but that other government officials who use formal intelligence or "horizon scanning" research as parts of their long-term planning processes are happy to have help in forecasting twenty or more years into the future.

Notes

1. Garthoff, *Soviet Leaders and Intelligence*, 1–16.
2. Garthoff, "Estimating Soviet Military," 135–86.
3. Ibid. See also Garthoff, "On Estimating and Imputing Intentions," 22–32.
4. Jervis, *Why Intelligence Fails*, 195.
5. Grabo, "Watch Committee," 376.
6. Lowenthal, *Intelligence*, 6th ed., 171–72.
7. Treverton, *Intelligence for an Age of Terror*, 22–23.
8. Grabo, *Handbook of Warning Intelligence*, 169–98; Shalev, *Israel's Intelligence Assessment*, 221.
9. Garthoff, "On Estimating and Imputing Intentions," 24.
10. Grabo, "Watch Committee," 363–85.
11. Shalev, *Israel's Intelligence Assessment*, 55.
12. Biddle, "Victory Misunderstood," 139–79.
13. The project's website is at http://www.correlatesofwar.org/.
14. Blainey, *Causes of War*, 293–94.
15. Handel, *Perception, Deception and Surprise*, 23–24.
16. Krepinevich and Watts, *Last Warrior*, 130–32, 181.
17. Bracken, "Net Assessment," 91.
18. Gentry, *How Wars Are Won and Lost*.
19. Krepinevich and Watts, *Last Warrior*, 181.
20. Garthoff, *Soviet Leaders and Intelligence*, 15.
21. Yogi Berra quote at http://www.goodreads.com/quotes/261863-it-s-tough-to-make-predictions -especially-about-the-future. Danish physicist Niels Bohr earlier said, "Prediction is very difficult, especially about the future." See https://www.goodreads.com/author/quotes/821936.Niels_Bohr.

CHAPTER 6

The "Indications and Warning" Analytic Method

In previous chapters, we mentioned the "indications and warning" (I&W) analytic method. In this chapter, we describe its development and assess its usefulness, limitations, and vulnerabilities. We also describe and analyze two variants of the method. Many of the factors addressed in chapter 5 affect use of the I&W method.

The Basic I&W Method

In the immediate post–World War II period, as we have seen, American leaders and intelligence officers worried about large-scale military and, to a lesser degree, other kinds of attacks by the Soviet Union and other communist countries on the United States or its friends. Intelligence people realized they needed techniques with some intellectual rigor to aid analytic processes and to more persuasively convince senior decision-makers that their warning methods, and thence their warning messages, were credible.

Therefore, the US IC developed what has become the basic, still widely used I&W method. We use the term "method" because it is a technique or an analytical approach, not a methodology in the sense philosophers of science use the term. British military intelligence developed and used a similar method before and during World War II and advised the CIA in the late 1940s on how to use indicator lists to monitor and assess threatening Soviet military activity.[1] Intelligence personnel who did such work initially were called "indications officers" and then "indications analysts."[2] Still later, they became "warning analysts"—the term still in use that we prefer because strategic warning analysts now also use analytic methods other than variants of the I&W approach.

Cynthia Grabo, an early participant in such work, described the purpose of the indicator lists the Watch Committee of the 1950s used:

An indicator list, simply defined, is a compilation of projected, anticipated or hypothetical actions which any nation might take in preparation for hostilities or other inimical actions. Such lists, often compiled without regard to whether it was likely or even possible to collect the desired information, proved of assistance to both collectors and analysts, provided they were not regarded as a bible of what to expect.[3]

Note the generic nature of the lists Grabo described. While analysts continue to keep generic indicator lists, they typically refine indicators used in actual warning problems to reflect variables including the purpose of threatening behavior and different force structures, doctrines, and operational practices of actors of intelligence interest.[4] As the I&W method evolved over time, its core version became more formal and now has trappings of intelligence doctrine even as the method has been adapted for other purposes, as we discuss below.[5]

Originally classified articles in *Studies in Intelligence* describe the early US approach to warning in considerable detail. Worried about a Soviet attack, analysts developed what by the late 1950s they called "indications intelligence," designed to provide "advanced strategic early warning."[6] Strategic warning was to be delivered "in advance of military operations, based on deductive conclusions about Soviet preparations" and was distinctly different from "operational early warning"—the receipt of information about an immediately unfolding attack derived by "mechanical means," or what we now call technical collection such as signals intelligence.[7] We now call such alerts "tactical warning."

The standard I&W method is relatively simple in concept when used for conventional military threat situations. The process of developing an indicator-based warning problem is roughly as follows. First, analysts identify a bad situation that might develop or already has developed but could get worse and needs to be monitored systematically. This means that some criteria, along the lines discussed in chapter 5, have been used to identify a threat. In current US defense and NATO warning terminology, the bad situation of concern is an "end-state," which is defined in fairly general terms that specify only the basic nature of the situation that intelligence wants to monitor. For example, the prospect that some Country A might invade Country B—if it appeared to be a potentially major problem and a greater-than-remote possibility—might be formally established as the "Country A–Country B Warning Problem."

Typically, a warning problem is assigned to one organization or specific analysts within an intelligence analytic organization, which often is the organization that proposed the warning problem or one that would monitor the situation of concern anyway. Thus, for example, in the DWN context, a designated warning problem involving a specific country is "owned," from the bureaucratic standpoint, by the intelligence element of the regional combatant command responsible for actual or potential US military activity in that country.[8] The organization responsible for the warning problem studies the situation, develops the approach to be taken to the warning problem, monitors the situation, and issues status reports or formal warning messages as appropriate. Combatant commanders typically raise or lower the alert status of their forces based on warning threat levels their intelligence staffs identify.

An organization charged with warning of such an event then has its warning analyst(s) identify several *possible* ways that Country A might try to invade Country B, which are called scenarios, to be developed more fully. Initially analysts might be relatively unconstrained in their imagination, later settling on scenarios that are more *plausible*. At the end of a (preferably) substantial analytic process in which warning analysts develop considerable expertise about Country A—including its leadership, military forces and doctrine, economic and social situations, and relationship with Country B—the warning organization establishes several (usually three to five) scenarios, which amount to hypotheses about how the end-state of concern might develop. This process should involve considerable study by individual analysts and discussion among analysts, perhaps using brainstorming or other collective techniques to coax the best ideas from the group. The actual number of scenarios chosen is a judgment call; too many scenarios are unmanageable, and too few limit possibilities to the detriment of analytical completeness.

Intelligence organizations sometimes identify "worst-case" scenarios, believing they help to challenge conventional wisdom and enable policymakers to respond appropriately to the gravest threats. We believe, however, that warning analysts generally should not posit such scenarios because they inappropriately prejudge likelihoods before analyses are complete.[9] This practice also biases future analyses and the messages that intelligence sends to consumers. Other negative effects include financially costly but unnecessary responses; excessive responses that appear threatening to other actors, thereby precipitating "security dilemma" situations; and the cry wolf syndrome when worst cases do not materialize.[10] Sometimes, moreover, worst-case scenarios become self-fulfilling prophesies. Reasonable alternatives to worst-case scenarios are "high-impact / low-probability" (HILP) scenarios that analysts judge to be unlikely but serious if they were to occur.[11]

For each scenario, analysts identify a path that could lead to the end-state. Scenario 1 might involve variables such as manpower mobilization, a surge of industrial production, leadership decisions, or propaganda campaigns linked sequentially or causally in processes whose major events are "indicators" of Scenario 1. Indicators should be judged to be likely to occur in specific ways as scenarios unfold—perhaps in temporal or causal relationship to each other in some cases—but should not be functionally directly linked to many other indicators. For example, diplomatic indicators should not be closely associated with economic indicators. Warning analysts do the same for all scenarios they identify. Scenarios should be appreciably different from each other, and the indicators for each should be as distinct from those of other scenarios as possible. Indicators can be of many sorts but should include military, political, economic, social, and technological factors.[12] I&W analysts should normally use a wide variety of functional and geographical indicators in each scenario to help ensure the independence of indicators and to enable various types of collection assets to provide relevant information about the status of indicators. There should be enough distinct scenarios and indicators to present alternatives that cover a plausible range of possibilities for realization of the end-state. Analysts then task collection assets to gather information that would enable timely recognition of movement toward the actualization of a scenario. When events associated with an ***indicator*** change, analysts have an ***indication*** of possible movement toward (or away from) the end-state.

Indicators should have several characteristics. They should be predictive, diagnostic, unambiguous, and collectible. Indicators are *predictive* if they consistently, causally precede the end-state of warning concern. They are *diagnostic* if they distinguish the emergence of one scenario as more likely than the others. Indicators are *unambiguous* if experienced analysts are unlikely to misinterpret them. And they are *collectible* if available collection assets can report movement toward or away from a designated end-state on a consistent, timely basis.[13] Infrequent reports on topics of interest render even logically good indicators poor choices; there is no point in identifying reports from key regime insiders as an indicator when an intelligence service has no reliable informants or has contact with them only sporadically. Because Israel long had good sources in Arab governments, it reasonably included such information in its indicator lists in 1973, but other states may not.[14] Hence, collection capabilities influence the selection of indicators, making analyst understanding of collection capabilities essential.

Academics see requirements for indicators similarly. Michael Handel specifies three essential characteristics of indicators.[15] Their actualization should be *necessary* for the worried-about event to occur; analysts will be sure the event of concern will not occur in different ways. They should be *unambiguous*; that is, the indicator should mean the warned-about event is likely to occur in the way hypothesized and does not suggest that other, unrelated or irrelevant events may occur. Third, indicators must be susceptible to intelligence *monitoring* in a consistent, reliable manner. Gregory Treverton similarly argues that indicators should have two qualities: uniqueness and visibility.[16] We think "uniqueness" equates to diagnosticity, while "visibility" means roughly collectibility.

With good indicators chosen and good collection assets in place, analysts monitor events for signs of change that might indicate an impending crisis or a diminution of tensions or a resolution of a problem that may suggest terminating the active monitoring of a warning problem. Analysts typically recognize that the indicators they select are not equally important, identify "critical indicators" for special collection and analytical emphasis, and know that indicators may change at different times and in different ways even if a scenario unfolds roughly as they anticipate. They weigh important indicators more highly than others in deciding whether to change warning status levels. There are no consistent quantities or qualities of indicators either necessary or sufficient to issue a warning message. Appreciable movements from one status level to another—in both directions—are reasons to issue warning messages. It is nearly as important to inform decision-makers that situations have become less, rather than more, threatening to enable them to concentrate on other, more important issues.

Aspects of this practice are illustrated in the scenarios and indicator lists US warning analysts developed in the early 1960s in an exercise to assess possible alternatives to the list(s) they actually used to monitor Soviet and Warsaw Pact military activity. This exercise was a self-critique of the warning processes US intelligence then used. Analysts developed seven scenarios of possible Soviet military actions. To our knowledge, the actual scenarios and associated indicator lists of that period and all others since remain classified. The exercise scenarios were:

  A. premeditated surprise attack
  B. preemptive attack
  C. escalation (limited war to general war)
  D. limited war
  E. guerrilla warfare
  F. diplomatic crisis with no military intent
  G. military suppression of internal dissent[17]

These scenarios vary dramatically in nature and impact. Scenarios F and G are not actual military threats to the West. Because they are general and quite distinct, there probably would have been little dispute among analysts about whether new intelligence information indicated the unfolding of one of these scenarios as opposed to another one. There is not *at this point* concern about whether, for example, a general attack might be focused on the northern or southern part of the Federal Republic of Germany—which are variants of the "premeditated surprise attack" scenario (A). Initially, analysts look for the major characteristics of the unfolding scenario for which indications are likely to be diagnostic.

To figure which of these scenarios might occur, analysts in the study developed 123 indicators.[18] Of them, twenty-eight indicators were useful for what the analysts thought were the three most dangerous scenarios: A, B, and C. These included activities that were diplomatic, political, economic, and military in nature. For scenario A—premeditated surprise attack—analysts considered important indicators to be

  1. deployment of medium-range ballistic missiles, intermediate-range ballistic missiles and associated equipment to satellite (Warsaw Pact members and other communist) nations
  2. rapid increase in the number of orbiting earth satellite vehicles
  3. unusually large and realistic maneuvers of Long Range Aviation units[19]
  4. major deployment of tankers and long-range bombers to forward bases
  5. intensive maintenance activity at submarine bases
  6. expanded submarine barrier operations[20]

For scenario B—preemptive attack:

  7. cancellation of leaves or marked restriction (on freedom of troop movement)
  8. release or delivery to combat units of specially controlled weapons and equipment
  9. widespread appearance of new cryptographic or transmission systems
  10. extensive interference with key Western communication systems
  11. abnormally large exercises at inter-army or higher level
  12. tightening of military security, such as new travel restrictions, etc.

13. abnormally high levels of activity in airborne forces units
14. withdrawals of significant naval surface units from the Black and Baltic Seas
15. intensive naval active-defense measures
16. major stand-down in tactical air forces for maintenance
17. general alerting of Soviet air defense forces
18. increased intelligence-collection efforts against key targets
19. active reconnaissance by aircraft, submarines, or surface vessels[21]

For scenario C—escalation (limited war to general war):

20. progressive reduction in size of Soviet bloc diplomatic missions in Western countries
21. consultation by regional satellite leaders with Moscow and Beijing
22. increased belligerency in official Soviet pronouncements and propaganda
23. sudden shifts, especially in crises, to softer propaganda themes
24. imposition of abnormally heavy censorship measures
25. widespread construction or expansion of shelters
26. evacuation of government, military, and technical personnel
27. conversion of industrial production from civilian to military items
28. cancellation of scheduled visits by Soviet scientists outside the Soviet bloc or their recall[22]

Analysts then weighed the indicators. They disagreed appreciably with each other about the relative importance of the indicators—a common occurrence. The analysts in the experiment also asked themselves whether these indicators were diagnostic—that is, whether they accurately distinguished one scenario from another. As noted, analysts should be able to answer affirmatively. Such differences of assessment mean that there rarely are clearly necessary or sufficient conditions for the actualization of an end-state of a strategic warning. Evidence that enemy troops have crossed a border renders a warning problem moot. Similarly, because some indicators are more important than others and identified indicators may be incomplete, simple counts of indications are likely to be misleading.

If the analysts had accepted these scenarios and indicators, they would have added them to collection priority lists, monitored events related to the indicators, compared events in news and intelligence reports to the lists and their understanding of Soviet practices generally, identified changes in activity types and levels, assessed the magnitude and importance of the changes as indications of worrisome activity, changed the status of indicators, and issued warning messages as appropriate.

More generally, when a warning analyst/organization becomes convinced that an event of concern is occurring or is about to happen—or a crisis situation is improving markedly—the responsible person or organization issues a warning message, which typically is short but addresses key changes and their implications. The message can be in a wide variety of formats—written, orally in person, by phone or email, and potentially other ways—but it must be timely and reach appropriate senior decision-makers in ways the recipients find persuasive. The DoD and the IC traditionally have had separate formal processes and formats for warning messages. IC warning typically has been produced consistent with DCI/DNI directives, when they existed. Senior warning officers, such as NIO/Ws, then used their informal contacts to further disseminate warning messages.

Warning messages typically reflect a change in the "status" of the warning problem—from normalcy through intermediate stages to some definition of a crisis from which there is little likelihood of additional strategic warning before a warned-about end-state occurs. Analysts using the I&W method traditionally also assign a color code and/or a symbol with a distinct shape (circle, triangle, etc.) to the warning status of both scenarios and individual indicators. Colors and symbols aid visual presentations of the current status of sets of warning problems or the multiple indicators of a single scenario. The longtime US use of green, yellow, and red to indicate increasing concern from normal to crisis, respectively, has led intelligence producers and consumers to call such graphical presentations "stoplight charts." These charts are a regular feature of military intelligence presentations, and some NIO/Ws, including Robert Vickers, used them to summarize warning assessments.[23]

Warning problems extend over variable but sometimes considerable periods of time, and new ones develop periodically, sometimes rapidly. The DoD now calls these warning problems "enduring" and "emerging" problems, respectively. The names are new; the concepts behind them are not. The current terminology is preferable, in our judgment, to a perspective John McCreary, a onetime head of the NWS, proposed in 1983—that warning issues should be characterized as "gradual" or "sudden."[24]

Enduring problems with long lives include the Cold War–era threat by Warsaw Pact forces to Central Europe and chronic worries about renewal of armed conflict on the Korean Peninsula.[25] Emerging problems can be of many sorts, potentially including surprise development of nonmilitary threats such as epidemic diseases and cyber threats as well as newly threatening military situations. Because warning problems often last for extended periods, major warning organizations such as the Joint Staff J-2 and the intelligence directorates of major US military commands monitor many warning problems. The number of warning problems has fluctuated over time in response to world events. In 1993, for example, the Joint Staff J-2 monitored 104 warning problems, one of which had 385 indicators.[26]

The combatant commands' warning elements long worked somewhat differently than did the Joint Staff J-2 and NIO/W systems.[27] While they, like the Joint Staff J-2, maintained watch centers alert for military crises, the combatant commands focused primarily on their regions or functions of responsibility and employed more junior people as warning personnel—mainly junior and middle-grade officers and noncommissioned officers. These personnel served short military tours and typically had modest training on warning and little background on their areas of responsibility. As a result, the commands developed a variant of the I&W method in which experienced analysts identified relevant indicators, which watch personnel then tracked in a binary "on-off" manner. That is, the indicator was present or not, and there were no critical indicators. Trouble could be spotted by counting a larger number of "on" indicators. This method purposefully did not allow for much analytic nuance; it was designed to be run by inexperienced people. This system led to construction of large indicator lists. For example, one combatant command around 1990 had lists of 660 and 275 indicators, respectively, for two of its major warning problems.[28] Finally, in the early 1990s, NIO/W Charlie Allen and a senior DIA warning officer convinced the commands to sharply reduce the size of their indicator lists and add nuance.[29] This move evidently helped considerably, enabling the I&W method the commands used to reach the sophistication of the method used in Washington in the 1950s.

Given the prominent US role in NATO and the usefulness of the I&W method, the DoD system became the NATO standard in the late 1980s.[30] NATO uses a four-part scheme of colors and symbols similar to the US method.

The British system that developed in the 1980s was slightly different.[31] The I&W system was based on a series of indicators collated into discrete groups, such as internal, external, political, economic, ground forces, naval forces, and air forces. These were further subdivided into command and control, communications, logistics, and so forth. Analysts decided whether these events or activities would make the Warsaw Pact more capable of posing a threat to NATO. Activities were measured against what was assessed to be a normal state. All indicators had specific intelligence collection assets directed against them.

The method also is used by other countries friendly to the United States. Israel, for example, used a variant of the I&W method in 1973. But because AMAN's scenarios anticipated conventional Arab attacks, not ones close to what actually occurred, the unusual activities Egypt's deception plan generated did not trigger a warning.[32] Israel identified indicators of whether Arab states had *capabilities* and *intentions* to attack Israel conventionally. The Israelis called activation of what we call indicators "telling signs" or "indicating signs."[33] AMAN warned in early October 1973 that Egypt had the ability to go to war but doubted its intentions until considerably later—hence its warning failure.

Limited evidence indicates that some non-Western countries, including Warsaw Pact countries, have developed similar methods and used them in crises.[34] For example, when leaders of the Soviet Union became concerned in November 1983 that the United States might be planning to launch a nuclear attack on the USSR under the guise of the NATO exercise Able Archer, which practiced nuclear weapons–related procedures, Soviet leader Yuri Andropov relied on a warning-focused Soviet intelligence effort known as RYAN (or RIAN, the Russian acronym for *Raketno Yadernoe Napadenie*, or nuclear missile attack). The then KGB chief Andropov earlier designed RYAN to monitor US war-planning activities and provide early warning of an American attack to the General Staff and senior civilian leaders.[35] The KGB and GRU, working together to some degree, apparently initiated the RYAN program in 1981 and eventually developed an integrated collection, processing, and analysis effort that tracked indicators of two major issues: an American *decision* to launch a nuclear war and US *preparations* for the initiation of nuclear war.[36] The Soviets brought other Warsaw Pact intelligence services into the effort. East Germany played a major role by, among other things, establishing an operations center that monitored a "catalog" of indicators of a US attack.

RYAN analysts monitoring Able Archer evidently decided it was only an exercise and persuasively communicated this judgment to senior Soviet leaders. While this episode is still shrouded in secrecy, what we know suggests that RYAN performed effectively as a warning analytic organization in this case, even though the Soviets generally believed their early-warning system was weak.[37] The Soviets de-emphasized RYAN soon after Able Archer, but it remained an active program until 1991.

Countries with small and/or fractured intelligence services are less likely to use the I&W method or have distinct warning organizations for several reasons. First, there may be no perceived threats worthy of a dedicated warning function. Second, the small size of a state and/or intelligence service may preclude creation of a dedicated function on grounds of resource priorities. Third, fragmented intelligence agencies that work together poorly or legal or policy decisions that separate intelligence from policy may obviate a perceived need for a warning function. According to Wilhelm Agrell, both of the factors in the last category applied to Swedish intelligence in recent decades.[38]

The I&W method merits some observations. First, it is a useful technique for large-scale military-threat situations, as evidenced by its longevity and wide acceptance. Its applicability is a direct result of the fact that large, equipment-heavy national military forces are organized and operate in ways conditioned by physics and their organizational doctrines, which make them relatively easy to observe and understand. The I&W method simplifies many analytic challenges because, as Gregory Treverton notes, if well done it helps convert mysteries into potentially solvable puzzles.[39] It does so by establishing expected relationships between variables using many techniques, including the structured analytic techniques of "backcasting" and "timelines." Backcasting posits events that may occur backward in time from the end-state, while timelines establish event order and duration.

The I&W method is therefore useful to both warning specialists and intelligence analysts generally. The method is relatively easy to use in monitoring operations and to explain to intelligence consumers, making it a comparatively transparent technique. The O/NE used the method to assess Soviet intentions in Cuba in 1962, leading to the infamous SNIE 85–3-62 discussed in chapter 3.[40]

Because of its virtues, the I&W method seems likely to remain the basic analytic approach for strategic military threat warning for the foreseeable future. Its flexibility means that it also is adaptable for use in a wide variety of other situations, including nonmilitary warning concerns. DWN doctrine says the I&W method is applicable to opportunity warning, which we believe is possible but unlikely given the more fleeting nature of opportunity warning and the resultant lack of detailed study necessary to build good scenarios and indicators.[41]

The method also has limitations and some undesirable features. First, it is primarily a military-threat-oriented method. While it is possible to use it for opportunity or nonmilitary-threat warning, governments apparently rarely use it in these ways. Logically, the method can occasionally spot an opportunity as a scenario is unfolding. Warning analysts would need to be alert to the possibility, however, because opportunities may be hard to see when they focus on evidence that events are moving toward what General Colin Powell, in his 1991 talk discussed in chapter 5, called a "bad" end-state.

Second, because the method involves identification of specific indicators chosen because of their relevance to a particular end-state, the method inherently is reactive, meaning it is primarily useful for monitoring identified and continuing, or enduring, warning problems. The analytic process that starts with assessing characteristics of an obviously worrisome end-state is inherently less helpful for newly emerging, still uncertain warning challenges that may be very different from all existing warning problems and therefore may be hard to identify before they become crises. Hence, different analytic techniques and expertise may be needed to identify emerging warning issues before they make newspaper headlines. Once issues are identified and studied, the I&W method may be applicable to them as "enduring" warning problems. In addition, because threatening, enduring problems are obvious, relatively easy to work, and are known to senior officials who ask about them, attention is less likely to be given to emerging issues.

Third, the method can be misused or misinterpreted. Because the basic approach is easy to master, there is danger that analysts may follow indicator lists, once developed, as a matter of rote without conducting periodic reassessments of perceived truths or assumptions to prevent obsolescence of an indicator. Without periodic revalidation, good indicators or scenarios can evolve into unchallenged assumptions about how an intelligence target is organized or behaves. The IDF made this error when it reified the Conception before the Yom Kippur War. Analysts also may casually adapt indicator lists from other warning problems without studying their issue sufficiently to ensure that the borrowed indicator list is appropriate. In addition, intelligence consumers sometimes see stoplight charts as excessively definitive descriptions of complex situations—a valid criticism of the commands' warning systems until the mid-1990s.[42] At the other extreme, some consumers too quickly reject stoplight charts as oversimplifications that are not credible.

Fourth, established warning problems become bureaucratic realities, with organizations and people committed to them emotionally and for reasons of organizational and/or career interests. Enduring warning problems therefore have a tendency to evolve into current intelligence issues that attract the concern of line intelligence analytic units, meaning they lose their unique value as warning topics. This slide into normalcy is a chronic risk for enduring warning problems and challenges warning intelligence managers to keep their focus on warning aspects of an issue and not current intelligence—a tough job when senior consumers' attention and kudos go to those who write on the hot topics of the day. As Cynthia Grabo observed long ago, warning done by specialized units is susceptible to degenerating into redundant, mediocre, and unwelcome current intelligence analysis.[43]

Fifth, the method is harder to use for nonmilitary threats primarily because, while the basics of military surprise have been established over the years and can be tracked through collection techniques well suited to military mobilizations that tend to display similar characteristics, characteristics of other types of threats and opportunities may not be as well established. Use of the I&W approach therefore requires extensive study of patterns of national decision-making behavior. It is possible to do so, and we discuss modifications of the basic I&W method below.

Sixth, the I&W method is vulnerable to deception. Because the basic method is well known and because military mobilization processes are fairly standard and readily identifiable, altering basic practices to deceive enemy warning personnel may be relatively easy. Deception doctrines such as *maskirovka* directly address this challenge. Knowledge of the specific indicators that warning personnel use makes deception easier. As discussed in chapter 2, British deceivers in 1944 identified German warning indicators—including the view that volumes of enemy bombing in specific areas indicated the Allies' priority concerns about the areas—leading the Allies to bomb the Pas-de-Calais extensively to suggest that they planned to attack there. The Allies also understood the doctrinally desirable characteristics of warning indicators noted above and designed their deceptions to trigger misleading German indicators with information derived from apparently independent sources. Then the Allies monitored, via Ultra intercepts mainly, how the Germans reacted to deceptive messages and physical actions that were parts of their broad deception effort, thereby manipulating other German indicators. While Operation Fortitude South was unusual, the idea of deceiving analysts who rely on discrete indicators is obvious. Hence, end-states of concern, scenarios, and indicators should be closely held, and warning analysts should master and use methods to identify deception activities. For these reasons, adversaries' warning scenarios and indicators may be high priorities for collection entities.

Two Variants of the I&W Method

Given the merits of the I&W method, variants of it have been developed for other purposes. In the first example below, an NGO adapted the method to identify genocidal threats to groups of people. The second adapts the I&W method to a new kind of military threat: the entrapment of states into launching optional wars that benefit manipulators of senior national decision-makers.

Monitoring Signs of Emerging Genocide

Genocide Watch uses an I&W-based method to monitor trouble spots around the globe for signs of emerging genocides.[44] Founded and run by Gregory Stanton, a professor at George Mason University, Genocide Watch developed a ten-stage process for identifying indicators of an emerging genocide. This means, in traditional I&W terminology, that Genocide Watch is concerned with only one end-state—which makes conceptualization of its project easier, although not necessarily its monitoring and analysis of specific situations. Stanton had many contacts in Rwanda before 1994, closely studied the 1994 genocide there, and has studied many others since 1994.[45]

The ten stages are analytical categories that typically consist of several related indicators. Movement through the stages indicates the degree of seriousness of an emerging situation. The ease of communication of movement through the numbered stages is similar to that of the stoplight charts of the traditional military I&W method. Unlike military warning analysis, Stanton also suggests ways (not shown here) that external actors can ameliorate or counter genocide-related activities, thereby mixing warning analysis with policy prescription—a practice anathema to the American IC that makes good sense for activists who seek to shape national governments' foreign and defense policies and do not have internal governmental means of communicating their messages.[46] Stanton defines the ten stages as follows:

1. **CLASSIFICATION:** All cultures have categories to distinguish people into "us and them" by ethnicity, race, religion, or nationality.
2. **SYMBOLIZATION:** We give names or other symbols to the classifications. We name people "Jews" or "Gypsies," or distinguish them by colors or dress; and apply the symbols to members of groups. Classification and symbolization are universally human and do not necessarily result in genocide unless they lead to dehumanization.
3. **DISCRIMINATION:** A dominant group uses law, custom, and political power to deny the rights of other groups. The powerless group may not be accorded full civil rights or even citizenship.
4. **DEHUMANIZATION:** One group denies the humanity of the other group. Members of it are equated with animals, vermin, insects or diseases. Dehumanization overcomes the normal human revulsion against murder. At this stage, hate propaganda in print and on hate radios is used to vilify the victim group.
5. **ORGANIZATION:** Genocide is always organized, usually by the state, often using militias to provide deniability of state responsibility (the Janjaweed in Darfur.) Sometimes organization is informal (Hindu mobs led by local [Rashtriya Swayamsevak Sangh] militants) or decentralized (terrorist groups.) Special army units or militias are often trained and armed. Plans are made for genocidal killings.
6. **POLARIZATION:** Extremists drive the groups apart. Hate groups broadcast polarizing propaganda. Laws may forbid intermarriage or social interaction. Extremist terrorism targets moderates, intimidating and silencing the center. Moderates from the perpetrators' own group are most able to stop genocide, so are the first to be arrested and killed.
7. **PREPARATION:** National or perpetrator group leaders plan the "Final Solution" to the Jewish, Armenian, Tutsi or other targeted group "question." They often use euphemisms to cloak their intentions, such as referring to their goals as "ethnic cleansing," "purification," or "counter-terrorism." They build armies, buy weapons and train their troops and militias. They indoctrinate the populace with fear of the victim group. Leaders often claim that "if we don't kill them, they will kill us."

8. **PERSECUTION:** Victims are identified and separated out because of their ethnic or religious identity. Death lists are drawn up. In state sponsored genocide, members of victim groups may be forced to wear identifying symbols. Their property is often expropriated. Sometimes they are segregated into ghettoes, deported into concentration camps, or confined to a famine-struck region and starved. Genocidal massacres begin. They are acts of genocide because they intentionally destroy part of a group.

9. **EXTERMINATION** begins, and quickly becomes the mass killing legally called "genocide." It is "extermination" to the killers because they do not believe their victims to be fully human. When it is sponsored by the state, the armed forces often work with militias to do the killing. Sometimes the genocide results in revenge killings by groups against each other, creating the downward whirlpool-like cycle of bilateral genocide (as in Burundi).

10. **DENIAL** is the final stage that lasts throughout and always follows a genocide. It is among the surest indicators of further genocidal massacres. The perpetrators of genocide dig up the mass graves, burn the bodies, try to cover up the evidence and intimidate the witnesses. They deny that they committed any crimes, and often blame what happened on the victims. They block investigations of the crimes, and continue to govern until driven from power by force, when they flee into exile. There they remain with impunity, like Pol Pot or Idi Amin, unless they are captured and a tribunal is established to try them.[47]

Genocide Watch is a typical NGO in that it relies on a network of similarly focused NGOs to help gather and assess "intelligence" information and to help disseminate warning messages it issues. Targets of warning messages are network partners, especially "gatekeeper" NGOs such as Human Rights Watch and International Crisis Group, senior national government officials, and international organizations such as UN agencies.[48] All of these targets are useful for achieving the ultimate goal of spurring government action. Genocide Watch, like other prominent advocacy NGOs, has good access to senior government officials due mainly to personal contacts. Many NGO officials, including Stanton, were once in government, and many government officials once were policy advocates as NGO staffers, academics, or think-tank employees.

The Simon-Skjodt Center for the Prevention of Genocide, a part of the United States Holocaust Memorial Museum, also monitors "early warning signs" of genocide to alert policymakers globally of a need to act to prevent genocide.[49] Its Early Warning Project employs a two-part method: (1) a "Statistical Risk Assessment" that calculates genocide dangers using a model based on historical cases of genocide and (2) judgments of an "Expert Opinion Pool" of observers.[50] The museum in 2008 published a book-length report on genocide prevention that discusses its I&W-like process for warning of emerging genocide.[51] Like other NGOs that perform warning-like functions, the museum integrates advocacy of its political agenda with its warning analysis.

Monitoring Perceptions of Vulnerability

Materially weak states and non-state actors, especially, increasingly manipulate major states to intervene in conflicts on their behalf. They typically do so by identifying and skillfully exploiting ethically based political vulnerabilities in their opponents and relevant third parties—or what scholars call norms, which are defined as collective views of appropriate behavior.[52] These attacks typically involve instrumental exploitation of aversion to civilian casualties in wars and, increasingly in recent decades, aversion to military casualties. While early variants of these exploitations were designed to defeat enemies that held the norms, beginning in the 1990s "weak" actors expanded their ambitions—and their inventory of manipulative skills—by framing conflicts in ways that demand external intervention to protect threatened civilians against the predations of their enemies. They thereby exploited an early variant of what later became known as the "responsibility-to-protect" (R2P) norm. For example, Bosnian Muslims in 1994 and 1995 and the Kosovo Liberation Army (KLA) in 1998 and 1999 exploited sensitivities to civilian casualties in US President Bill Clinton and several other NATO leaders to induce NATO interventions in 1995 and 1999, respectively, on their behalf against their common enemy, the Serbs. Both groups used several techniques—including information operations that misrepresented the numbers and causes of civilian deaths and committing atrocities against their own people for purposes of blaming the Serbs—to effectively induce NATO's intervention.

In Libya in 2011, with R2P more firmly established as an international norm, rebels trying to overthrow the Muammar el-Qaddafi regime successfully convinced Western European and American leaders, especially French President Nicolas Sarkozy and British Prime Minister David Cameron, that Qaddafi intended to kill civilian opponents of his regime and to have his troops systematically rape civilian women and had distributed Viagra to troops to aid that effort.[53] These accusations had no basis in fact, but they convinced the UN Security Council to authorize an ethically motivated humanitarian protection mission, which NATO leaders then converted to a regime-change mission.[54]

For intelligence professionals, these cases represent a threat-warning challenge of a dramatically different sort than those that worried Cynthia Grabo. In such cases, manipulative non-state actors induce stronger states to act under deceptive circumstances.[55] KLA leaders have been publicly candid about their efforts to manipulate President Clinton's normative sensitivities to entice him to attack their Yugoslav enemies. They saw Clinton's sensitivities as exploitable political vulnerabilities and developed an "attack" strategy designed not to harm the United States and NATO but to lead them to voluntarily start an optional war—that is, a war not fundamental to core material national interests. The threat therefore is the unnecessary expenditure of military resources, political capital, and lives that such manipulation may entail—not physical attack by another state.

Because of the substantial evidence trail, warning professionals might have been able to detect the norm-derived "attack" on the United States and NATO if they had been monitoring the KLA's perceptions of the ethical vulnerabilities of Clinton, other NATO leaders, and electorates in NATO countries.[56] KLA leaders evidently studied Clinton closely and created reality on the ground that the KLA and its friends framed in ways they believed would be sufficiently morally repugnant to Clinton personally to induce him to launch an optional war. Had US intelligence analysts been monitoring the KLA's perceptions of Clinton's vulnerabilities, they might have been able to warn him that he was being manipulated to serve the KLA's political goal of generating external military and diplomatic assistance to help achieve independence for Kosovo. Analysts would have had to understand the mechanisms of influence on norm-driven national decision-making and developed indicators: (1) goals achievable by vulnerability exploitation, (2) perceptions of (and actual) vulnerabilities in relevant actors, and (3) the initiation of various types of vulnerability exploitation. They also needed (4) measures of success of exploitation attempts and (5) appreciation of the consequences of successful or failed exploitation.[57]

The Kosovo case suggests a general model of norm-based manipulation of vulnerabilities of both states and national leader state actors, enabling production of a generic warning indicator list appropriate to monitoring emergence of a new kind of threat to liberal states. The list that follows should be refined in practice to account for situational peculiarities. Indicators come in six general groupings.

1. *Actor goals achievable by norm-based manipulation of others.*
   a. An actor must be materially weak vis-à-vis its enemy, have little prospect for military success on its own, and be able to identify an external actor or actors whose intervention(s) can significantly advance its cause.
   b. A formal alliance structure that prospectively could provide external aid does not exist.
   c. There are political obstacles to direct, politically motivated assistance by outsiders, including domestic politics, diplomatic pressures, international humanitarian law, or the UN Charter's prohibition on the use of force except with Security Council authorization or for self-defense.
2. *Background vulnerability.* A society or national leader has demonstrated a strong norm-based bias against a specific individual, group, country, or political-military practice. Or the leader shows a strong preference for foreign intervention in:
   a. Speeches, writings, or actions that indicate or suggest a norm-based political vulnerability—and contain terms, images, analogies, metaphors, or other frames of reference useful for norm-based manipulation.
   b. Generic threats of governmental action to redress humanitarian wrongs.
   c. Strong interventionist sentiment in principal advisors or important political constituencies.
3. *Potential attacker's perceptions of target vulnerability.*
   a. Actors perceive vulnerabilities in enemies, including those of leaders or target societies more generally.

    b. Actors perceive vulnerabilities in potential de facto "allies," including those of leaders or society more generally.

4. *Situational opportunity for vulnerability exploitation.* A humanitarian crisis emerges in which interventionist sentiments rise.

    a. Civilian suffering and/or casualties mount.

    b. External pressures for action grow—among allies, in the UN, or by influential NGOs.

5. *Initiation of vulnerability exploitation.*

    a. Rhetoric heats up, with the initiation of information campaign(s) aimed at relevant governments and NGOs, with prominent use of terminology designed to evoke sympathy or legal obligations—what Roland Paris calls a "metaphor war."[58] Also useful are terms of UN Security Council resolutions and the language of international humanitarian law (IHL). Clinton's favorites in 1999 included "genocide," "concentration camps," "powderkeg," and the Holocaust.[59]

    b. The manipulator, or attacker, publicizes actual enemy violations of IHL.

    c. The attacker exaggerates or distorts actual enemy violations of IHL.

    d. The attacker creates casualties directly or indirectly—as by placing civilians in areas likely to be bombed or feeding bogus intelligence information to enemies—for purposes of generating casualties or other IHL violations for blame on an enemy.

    e. The attacker argues that external intervention is necessary to protect against further outrages or to punish perpetrators of internationally recognized crimes.

6. *Consequences of successful or failed manipulation*—designed to tell whether actions have been successful.

    a. Target country or group of countries threatens the enemy with a variety of actions, including military action, economic or other sanctions, diplomatic recognition of secessionist groups, military assistance, and consensual deployment of peacekeeping, peace enforcement, and potentially other personnel.[60]

    b. Target country or group of countries engages the enemy militarily.

    c. External aid enables accomplishment of the manipulator's goals.[61]

This kind of warning problem presents unusual advantages and challenges. Among its greatest uses: the method can help identify perceptions that can identify intelligence-target intentions, something the traditional I&W method, with its focus on variants of threats of military attack, does not do well. But the warning challenge is greater than usual because effective warning in such cases requires persuading senior leaders that people they thought were good people, who were "friends," in fact were playing them for fools—something leaders are not likely to want to hear. Because this kind of manipulation was successful in the Balkans in the 1990s and in Libya in 2011, and the techniques are widely known, we expect this modified version of the basic I&W method to be useful for the foreseeable future.[62]

Notes

1. For some history on British assistance, see "Nightwatch: A Brief History of Indicators Analysis," Public Intelligence Blog, October 12, 2012, http://www.phibetaiota.net/2012/10/nightwatch-a-brief -history-of-indicators-analysis/.

2. Ramsey and Boerner, "Study in Indications Methodology," 75.

3. Grabo, "Watch Committee," 365; Patton, "Monitoring of War Indicators," 62–64. See also Director of Central Intelligence, "Watch Committee."

4. Lowenthal, *Intelligence*, 6th ed., 179–80.

5. Patton, "Monitoring of War Indicators," 55–68; Ramsey and Boerner, "Study in Indications Methodology," 75–94.

6. Ibid., 55.

7. Ibid.

8. The DoD divides the world into segments that are the responsibility of specific regional military commands, which have primary DoD responsibility for any military action the United States is taking or may take. Hence, commands' intelligence directorates closely follow events in their areas of responsibility.

9. For good critiques of worst-case scenarios, see Betts, "Analysis, War, and Decision," 65–66, 74–75, 88; Handel, "Intelligence and Problem of Strategic Surprise," 247–48; Herman, "Intelligence and Assessment," 773–82; and Kent, "Crucial Estimate Relived," 116. For other views, see Arcos and Palacios, "Impact of Intelligence."

10. In a "security dilemma," one state's efforts to improve security by increasing its armaments precipitates a countering response by another, leading to an arms race that does not improve either state's security. See Jervis, "Cooperation under the Security Dilemma."

11. Davis, "Strategic Warning: Intelligence Support," 181.

12. Grabo, *Anticipating Surprise*, 51–76.

13. ADWS brochure.

14. Bar-Joseph, "Question of Loyalty."

15. Handel, "Intelligence and Problem of Strategic Surprise," 20.

16. Treverton, *Intelligence for an Age of Terror*, 42–45.

17. Ramsey and Boerner, "Study in Indications Methodology," 76.

18. Ibid., 77–78.

19. "Long Range Aviation" was the strategic bomber part of the Soviet air force.

20. Ramsey and Boerner, "Study in Indications Methodology," 77–78.

21. Ibid.

22. Ibid.

23. Vickers used stoplight charts in his weekly, one-page "Watch List" publication that typically contained about a dozen items. Source: authors' discussion with Robert Vickers, February 8, 2017.

24. McCreary, "Warning Cycles," 72.

25. Joint Chiefs of Staff, Defense Warning Staff, J2 Warning, *(U) Defense Warning Network Handbook*.

26. Authors' discussion with Robert Dunfield, May 13, 2017.

27. Detail in this paragraph is from Ron Woodward, who worked and taught warning in the DoD for twenty-eight years.

28. Gordon discussion with Ron Woodward, June 11, 2017.

29. Ibid.

30. Authors' discussion with Robert Dunfield, who worked this issue, May 13, 2017.

31. Material in this paragraph was provided to Joseph Gordon by John Tolson, September 1, 2017. See also Hughes-Wilson, *Military Intelligence Blunders*, 1–15.

32. Lowenthal, *Intelligence*, 6th ed., 180.

33. Shalev, *Israel's Intelligence Assessment*, 11–12; Bar-Joseph, *Angel*, 106, 172, 222; Hershkovitz, "'Three-Story Building'"; Jones, "'One Size Fits All,'" 278.

34. Glantz, "Soviet Operational Intelligence," 20, 21, 24.

35. Fischer, "1980s Soviet War Scare," 186–87; Adamsky, "1983 Nuclear Crisis," 24–27; Andrew, *For the President's Eyes Only*, 463, 473; Barrass, "Able Archer 83," 7–30; Fischer, "Anglo-American Intelligence," 75–92; Scott, "Intelligence and Risk of Nuclear War," 759–77; Pry, "Ideology as a Factor"; Fischer, "Scolding Intelligence."

36. Adamsky, "1983 Nuclear Crisis," 19–21; Scott, "Intelligence and Risk of Nuclear War," 765.

37. Barrass, "Able Archer 83," 12, 16.

38. Agrell, "Sweden," 239–63.

39. Treverton, *Intelligence for an Age of Terror*, 155.

40. Kent, "Crucial Estimate Relived," 115.

41. Joint Chiefs of Staff, Defense Warning Staff, J2 Warning, *(U) Defense Warning Network Handbook*, 43.

42. Authors' personal experience with intelligence consumers.

43. Grabo, *Handbook of Warning Intelligence*, 15–19.

44. See Genocide Watch's website at http://genocidewatch.net/.

45. Stanton, "Rwandan Genocide," 6–25.

46. Gentry, "Toward a Theory."

47. Excerpts from Gregory H. Stanton, "The Ten Stages of Genocide," Genocide Watch website at http://www.genocidewatch.org/genocide/tenstagesofgenocide.html, accessed June 1, 2016.

48. Carpenter, "Vetting the Advocacy Agenda," 69–102; Deibert, "Deep Probe," 175–93.

49. See Holocaust Museum website at https://www.ushmm.org/confront-genocide/about, accessed January 26, 2017.

50. For details, see Holocaust Museum website at https://www.ushmm.org/confront-genocide/how-to-prevent-genocide/early-warning-project, accessed January 26, 2017.

51. Albright and Cohen, *Preventing Genocide*, especially ch. 2, 17–33.

52. Gentry, "Norms as Weapons of War," 11–30; Gentry, "Instrumental Use of Norms."

53. Riley, "Deceived to Intervene," 35–46.

54. Kuperman, "Model Humanitarian Intervention?," 105–36.

55. In a similar but bizarre case, Macedonian officials in late 2001 murdered several innocent South Asian migrants in a botched effort to show to the United States that Macedonia, too, had a "terrorism" problem. See Nicholas Wood, "A Fake Macedonian Tale That Led to Deaths," *New York Times*, May 17, 2004, http://www.nytimes.com/2004/05/17/world/a-fake-macedonia-terror-tale-that-led-to-deaths.html.

56. Gentry, "Warning Analysis."

57. Ibid., 66.

58. Paris, "Kosovo and the Metaphor War," 423–50.

59. Ibid., 435–38.

60. Kuperman, "Moral Hazard," 52.

61. Gentry, "Warning Analysis," 80–82.

62. Riley, "Deceived to Intervene."

CHAPTER 7

Other Warning
Analytic Techniques

Over the years, states' intelligence services, other government agencies, and many private sector actors and academics have developed techniques useful for strategic warning analyses. This chapter discusses some techniques that complement the basic I&W method. Some are especially useful for identifying emerging warning issues. We regard these techniques as valuable tools in a "toolkit" of analytic methods that warning analysts might find differently useful in addressing various situations.

In the past two decades or so, a large number of articles, pamphlets, and books on "structured analytic techniques" and "critical thinking" have been published with the goal of improving intelligence analysis largely by helping analysts to avoid avoidable mistakes.[1] In general, these techniques apply insights from psychology and the social sciences to add rigor to analysis. Many intelligence services, including most US agencies, make SATs major parts of their new analyst training programs.[2] Most SATs were designed with line intelligence analysts in mind—not warning specialists—and they therefore apply to only a limited extent to strategic warning analysis. They generally are too simple and rote to address emerging warning problems. There are exceptions, however, and we mention in this book some of the several dozen SATs that various authors have proposed, including techniques known as red teaming, brainstorming, and backcasting. As we have seen, warning specialists developed one prominent SAT—the I&W method—to cope with the distinctive challenges of military threat warning. We therefore present in this chapter an eclectic set of questions, analytical approaches, and theories that we think are variously useful in addressing warning analytic challenges.

Richard Betts suggests that warning analysis is different from current intelligence and research analysis because line units usually use variants of "normal theory," while warning analysis requires use of different approaches, which in aggregate he calls "exceptional thinking."[3] Betts argues that recognition of historical behavioral patterns and conventional ways of assessing them are appropriate for analysis of most intelligence problems but that for unusual situations analysts must think differently, and switching from one mode to the other is intellectually hard. We think it is difficult when organizational and institutional incentives value a set of skills—most especially the ability to summarize information into short, punchy current intelligence articles—that have different purposes than strategic warning messages. This incompatibility of essential skills and perspectives between warning and conventional analysis is the primary reason warning specialists long have recommended the creation and effective use of specialized warning functional units to complement, not replicate or replace, line units' research analyses and current intelligence production. As Mark Lowenthal notes, long-term research and current intelligence require different analytic skills, and warning analysis is different still.[4]

But how can analytic organizations in aggregate, and specialized warning units if they exist, know when to set aside normal theory and adopt effective variants of exceptional thinking? History indicates that in most cases of significant warning failure, a single intelligence analyst or small number of analysts accurately assessed the situations and so advised their colleagues and superiors but were unable to convince them to accept their unconventional assessments, meaning their organizations declined to issue warnings.[5] Hence, key questions for intelligence professionals and scholars are: how can intelligence managers and analysts know which kind of exceptional thinking is appropriate for an emerging issue, and which analyst, possibly quite junior ones, will think exceptionally well in new and different situations? How can managers accurately select kernels of insight when other novel perspectives on the same situation turn out to be badly mistaken? And how can managers build structures and procedures that encourage prescient analyses—not punish creativity when it sometimes leads to odd and incorrect conclusions?

Unfortunately, there are no good answers to these questions. But we think the following techniques can help warning analysts in some cases. Per Betts, they reflect aspects of exceptional thinking.

Horizon Scanning

One manifestation of the widespread perception that the world is becoming more complex is a set of analytic approaches generically known as "horizon scanning." The term is sometimes associated with a quest to achieve "strategic foresight."

There is not, however, any widely accepted horizon-scanning process as formal as the venerable I&W method. Indeed, several variants of horizon scanning are in use. The basic idea behind all variants is that analysts must be alert and imaginative to identify as far away as possible (in distance and time) emerging trends of importance to give decision-makers time and insight to respond effectively. This family of approaches appears increasingly frequently in both government and business intelligence literatures, mainly outside the United States. Government officials in agencies not normally considered parts of security establishments now seem to use the term more frequently than do intelligence officials.

To our knowledge, the earliest significant reference to the horizon as metaphor for intelligence analysis was the admonition of the then CIA deputy director for intelligence Robert Gates to CIA analysts in the mid-1980s to develop ways to look "over the horizon" for emerging trends that American policymakers did not yet know would one day concern them greatly.[6] The IC largely abandoned this approach, however, as it concentrated on current intelligence.

Several British intelligence and non-intelligence agencies have adopted variants of horizon scanning, partly in response to Lord Butler's recommendation in his autopsy of 2003 Iraq War intelligence-related problems. In 2008, the Cabinet Office created a Strategic Horizons Unit, which it soon largely abandoned.[7] In 2011, the British government enjoined British intelligence to do horizon scanning for security implications of the then recent Eurozone economic troubles.[8] As of 2014, the Cabinet Office was the center of a broad, government-wide set of groups that conducted horizon scanning focused on specific issues of interest.[9]

The British Department of Environment, Food and Rural Affairs in 2009 defined "horizon scanning" as "the systematic examination of potential threats, opportunities and likely developments including but not restricted to those at the margins of current thinking and planning. Horizon scanning may explore novel and unexpected issues as well as persistent problems or trends."[10]

The British are developing methods that are beginning to reach the formality of the traditional military I&W approach.[11] They also have adopted a metaphor that is useful: the "cone of plausibility," also known as the "futures cone" (see figure 7.1).[12]

As analysts look forward from the point of the cone some thirty years, evaluating resource, social, political, technological, and military variables, they see an expanding set of possibilities, which range from the "probable," or most likely, events in the center of the

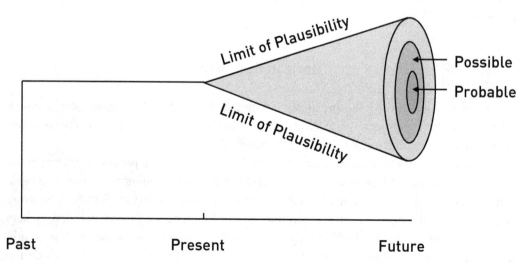

Figure 7.1 Cone of Plausibility

cone, to less likely but "possible" events and then "plausible" but unlikely events at the outside of the cone.[13] The goal is to identify possibilities in the "probable" core of the cone. There is not, unfortunately, a set of suggestions for ways to keep analyses in general or warning messages focused on the center of the cone.

The British approach is broad. It encompasses opportunities as well as threats, and, like all other horizon-scanning varieties, it emphasizes what the US Defense Warning Network calls "emerging" warning problems—precisely the issues that the I&W method, with its carefully constructed scenarios and empirically validated indicator lists, is ill equipped to address.

Another prominent variant is the Risk Assessment and Horizon Scanning (RAHS) analytic approach adopted by the government of Singapore.[14] RAHS features a network of analysts from throughout the government of Singapore who monitor emerging events imaginatively and share their insights. It is designed to detect "faint signals" of impending change that analysts frequently miss—a recognition of the insights of Roberta Wohlstetter and others about "signals" and "noise." RAHS has no standard analytic technique like the I&W method. Instead, RAHS uses information technology to assemble data of potential interest. But, in contrast to some information-technology programs, the Singaporeans see computer technology as an aid to analysis by smart people—not a technology-focused "Big Data" solution.[15] The idea for this effort came, in significant part, from Dave Snowden, once an employee of the International Business Machines Corporation and later head of his own company, known as Cognitive Edge, who developed a similar process for businesses.

This approach encourages analysts to imaginatively consider new events and new analytic techniques and to share insights widely. By networking people with diverse "thought patterns," Singapore hopes to be able to overcome the "stove pipes" that the 9/11 Commission in the United States concluded was a cause of the US failure to apprehend the 9/11 attackers.[16]

People in some countries use the term "horizon scanning" in association with forecasting national or subnational governments' medical needs. In Sweden, for example, Björn Wettermark of the Stockholm County Council uses horizon scanning to forecast future demand for pharmaceuticals.[17] And the Canadian Agency for Drugs and Technologies in Health (CADTH), a consortium of government agencies from across Canada created in 1989, uses horizon scanning to forecast the emergence of important new health care technologies.[18]

Another variant is the Eco-Innovation Observatory, an EU project that provides a repository of databases for the structured collection and analysis of an extensive range of "eco-innovation information" gathered from across the EU and key economic regions around the globe. Use of the database, combined with input from experts and practitioners in the environmental fields, is designed to enable understanding of eco-innovation processes and developments over the past two decades and the determination of likely trends for the next twenty years. The observatory periodically issues Horizon Scanning and Foresight Reports. Features of the project include

- Collection and analysis of data on future market and technology trends, liaison with other initiatives at European and national levels.
- Foresight activities to gather expert opinions on key emerging eco-innovation fields and issues, and the potential impacts on future markets.
- Development of a European eco-innovation scoreboard, assessing indicators at country, sector and thematic levels to identify strengths and weaknesses.
- Publication of an annual report on recent trends and emerging markets for eco-innovation.
- Thematic reports addressing specific technological and "horizontal" issues, such as consumer acceptance and public procurement.
- Country reports presenting country-level data and trends.
- Provision of market and technology intelligence tailored for [subject matter experts], including trends in financing.[19]

In addition, the government of Switzerland is assessing the horizon-scanning concept and has published an insightful analysis of the technique.[20]

Surveillance versus Reconnaissance

The RAHS approach is similar in some respects to a longer-lived philosophy of warning intelligence and, to some degree, of intelligence analysis more generally: the idea that intelligence conducts both *reconnaissance* and *surveillance*. Former NIO/W Ken Knight uses the terms to describe aspects of the warning function.[21] Sherman Kent also identified "surveillance" as a key task of intelligence in his 1949 book.[22] The concepts are distinct but complementary.

Surveillance, in Kent's and Knight's similar perspectives, refers to the function of monitoring events of known importance. This means, for example, watching issues such as the evolution of Soviet nuclear weapons during the Cold War and the activities of radical extremist groups, especially since 2001. In the vernacular of US defense warning doctrine, this concept equates to monitoring "enduring" warning problems. The Australian DIO defines surveillance as "monitoring the enduring threats."[23]

Reconnaissance, on the other hand, looks for new issues of importance, or emerging warning issues. The Australians similarly define reconnaissance as "recognizing and characterizing novel emerging threats and opportunities in order to avert/mitigate/shape the strategic environment."[24] Soldiers on reconnaissance patrols may know the types of circumstances they are likely to be most concerned about, but they look for specific activities that are new or threatening or offer an opportunity for an ambush, for example. In strategic warning, reconnaissance requires alertness to new issues or imaginative new ways of looking at old problems. Singapore's RAHS, using different terms, conducts reconnaissance activities designed to produce threat warning successes.

Anticipatory Intelligence

The ODNI and most of the US IC, but evidently no other national intelligence service, in recent years began to use the term "anticipatory intelligence" to refer, usually in vague ways, to future events. The CIA, however, does not teach the concept in its new-analyst courses, and CIA people apparently use the term rarely.[25] We confess that when we first heard the term, we both thought it was a joke. Our next reaction, after learning that ODNI people were serious about the term, was that it is an oxymoron. After all, by virtually all definitions, intelligence focuses on assessing the likelihood of future events and their implications. Intelligence is not history. While analysts often study the past, they do so to help them better understand the present and the future.

Anticipatory intelligence is commonly used in the United States in two ways: (1) as awareness that, despite the contemporary fixation on current intelligence, there really should be a future orientation to some types of intelligence, and (2) as vague recognition of the importance of the warning function in the broad sense that we use in this book. The first edition of *The National Intelligence Strategy of the United States of America*, issued by the ODNI in 2005, says that one IC "mission objective" is to "*anticipate* developments of strategic concern and identify opportunities as well as vulnerabilities for decision-makers" (emphasis added).[26] This is a fairly standard intelligence task, but it seems to be the origin of the anticipatory intelligence concept that commonly now is seen as a new type of intelligence analysis. In 2010, Wayne Michael Hall and Gary Citrenbaum, in a book on intelligence analysis, devoted a chapter to anticipatory intelligence, but there is not a single entry in the book's index for warning.[27] We think the term became more commonly used within the IC after its perceived failure to anticipate the Arab Spring of 2011.

The 2014 version of *The National Intelligence Strategy* continues to cite anticipatory intelligence as one of the IC's mission objectives: to "detect, identify, and warn of emerging issues and discontinuities."[28] It defines anticipatory intelligence as "the product of intelligence collection and analysis focused on trends, events, and changing conditions to identify and characterize potential or imminent discontinuities, significant events, substantial opportunities, or threats to U.S. national interests."[29] To accomplish these general goals, the document says the IC will do the following:

- Create capabilities for dynamic horizon-scanning and discovery to assess changing and emerging conditions and issues that can affect U.S. national security.
- Deepen understanding of conditions, issues, and trends to detect subtle shifts and assess their potential trajectories, and forecast the impact on U.S. national security thus generating opportunities to alert or warn.
- Develop integrated capabilities to create alerts within the IC and to provide timely and relevant warning to our customers.[30]

These are general objectives that any competent intelligence service might identify as standard tasks. Such language does, however, reflect the fact that the ODNI and most IC agencies do not now have warning programs as they have traditionally been widely understood. The term and concept are compatible with the strong version of the EAAWA model that DNI Clapper established as IC policy.

Gregory Treverton, who was chairman of the NIC from 2014 to 2017, sees anticipatory intelligence and warning as performing distinct missions. Treverton sees warning as intelligence analysis with imminent ramifications for policy. In contrast, he believes, anticipatory intelligence focuses on longer-range trends of intelligence interest that may not have immediate policy relevance.[31] If anticipatory intelligence works well, it can stimulate collection on interesting trends, thereby helping the warning function. Treverton adds, though, that he does not think the term is helpful.[32] We go further: the anticipatory intelligence concept damages the strategic warning function.

The Global Trends Projects

In 1997, the NIC, the senior-level analytic group that DCI Stansfield Turner created in 1979 and that now reports to the DNI, published the first in a series of unclassified reports about what the NIC calls "global trends."[33] The first report, *Global Trends 2010*, examined trends likely to influence global events in 2010. Since then, reports have been issued every four years, following US presidential elections, with target dates roughly two decades in the future. In January 2017, President-elect Donald Trump received the sixth iteration, *Global Trends: The Paradox of Progress*, which looks ahead to 2035.[34]

The series is an unusual effort for an intelligence agency. While senior US government officials are the primary intended audience—and the budgetary rationale for the project—the NIC also wants to communicate with a much broader, diverse group of people, including many who are not in government but who influence governments globally. It engages experts from all over the world and invites public input and discussion. It is widely known, read, and cited as an authoritative source of informed speculation about the future. It seeks to identify emerging trends of many sorts, including "economics, demography, ecology, energy, health, governance, security, identity, and geopolitics—and understand their implications for peace, security, and prosperity worldwide."[35] The series discusses likely and possible influences on the evolution of global affairs but does not make specific predictions or forecasts, does not definitively assess any situation (the estimates function), and does not specifically warn of impending dire events or opportunities. Therefore, it does not deal with issues that the IC believes merit specific, senior-level decisions in the relatively near future.

The British MoD publishes a similar series titled Global Strategic Trends, which is prepared by the MoD's Development, Concept and Doctrine Centre.[36] The purpose of the Global Strategic Trends documents is to provide unclassified assessments of likely drivers of major global events and trends the British government should consider when thinking about British defense (and other) needs. The reports explain why anticipated trends have both *benefits* and *risks* for the United Kingdom. They use the word "threat" liberally but do not as frequently use the term "opportunity." The Global Strategic Trends documents also use the cone of plausibility as an explanatory device.

Hence, the British and American global trends reports are not warning reports in the traditional sense. They do not ask policymakers to make decisions in the near future in response to specific, developing situations. Yet, we argue, they perform aspects of the strategic warning function by identifying possible future events and their drivers, and they encourage decision-makers of many varieties—as well as people who may be in positions of power in the future—to think about emerging and evolving issues and how they may wish to react to, or influence the course of development of, those trends in the future. The reports focus research and thinking to help perform the strategic intelligence function of uncertainty reduction. Hence, we consider the global trends process to be one of several influences that have broadened the scope of strategic warning, and we see its success and popularity as influencing the evolution of the warning function.

Strategic Futures

Parts of the academic community, some governments, and some think tanks conduct versions of the Global Trends project that they call "strategic futures."[37] These efforts typically feature aspects of the futurologist thinking and writing that people such as Alvin and Heidi Toffler did for years.[38]

We generally do not regard such work as "warning" for several reasons. The time frame of such work typically exceeds dramatically the attention span of most senior government leaders, meaning they are not designed to recommend an immediate policy response or opportunistic action. And, critically, many strategic futures projects reflect activist political agendas and are designed to influence governments' thinking about scientific, ideological, or other issues—a prominent difference from all government warning functions and institutional arrangements. For example, the Frederick S. Pardee Center for International Futures of the University of Denver's Josef Korbel School of International Studies has an activist mission: "to explore, understand, and shape alternative futures of global change and human development."[39] The center has built a model, called International Futures, which it uses to understand "global systems" and to forecast the futures of 186 countries through the year 2100.[40]

Closer to warning, the Atlantic Council produces "strategy papers" that assess issues of importance in the medium future—five years ahead. In early 2017, for example, it published *Europe in 2022: Alternative Futures*, which examines ways the EU could evolve.[41] As with other strategic futures work, this project is designed to serve the informational and analytic needs of a broad audience. Unlike some others, it is politically neutral. It does not, however, have the core warning attribute of specifically calling for senior-level action to address a tangible issue. Like the global trends projects, futures analyses have found a niche and serve to extend the functional scope and temporal reach of strategic warning.

Social Science Theories and Approaches

Academic studies typically feature theorizing about the causes of phenomena. Theories by definition simplify reality, meaning many theories are too simplistic to be of practical use to decision-makers. Moreover, many of them fail to pass commonsense tests, largely explaining why the word "theory" has such a bad reputation among decision-makers and intelligence officers. But there are exceptions to this generalization that intelligence and policymakers should not ignore. Good theorists ask important questions and offer insightful ways to perform strategic warning analysis. Intelligence services monitor social science research to some extent and occasionally borrow directly or modify social science methods for intelligence purposes.[42]

Several general approaches are relevant to issues of warning methods, deception techniques, and the causes of surprise. These are useful, we believe, for both students of warning intelligence and intelligence practitioners. They are especially helpful for assessing the more complicated part of the capabilities/intentions dichotomy in threat warning—identification of actors' intentions. None of these approaches, questions, and theories is a panacea, but they are useful additional analytic tools. The traditional I&W method remains viable.

Deterrence Theory

Especially after the onset of the Cold War in the 1950s, think tank researchers and government officials developed detailed theories and then policies devoted to deterring hostile actions by adversaries. In doing so, they studied the typical reactions of leaders to different types of stimuli, including threats of retaliation. Among the most (in)famous of the policies that emerged from these studies was the mutual assured destruction (MAD) doctrine and associated nuclear weapons–targeting policies the United States designed to dissuade the Soviet Union from contemplating major attacks. Like other deterrent policies, MAD was designed to convince the Soviets to refrain from actions they might have considered if the cost-benefit trade-off of the contemplated action appeared attractive by altering their perceptions of benefits and costs, including the likelihood of success of actions.[43] Deterrence theory has been applied to other problem areas and actors, including states and non-state actors. Hence, understanding how leaders—including their own government's leaders—perceive the deterrent threats of others and make associated cost-benefit analyses can help warning analysts assess how foreign leaders may react to threats or deterrent messages, leading to better warning of threats and messages of reassurance that deterrent polices seem to be working.

Political scientist Janice Gross Stein applied deterrence theory to deception theory and warning.[44] Deterrence theory, while relevant in many other areas, is especially applicable to military threat warning and military deception. Stein identified five factors that affect senior leaders' decisions about whether the deterrent action(s) of others are effective. These factors can become, per Andrew Marshall, topics of some of the "right questions" warning analysts should ask themselves.[45] Aspects of the factors may be elements of scenario development and indicator lists or of use when interpreting incoming intelligence information. We convert Stein's five factors into questions:

1. How does the target of deterrence see the balance of interests among the relevant actors? Sharply different types and levels of national or other interests among actors are likely to influence actors' resolve and thereby the effectiveness of deterrent actions.
2. Do the targets of deterrence see other actions as plausibly effective alternatives to the military or other actions deterrence policy is designed to thwart? That is, does a deterrence policy actually cover all possible ways a state may achieve goals the policy is designed to prevent?
3. How does the target of deterrent actions see prospects for success of its planned action?
4. How does the prospectively deterred actor see the international situation, particularly the attitudes, policies, and actions of its allies and arms suppliers?
5. How does the target of deterrent actions assess the costs it is likely to bear in a conflict? Perceptions of high costs in terms of losses—in absolute and comparative terms—to a prospective attacker are likely to make deterrence more effective.[46]

In the 1973 Arab-Israeli War case discussed in chapter 2, Israeli Major General Zeira and others who shared his belief in the Conception were convinced that demonstrable Israeli military might and Egyptian military weaknesses made any major war unthinkable for Egypt. Therefore, they believed, Israel had clearly attained an ability to deter Egypt. But that deterrence applied only to a scenario involving an Egyptian attempt to reconquer the Sinai, not limited war to achieve the political-military goals Sadat actually hoped to achieve. All five of Stein's factors help explain Israel's mistake in this case.

Dima Adamsky has shown how American overestimation of Soviet nuclear strength in the 1970s led Presidents Carter and Reagan to increase US nuclear preparedness, conduct exercises, and leak selected information designed to forestall feared Soviet aggressiveness—a form of deterrence.[47] US officials identified Soviet leaders' fears for their own safety and so let it be known that US nuclear weapons targeted decision-making leaders personally. But the Americans badly forecast Soviet reactions. Instead of reducing Soviet "aggressiveness," these moves increased Soviet fears of American belligerence. Better understanding of deterrence theory or their Soviet targets might have led US leaders to practice deterrence differently. Appreciation of likely Soviet reactions to types of US deterrence-motivated moves, as well as understanding of Soviet intelligence-collection and analytic capabilities, might have enabled US intelligence to warn of unintended—and potentially dangerous—Soviet reactions to US moves. Intelligence analysts did not, however, know what other elements of the US government were thinking and doing, making intelligence warning in this arena impossible.[48] This is a significant issue for many countries.

Prospect Theory

Prospect theory can help warning analysts by seeing behavioral biases of intelligence targets that spring from leaders' perceptions that their situations are generally favorable or unfavorable. Psychologists Daniel Kahneman and Amos Tversky developed prospect theory, which holds that people make different kinds of decisions based on whether they think their actions involve risks to perceived personal losses or gains.[49] Their original experiments concerned gambling wins and losses. Kahneman and Tversky found that people are more conservative about risking their winnings (what they called the "domain of gains") and more risk-taking if they are losing (the "domain of losses"). When losing, people take bigger chances by "doubling down" to recoup losses than when they have winnings they want to protect. Kahneman and Tversky soon turned their insights to the study of the economic choices of individuals, leading to major contributions to behavioral economics and earning Kahneman a Nobel Prize in economics in 2002. (Tversky died in 1996.)

Political scientists soon applied prospect theory to analyses of foreign policy decision-making, sometimes in ways directly applicable to warning analysis.[50] For example, Victor Cha used prospect theory in 2002 to explain North Korea's foreign policy and to recommend US policy responses in a way directly applicable to strategic warning.[51] Cha urged US policymakers to recognize that North Korea was in decline, probably in absolute terms but certainly vis-à-vis its archrival South Korea, and to recognize that Pyongyang correspondingly saw itself in the "domain of losses," where national leaders are unusually prone to take risks—to "double down"—even if chances for success are low. In the North Korean case, risky actions could include military strikes on the South or other types of "reckless" behavior. Cha therefore recommended US policies that would enable North Korea to see an improved situation as possible, thereby keeping the then Kim Jong-il regime in the less dangerous domain of gains. Cha's insights may be more relevant as we write.

The lesson for warning is that intelligence assessments that a national leader sees his or her situation in the domains of gains (or losses) should suggest a lesser (or greater) chance of initiation of hostilities or other seemingly irrational behavior by the actor than might otherwise seem likely. This suggests development of new, psychology-based indicators in addition to standard military, political, economic, technological, and social indicators—and associated collection priorities.

Had Israeli intelligence personnel anticipated prospect theory, which Kahneman and Tversky first articulated in 1979, they might have concluded that President Sadat recognized that his domestic political situation and his relationships with the Soviets and Arab benefactors were poor and that this position in the "domain of losses" suggested that he might be willing to take unusual risks to improve his situation. Would Israeli analysts have been able to divine Sadat's exact strategy? Perhaps not. But contemplation of the significance of the big needs that he and Egypt clearly had—including return of the territory of the Sinai and improving their collective self-image—in the context of his limited powers might have encouraged the analysts to imaginatively assess unconventional options Sadat had to improve his situation—and to rely less on conventional military logic.

Anticipating Mistakes

Leaders regularly make mistakes. Warning analysts therefore should build into their assessments possibilities that both foreign leaders and their own leaders, whom foreign intelligence services study and make decisions about, will make significant errors in judgment. Such errors contribute to policies and actions that do not, to external observers, seem "rational"—and therefore do not seem likely. Robert Gates argued in 1973 that the IC's poor record of anticipating Soviet intentions was caused in part by misreading the competence and rationality of Soviet decision-making processes.[52] Later, Gates as DCI displayed on his desk the maxim "As a general rule, the best way to achieve complete strategic surprise is to commit an act that makes no sense or is self-destructive."[53] We have seen that Sherman Kent attributed his mistake in 1962 about whether the Soviets would put nuclear missiles into Cuba to his judgment that the Soviets would not take an action that would fairly obviously damage their interests.[54]

Parts of the intelligence and foreign policy decision-making literatures try to explain why leaders make mistakes.[55] For example, James Wirtz attributes American intelligence failure to anticipate the Tet Offensive of 1968 partially to a correct US assessment that North Vietnam overestimated its chances of sparking a "general uprising" in South Vietnamese cities accompanied by an unwillingness to believe Hanoi would act on the basis of its misperception.[56] More generally, Wirtz suggests that three types of mistakes recur in surprise attack situations: (1) attackers mistake the advantages of a surprise attack for an advantage in war in general, (2) attackers fail to accurately anticipate victims' responses to the attack, and (3) attackers and victims misunderstand each other for cultural reasons.[57] Similarly, the lack of Western understanding of Soviet fears about President Reagan's intentions contributed to delayed appreciation of the nature and significance of the Able Archer crisis of 1983.[58] Robert Jervis suggests that one reason the intelligence communities of the world so badly erred in their assessments of Iraq's WMD programs in 2002 was that "Saddam did *not* have a plan, his control was less than complete, and the regime was less than fully competent."[59]

Such errors do not occur because analysts commit the cardinal mistake of "mirror imaging." Rather, analysts who understand that foreign decision-makers think differently and have different goals and worldviews do not accurately anticipate decisions or actions that reflect foreign leaders' information inadequacies, bureaucratic politics, personal biases and emotions, and potentially a host of other hard-to-see factors. Leaders make such mistakes for reasons that recur, meaning warning analysts can also learn about mistakes their own national leaders—their intelligence consumers—may make by studying the mistakes of other leaders.[60]

By observing their own leaders, warning analysts may also be able to craft warning messages in ways that help their principals to avoid or ameliorate such errors or help them appreciate why foreign leaders misunderstand them. For example, Soviet Foreign Minister Andrei Gromyko once complained to US Ambassador J. L. Bean, "You're so unpredictable. We can't count on American policy."[61] And, because senior decision-makers sometimes ask intelligence to study topics that interest them, intelligence can educate, inform, and warn about issues decision-makers care about—a highly desirable situation for intelligence people. Yet many national intelligence cultures, especially strongly in the United States, prohibit assessment of their own countries and their leaders. This is problematic because foreign intelligence services and leaders study American leaders closely and act on the basis of judgments they reach.[62]

The challenge of understanding the perceptions of others is substantial. Robert Jervis suggests that the "fundamental cause" of intelligence analytic errors is that people around the world see things differently and that grasping the worldviews of others is difficult.[63] He calls this challenge the "Rashomon effect" after a Japanese fable in which participants in an event saw the course of events very differently.[64]

Misperceptions occur for many other reasons. People rely more strongly on personal experiences than on vicarious learning. They rely on heuristics, generated largely by their education and experiences, to guide their decision-making. Intelligence reporting and analysis can be incomplete or erroneous. Leaders may be hobbled by domestic political or government bureaucratic constraints.[65] Like Stalin and Hitler, they sometimes have acute biases and blind spots. They rely on mistaken lessons, irrelevant or badly chosen historical analogies, and inappropriate theories to guide their decision-making. The literature on terrorist decision-making notes that terrorists tend to firmly embrace at emotional levels misperceptions that enable them to wage the difficult, sometimes nearly hopeless struggles they conduct; these psychological tendencies, too, are not always obvious.[66]

Neta Crawford argues that emotion is a major but understudied part of national security decision-making.[67] Leaders have emotions, including fears and hates, which cloud decision-making processes. Warning specialists who understand the role of emotion in general, and the particular emotions of specific leaders, may be better situated to anticipate policy successes and mistakes.

Analysts can try to understand the situations of their analytic targets—and have what is sometimes called "empathy" with them—but still err in assessing their intentions. The warning challenge is to study people, foreign policy–making institutions, and processes and to anticipate important judgmental errors. This kind of analysis requires substantive expertise about the psychology of leaders, political cultures, and decision-making institutions.

Moreover, warning specialists who focus on threats face unique challenges. Psychologists long have noted that people in general are prone to see unfavorable intentions in others' decisions, while they tend to see their own aggressive or mistaken actions as unavoidable given their situations. Consequently, threat warning analysts are likely to make excessively harsh judgments about the policies of adversaries and to dismiss others' perceptions of one's own country's actions as precipitating factors.

Leaders often have help in making mistakes. As noted, leaders sometimes ignore or disregard warning messages because they have interests and/or political pressures that lead to ineffective decisions inconsistent with warning messages. Jared Diamond goes a step further, arguing that societies collectively sometimes make bad decisions, which sometimes are fatal.[68] Diamond focuses mainly on environmental challenges, but his points about how whole societies err also apply to political, economic, social, and military affairs. Diamond suggests that while the details of societal failure differ dramatically, errors occur in four general ways. Societies (1) fail to anticipate problems before they arrive, (2) fail to perceive the emergence of problems, (3) recognize the arrival of challenges but do not try to address them, or (4) try to solve problems but fail to do so.[69] We agree with Diamond that category 3 is most common and most interesting—and where warning analysts should look for emerging warning issues. In modern democracies, interest-group politics frequently generate decisions that benefit small groups at the expense of the whole or even the groups' long-term interests. Some of these decisions are strategically important.

Because these patterns are known, actors occasionally use an apparently illogical or irrational strategy to generate surprise against actors who expect greater "rationality." President Nixon, for example, sometimes feigned irrationality to help him deal with the Soviets. And General Douglas MacArthur in 1950 argued to skeptical American military colleagues that the Inchon landing he proposed was so obviously difficult that the North Koreans would not expect it, thereby enhancing its chances of success.[70] MacArthur was right. The North Koreans were surprised, and the landing was successful.

Political Leadership Profiles

Senior decision-makers often rely on their personal experiences to make decisions. Many have distinctive worldviews that influence their decisions. Understanding such characteristics can help intelligence analysts assess how individual people will act or react in some circumstances. Some intelligence services therefore conduct biographical research and produce biographical sketches of senior political and military leaders for consumers who deal with foreign dignitaries. Biographical intelligence can also identify and assess variables relevant to warning analysis.

As we saw in the case studies of chapter 2, successful warning analysts and deceivers studied their targets carefully. Churchill beat the analysts of the JIC to a forecast that Germany would invade the Soviet Union by making judgments based on his understanding of Hitler the man, not the current flow of intelligence information. The Twenty Committee crafted its deception campaign based on its understanding of Hitler's experiences and judgments—such as his respect for Generals Patton and Thorne. Hitler and his planners made and adjusted their deception themes in 1941 based in part on their study of Stalin. And Sadat designed his attack plan in part based on his judgment that Israelis generally were "arrogant" about the military superiority of the IDF and were politically vulnerable to long and costly wars. The deceivers practiced a variant of what is now known as political psychology.[71]

The CIA is among the intelligence services that conduct psychological and medical analyses of foreign leaders. Dr. Jerrold Post, for example, conducted political psychological analyses of world leaders for the CIA before becoming professor of psychiatry and director of the Political Psychology Program at the George Washington University. Post's prominent "patients" included Saddam Hussein, Anwar Sadat, Menachem Begin, and, after he left CIA, Bill and Hillary Clinton.[72] The physical ailments of national leaders may also help identify health-related ambitions associated with leaders' perceptions that they may have little remaining time to live, preparations for departure from power, or decision-making incapacity due to illness. Such infirmities often are tightly held secrets.[73] For example, the shah of Iran suffered from cancer in 1978 when he unsuccessfully battled the revolutionary forces that eventually deposed him, but his French doctors did not inform even French intelligence of his condition. Knowledge that the shah was gravely ill might have made American intelligence analysts less inclined to believe the shah could weather his political challenge, providing warning of the revolution and avoiding an embarrassing intelligence failure.[74] In addition, states may seek to hide the extent of infection of elite groups by diseases such as HIV/AIDS. While an epidemic among elites may not be an immediate crisis, it could damage local and regional confidence in infected leaders. It could also provide a warning opportunity: key leaders might keenly appreciate an offer of treatment.

The academic world has addressed this issue to some extent.[75] Alexander George produced foundational books on psychological aspects of national leadership.[76] Nathan Leites took a political approach to understanding group and personal behavioral tendencies, which he called "operational codes."[77] George applied the operational code approach directly to assessing political leaders and their decision-making.[78] Stephen Dyson and Matthew Parent more recently evaluated the content of Russian leader Vladimir Putin's public speeches and written communications, helping to explain why Putin has repeatedly surprised and confounded Western political leaders and scholars.[79] And Robert Jervis, like George, has insightfully combined psychology with political analysis.[80] We think this general approach is a promising way to understand how national leaders see their environments, develop and use leadership philosophies, and make and implement decisions. It therefore is potentially useful for both threat and opportunity warning. It can also complement analyses that mainly employ other insights, such as prospect theory.

Political Demography

Political demography offers a way to identify states at risk of instability by specifying demographic patterns that in the past have been associated with political instability. Richard Cincotta, formerly a consultant to the US NIC, notes that states that have a high percentage of youth, defined as people fifteen to twenty-nine years of age constituting more than 40 percent of the population of working age (fifteen to sixty-four years), have high risks of instability and thence of authoritarian regimes that employ strong measures to control the excesses of youth.[81] When youth bulges shrink, states tend to become stable democracies, according to Freedom House measures of political rights and civil liberties.

Such forecasts are unusual in that they can address the distant future—outside usual time horizons of warning—due to the stability of demographic patterns.

Demography can be used to address more immediate warning issues. For example, some countries, including several in Latin America, became democracies before their demographic time and are prone to regress. Tracking the key measure of youth bulge when it is big can tell a warning analyst whether there is an above-average likelihood of political instability that could lead to reduced measures of political freedoms and civil liberties. Alternatively, statesmen may worry that countries experiencing stress in the form of rising terrorism may be likely to become more authoritarian. Cincotta argues that the demographic patterns of Tunisia suggest that it may be able to withstand its strains effectively.[82]

This technique identifies a consistent correlation between something easily measured and a topic of intelligence importance. It helps because it can fairly reliably suggest to analysts where they might profitably undertake detailed analyses to confirm the correlation and to identify causal relationships that are important to explain to senior decision-makers.

Hybrid Theoretical and Other Approaches

Some analysts address complicated issues by using many analytic approaches, theories, and paradigms in combination. One such effort is Stuart Kaufman's assessment of the causes of ethnic wars.[83] Kaufman argues that several standard explanations—including ancient hatreds, manipulative leaders, economic deprivation, and mutual insecurities leading to what political scientists call a "security dilemma"—all are sometimes valid, but they depend on activation by nationalist symbols that legitimize violence against another group.[84] He argues that actors and circumstances variously shape the development of ethnic violence but symbolic politics that legitimizes violence must be present for violence to occur. Kaufman's argument suggests that a good warning indicator of ethnic violence is the presence of symbols on both sides that preclude compromise and legitimate bloodshed. Other variables are less critical.

Game Theory

Some theorists believe game theory offers insights into the nature of strategic surprise, and thence to warning intelligence.[85] Robert Jervis suggests that game theory applies to international politics because leaders interact dynamically, trying to understand and anticipate others' behavior.[86] Robert Axelrod and Thomas Schelling also have applied game theory to aspects of international relations.[87] Players try to understand and anticipate others' moves, which involves use of strategy. Players sometimes strive for surprise, meaning they do things that do not at first blush seem reasonable but are effective for generating surprise. Behavior that appears to be irrational or costly to one's self is virtually always a good way to generate surprise. Some theorists have applied game theory to specific historical events. Steven Brams, for example, likens the Cuban Missile Crisis to a game of "chicken."[88] The crisis was more complicated than Brams argues, but we believe warning professionals can learn from this literature.

War games long have been used to simulate decision-making under complexity. Good war games can be extremely insightful, while ones done poorly or to support a favored policy or strategy may be worse than useless.

Big Data and Other Statistical Approaches

Social scientists long have used statistics for many purposes, including establishing correlations between phenomena and pointing to possible causal relationships. Statistical methods typically use data sets that are built in ways conducive to computer manipulation. The "Big Data" approach is different: computers analyze large amounts of somewhat incompatible data to find patterns, which are always correlations, not causal relationships.[89]

Traditionally, social scientists look for relationships between phenomena of interest—what they often call dependent variables—and potential causes, or what they call independent variables. Scholars of many types of conflict and other issues look for such relationships. Sometimes it is easy to see why relationships exist: wars are more common between neighboring states than between countries on opposite sides of the world. But the causal nature of relationships often is less clear, even when correlations are statistically significant. Barbara Harff, for example, examined the causes of genocide and mass political murders and found six variables, or what she explicitly called indicators, of fifty-five instances of such killing:

1. the presence of political instability
2. a previous genocide
3. ideological orientation of the ruling elite
4. regime type: the presence of autocratic rule
5. ethnic character of the ruling elite—they are members of an ethnic minority
6. trade openness[90]

Note that several of these "indicators" are similar to the stages of Genocide Watch's model of the development of genocide discussed in chapter 6 but that others, such as trade openness, are findings of statistical correlation. Causal mechanisms are not clear and may be indirect. Nevertheless, it makes sense for warning officers to investigate the causes of interesting correlations and to keep such relationships on "indicator" lists.

Technologists, especially, make big claims for "Big Data."[91] Big Data analytic techniques have some uses in intelligence, including the "network analysis" useful in CT work, which once was done by hand by placing information on paper file cards. Big Data may help address other tactically oriented puzzles and be useful for identifying media and other public data suggesting the emergence of political instability in a country or region. Despite technological help in establishing correlations, analysis is always required to establish causation and meaning.[92] Effective use of Big Data may also require analysts to ask a "right question" to guide computer runs and be expert enough to make sense of patterns that computers find.

Such techniques are less useful for strategic warning, however, because warning analysts need to know why and how *future* events are going to unfold in order to forecast patterns that have not yet emerged and to explain to skeptical senior leaders why they should accept warning messages. As Gregory Treverton observes, the IC collects "too much data and too little information."[93] Still, statistical relationships, especially when the pursuit of good questions finds interesting correlations between relevant variables, may identify issues that merit detailed qualitative assessment of causal relationships and their implications. Big Data may be useful for monitoring some warning problems with established scenarios and indicators, but its utility for identifying emerging issues is likely to be modest even if warning analysts are astute and use statistical techniques to test hypotheses they establish for other reasons.

Data have to be good to be useful. While Big Data techniques can sort messy data sets, underlying data still must be relevant to a warning problem. Their use is reduced if countries block large-scale data collection for privacy reasons or introduce deceptive information, as some countries have done in the past.[94] Hence, we are skeptical about the many fantastic claims for Big Data while remaining open-minded about the possibility that in some cases Big Data methods may help strategic warning intelligence. We think it is much more likely to be useful for other intelligence purposes, including tactical warning.

Social Media

Social media may, in some cases, provide early warning of important issues. They received considerable attention in 2011 when Twitter, especially, seemed to contribute markedly to the rapid spread of demands for political change associated with the Arab Spring.[95] Social media can also provide warning of more localized events, such as riots in the aftermath of a police shooting of a seemingly innocent person.[96] Public health officials scan social media for indications of outbreaks of disease.[97] And they can indicate impending food shortages or other humanitarian crises, proving warning to humanitarian NGOs and aid agencies. Our sense is that warning situations in which social media are likely to be helpful mainly are short-term and tactical in nature, but recurrent short-term operating patterns or communication of enduring goals may yield understanding useful for strategic warning.

Social media are now a major arena of political contestation involving large numbers of actors, meaning they offer significant opportunities for deception, including manipulation of message content and the identities of participating actors.[98] Correspondingly, social media pose appreciable and perhaps unique warning analytic challenges. Media technologies and their uses are evolving rapidly, making their impact on the course of political and other events unclear—but worthy of continuing investigation.[99]

Crowdsourcing

Another favorite of technologists and social media aficionados is "crowdsourcing"—the assembly of large groups of people, usually online, that provides collective wisdom about issues that has sometimes been excellent.[100] In the intelligence world, "futures markets" that enable large numbers of analysts to bet on the outcomes of intelligence issues are under investigation.[101] We accept the possibility that these methods may eventually become a useful tool in intelligence collection and analysis generally and sometimes may be useful for tactical warning, but we see little likelihood that they will help strategic warning analysts identify emerging warning issues. If an issue has attracted a widespread, popular following, it probably has developed to the point that policymakers are aware of it, current intelligence tracks it, and it is no longer a strategic warning issue.

IARPA's Aggregate Contingent Estimation (ACE) program is a variant of crowdsourcing—an effort to develop better ways to elicit, weigh, and combine groups of analysts' forecasts to divine better ones.[102] This idea runs counter to the historical record that on most important warning issues small numbers of especially insightful people, not most analysts, were prescient. We therefore are skeptical that this effort will aid strategic warning, though it might help improve short-term predictions and tactical warning. IARPA's Open Source Indicators (OSI) program seeks to develop ways in which automatic processing of open-source data can "anticipate and/or detect significant societal events, such as political crises, humanitarian crises, mass violence, riots, mass migrations, disease outbreaks, economic instability, resource shortages, and responses to natural disasters."[103] Successful methods will "beat the news."[104] This, too, may help tactical warning but also seems unlikely to be a significant strategic warning tool.

Climate Change a Warning Issue?

Much attention in recent years has been devoted to whether humans are altering the planetary climate, to what degree, and with what consequences. The IC produced an NIE on the subject in 2008. Much of the concern involves long-term issues well beyond the normal time horizon of security-focused warning. The discussion also is prominent and controversial, arguably leading to a conclusion that warning units should focus on other problems. But analysts increasingly are looking at the possibilities that climate change may trigger more traditional security concerns, including migration and territorial disputes caused by changing coastlines in the relatively near term.[105] Andrew Marshall's Office of Net Assessment commissioned a study of the security impact of climate change.[106] Among the most worrisome issues is the apparent historical recurrence of rapid temperature changes only in discrete regions of the world. While we do not suggest a major effort here, warning units may want to monitor ongoing studies on possibilities for what now appear to be low-probability but high-impact consequences of climate change.

Political Instability Modeling

Sometimes line analytic units develop tools and processes useful for warning as well as other forms of analysis using social science methods.[107] For example, in the 1980s, CIA Deputy Director for Intelligence Robert Gates directed his Political Instability Branch to prepare closely held papers on the "prospects for dramatic political change" and to monitor threats to political instability around the globe. This branch, then headed by Randy Pherson, published the *Political Instability Quarterly*, which monitored conditions in thirty-six countries. The goal of the unit was to develop a capacity to warn US policymakers that instability was likely to break out in a country at least six months before appreciable instability occurred. According to Pherson, the process worked well. The branch did not miss an event for the two-and-a-half-year run of the publication, which ceased as part of a management decision to redirect resources to other issues. Since 1994, the US government has also sponsored a Political Instability Task Force—a group of academic experts who monitor political instability, state failure, and resultant consequences, including genocide.[108] In addition, "The State Failure Project: Early Warning Research for U.S. Foreign Policy Planning" tried to identify indicators of political instability.[109]

The Political Instability Branch also developed a method for predicting major increases in political-military tensions as a precursor to a military coup. The branch tracked countries vulnerable to coups and published key findings on a quarterly basis. One of the better calls was that junior military officers in one country were about to launch a coup against its president. Country-focused analysts dismissed the unit's findings as overreaching despite the fact that a separate Political Instability Branch study using an expected utility analysis methodology for forecasting political outcomes also predicted that the president's remaining time in power was limited. When presented with these two warning assessments, the relevant regional NIO scheduled a community-wide meeting the next week to assess the likelihood of a coup, which occurred a few days before the meeting was to be held. A key lesson Pherson learned from this incident was the need to always include analysts from relevant line analytic units in any warning analysis project.

The military coup methodology also proved successful in providing opportunity warning that enabled the US government to help prevent at least one military coup. When his group's analysis identified the potential for a coup in a Latin American country that generated little interest among policymakers at the time, Pherson alerted the NSC principal staff officer for Latin America, who called the State Department to alert the US ambassador in the country to the threat and to focus the embassy's attention on several of the key indicators. The ambassador responded the following day that the embassy had not been paying attention to the indicators and concurred with the analytic conclusions. Embassy officers subsequently took remedial action to reduce tensions, and no coup occurred—possibly indicating a warning success.

But identifying signs that general dissatisfaction may at some point lead to political instability is hard.[110] The IC received considerable criticism for not warning of the outbreak of the Arab Spring in 2011. The issue was not the presence of general unhappiness but rather identification of "triggers" of outbursts, a more difficult challenge.[111] We think economist Timur Kuran developed a particularly insightful rationalist model that explains why the revolution of 1989 in Eastern Europe burst forth so apparently suddenly.[112] Kuran argues that people in Eastern European police states carefully weighed the costs of expressing their true feelings against the benefits of free expression and quickly became more willing to defy regimes when the net costs of defiance evidently declined in the fall of 1989. Kuran's model is adaptable to other situations.

Understanding and Unmasking Deception

Intelligence analysts face many challenges, but one that especially troubles warning analysts is dedicated opposition from adversaries' (and sometimes "friends'") D&D efforts. The intelligence literature is most clear about principles of deception involving surprise military attack, which is common but is arguably a relatively simple version of deception. As discussed in chapter 6, the Kosovo Liberation Army's successful deception campaign targeting NATO political leaders had other goals.[113]

While a detailed treatment of counter-deception theory and techniques is beyond the scope of this book, we believe the case studies, historical lessons, and theories discussed herein are consistent with much of the counter-deception literature. We highlight here some of the factors that warning analysts and students of strategic warning should keep in mind when assessing the use and effectiveness of deception techniques.

First, actors use strategic deception in the hope of gaining appreciable advantages, usually vis-à-vis an opponent. This means warning analysts should be alert for situations in which there are significant incentives to generate surprise or misunderstanding in opponents or third parties.[114] A core lesson of history, shown in the Chinese intervention in Korea in 1950, the Tet Offensive of 1968, the Yom Kippur War of 1973, and the Kosovo Liberation Army's deception of 1998–99, is the tendency of intelligence analysts and decision-makers to focus on military factors and downplay or ignore underlying political motivations and incentives.

Second, there must be opportunities to use deception, such as a still-evolving "policy space" that deceivers want to influence. Deceivers are less likely to attempt to influence policy positions they perceive to be firm.[115] A mediocre (not poor) opposition intelligence service that has some credibility with decision-makers facilitates deception by providing an easy target that can help mislead decision-makers—the ultimate target of deception activities.[116]

Warning specialists can appreciably help themselves by understanding principles deceivers use to craft their campaigns. James Bruce and Michael Bennett identify four general principles of deception, which all appear in most cases:

1. Truth: All deception works in a context of what is true.
2. Denial: Denying targets access to key aspects of the truth is a prerequisite for all deception.

3. Deceit: All deception requires some deceit.
4. Misdirection: Deception depends on manipulating what the target perceives.[117]

Michael Handel argues that deceptively provided information should be 90 percent true.[118] The risk of providing accurate operational information can be mitigated by passing low-grade informational "chicken feed," information deceivers believe their intended victims already know, or perishable information provided too late for victims to use. The Twenty Committee, as discussed in chapter 2, used all of these techniques in 1944.

Deceivers know and rely on the cognitive biases of people and the vulnerabilities of standard analytic techniques.[119] They study the personality traits and quirks of key decision-makers such as Hitler and Stalin. They usually rely on moderately able analysts' abilities to assess and develop the messages they want to convey, believing that assessments their targets develop from seemingly credible, apparently independent sources improve targets' confidence in their intelligence misjudgments. In Betts's terminology, deceivers exploit the normal theory that usually works well. Put differently, deceivers understand and exploit the vulnerabilities of doctrinally established analytic "tradecraft."

Deceivers also target the foibles of intelligence organizations, including time pressures and the common requirement that organizational judgments require appreciable review and coordination processes. Adding "noise" per Wohlstetter can help prolong intra-organizational debates on warning issues, paralyzing decision processes, delaying dissemination of warning messages, or leading organizations to water down warning messages to gain consensus. As we have noted, warning failures often occur because intelligence analysts disagree about the meaning of unfolding events.

Donald Daniel and Katherine Herbig categorize most deceptions as being of two types: ambiguity-enhancing (A-type) and misleading (M-type).[120] A-type deceptions ensure that signals, per Wohlstetter, are embedded in large amounts of noise, confusing victims about the real intentions of deceivers. Germany in 1941 and Egypt in 1973 used this type of deception. M-type deceptions aim to mislead victims about small numbers of important details. In 1944, British deceivers aimed to mislead Germany about only one detail: the location of the invasion Germany expected.

How can line analysts detect purposely low-grade information they receive when they usually are happy to get most any accurate data? And how can they identify what is missing or misleading? We suggest that "extraordinary thinking" generally is needed to spot unusual patterns of reporting and inconsistencies (or unusual consistencies) not normally evident in reporting and to accurately assess their meaning. We suggest that at least four factors can help spot such deceptions: (1) a critical, introspective outlook, (2) knowing and understanding the history of deception and why deceptions succeeded (or not), (3) understanding principles of counter-deception such as those Bruce and Bennett enumerate, and (4) mastering techniques such as the I&W method and counter-deception techniques.

Barton Whaley and Jeffrey Busby argue that all deceptions potentially can be discovered and countered.[121] We are less sanguine but are convinced that intelligence officers can and should identify, and counter or exploit, some deceptions. In a course he developed in the 1980s, Richards Heuer taught a deception "checklist" featuring a series of questions under the following headings that analysts should ask themselves: (1) evaluation of sources of information, (2) evaluation of evidence, (3) the "Opposition Perspective," and (4) past opposition activities in the deception arena.[122] Using such devices, we suggest that the Knorr-Betts baseball analogy is useful here too. Warning analysts should aspire to increase their "batting average" of deceptions countered. We think Michael Bennett and Edward Waltz have written a fine book on countering deception, and we recommend it to warning analysts.[123]

Notes

1. Heuer, *Psychology of Intelligence Analysis*; Moore, *Critical Thinking and Intelligence Analysis*; Pherson and Pherson, *Critical Thinking for Strategic Intelligence*; Clark, *Intelligence Analysis*; Cooper, *Curing Analytical Pathologies*. For reference to the lack of evidence that SATs work, see Chang and Tetlock, "Rethinking Training of Intelligence Analysts," 909.

2. State/INR does not have such requirements.

3. Betts, "Warning Dilemmas," 828–23; Betts, *Enemies of Intelligence*, 55–62. Jack Davis agreed with Betts. See Davis, "Strategic Warning: Intelligence Support," 180.

4. Lowenthal, *Intelligence*, 6th ed., 79.

5. Grabo, *Handbook of Warning Intelligence*, 423.

6. Personal experience of John Gentry.

7. Gustafson, "Strategic Horizons," 590.

8. Cormac, "Secret Intelligence and Economic Security," 100.

9. For members, see "Membership of Horizon Scanning Programme Groups," August 2014, https://www.gov.uk/government/uploads/system/uploads/attachment_data/file/352238/Membership_of_the_CSAG_GOSH_CoIs_and_Roundtables_September_2014.pdf.

10. As cited in Gustafson, "Horizon Scanning," 592.

11. United Kingdom Government Office for Science, *Scenario Planning*, October 2009, at http://webarchive.nationalarchives.gov.uk/20140108141323/http://www.bis.gov.uk/assets/foresight/docs/horizon-scanning-centre/foresight_scenario_planning.pdf.

12. Gustafson, "Horizon Scanning," 598–600; Voros, "Generic Foresight Process," 10–21.

13. Gustafson, "Horizon Scanning," 599.

14. For details, see Quiggin, *Seeing the Invisible*; and Chong et al., *Risk Assessment*.

15. Lim, "Big Data and Strategic Intelligence," 619–35.

16. National Commission on Terrorist Attacks upon the United States, *Final Report*.

17. See PowerPoint briefing of Björn Wettermark, "Horizon Scanning and Forecasting Drug Utilization in Sweden," presented in May 2015 in Warsaw, Poland, http://www.piperska.org/sites/default/files/Wettermark_Horizon_scanning_and_forecasting_in_Sweden.pdf.

18. See CADTH website, https://www.cadth.ca/about-cadth/what-we-do/products-services/horizon-scanning, accessed June 2, 2016.

19. See website of Eco-Innovation Observatory, http://www.eco-innovation.eu/index.php/about-us.

20. Beat Habbeger, *Horizon Scanning in Government: Concept, Country Experiences, and Models for Switzerland* (Zurich: Center for Security Studies, 2009), http://www.css.ethz.ch/content/dam/ethz/special-interest/gess/cis/center-for-securities-studies/pdfs/Horizon-Scanning-in-Government.pdf.

21. Authors' communication with Ken Knight on several occasions in 2014 through 2017.

22. Kent, *Strategic Intelligence*, 152–55.

23. Australian Ministry of Defence pamphlet titled "Australian Defence Warning System: Providing Strategic Warning," no date.

24. Ibid.

25. Authors' discussion with a Kent School instructor, January 2017.

26. Director of National Intelligence, *National Intelligence Strategy, 2005*, 5.

27. Hall and Citrenbaum, *Intelligence Analysis*, 167–85.

28. Director of National Intelligence, *National Intelligence Strategy, 2014*, 6.

29. Ibid., 8.

30. Ibid.

31. Authors' discussion with Gregory Treverton, April 6, 2017.

32. Gregory Treverton email to Gentry, June 23, 2017.

33. For more information, see the NIC website at https://www.dni.gov/index.php/global-trends -home.

34. Available at https://www.dni.gov/files/images/globalTrends/documents/GT-Full-Report.pdf.

35. For more information, see the NIC website at https://www.dni.gov/index.php/global-trends -home.

36. Gustafson, "Strategic Horizons," 593; United Kingdom Ministry of Defence, *Global Strategic Trends*.

37. Muller, "Improving Futures Intelligence," 382–95.

38. For example, Alvin Toffler, *Future Shock* (New York: Random House, 1970); and Alvin Toffler and Heidi Toffler, *War and Anti-War: Making Sense of Today's Global Chaos* (New York: Grand Central, 1995).

39. Pardee Center website at http://pardee.du.edu/, accessed May 28, 2016.

40. Ibid.

41. Mathew Burrows and Frances G. Burwell, *Europe in 2022: Alternative Futures* (Washington, DC: Atlantic Council, March 2017), http://www.atlanticcouncil.org/images/publications/Europe_in_2022 _web_0329.pdf.

42. For example, CIA's Office of Russian and European Analysis produced a useful guide for its analysts titled "(U) Anticipating Strategic-Level Surprise," CIA-DI-12–01775, January 2013.

43. Jervis, *How Statesmen Think*, 191–215.

44. Stein, "Military Deception, Strategic Surprise," 94–122.

45. See also Davis and Grabo, "Strategic Warning and Deception," 38.

46. Stein, "Military Deception, Strategic Surprise," 99–106.

47. Adamsky, "1983 Nuclear Crisis."

48. Ibid., 34.

49. Kahneman and Tversky, "Prospect Theory."

50. Jervis, *How Statesmen Think*, 85–103; Mercer, "Prospect Theory and Political Science," 1–21; Jervis, "Political Implications of Loss Aversion," 187–204.

51. Cha, "Hawk Engagement," 40–78.

52. Gates, "Prediction of Soviet Intentions," 39–46.

53. Andrew, *For the President's Eyes Only*, 538.

54. Kent, "Crucial Estimate Relived," 118.

55. Mandel, "On Estimating Post–Cold War," 194–215.

56. Wirtz, *Tet Offensive*, 83–84.

57. Wirtz, "Miscalculation, Surprise," 4–5.

58. Barrass, "Able Archer 83," 22–26.

59. Jervis, "Reports, Politics, and Intelligence Failures," 23.

60. For a good analysis of what many Soviets later considered to be a policy error, see Valenta, *Soviet Intervention in Czechoslovakia*.

61. Ibid., 129.

62. For example, see Jervis, *Why Intelligence Fails*, 72–73.

63. Ibid., 175–78.

64. Ibid.

65. For example, see Valenta, *Soviet Intervention in Czechoslovakia.*

66. McCormick, "Terrorist Decision Making," 490–95.

67. Crawford, "Passion of World Politics," 116–56.

68. Diamond, *Collapse,* esp. 419–40.

69. Ibid., 421.

70. Betts, "Strategic Surprise for War Termination," 152.

71. Jervis, *How Statesmen Think.*

72. Post, *Psychological Assessment of Political Leaders.*

73. McDermott, "Use and Abuse of Medical Intelligence," 491–520.

74. Jervis, *Why Intelligence Fails,* 15–108.

75. Hermann, "Explaining Foreign Policy Behavior," 7–46; Larson, "Role of Belief Systems," 17–33.

76. George, *Presidential Decisionmaking*; George, *Bridging the Gap.*

77. Leites, *Study of Bolshevism.*

78. George, "Operational Code," 191–222.

79. Dyson and Parent, "Operational Code Approach"; Marten, "Putin's Choices," 189–204.

80. Jervis, *How Statesmen Think*; Jervis, *Perception and Misperception.*

81. Cincotta, "Half a Chance," 10–18.

82. Cincotta, "Will Tunisia's Democracy Survive?"

83. Kaufman, *Modern Hatreds.*

84. Ibid., 203–21.

85. Levite, *Intelligence and Strategic Surprise,* 2.

86. Jervis, *How Statesmen Think,* 3, 141–42.

87. Axelrod, *Complexity of Cooperation*; Schelling, *Strategy of Conflict.*

88. Steven J. Brams, "Game Theory and the Cuban Missile Crisis," *Plus,* January 1, 2001, https://plus.maths.org/content/game-theory-and-cuban-missile-crisis.

89. Cukier and Mayer-Schoenberger, "Rise of Big Data," 28–40.

90. Harff, "No Lessons Learned from Holocaust?," 65–73.

91. Hare and Coghill, "Future of Intelligence Analysis Task," 858–70.

92. Spielmann, "I Got Algorithm," 525–44; Lim, "Big Data and Strategic Intelligence."

93. Treverton, *Intelligence for an Age of Terror,* 9.

94. Lahneman, "IC Data Mining," 700–723.

95. Rovner, "Intelligence in the Twitter Age," 260–71.

96. Omand, Bartlett, and Miller, "Introducing Social Media Intelligence," 801–23.

97. Ibid., 803.

98. For examples, see Riley, "Deceived to Intervene."

99. Lynch, Freelon, and Aday, *Syria's Socially Mediated Civil War.*

100. Stottlemyre, "HUMINT, OSINT, or Something New?," 578–89.

101. Treverton, *Intelligence for an Age of Terror,* 150.

102. IARPA, https://www.iarpa.gov/index.php/research-programs/ace, accessed February 18, 2017.

103. IARPA, https://www.iarpa.gov/index.php/research-programs/osi, accessed February 28, 2017.

104. Ibid.

105. Dupont, "Strategic Implications of Climate Change," 42–54.

106. Ibid., 42–44.

107. Details of this section provided by Randy Pherson in an email to the authors, December 20, 2016.

108. Albright and Cohen, *Preventing Genocide,* 24.

109. For a description, see Daniel C. Esty, Jack Goldstone, Ted Robert Gurr, et al., "The Failed State Project: Early Warning Research for U.S. Foreign Policy Planning," paper presented at a conference called Failed States and International Security: Causes, Prospects, and Consequence, Purdue University, February 25–27, 1998, http://www.comm.ucsb.edu/faculty/mstohl/failed_states/1998/papers/gurr.html.

110. Alexseev, "Early Warning, Ethnopolitical Conflicts," 191–213.

111. George and Wirtz, "Warning in Age of Uncertainty," 220–21.

112. Kuran, "Now Out of Never," 7–48.

113. For another motive, see Katz, "Deception and Denial in Iraq," 577–85.

114. Knorr, "Strategic Surprise," 173–93.

115. Morgan, "Opportunity for a Strategic Surprise," 195–245.

116. Gentry, "Warning Analysis."

117. Bruce and Bennett, "Foreign Denial and Deception," 201.

118. Handel, *Military Deception*, 25.

119. Kass and London, "Surprise, Deception, Denial and Warning," 59–82.

120. Daniel and Herbig, *Strategic Military Deception*.

121. Whaley and Busby, "Detecting Deception," 181–221.

122. Heuer, *Rethinking Intelligence*, 34.

123. Bennett and Waltz, *Counterdeception Principles*.

CHAPTER 8

Cognitive, Psychological, and Character Issues

Intelligence analysis, as Mark Lowenthal often says, is an "intellectual activity."[1] It requires native intelligence, knowledge, dedication, and patience. Warning analysis is a special kind of analysis. It requires a distinctive combination of qualities to identify new warning issues and to develop appropriate, persuasive ways to address them. It is hard work subject to many challenges, not the least of which are normal physiological, or cognitive, features of the human brain.

Psychologists have learned a great deal about how people address complicated intellectual challenges and have applied these lessons to foreign policy decision-making.[2] In recent years, students of intelligence analysis have adapted many of these lessons for use in addressing intelligence analytic problems. Psychological understanding of "mindsets and biases" has been a major stimulus in the development of structured analytic techniques, for example.[3]

Practitioners of deception also study the intellectual and psychological strengths and weaknesses of their target intelligence producers and consumers. They learn how psychological vulnerabilities have been successfully exploited in the past to help them fool their targets in the future.[4] Prominent student of deception Barton Whaley notes that deception is an aspect of "applied psychology" that especially falls within the arena of what psychologists call misperception.[5] We therefore discuss in this chapter the special mental challenges of strategic warning analysts, including the difficulties of detecting the efforts of those who try to deceive them.

Knowledgeable students of the strategic warning function and experienced practitioners consistently state that some personality traits characterize successful warning analysts and argue that they are identifiable and recruitable but are only partly trainable. Given the institutional cultures and incentive systems of national intelligence services and government bureaucracies, which often discourage warning, such analysts are even harder to nurture and to retain, especially when they work in intelligence organizations that have adopted the EAAWA philosophy. We therefore in this chapter also discuss these special character traits.

Confirmation Bias

One of the well-recognized cognitive errors of intelligence analysis generally, confirmation bias, is especially pernicious in warning specialists because deceivers rely on it to build deception campaigns. Knowing analysts' (and decision-makers') personal experiences, beliefs, and expectations helps deceivers to identify the types of true but partial and therefore misleading information consistent with established beliefs and biases, along with denial of other types of relevant information and carefully selected false information, that will lead their targets to reach the incorrect conclusions they desire.

We have discussed three examples of exploitation of this kind of vulnerability—in both intelligence analysts and decision-makers. In 1941, Germany identified many of Stalin's biases—such as his paranoia that Churchill was trying to start a Soviet-German war to destroy Soviet socialism—leading to alteration of its rumor campaign to feed Stalin "evidence" he expected to see, which diverted Stalin from Hitler's real intent. British deceivers in 1944 arranged additional air strikes on the Pas-de-Calais region after they became aware that German intelligence and leaders expected the Allies to bomb most heavily where they planned their landing. And the KLA arranged "facts on the ground" and used emotive language consistent with what President Clinton expected to see about the Serbs he had come to despise.

Even when there is no active deception effort, analysts experiencing confirmation bias are less receptive than they should be to relevant new information inconsistent with their beliefs.[6] This phenomenon is exacerbated when line analytic units develop corporate positions on analytic issues that are resistant to change. In these environments, analysts and their managers deny the relevance of new information that is inconsistent with established views or see it as confirmation of their preconceptions. Israelis' reification of the Concept in 1973 and AMAN's monitoring of Egyptian military activity through this lens is a classic example of this phenomenon. But the phenomenon is common elsewhere too. Former Chairman of the NIC and Assistant Director of Central Intelligence for Analysis and Production John Gannon regularly saw analytic organizations develop corporate views that were hard to dislodge.[7] Similarly, CIA analysts were stubbornly committed to what turned out to be incorrect judgments about the meaning of Iraqi possession of aluminum tubes, which led to errors in the 2002 NIE on Iraq's WMD programs.[8] To counter this tendency, analysts must have low tolerance for established wisdom that establishes the plausibility of potential analytic judgments, and they must regularly revisit established views and assumptions.[9]

To counter or at least ameliorate this vulnerability, analysts, managers, and the decision-makers they support must remain as open-minded—and as continuingly skeptical—as possible and regularly reassess once-accurate judgments that may have become unchallenged assumptions. The employment of experienced intelligence analysts with different backgrounds to check and challenge assessments is another useful way to help prevent deception success by exploiting the dysfunctions of the confirmation bias.

Mirror Imaging

A much-discussed pathology, variants of mirror imaging—expecting others to act as one would oneself—frequently occur and are exploitable. British deceivers in 1944 exploited Hitler's mirror imaging when they named Generals Patton and Thorne to "command" notional American and British armies that were key parts of their deception plan. Because the deceivers knew Hitler respected the generals and that he thought the Allies would think similarly, they named Patton and Thorne to "command" the most important Allied units—the ones leading the invasion of the Continent. The antidote for mirror-imaging is awareness of the tendency, development of expertise, and empathy for another's situation without putting oneself into the other fellow's shoes.

Excessive Intellectual and Bureaucratic Routine

The propensity of dedicated warning organizations to establish routine publication schedules—typically weekly reports in the United States and the United Kingdom—runs several risks. It encourages publication of "warning" messages whether real warnings are warranted or not. A firm publication schedule of a formal journal degrades warning messages into current intelligence articles, which damages their quality, runs afoul bureaucratically of line analytic units' work on similar subjects, and desensitizes consumers to the importance of warning messages as special communications about important issues.[10] Gregory Treverton argues that periodic reports serve a useful "curation" function: they remind senior consumers of what they previously were warned about.[11] We accept that this sometimes occurs, but we are unaware of any weekly warning product that was appreciably and regularly viewed positively by senior policy officials, which is consistent with survey findings of NIO/Ws Charlie Allen and Robert Vickers. We therefore agree with Jack Davis that warning issues should be chosen carefully to maximize consumer interest and receptivity to warning messages.[12] Dedicated warning units should, we believe, avoid regular schedules for genuine warning messages and warn only when situations meet an important threshold: the message asks for, or alerts decision-makers about, the possibility of a need to make a policy decision. The latter criterion permits alerts about evolutionary changes that may eventually become important issues but keeps analyses more focused on warning than most current intelligence pieces.

Waiting for Evidence

Strategic warning is about making good judgments in the face of substantial uncertainty. But both analysts and decision-makers frequently, especially when a warning-induced decision may be intellectually difficult or costly, choose to wait until the situation clarifies and there is more evidence. This tendency is especially apparent when analysts and their managers fear criticism for making a mistake—which is largely a function of the degree of mutual trust they have with their decision-making consumers.[13] This tendency is understandable to a degree, but it is also a recipe for dallying to the point that timely warning is impossible. To a considerably greater extent than line analysts, warning analysts must make difficult assessments wisely and convey them with candid assessments of degrees of confidence to decision-makers who might rather wait and who will wait if they do not trust the judgment and discretion of intelligence personnel. This requires a degree of intellectual courage that intelligence professionals do not consistently demonstrate.

In his short talk to military warning professionals in 1991 that we mentioned in chapter 5, the then chairman of the Joint Chiefs of Staff, General Colin Powell, addressed the confidence issue by encouraging his warning people to continue to approach him with warning concerns if they were worried.[14] He said he would respect the initiative even though he might find warning messages unpersuasive. This kind of senior leader's trust and encouragement goes a long way toward encouraging warning analysts. But Powell also cautioned his warning personnel against excessive warning. Warning about everything, he said, means warning about nothing.

Desirable Warning "Personality" Characteristics

It is striking that virtually all warning specialists in government and business, and students of deception, argue that there is something special about the personal characteristics of successful practitioners of strategic warning and deception. They find that few people make good warning analysts. Some of these observers also note traits that are consistently dysfunctional in analysts and managers of strategic warning functions. If mental and psychological needs of the warning function are indeed unusual, the ramifications for warning and the institutions that practice it but do not choose their personnel carefully are potentially significantly negative. We also discern different types of senior managers of warning and offer a two-part typology.

The best insights come from people who have directly studied warning analysts and practitioners of deception. In chapter 2, we saw an unusually good example of the eclectic skills of deceivers in the members of the Twenty Committee—people who were professors, lawyers, entertainers, poets, and practical jokers. Few of them worked for the government before the war or continued to work for the government after 1945. Similarly, many of the Allies' cryptologic breakthroughs during World War II were achieved by temporary government employees.[15] This pattern suggests that the organizational cultures of government bureaucracies may be impediments to the recruitment and retention of good warning analysts—a hypothesis in need of further specification and research.

Cynthia Grabo devoted a section of her book to the personality traits strategic warning analysts should have. With some twenty years of experience watching warning analysts on rotational assignments come and go, Grabo identified characteristics of good warning analysts, including "basic intellectual attributes," such as insatiable curiosity, aptitude for detailed research, imagination, a retentive memory, and recognition of what is important, and "attributes of character or temperament," including motivation, capacity for hard work, and initiative.[16] Grabo made clear she believed these traits are not common in intelligence analysts.

Prominent, experienced warning analysts universally, to our knowledge, agree with Grabo. For example, former NIO/W Mary McCarthy wrote in 1998, "The 'art and science of assessing threats' . . . requires laborious, methodical, rigorous analytic work; it requires imagination, and it requires a diversity of outlooks. With the exception of a few notable pockets of excellence, the [US Intelligence] Community would appear to need a boost in all three departments."[17] We emphasize that McCarthy noted the importance of diversity in "outlooks"—or mental perspectives—not race or gender or other demographic characteristics.

Barton Whaley later suggested similarly that there are personality types well suited to conducting military deception. He identified four characteristics as especially important and recommended that the issue of character be a topic of future research.[18] Whaley thought good deceivers among military planners, and by extension others, should

1. be iconoclastic, prepared to break procedural rules to make one's own in order to accomplish the larger mission;
2. have an odd sense of humor by appreciating the pleasures of deceiving others;
3. have an empathic mind by knowing one's enemies; and
4. have an "alert mind" or a "prepared mind" that is flexible and open to new and unusual events. This characteristic "tolerates the absurd, the ridiculous. It notices the anomalies, the discrepancies, the incongruous happenings that crop up from time to time."[19]

This logic makes sense because warning personnel and deceivers each try to understand and exploit each other's situations, goals, and psychological, analytical, and institutional propensities at individual and group levels. Are such people born or made? Whaley says such traits are a mix of personality and experience, of genetics and learning.[20]

Jon Latimer, a retired British Army officer who writes on deception in war, believes that

> the most effective deceivers display an unorthodoxy of thought that is usually little appreciated in a peacetime army. Perhaps more than any other branch of military endeavor, successful deception is an art rather than science, although science increasingly provides

the technical means by which deception is created. Many of the best practitioners have had backgrounds in both the visual and performing arts, but the art of deception is most successful when applied patiently, with proven techniques guided by solid principles.[21]

Michael Handel argues that the effective practice of deception is a "creative art," not a science or a craft; for that reason, it is hard to teach deception to someone who does not have "an instinct" for it.[22] If one accepts our belief that warning analysis and deception share many characteristics and that in their chronic dynamic interactions they must know each other well to be effective, then we assert that Handel and Latimer also argue that warning analysis contains an element of art. Handel also says there probably is no way to become good at deception except through experience.[23] Handel's and Latimer's views implicitly suggest that the IC's practice of giving new analysts a few hours of training on warning as part of the EAAWA approach to warning is likely to fail.

Dave Snowden, one of the developers of Singapore's Risk Assessment and Horizon Scanning process, says that people who best do RAHS work are people who are comfortable with "abstraction and change. This means people with broad experience or people who have a classic liberal education."[24]

Warning specialists often try to place themselves in the position of their intelligence targets, also a characteristic of red teaming, which potentially can also be useful for line analysts and deceivers. It is one of the standard SATs now widely taught. The concept of the red team goes back at least as far as World War I, when some armies established groups tasked with trying to anticipate what their enemies were thinking and thus planned to do.[25] This can be done in many ways. For example, the German military in late 1939 and early 1940 ran a series of exercises in which they tested competing war plan proposals against likely French responses; the final plan reflected lessons of the exercise play of an intelligence officer who had extensively studied senior French military officers' decision-making processes and behavior and who acted roughly as French military chief General Maurice Gamelin actually did during the war.[26] Few people can do this well.

In 1974, in direct response to the Yom Kippur War, Israeli military intelligence established a new analytic unit that both had oversight responsibilities over the Research Department—by assessing the completeness and soundness of regular analyses—and periodically issued assessments that specifically reached conclusions opposite to the Research Department's best assessment.[27] The latter role has elements of red teaming.

Micah Zenko argues that special personality characteristics are essential to performing well on red teams: "Red teaming requires a distinct personality type—open-minded, creative, confident, and a little odd, while maintaining the ability to relate and communicate with the targeted institution without coming across as antagonistic."[28]

Ben Gilad, who is a business intelligence specialist, says the best business warning analyst has skills and traits often considered contradictory: "someone who is a detail-oriented, big-picture type of person, fearless and full of self-doubts, a great political networker introvert, analytical to a fault with a sixth sense . . . and, finally, a broad-minded, focused person."[29] He adds that analysts also must have an ability to synthesize—that is, to "paste together a puzzle of emerging reality from a variety of unrelated bits"—and integrity.[30] In business environments usually much smaller than governments, Gilad identifies four variables that help determine whether the "competitive early warning" function will work well: (1) company culture, (2) top management's decision-making style, (3) the chief executive's personality, and (4) the warning analyst's skills and personality.[31] All of these characteristics also are relevant to government intelligence services.

James Wirtz notes that states collectively are much more susceptible to being surprised, and less interested in using deception themselves, if they see themselves as relatively strong materially vis-à-vis a prospective enemy but that people become much more receptive to warning after they experience a traumatic failure.[32] Implicitly this finding also applies to the organizational cultures of intelligence agencies. Wirtz illustrates his point by comparing the poor warning performance of US intelligence and senior intelligence consumers before the Pearl Harbor attack of December 1941 with the excellent performance by some of the same individuals only six months later in the intelligence preparation for the Battle of Midway. Wirtz argues that the "cognitive framework" of people makes a big difference in whether they are receptive to unconventional ideas.[33] We extend the argument to suggest that good warning personnel are relatively immune to what might be called the "political climate of the times" and that they are able to retain a degree of curiosity and skepticism when most others around them, including the people leading their organizations, are sanguine. This trait is especially important when a temporarily benign international security situation leads consumers and intelligence leaders to pay less attention to threat warning intelligence.

Philip Tetlock and his colleagues include in their report of their two-year study for the IC about how to improve forecasting, or prediction, an assessment of the personal character traits of successful forecasters. While these are important for strategic analysts generally, they are especially relevant for warning analysts. The abstract of a paper summarizing the conclusions of Tetlock's study says:

> We report findings from a geopolitical forecasting tournament that assessed the accuracy of more than 150,000 forecasts of 743 participants on 199 events occurring over 2 years. Participants were above average in intelligence and political knowledge relative to the general population. Individual differences in performance emerged, and forecasting skills were surprisingly consistent over time. Key predictors were (a) dispositional variables of cognitive ability, political knowledge, and open-mindedness; (b) situational variables of training in probabilistic reasoning and participation in collaborative teams that shared information and discussed rationales . . . ; and (c) behavioral variables of deliberation time and frequency of belief updating. We developed a profile of the best forecasters; they were better at inductive reasoning, pattern detection, cognitive flexibility, and open-mindedness. They had greater understanding of geopolitics, training in probabilistic reasoning, and opportunities to succeed in cognitively enriched team environments. Last but not least, they viewed forecasting as a skill that required deliberate practice, sustained effort, and constant monitoring of current affairs.[34]

Expertise, and the willingness to constantly replenish it, also is important. Tetlock concluded that people with expertise are better forecasters. David Mandel and Alan Barnes reached similar conclusions in a study of the forecasting accuracy of assessments of the Canadian Intelligence Assessment Secretariat, an analytic component of the Canadian Privy Council Office, which found that "experienced" analysts forecast better than junior analysts.[35] We emphasize that Tetlock's pointed message in this and other studies differs markedly from the interpretation of his work common in the IC—that expertise is detrimental to sound analysis. Tetlock specifically says his findings have often been misrepresented.[36]

Rose McDermott suggests that personality tests be used more to identify characteristics particularly relevant to intelligence analysis in general, including open-mindedness or the absence of premature cognitive closure.[37] By implication, such testing might also be useful for finding people with the characteristics Grabo and others identify as desirable.

Barton Whaley cites former IDF chief of intelligence Major General Eli Zeira as saying he similarly thought three personality factors were important in intelligence analysts, implicitly including warning specialists: (1) people who succeeded because they threw away the rule book, (2) persons with unusual senses of humor, and (3) magicians.[38] Zeira's words make some sense, although in practice, as described in chapter 2, Zeira seriously damaged Israel's warning capacity in 1973, and Uri Bar-Joseph cites Zeira and the chief of Branch 6 of AMAN's Research Department, Lieutenant Colonel Yona Bandman, as displaying personality traits that then were, and we think generally are, dysfunctional, including "authoritarian and dogmatic" personalities and an excessive need for cognitive closure.[39] Zeira is among many analysts who mention magic in the context of deception and warning.

Warning officers with the traits noted above are harder to fool than other intelligence analysts. Genuinely inept intelligence people are difficult to target because they have little ability to solve intelligence analytic puzzles, leading deceivers to overestimate their analytic capabilities and leading to missed deception messages; this is not an IC problem. Mediocre analysts are easiest to fool because they know basic analytic tradecraft but not much more, meaning that deceivers need do little more than exploit the "tradecraft" practices training courses emphasize. People with mediocre warning skills—a core feature of the EAAWA model—may, when working against competent deceivers, therefore be worse than useless. The best defense against competent deceivers is first-rate individual analysts and teams that identify inconsistencies in collected information that others miss. History suggests strongly that only a cadre of professional warning specialists can even fairly consistently provide this kind of defense to analytic organizations by advising, cajoling, prompting, and challenging line analysts stuck using normal theory when exceptional thinking is required.

We agree therefore with the Royal Navy's chief of intelligence during World War II, Admiral John Godfrey, who said, "It is quite useless, and in fact dangerous to employ people of medium intelligence" in intelligence.[40] Godfrey added, "Only men with first class brains should be allowed to touch this stuff. If the right sort of people can't be found, better keep out altogether."[41] The especially important lesson for warning is that only specially selected, capable people are likely to be successful warning analysts. This standard argues strongly against the EAAWA model of strategic warning embedded in the US concept of "anticipatory intelligence."

Our summary assessment is that there are in fact personality types and mental characteristics especially suited—and others not well suited—to the warning function. We here distill the observations of others and add some of our own to generalize about traits of successful strategic warning analysts and senior warning officers as people. These characteristics are especially applicable to the small number of people who are career warning officers:

- Good warning analysts are unusually bright, creative people who are curious and hard working. They develop enough expertise on their subjects to enable them to understand normalcy and change without becoming captives of their subjects. They are willing to learn new things and to move readily to new subjects. They ask "why?" a lot.
- Effective warning analysts must be moderately unorthodox in intellectual outlook—willing to question conventional wisdom and identify different "right" questions without becoming operationally dysfunctional by being excessively confrontational. Virtually all warning analysts work in bureaucracies, and all must communicate with senior decision-makers, meaning they must develop and maintain reputations for imaginative competence, reliability, and trustworthiness.
- They must be able to get along with most people even as they challenge the strongly held views of others.
- They must be modest in career aspirations and in their bureaucratic quest for kudos. Warning is a lonely business. Success comes infrequently and may appear to be a policy success. Warning analysts are well aware of the old intelligence professionals' saying "There are policy successes and intelligence failures." Moreover, warning is rarely a career-enhancing line of work in bureaucracies that use the quantity of published intelligence products as a performance measure because warning "production" should be selective and hence intermittent. Senior leaders often do not welcome threat warnings even if they recognize warnings as appropriate, meaning warning analysts may not receive kudos from senior consumers. Many good American analysts, at least, long have recognized this situation and sought to avoid lengthy assignments to warning positions.[42] Career warning analysts must accept that reality. Such people are rare.

We think a related series of personality characteristics are especially helpful for warning officers who serve rotational assignments in dedicated warning organizations:

- They should have as many of the personal characteristics of curiosity, willingness to question, and so on as do the career warning personnel discussed above.
- As short-timers in warning, they should have experience, be moderately senior, and be genuine experts in some area(s). Expertise helps them on issues they know and gives them insights into the kinds of issues other analysts follow. They then become knowledgeable amateurs who can perform "red team functions."

- They should receive some specialized training in warning methods that they normally would not receive—or need—as line-unit analysts or managers.[43]

We add that warning officers of this sort are likely to be found only if their organizations, meaning the leaders of those organizations, accept warning as an important analytic function. As we have seen, this is not always the case.

Zeira's insights and his own fairly obviously dysfunctional leadership point to a core challenge for intelligence agencies: the selection of leaders of warning analysts also is critically important. The history of US NIO/Ws shows dramatic differences in the approaches of leaders. Some, such as John Bird and Robert Vickers, worked collegially and tried to ensure that the warning function succeeded regardless of which person or organization received kudos—a necessary characteristic of the hybrid model—while other NIO/Ws more aggressively warned, sometimes to the detriment of analytic insight, in ways that occasionally rankled other intelligence officers.

The biographies and practical operational experience of senior warning officers suggest that personality type matters here too. We believe the terms "contrarian" and "collegial" usefully describe two ideal types of warning leadership. In the US context, NIO/Ws Bird and Vickers took seriously their mandates to work closely with fellow NIOs and line analytic units and did so to the maximum extent possible, earning our label "collegial" even though they sometimes disagreed substantively with other analysts. This term does not imply that they simply took votes and passed along consensus judgments. Rather, it means that they sought to involve key intelligence actors in warning to the extent possible and to reach good analytical results in collaborative, non-confrontational ways. They saw their role as trying to produce warning success for the IC as a whole—not for themselves, their offices, or their components.

Contrarians tended to be more willing to make unilateral decisions (themselves as individuals or within their offices), to hold strong views in the face of significant evidence to the contrary, and to revel in being different. They sometimes seem to be happy to be Cassandras. Former Chairman of the NIC John Gannon described one such NIO/W contrarian as "high decibel"—which was not a compliment.[44] As we have argued, possession of different perspectives is an important attribute in a warning officer, but the difference must be supported by evidence and a record of analytical success. Otherwise, the cry wolf syndrome quickly appears and the credibility of warning suffers. While NIO/W David McManus's difference with established views in 1983 generated controversy at the time, his insights were good, and, when emerging facts resolved the issue, personal relationships were not damaged. In contrast, the contrarian perspective can bruise relationships, damaging the ability of warning professionals to warn persuasively in the future. Major General Zeira in 1973 displayed a contrarian perspective that was both analytically incorrect and seriously dysfunctional by quashing alternative views. We believe this perspective affected the performance of NIO/Ws on occasion as well.

Former NIO/W Charlie Allen in 2017 described himself as fitting the contrarian type.[45] He defended his approach but recognized that it often caused problems.[46] While firmly backing the idea of restoring the office of NIO/W, he said the new office should not institutionalize his ways.[47] We concur.

Notes

1. Lowenthal, "Towards a Reasonable Standard," 307.
2. Jervis, *Perception and Misperception*; Jervis, "Hypotheses on Misperception."
3. Heuer, *Psychology of Intelligence Analysis.*
4. Hesketh, *Fortitude,* 4; Kahn, *Hitler's Spies*, 486.
5. Whaley, "Toward a General Theory of Deception," 178–92.
6. Shelton, "Roots of Analytic Failures," 637–55.
7. Authors' discussion with John Gannon, March 16, 2017.
8. Jervis, *Why Intelligence Fails*, 146–50.
9. Ibid.
10. Davis, "Strategic Warning: If Surprise Is Inevitable," 14.
11. Authors' discussion with Gregory Treverton, April 6, 2017.
12. Davis, "Strategic Warning: Intelligence Support," 185.
13. Gentry, "Intelligence of Fear," 11, 13–16.
14. Unclassified video in authors' possession.
15. Budiansky, *Code Warriors*, 62–63.
16. Grabo, *Handbook of Warning Intelligence*, 102–12. See also Smith, "Good Intelligence Analyst," 181–85.
17. McCarthy, "Mission to Warn," 20.
18. Whaley, *Practise to Deceive*, xviii.
19. Ibid., 194–205.
20. Ibid., 205.
21. Latimer, *Deception in War*, 4.
22. Handel, *Perception, Deception and Surprise*, 27–28.
23. Ibid.
24. As quoted in Quiggin, *Seeing the Invisible*, 220.
25. Kent, "Crucial Estimate Relived," 117.
26. May, *Strange Victory*, 240–68.
27. Shalev, *Israel's Intelligence Assessment*, 213–18.
28. Zenko, *Red Team*, 235. See also pp. 11–14.
29. Gilad, *Early Warning*, 247.
30. Ibid., 248.
31. Ibid.
32. Wirtz, "Theory of Surprise," 101–16.
33. Ibid., 112.
34. Mellers et al., "Psychology of Intelligence Analysis."
35. Mandel and Barnes, "Accuracy of Forecasts," 10987.
36. Tetlock and Gardner, *Superforecasting.*
37. McDermott, "Experimental Intelligence," 93–95.
38. Whaley, *Practise to Deceive*, 195.
39. Bar-Joseph, *Watchman Fell Asleep*, 250–51.
40. McIntyre, *Operation Mincemeat*, 29.
41. Ibid., 30.

42. Grabo, "Watch Committee," 373.
43. Thanks to John Gannon for this suggestion.
44. Authors' discussion with John Gannon, March 16, 2017.
45. Gordon discussion with Charlie Allen, March 17, 2017.
46. Ibid.
47. Ibid.

CHAPTER 9

Producers of Warning Intelligence beyond Formal Intelligence Communities

Strategic warning increasingly is produced by organizations other than national intelligence services and defense ministries and is consumed by people other than senior national leaders. This evolution reflects both the need for warning intelligence for new purposes and efforts by new groups to innovate. This chapter briefly discusses some of these actors and ways they are remaking and using variants of warning intelligence. We think some of these techniques may be useful widely, but others are narrowly applicable to specific types of warning issues.

Homeland Security

The rise of violent extremism in recent years has led states to increase intelligence attention to domestic threats. This evolution appreciably extends the functional scope of warning, extends the range of actors involved in warning by including domestically focused police organizations, alters the substance of warning analysis, and complicates the challenge of persuasively communicating warning messages by expanding the number of target audiences.

Domestic terrorism has not belonged within the bailiwick of strategic warning because, in the traditional view, the deaths of small numbers of people, while unfortunate, do not pose major threats to states. The fatalities caused by all terrorist attacks to date in all countries of the world—including the 9/11 attacks that destroyed several large buildings in New York City, damaged the Pentagon, and killed nearly 3,000 people—amount to those of a medium-sized battle in conventional wars. Hence, terrorist attacks historically have been considered tactical events.[1] Even chemical or "dirty bomb" radiological attacks that some terrorist groups are said to be developing capacities to conduct would not pose major threats to states as a whole. Moreover, law enforcement agencies traditionally use intelligence to track down "terrorists" as criminals after they committed crimes and often see intelligence as a means to generate evidence admissible in criminal trials, not to warn about future events. The FBI by many accounts has had a hard time adjusting to a new organizational mandate to anticipate and prevent attacks rather than prosecuting perpetrators of crimes.[2]

But concepts change over time, and intelligence pays more attention to terrorism for at least two major reasons. First, national governments worry about the possibility that non-state actors may acquire WMD that heretofore only states possessed, thereby possibly moving into the strategic warning arena as traditionally defined. Al-Qaeda, for example, long has been said to want to acquire nuclear materials, and the Islamic State began using chemical weapons in 2014. Second, and more important we believe, the concept of "strategic" is changing. Electorates and national leaders see even small terrorist attacks as being very important, meaning national leaders see maintenance of security against terrorist attacks as strategically important to their political careers. In this sense, states' security concerns and hence intelligence priorities have been personalized and politicized to a substantial degree.[3] Consequently, states spend much more time and effort on CT and other domestic security-focused intelligence than they formerly did and try to anticipate, and thereby prevent, new terrorist attacks.

Threats from transnational groups and "lone wolf" attacks inspired by distant groups often have both domestic and international components. Hence, the traditional boundaries between foreign and domestic intelligence and between strategic and tactical intelligence are blurring in ways that complicate the definitional distinction between strategic and tactical warning intelligence—and arguably the conduct of both varieties of warning by confusing jurisdictional boundaries.[4] The United States long has clearly distinguished foreign intelligence information from evidence admissible in criminal trials, adding a major impediment to information sharing that has been ameliorated but not eliminated since 2001. The creation of the National Counterterrorism Center (NCTC) in 2005 complicates matters further by giving a new organization foreign and domestic responsibilities that include traditional intelligence activities, operational oversight, and some CT-related policymaking responsibilities.

The traditional I&W approach—developed to anticipate interstate wars between conventional military forces—is not well suited to handle most CT-related intelligence issues. First, no end-state can easily be identified; a generic worry about terrorism usually is not specific enough to enable generation of specific scenarios and indicators useful for strategic warning. Second, techniques of attack vary dramatically based on several factors—including the nature of the target, attacker assets, and security measures—making it hard to develop scenarios and indicators with broad applicability or permanence. It may, however, be possible to do so for groups that operate regularly or specific types of activities that recur.[5] Third, it is virtually impossible to use a standard I&W method to identify new (or "emerging") terrorist groups or new operating areas or practices; traditional police methods evidently often work better.[6] Intelligence-informed police work expanded sharply after 9/11, however, especially via the "fusion center" concept, which assembles in one place many police and intelligence organizations that share information on persons and groups of interest.[7]

Whereas strategic warning of the sort that concerned Cynthia Grabo was mainly analytical and concerned states, the new homeland security paradigm involves identifying individual people with malicious intentions, meaning it is largely a data-collection-and-assembly challenge. Whereas traditional strategic warning often has a significant mystery component, homeland security intelligence mainly is about solving puzzles—finding individual people at specific places and times, enabling security forces to capture or kill them. The new breed of "targeting analysts" does this work. This challenge involves use of traditional techniques such as link analysis to establish relationships between people and groups as well as use of some new analytical techniques, including "Big Data" searches for relationships or correlations that then can be evaluated using traditional analytic means.[8] Only in this narrowly tactical arena does the critique that the IC failed to "connect the dots" before 9/11 make any sense. One can imagine a detailed study of a group that generates understanding of ideological/theological principles or organizational cultures that can help identify planned attacks or other hostile acts, but most tactical CT warning work involves skills of targeting analysts.

Another fundamental difference between CT-focused warning and traditional strategic warning is the audience of warning messages. Whereas traditional strategic warning intelligence focuses on a relatively few senior national leaders who have considerable freedom in the ways they react to warning messages, in the CT realm a large and diverse audience often includes law enforcement agencies, regional and local political leaders, and the general public.[9] This means senior leaders' flexibility to use warning intelligence may be restricted by domestic political pressures. In the post-9/11 period, several countries developed public-alert warning mechanisms, usually by domestic agencies such as DHS in the United States, that are designed narrowly to communicate terrorism-related threat messages to the public. Such systems also exist in Australia, Belgium, France, Ireland, the Netherlands, and the United Kingdom. These typically have graphic display devices that look a lot like the traditional I&W display system, featuring four or five threat levels and perhaps color coding in the tradition of stoplight charts.

These alert communications mechanisms focus on immediate (tactical) threats and are not, by themselves, warning systems that combine collection and analysis to produce and communicate intelligence. For example, in the United States in the wake of the 9/11 attacks, President George W. Bush signed Homeland Security Presidential Directive 3 on March 12, 2002, creating the Homeland Security Advisory System (HSAS), about which DHS said, "The advisory system will be the foundation for building a comprehensive and effective communications structure for the dissemination of information regarding the risk of terrorist attacks to all levels of government and the American people."[10] The government gave colors to alert levels, which it changed regularly in 2002–6, generating much popular impatience because the thresholds of threat were unclear and none of the heightened threat levels preceded actual attacks, generating the cry wolf syndrome. (It is not apparent that the alerts discouraged planned attacks.) The five threat levels of the HSAS were green (low), blue (guarded), yellow (elevated), orange (high), and red (severe). The threat level then remained constant from 2006 to 2011, when DHS announced a new system, the National Terrorism Advisory System (NTAS), which replaced the previous color-code system.[11]

The NTAS features two levels of "alerts": elevated and imminent. DHS did not issue any alerts under this system. In December 2015, DHS added a new message form—the NTAS "Bulletin"—to provide information to the public. Also in December 2015, DHS Secretary Jeh Johnson ordered another review, which apparently was still going on as President Barack Obama left office. Thus, the United States retains a questionably effective public-alert system that is not a genuine warning system.

Alert systems such as HSAS and NTAS differ markedly from strategic warning systems focused on senior national leaders and pose challenges to intelligence officers. Local leaders typically are less schooled in intelligence practices and capabilities than national leaders, and the public is more ignorant of intelligence matters than leaders and therefore frequently less tolerant of intelligence errors.[12] To protect themselves, intelligence people may be more willing to warn on partial evidence, but they run a risk of more easily generating antipathy to warning or desensitization via the cry wolf syndrome. The public systems have frequently been criticized for several other reasons: their background logic is unclear; they warn excessively and too stridently, as did the Bush administration using HSAS; or they change status levels too infrequently, as Obama's DHS did (perhaps overlearning lessons of the Bush years), making them appear to be unresponsive to changing threats and leading to questions about systems' efficacy.[13] In contrast, the Dutch systems, as discussed in chapter 4, are integrated intelligence and warning systems that target different parts of Dutch society and seem to work fairly well in that they have achieved significant public acceptance. Hence, types of persuasive communication and the politics of warning intelligence in the homeland security arena differ dramatically from those of warning focused on external military threats.[14]

Medical/Health/Biological Warning

Growing concern about health-related terrorism in the form of biological weapons and the emergence of infectious diseases have increased discussion of the intelligence role in monitoring, and warning of, emerging and continuing biological threats.[15] The definitions of such threats remain disputed, however.[16] While a role for traditional foreign intelligence activities is clear when states develop biological weapons and in cases of transnational biological terrorism, intelligence on general health issues is likely to remain secondary to the work of domestic and international public health services. The World Health Organization (WHO) has a widely recognized mandate to warn of the emergence of new pandemic diseases and the re-emergence of known diseases. Unlike traditional intelligence warning entities, the WHO and public health agencies also make health-related policy decisions and act operationally to address threatening situations.[17] When outbreaks occur, members of the medical community also become intelligence "collectors." While in some cases, such as the influenza outbreak of 1918–19 that killed some fifty million people globally, the consequences of pandemics are large, the warning functions are largely tactical in nature.

Medical intelligence, like other varieties of intelligence, can fail. Many in the public health community in 2014 thought the Ebola virus would not be a major epidemic threat. Ebola for decades afflicted parts of equatorial Africa but had not previously appeared in West Africa. Factors unique to West Africa, including a lack of preparation for the outbreak, the spread of the disease to urban areas, and movement of infected people across national borders, exacerbated the crisis.[18] These failures occur even though diseases, unlike states, do not field dedicated D&D efforts.

Security-focused intelligence services seem unlikely ever to be able to match the epidemiological and other scientific/medical skills of health-focused organizations such as the Centers for Disease Control and Prevention or the National Institutes of Health in the United States or the WHO.[19] We expect that public health is best ensured through exchange of information by networks of transparent public health agencies.

Nevertheless, foreign intelligence services can play a role in health-related situations in at least two general situations: (1) identifying the nature and extent of communicable diseases when states seek to hide the nature of a public health problem and (2) tracking and stopping plans for attacks using biological agents against people, crops, and animals. Patrick Walsh suggests that traditional warning methods can be used in some such cases—as by convening red teams to identify plausible biological attack scenarios for which indicators can be developed that in turn help guide collection and analysis.[20] Elizabeth Prescott observes that new diseases such as severe acute respiratory syndrome (SARS) and the threat of biological terrorism suggest a need for a better global disease-monitoring system.[21] Intelligence could play a role in this network, and the persuasive skills of warning organizations might help policymakers respond effectively.

The Ebola outbreak in West Africa became a warning issue for the US Defense Warning Network when President Obama in 2014 ordered US troops to help combat the disease by providing medical infrastructure and transportation for infected persons.[22] Defense warning personnel monitored the disease's ebbs and flows because US troops were susceptible to it. More generally, possible use of US troops in support roles in future outbreaks makes such diseases an ongoing concern at the Pentagon. Whether DoD's small part in struggles against epidemic diseases passes the threshold of strategic is debatable, but its significance to senior US government officials makes it an issue for defense intelligence officials with strategic-level warning responsibilities.

Cyber Warning?

The cyber realm increasingly is both a domain of interstate conflict—in addition to traditional ground, naval, air, and space domains—and an arena of espionage and criminal activity. In the US government, numerous agencies have responsibilities for aspects of these issues under formal US government policy, including Obama's Presidential Policy

Directive 41, "United States Cyber Incident Coordination."[23] Many US efforts are devoted to cyber defense, while others, particularly in DoD and the IC, evidently also have offensive components. A small effort is devoted to warning of cyber-attacks concerning civilian infrastructure.

Is it possible to warn of cyber-attacks? Cyber-threat scenarios require a different set of indicators than do conventional military threat scenarios, and it is not clear that an I&W-like approach makes sense.[24] The details of existing cyber warning efforts are obscure, but cyber warning appears to be the responsibility of several US organizations. In the intelligence realm, the Cyber Threat Intelligence Integration Center (CTIIC)—the newest of four functional "centers" of the ODNI that combine operations, analysis, and policy generation (in some cases) in single organizations—has primary responsibility for cyber-related intelligence. Among its five major responsibilities is ensuring that "indicators of malicious cyber activity and, as appropriate, related threat reporting contained in intelligence channels are downgraded to the lowest classification possible for distribution to both US Government and US private sector entities."[25] This wording suggests a warning function that includes both strategic and tactical warning.

IARPA is conducting a multiyear study known as Cyber-attack Automated Unconventional Sensor Environment (CAUSE), which aims to develop automated methods to "forecast and detect cyber-attacks significantly earlier than existing methods."[26] The project seeks to observe early stages of attacks, such as reconnaissance, planning, and delivery that may enable warning of significant cyber-attacks before they are most damaging.

The DHS conducts cyber warning–related activities. DHS runs the National Infrastructure Coordination Center (NICC), which is an operations center that monitors critical infrastructure of the United States as a whole for the federal government.[27] The NICC is a part of DHS's National Protection and Programs Directorate. The NICC appears to have tactical warning functions only. DHS's National Cyberspace Protection System (NCPS) has a series of technologies, collectively known as EINSTEIN, that include detection, analytics, intrusion prevention, and information sharing.[28] Again, we judge this set of tasks to implicitly include a warning function that mainly is tactical in nature.

Economic Warning

Central banks, financial regulators, and major private-sector economic actors are keenly interested in anticipating financial and other economic crises and opportunities. They variously want to be able to intervene to prevent or mitigate the effects of macroeconomic crises or make money. Some states help their businesses prosper by identifying business opportunities and by stealing or protecting sensitive technologies, for example. They may also warn of aggressive actions by other states, including emerging regulatory regimes, aimed at their government or those of friends or important third parties. Given that regulators' control of the global economy is substantial and in many ways growing, and the fiscal policies of most national governments in different ways have put huge strains on the global economy, key objects of economic warning analysis potentially include government policies as well as the vicissitudes of markets. Per Gregory Treverton, these threats come with and without threateners.

States' intelligence warning organizations variously address such economic issues for several reasons. First, states sometimes try to identify opportunities for attacking other states' economic vulnerabilities with politically motivated sanctions.[29] Some countries' intelligence services, such as those of the United States, emphasize economic issues that affect military capacities; therefore, CIA devoted considerable resources to monitoring and assessing Soviet defense-related economic activity but little to other types of economic information.[30] Unsurprisingly, US economic warning intelligence in total evidently has not performed well, although some former NIO/Ws rate economic warnings among their successes.[31] Other countries place much more emphasis on economic intelligence but often place monitoring operations in policymaking organizations such as finance and foreign ministries. The Soviet Union and its allies used their intelligence services to acquire military-related and other sensitive technologies in the West, thereby helping to thwart the Cold War–era multilateral strategic economic embargo regime known as the Coordinating Committee for Multilateral Export Controls (CoCom).[32]

Second, many states care a good deal about economic issues and focus collection assets on acquiring economic information or technologies from other states and private firms. These activities are parts of normal collection and analytic components of intelligence services, not warning, and defenses against such activities are normally counterintelligence and law enforcement jobs. Countries often mentioned as using intelligence assets to support domestic firms include France and Israel but not the United States, which long has chosen not to support its businesses with economic intelligence.[33]

Third, important technological surprises, which most states care about, are usually best addressed by scientific and technologically focused intelligence units, not warning entities, or better yet commerce ministries, businesses, and research entities, including universities. Warning entities can, however, support and publicize effective warning messages produced by others.

Fourth, and perhaps most important, government fiscal irresponsibility that generates large debt burdens and bizarre, by historical standards, monetary policy is a major cause of the structural component of global economic instability. Intelligence service leaders have no interest in pointing out to their political masters that they are part of the problem; intelligence personnel recognize the political attractions of fiscal irresponsibility and see no reason to alienate their bosses pointlessly. Instead, critiques of excessive deficit spending, structural problems in labor markets caused by government regulations, and the dangers of excessively aggressive monetary policy appear largely in the financial press.

Central banks and international economic organizations such as the International Monetary Fund (IMF) and the World Bank warn of financial panics.[34] Identification of impending crises can serve several policy purposes, including alerting vulnerable governments to their problems and convincing or pressuring them to alter destructive policies or initiate rescue operations, often in the form of emergency loans that contain strings or "conditionality," meaning governments must alter policies in specified ways to gain or retain access to the funds. The IMF, central bankers, and academic macroeconomists have identified conditions that historically seem to have caused financial crises. Hence, they have identified both types of scenarios and associated indicators that are similar to the traditional I&W model.

Federal Reserve Board economists study history, identify factors that significantly affect macroeconomic performance, and develop econometric models that integrate well-specified indicators systematically and create I&W-like scenarios. Important variables include interest rates, general price levels, prices of major items such as housing, and prices of important raw materials such as crude oil. Economists often create "alterative scenarios" generated by differing judgments or assumptions about the values of key indicators. They also study which indicators work best to forecast events of special policy interest, such as recessions.[35] This "normal theory" usually works fine. But sometimes unusual conditions develop, the models do not work well, and "exceptional thinking" comes too late. Such an event happened in the United States in 2008. Recognizing this failure, economists since then have developed other models, some designed specifically for crisis situations.[36]

In 2013, former chairman of the Federal Reserve Alan Greenspan analyzed the failure of the Fed, and economists generally, to anticipate the global financial crisis of 2008, arguing that standard econometric models inadequately accounted for what he called "animal spirits."[37] Borrowing the concept from John Maynard Keynes, Greenspan argued that psychological factors—including ambitions and fears such as risk aversion, preference for receiving economic returns sooner rather than later, and desire for "conspicuous consumption" compared to one's peers ("keeping up with the Joneses")—largely accounted for the crisis.[38] Such herd behavior drives economic booms and busts. Greenspan asserted that such factors are more regular and understandable than many economists believe and suggested they be better integrated into economic models to improve forecasting accuracy. We think these emotional factors also influence political and military decision-making and that warning analysts can learn a lot from behavioral economics.[39]

Earthquake and Volcano Warning

While they are the subjects of physical science and are largely tactical in nature, the processes of scientific warning about earthquakes, tsunamis, and volcanic eruptions bear some resemblance to the typically political-military topics of intelligence services' warnings to national leaders.[40] For geologic events, study of fault zones and volcanoes has produced general understanding of key geophysical factors that produce seismic events. Scientists have produced "indicator lists" of especially diagnostic events. Geologists "collect" relevant information using seismic, Global Positioning System (GPS), and other instruments at carefully selected locations. When indications develop that major seismic events are likely soon, scientific warners recommend that political leaders consider defensive actions that may entail appreciable costs. Scientists rely on their credibility—typically a function of scientific credentials and previous warning successes—to convince politicians that costly actions are immediately warranted. Tangible costs include the financial and economic opportunity costs of evacuations. There are political risks too. Failure to act in response to an accurate warning may cost lives and damage the political careers of leaders who did not act promptly, while what seems to have been an unnecessary evacuation will generate other recriminations.

Geologists often successfully warn in this fashion. For example, geologists of the United States Geological Survey (USGS) persuasively warned of the impending eruption of Mount Pinatubo in the Philippines in 1991, enabling an evacuation that undoubtedly saved many lives.[41] The USGS has formal monitoring and warning systems and partners with other US government agencies and other national governments to share scientific information and warnings about imminent threats. The USGS's Volcano Notification Service alerts interested people (by email) of threatening activity. It posts on its website a color-coded chart showing the activity status of volcanoes in the western United States, including Alaska and Hawaii.[42] These activity-level characterizations—known as "unassigned," "normal," and "elevated"—are similar to I&W military-threat-indicator status levels displayed on stoplight charts.

Business Warning

Commercial firms face considerable uncertainties from changing business environmental factors, competitors, and sometimes damaging attacks by states in the form of regulatory, tax, and other policies. Hence, businesses unsurprisingly have developed intelligence functions internally, private "intelligence agencies" have developed and thrived, colleges and private academies provide training in business intelligence, and a literature on business intelligence emerged in the 1970s and blossomed in the 1980s. Business intelligence efforts have gone in a number of directions. While some are the private equivalent to the current and research analyses of government intelligence services, others are roughly the equivalent of the estimative and warning functions. But private business intelligence entities often also have policy advisory roles that go far beyond the functions of most government intelligence organizations.

One of the earliest and most successful commercial intelligence firms is Oxford Analytica, founded in 1975 and based in Oxford, England. It provides, for paying customers that are private-sector actors and some government agencies, analysis and advisory services.[43] It covers many subjects, including the political and military topics that government warning functions primarily focus on as well as business and societal issues outside normal government purviews. Oxford Analytica has developed a business model that includes an organizational culture, collection and analysis methods, and relationships with clients that differ from many government intelligence services.

Oxford Analytica has four offices: Oxford, New York, Paris, and Tokyo. Its core staff works closely with some 1,400 part-time contributors who are experienced experts in their fields and whose identities are confidential. Oxford Analytica thereby has recruited in the same people both collection and analysis assets who provide information and judgments on proprietary bases. This approach differs dramatically from current practice at US intelligence agencies. Oxford Analytica's full-time staff interacts closely with customers, providing advisory services—that is, advice on policy issues—a role proscribed by the political cultures of most national intelligence services. Its part-time contributors include academics, former senior policymakers, former government regulators, and business people, meaning its employees have credibility with current policymakers who actually are paying customers, thereby tangibly demonstrating their trust. In August 2016, Oxford Analytica had on its board of directors Lord Butler of Brockwell; Sir Colin McColl, former chief of the UK Secret Intelligence Service; former US Senator Bill Bradley; former US Undersecretary of State and first Director of National Intelligence John Negroponte; David Low, a former US NIO for transnational threats; and Robin McConnachie, former advisor to the Bank of England.[44] The "outreach" of Oxford Analytica staffers and directors is an expanded version of one of the responsibilities of national intelligence officers in the US IC.

Oxford Analytica plausibly claims it has built a successful business because its expert analysts have a solid record of successful "predictions." As we have noted, most government intelligence agencies worry about their reputations and resist reporting any kind of analytic performance. Its senior staff identify emerging issues of interest to its customers—a classic warning function. It can call selectively on its network of experts to address emerging issues, meaning it does not have agency and sub-agency stovepipe constraints on deploying the best talent available to each issue it addresses.

Stratfor, founded in 1996 and based in Austin, Texas, does similar work.[45] It focuses on producing accurate forecasts that provide its customers with opportunities. As does Oxford Analytica, Stratfor provides both analyses and advisory services. Like Oxford Analytica, it stresses its record of performance. Eurasia Group, founded in 1999, does similar work.[46] Many others operate similarly.

A core function of private intelligence firms working for private companies is assessing "political risk." Governments sometimes are unpredictable and capricious, and firms typically want to avoid damage from government actions, not engage governments politically. Elections often bring substantial new challenges (and opportunities) in the form of the ideological agendas of winners. Hence, business intelligence firms warn of the implications of possible actions by all governments in the world.

A particularly lucid treatment of the conduct of warning intelligence *within* commercial firms is a book by Benjamin Gilad, a founder and still leader of the Fuld-Gilad-Herring Academy of Competitive Intelligence, based in Boston, Massachusetts.[47] Gilad argues that the warning-related part of business or competitive intelligence, or what he calls "competitive early warning" (CEW), has many features similar to the military threat literature and I&W analytic method discussed above but also some appreciable differences that we believe are noteworthy.[48]

For Gilad, CEW is a strategic function designed to prevent surprises by encouraging chief executive officers (CEOs) to act to fend off risks in four general areas of environmental change: (1) technology, (2) government regulation, (3) social and demographic changes that affect market preferences, and (4) competitors' actions.[49] Companies as whole organizations identify and prioritize risks, develop scenarios about how they could develop, and agree on indicators of them.[50] Gilad writes, "Also known as signposts, indicators are specific questions or targets for collection, assigned to specific employees identified as gateways to this information, that signify a particular scenario is emerging. Indicators can be quantitative or qualitative."[51]

The firm as a whole agrees on indicators in ways similar to the scenario- and indicator-generation processes of the I&W method. This process is dependent on analyst expertise, not simply gathering data or presenting tactical information, which Gilad defines in a way similar to national intelligence agencies' contemporary definition of "current intelligence"; because warning messages must be focused to ensure credibility and relevance, they must be issued intermittently only as needed.[52] Hence, Gilad warns against what has been a recurrent problem for warning in the US IC: devolution of the warning function into current intelligence and of warning units into redundant current intelligence shops focused on "production" as the measure of organizational success. He implies as well that he opposes the EAAWA approach to strategic warning.

Identification of business risks (Gilad also uses the term "uncertainty") is a "seamless" process that links competitive intelligence analysis with strategic planning and senior decision-making to mitigate risks and to identify and exploit opportunities.[53] This process merits several comments. First, CEW is primarily an analytical process; it may sometimes use special insights of business observers, but it does not involve collection or extensive reliance on "data." Gilad argues that data alone—without analysis—are useless.[54] Second, when CEW processes work, there is no gap between intelligence producers and consumers. Gilad rejects the basic Sherman Kent "distance" argument in favor of a system more like Britain's JIC process, which integrates the work of intelligence, policy, and operations personnel. Third, the seamless integration of intelligence with "operators" who do strategic planning is more similar to the activities of tactical military intelligence personnel than to those of strategic warning analysts, even though the intent is strategic in nature. Fourth, the process of generating executive action is critical but may fail because CEOs sometimes are uninterested in acting for reasons similar to those of national political leaders. Gilad therefore makes an argument close to John Bird's philosophy cited in chapter 1: the persuasiveness of a warning message is both essential and often the hardest part of the process.[55]

NGOs' and International Organizations' Warning

Nonviolent non-state actors, especially international organizations such as UN agencies and private NGOs with both humanitarian assistance and advocacy roles, use warning-like methods to alert NGO networks, governments, and UN leaders, directly and indirectly via the networks, of emerging situations they deem undesirable and to urge action.[56] These organizations became much more active in the 1990s as a result of several factors, including humanitarian disasters and growing outrage over events such as the Rwanda genocide in 1994 and the massacre of several thousand Bosnian Muslims near Srebrenica, Bosnia, in July 1995. We anticipate that these organizations will increasingly be both users of warning-like techniques and innovators in developing new and modified such techniques.

For many years, the UN had nothing approximating an intelligence capacity, let alone a warning function.[57] A belief that "intelligence" implied secret activities incompatible with the UN's mission and culture was a major impediment. Cold War tensions and the ability of the rival superpowers to veto Security Council resolutions kept UN field activities to a minimum, limiting needs for tactical intelligence. But with the demise of the USSR and a more cooperative relationship between Washington and Moscow in the 1990s, UN peace operations expanded and with them the need for UN intelligence. The then Secretary-General Boutros Boutros-Ghali observed in 1992 in his widely acclaimed report *An Agenda for Peace: Preventive Diplomacy, Peacemaking and Peace-Keeping* that the UN badly needed to develop an early warning system focused on political instability and emerging conflicts that might require UN intervention.[58] In response, NGOs, international organizations such as the Organization for Economic Cooperation and Development, and UN organizations such as the Department of Political Affairs and the Office for Coordination of Humanitarian Affairs developed early warning mechanisms to identify the onset of political instability.[59]

These efforts help address the UN's chronic need for warning in at least two general arenas. First, the Security Council and the Secretariat, especially, need warning of the emergence of crises so they can act in a timely and effective manner. Second, the large (by Cold War standards) number of UN field missions, especially but not exclusively peace-keeping operations, require intelligence about political-military developments to effectively plan operations and to identify threats to (and occasionally opportunities for) UN personnel and the civilians the peacekeepers are deployed to protect.

The UN has not, however, developed anything close to a strategic warning mechanism like those of most of the states discussed in this book. The primary reason is that most states do not want to give the UN independent intelligence (and military) capabilities, which would give the UN undesirable operational independence, potentially threatening the interests of the permanent five Security Council members, especially. Given the broad membership of the UN and sensitivities about intelligence sources and methods, few states are willing to give the UN sensitive intelligence. And some UN partisans still see the organization as too good to be tarnished by the allegedly dirty business of intelligence.

Nevertheless, the clear needs of UN personnel in the field for information about local events and analysis of the information have led to the creation of limited tactical intelligence capabilities, including warning. The Department of Peacekeeping Operations now has an intelligence analytic capacity and open-source collection means in its Situation Centre.[60] Major UN agencies also have modest information-gathering and analysis units that share information and assessments. And field units now normally have modest collection and analysis capabilities.[61] The result is a UN system that has appreciable intelligence capabilities.[62] These intelligence functions have begun to help improve field operations.

Some NGOs use methodologically sound analytic processes to assess the threats and opportunities they warn about. The Fund for Peace, for example, publishes its annual Fragile States Index, based on a proprietary indicator-based model that contains social, economic, political, and military indicators.[63] A numerical index indicates risk of instability, and the annual report contains color-coded maps and tables that resemble I&W stoplight charts. Other, more ideologically motivated NGOs use social science techniques to rationalize their advocacy.

As discussed in chapter 6 in the content of Genocide Watch's application of the I&W mode, many humanitarian NGOs have developed what amount to indicators of emerging humanitarian crises due to both natural disasters and human conflicts.[64] Recognition of an impending crisis leads NGOs to alert governments and international organizations such as the UN High Commissioner for Refugees and the World Food Programme, for example, performing a warning function by publicizing the crisis, raising public awareness in ways that increase fund raising, and pressuring governments to act.[65] These steps often occur simultaneously, again showing a mode of operation different from that used by the US IC. Genocide Watch is a typical NGO in that it relies on a network of similarly focused NGOs to help gather and assess "intelligence" information, and its network connections help with disseminating warning messages. Targets of warning messages are network partners, senior national government officials, and international organizations such as UN agencies. Many prominent "advocacy NGOs"—NGOs that advocate political programs and policies but do no humanitarian field work, such as Genocide Watch—have good access to senior government officials due mainly to personal contacts of their leaders. Many NGO officials were once in government, and some senior government officials once were NGO staffers, academics, or think tank employees—generating networks useful for effective advocacy of their political agendas. NGOs therefore have wider latitude for advocacy than most government intelligence agencies. Their access to senior decision-makers also often is better because it is based on personal relationships of friendship and trust. Government warning professionals can both learn from the warning-related successes of advocacy NGOs and should always remember that such NGOs are competitors for the time and attention of senior decision-makers.

Notes

1. Luikart and Ang, "Transforming Homeland Security," 69–77.
2. Tromblay, "Threat Review and Prioritization Trap," 762–70; Svendsen, "Federal Bureau of Investigation," 371–97; Zegart, *Spying Blind*.
3. Hulnick, "Indications and Warning," 593–608; Wirtz, "Indications and Warning."
4. Clarke and Eddy, *Warnings*.
5. Sirseloudi, "How to Predict."
6. Dahl, "Plots That Failed," 621–48.
7. Sullivan and Wirtz, "Terrorism Early Warning," 18.
8. Lim, "Big Data and Strategic Intelligence."

9. Treverton, *Intelligence for an Age of Terror*, 187–88.

10. DHS website, https://www.dhs.gov/homeland-security-advisory-system, accessed April 27, 2017.

11. Ibid.

12. Strachan-Morris, "Threat and Risk," 172–86.

13. John Hudson, "Obama's Terrorism Alert System Has Never Issued a Public Warning—Ever," *Foreign Policy*, September 29, 2014, http://foreignpolicy.com/2014/09/29/obamas-terrorism-alert -system-has-never-issued-a-public-warning-ever/.

14. Freedman, "Politics of Warning," 379–418.

15. Walsh, "Managing Emerging Health Security Threats," 359–62; Koblentz, "Biosecurity Reconsidered," 96–132; Wilson, "Signal Recognition," 222–30.

16. Koblentz, "Biosecurity Reconsidered," 104–7.

17. Ibid., 123, 126.

18. "Factors That Contributed to Undetected Spread of the Ebola Virus and Impeded Rapid Containment," WHO, January 2015, http://www.who.int/csr/disease/ebola/one-year-report/factors/en/.

19. Garrett, "Biology's Brave New World," 42–46.

20. Walsh, "Managing Emerging Health Security Threats," 355.

21. Prescott, "SARS," 207–26.

22. Tom Vanden Brook and David Jackson, "More U.S. Troops Being Sent to Battle Ebola," *USA Today*, October 3, 2014, http://www.usatoday.com/story/news/world/2014/10/03/ebola-pentagon /16650617/.

23. For its language, see "Presidential Policy Directive: United States Cyber Incident Coordination," White House, July 26, 2016, https://obamawhitehouse.archives.gov/the-press-office/2016/07/26 /presidential-policy-directive-united-states-cyber-incident.

24. DeMattei, "Developing Strategic Warning Capability," 81–121; Wirtz, "Cyber Pearl Harbor."

25. CTIIC website at https://www.dni.gov/index.php/ctiic-who-we-are.

26. IARPA website at https://www.iarpa.gov/index.php/research-programs/cause.

27. DHS website at https://www.dhs.gov/national-infrastructure-coordinating-center, accessed April 27, 2017.

28. DHS website at https://www.dhs.gov/national-cybersecurity-protection-system-ncps, accessed April 27, 2017.

29. Feaver and Lorber, *Diminishing Returns?*

30. Zelikow, "American Economic Intelligence," 164–77.

31. George and Wirtz, "Warning in Age of Uncertainty," 221–22.

32. Libbey, "CoCom, Comecon," 133–52.

33. Zelikow, "American Economic Intelligence."

34. Sharma, "Asia's Economic Crisis," 27–52.

35. Travis Berge, Nitish Sinha, and Michael Smolyansky, "Which Market Indicators Best Forecast Recessions?," *FEDS Notes*, August 2, 2016, https://www.federalreserve.gov/econresdata/notes/feds-notes /2016/which-market-indicators-best-forecast-recessions-20160802.html.

36. For example, Pablo Guerrón-Quintanay and Molin Zhong, *Macroeconomic Forecasting in Times of Crises*, Finance and Economics Discussion Series (Washington, DC: Federal Reserve Board, 2017), https://www.federalreserve.gov/econresdata/feds/2017/files/2017018pap.pdf.

37. Greenspan, "Never Saw It Coming," 88–96.

38. Ibid., 88–91.

39. See also Akerlof and Shiller, *Animal Spirits*.

40. Bhardwaj, Sharma, and Kumar, "Multiparameter Algorithm," 1242–64.

41. For an account of successful warning of the eruption of Mount Pinatubo in 1991, see "Mt. Pinatubo Explosion at Clark Air Base, Philippines Part 1," YouTube, https://www.youtube.com/watch ?v=SMe0VPQftsc, accessed May 23, 2016.

42. USGS, "Volcano Hazards Program," at http://volcanoes.usgs.gov/index.html; and USGS, "Earthquake Hazards Program," at http://earthquake.usgs.gov/research/earlywarning/, both accessed May 23, 2016.

43. Oxford Analytica website at http://www.oxan.com/, accessed August 26, 2016.

44. Oxford Analytica website at https://www.oxan.com/about/people/international-advisory-board/, accessed August 26, 2016.

45. Stratfor website at https://www.stratfor.com/, accessed August 26, 2016.

46. Eurasia Group's website at http://www.eurasiagroup.net/, accessed February 18, 2017.

47. The academy's website is http://www.academyci.com/mission/, accessed May 9, 2016.

48. Gilad, *Early Warning*. See also Herring, *Measuring Effectiveness of Competitive Intelligence*.

49. Gilad, *Early Warning*, 72–74.

50. For another view of business-focused scenario generation as an analytic technique, see Schwartz, *Art of the Long View*.

51. Gilad, *Early Warning*, 116.

52. Ibid., 127, 142.

53. Ibid., 59–60.

54. Ibid., 19.

55. Ibid., 134.

56. Gentry, "Toward a Theory."

57. Chesterman, "Does the UN Have Intelligence?"

58. Boutros-Ghali, "Agenda for Peace," paras. 26–27.

59. Organisation for Economic Co-operation and Development, *Preventing Violence*; Ekpe, "Intelligence Assets of the United Nations," 384–87.

60. Dorn, "Intelligence at UN Headquarters?"; Johnston, "No Cloak and Dagger Required."

61. Dorn, "Intelligence-Led Peacekeeping"; Rietjens and de Waard, "UN Peacekeeping Intelligence."

62. Zenko and Friedman, "UN Early Warning," 21–37.

63. Fund for Peace, "Fragile States Index 2016," http://library.fundforpeace.org/library/fragilestatesindex-2016.pdf, accessed May 25, 2017.

64. Clarke, "Early Warning Analysis," 71–97; Stanton, "Rwandan Genocide."

65. Gentry, "Toward a Theory."

CHAPTER 10

Dealing with Senior Intelligence Consumers

Richard Betts argues that warning failures usually have one of two causes. Either warning data or assessments do not flow well through the intelligence system, or senior decision-makers reject warning messages that contradict their strategic estimates or assumptions.[1] Most of this book has addressed aspects of the first problem. In this chapter, we consider the second problem and its consequences, and we discuss how intelligence can help senior decision-makers make fewer warning-related mistakes.

Senior national leaders—elected as well as career civilian and military officials—are typically smart and experienced people who have overcome significant challenges to reach positions of significant authority. They have personal, political, and ideological agendas, and they virtually always have constituencies they want to reflect and please. They frequently work hard to convince reluctant audiences to support their programs, sometimes using intelligence selectively for this purpose.[2] Senior political leaders of states and the military leaders of national armed forces are busy people. They tend to have little patience for wide-ranging philosophical discussions and give their intelligence people modest amounts of their time. They are confident people who need to, and like to, act decisively to further their agendas.[3] Senior political leaders therefore like intelligence that supports their programs. Some appreciate warnings that their preferred policies may run into trouble, but others react in a viscerally negative way when intelligence delivers unwelcome messages, attacking messengers as well as messages.[4] In other cases, intelligence has difficulty gaining the attention of senior leaders when their focus lies elsewhere.

Leaders are, therefore, differently inclined than are most intelligence analysts, who self-select into jobs that require at least some reflection about complex issues and are supposed to be, and usually are, politically neutral.[5] John McLaughlin, a longtime CIA analyst and former deputy DCI, argues that these differences amount to a fundamental cultural difference between the worlds of intelligence and policymaking.[6] A key job for intelligence professionals is to make the "worlds" interact in ways that primarily serve leaders but also are mutually beneficial.

Senior political leaders often know a great deal about world affairs, but their knowledge is incomplete and sometimes misleads them when it is applied to new and different situations. Alexander George argues that US presidents have different decision-making styles and they differentially use several techniques to reduce the tensions—the psychological costs—of making difficult decisions.[7] As we have argued, warning is often about suggesting to leaders that they make decisions they would rather not make; hence, understanding how specific leaders respond to stress can be the difference between persuasive and unpersuasive warning. Leaders misperceive world events based on limited information and often see events through their own cultural lenses—that is, they frequently "mirror-image." They make decisions based on an idiosyncratic, personal understanding of history.[8] Foreign policy analysts have documented that leaders frequently use historical analogies to both make decisions and to communicate them to their constituents, often in ways that purposefully or inadvertently misrepresent history or apply it in questionable ways.[9] American political leaders tend to see foreign adversaries as latter-day Hitlers and difficult military situations as Vietnam-like "quagmires," for example.

Psychologists have demonstrated that people, including national political leaders, rely heavily on personal experiences when making decisions and that they value information consistent with their beliefs—not necessarily their desires—more than information inconsistent with their perceptions or assumptions; they thereby demonstrate "confirmation bias." As we saw in chapter 8, this bias also is a major issue for analysts and a vulnerability that deceivers exploit. Confirmation bias in intelligence consumers adds to the challenges of warning specialists in two major ways. First, deceivers target decision-makers, not just intelligence analysts, thereby strengthening and/or distorting their misperceptions and making persuasive communication of warning messages more challenging.[10] Second, selective confirmation biases tend to distort decision-makers' receptivity to intelligence generally. Hence, warning professionals should be especially alert to such biases in the leaders they serve and work to reduce them—a tough task that requires close relationships of mutual trust.

Leaders have many information sources that compete with intelligence, including family, friends, political advisors, activist NGOs, the media, and world leaders with whom they interact personally. These sources sometimes deceive and mislead national leaders to influence national policy decisions in ways that favor their political, ideological, or material interest-based goals. Intelligence is less likely to meaningfully inform decision-makers about controversial, important issues they believe they understand well.[11] Hence, intelligence always, and arguably in the modern wired world increasingly, has significant competitors for the time and attention of key consumers.[12]

Senior leaders' receptivity to intelligence varies widely. McLaughlin, who regularly dealt with consumers and did a rotational assignment to a policy office at the State Department, says that US intelligence consumers come in two varieties: (1) people who know how to interpret and use intelligence and (2) those who do not or will not use intelligence, even if they understand it.[13] The latter include people who distrust or dislike intelligence organizations, making these consumers hard to serve well; it makes good sense for intelligence to avoid if possible reaching that point in intelligence producer-consumer relationships. It also makes sense for intelligence people to educate consumers to the (usually limited) extent possible about the capabilities and limitations of intelligence.[14]

Leaders tend to stick with their decisions once made, even when they do not seem to be going well.[15] Sometimes this makes sense: forecasts sometimes are erroneous, situations change, and the costs of switching policies in midstream may generate perceptions of indecisiveness that are more politically costly than even an obvious policy failure. Senior leaders may develop commitments to even seriously troubled policies that make them resist new warnings. The obvious lesson for intelligence is to know when windows of intelligence opportunity exist, to warn before policy commitments become firm, and to move on to other issues after policymakers understand a situation and have made their policy decisions.

Intelligence people, in turn, seeing only part of the complex world of senior decision-making, are prone to blame senior leaders for not taking their advice and for attributing the irrelevance of their messages to the ineptitude, ideologies, or biases of their consumers. The arrogant view that consumers should take their advice is widespread among American intelligence analysts.[16] The arrogance is particularly incongruous given the IC's cultural legacy of Sherman Kent that values distance between producers and consumers and eschews any direct intelligence role in the making of specific policies.[17] As we write in the first half of Donald Trump's presidency, intelligence producer-consumer relations again are strained. We assign responsibility for the situation to both the White House and the IC but not equally so. Given the asymmetrical relationship between intelligence and presidents, poor presidential treatment of intelligence organizations and people is unwise but legitimate, while politically, ideologically, or bureaucratically motivated rebellion in the bureaucracy (independent of resistance to efforts to politicize intelligence) is always wholly inappropriate.[18]

Even before Trump's 2016 presidential campaign, the IC displayed characteristics that negatively affected general relationships with senior executives, meaning that they also affected the performance of warning intelligence. Robert Jervis, who has been a CIA consultant since 1978, wrote in 2010:

> With some reason, [Republicans] see intelligence analysts as predominantly liberals. Their suspicions that intelligence has sought to thwart and embarrass the administration are usually false, but to the extent that the worldviews of most intelligence officers are different from those of the Republicans, the latter are justified in being skeptical of IC analysis on broad issues. For their part, intelligence analysts, like everyone else, underestimate the degree to which their own interpretations of specific bits of evidence are colored by their general predispositions and so consider the leaders' rejection of their views closed-minded and ideological. Although not all people are equally driven by their theories about the world, there is a degree of legitimacy to the leaders' position that members of the IC often fail to grasp. President Ronald Reagan and his colleagues, including DCI Bill Casey, probably were right to believe that the IC's assessments that the Soviet Union was not supporting terrorism and was not vulnerable to economic

pressures were more a product of the IC's liberal leanings than of the evidence. They therefore felt justified in ignoring the IC when they did not put pressure on it, which in turn led to charges of politicization.[19]

Any such systematic political, ideological, or cultural bias within intelligence services makes the collective intelligence quest for objectivity much more difficult but in different ways when Republicans or Democrats occupy the White House. Republicans will tend not to trust intelligence for the reasons Jervis articulates, and Democrats will get support they want but perhaps not the objective analysis they need.[20] Producer-consumer "distance" and the associated, alleged virtue of "speaking truth to power" enable analysts and analysts' managers to rationalize their own biases as objectivity.[21] Both situations damage the intelligence function.

While we do not favor politicization of any sort by intelligence producers, we suggest that standards of politicization in the warning arena, which explicitly asks policymakers to make decisions that could entail action, are different than in other areas of analysis. If senior leaders have already made policy decisions and invested political and material capital in a policy venture, they are likely to both ignore and resent new information that contradicts earlier information and questions the wisdom of their decisions. Moreover, spurned warnings might damage the warning function's relationship of trust with the leaders, meaning it may be better to do what John Gentry has called "politicization by omission"—decide not to address an otherwise relevant intelligence issue because it will have no policy relevance.[22] DCI Richard Helms took this stance by not sending to President Nixon an assessment that the military incursion into Cambodia Nixon ordered in 1970 was unlikely to be effective after Helms learned that Nixon was firmly committed to the action.[23] Helms was criticized internally at CIA for this "politicization"—we suspect mainly by intelligence people who opposed Nixon's policies—but we understand why he did so and believe that under the circumstances he made a good decision. Details of more recent examples are not in the public domain.[24] These troubles are much less of a problem in systems in which producers and consumers frequently interact, as in the British JIC.

For such reasons, we support the view, often associated with former DCI Robert Gates, that apolitical intelligence should be close to policymaking to ensure its relevance, and we think the strong version of Kent's advocacy of intelligence producer-consumer "distance" has become counterproductive.[25] But we reject the view of some that policy relevance requires an overwhelming focus on current intelligence. The British JIC example illustrates that close intelligence contacts with policy implementers does not necessarily generate appreciable objectivity problems.

Challenges to Good Intelligence Producer-Consumer Relations

There is no shortage of history about relationships—sometimes good, often troubled—between intelligence and senior consumers.[26] There also is an extensive literature on episodes in which senior leaders ignored or rejected intelligence advice—or more generally information from any source—that might have helped prevent policy debacles. We discussed some of them in chapter 2. Recall that Hitler declined to ask his intelligence personnel if Germany could achieve his goals by conquering the USSR just to the Urals, which was his plan; he was supremely confident in his political-military acumen, which at times was quite good. Stalin distrusted both his intelligence officers and their human assets—leaving himself the chief intelligence analyst who consequentially misread Hitler's intentions. And Churchill, while appreciating intelligence, saw British intelligence officers as unable to understand foreign situations that were clear to him, including his view of Hitler's character—leading him to be his own chief analyst much of the time.

In the United States, many anecdotes illustrate the attentiveness of presidents to intelligence in general and of their attitudes, including sometimes obvious biases, toward and about intelligence agencies and specific personnel. These stories are mainly about current intelligence and estimates, but they suggest how presidents and other senior leaders may have regarded warning messages. The short cases that follow suggest some of the decision-making styles intelligence professionals should be able to identify and to serve.

President Franklin Roosevelt used a foreign policymaking style that Alexander George calls the "competitive management model."[27] Roosevelt encouraged competition and conflict among his subordinates and advisors, gave them overlapping responsibilities, and ensured that they did not communicate much among themselves. During World War II, as the nascent IC grew dramatically, Roosevelt showed an unusual preference for HUMINT and covert action but little interest in the SIGINT reporting that was the primary US collection source during the war.[28] These characteristics would have had appreciable ramifications for warning intelligence—if it had existed then. First, warning intelligence would have had to reach the president personally; subordinate decision-makers had much less power than in other administrations. And warning messages would have been much more compelling if warning messages had emphasized HUMINT sources. Knowing these characteristics would have required close observation of the president and a relationship of trust that Roosevelt developed with few of his advisors.

President Harry Truman made decisions as if he were a chairman of the board, Alexander George argues, receiving information from many sources, weighing the arguments, and then making a decision; George calls Truman's style the "formalistic" model.[29] Within the intelligence realm, Truman liked to read raw intelligence reports and to make up his own mind about the meaning of foreign developments.[30] He asked that his daily intelligence reports contain no estimates or forecasts; the Central Intelligence Group in 1946, and then CIA in 1947 and later, responded by creating a daily summary of reporting that covered key issues and eliminated the redundant reports he had been getting.[31] In a survey of US policymakers in the early 1950s, Roger Hilsman found that many also wanted to make their own decisions based on "facts, not analysts' judgment."[32] Presumably warning professionals would have had to be unusually careful to articulate the logic of their reasoning when presenting a warning to Truman and similarly minded senior officials.

President Dwight Eisenhower knew intelligence well. As a career US Army officer and as commander of Allied forces in Europe during World War II, Eisenhower used intelligence a lot. He also commanded NATO forces in Europe in the early Cold War era. As president, he displayed considerable confidence in DCI Allen Dulles, and he directed the CIA to undertake several risky covert actions, including regime-change operations in Iran in 1953 and Guatemala in 1954.[33] Ike's national security decision-making operation—the NSC and its staff—was formal, requiring intelligence support in structured ways. George calls this a different variant of the "formalistic" model.[34] Eisenhower was open to intelligence messages and effectively built intelligence into his foreign policies, sometimes in prominent ways. For example, he personally authorized U-2 flights over the Soviet Union and halted them after Francis Gary Powers was shot down in May 1960—sparking a diplomatic row that led to the cancellation of a planned summit meeting with Soviet leader Nikita Khrushchev.

President John Kennedy's decision-making structure initially included a haphazard reading of intelligence briefs and undisciplined decision-making processes that frustrated his national security advisor, McGeorge Bundy.[35] George calls it the "collegial" model, one Jimmy Carter also used.[36] Kennedy became disenchanted with intelligence after the Bay of Pigs debacle in 1961—a fiasco for which both he and CIA bear significant responsibility.[37] Kennedy eventually began to pay more attention to intelligence, and CIA produced a tailored daily briefing for him called the *President's Intelligence Checklist*.[38] Kennedy used intelligence well during the Cuban Missile Crisis of October 1962 but ignored CIA warnings that the war in Vietnam, to which Kennedy increased American commitments dramatically, was going badly and was not likely to end successfully. The CIA also warned that Vietnam's President Ngo Dinh Diem, whom Kennedy supported, was a problematic leader but that there was no obvious replacement for him.[39] Kennedy administration officials ignored the warning and tacitly approved the November 1963 coup that killed Diem and his brother, precipitating an extended period of political instability in Saigon that appreciably damaged the war effort.

President Lyndon Johnson valued personal relationships and took as personal slights intelligence information and judgments inconsistent with his perceptions and his domestic programs.[40] Johnson disliked both bad news and the people who delivered it.[41] He did not like DCI John McCone (a Kennedy administration appointee and a Republican), gave him little time, and did not appreciate warnings that the war in Vietnam probably would continue to go badly.[42] McCone therefore resigned in April 1965. Johnson replaced him with retired Vice Admiral William Raborn, a fellow Texan with whom he got along well but who knew little about intelligence, and then with Richard Helms, a career intelligence officer he personally liked.[43] He stated his view of intelligence in an earthy comment that Helms overheard at a White House dinner:

> Let me tell you about these intelligence guys. When I was growing up in Texas, we had a cow named Bessie. I'd go out early and milk her. I'd get her in the stanchion, seat myself and squeeze out a pail of fresh milk. One day I'd worked hard and gotten a full pail of milk, but I wasn't paying attention, and old Bessie swung her shit-smeared tail through the bucket of milk. Now, you know that's what these intelligence guys do. You

work hard and get a good program or policy going, and they swing a shit-smeared tail through it.[44]

It seems unlikely that Johnson could have been enamored of an IC committed to objective analysis, but the IC considered "cooking the books" to curry favor with LBJ to be a solution worse than the problem he presented. Instead, intelligence worked for senior officials with access to Johnson. In fact, Secretary of Defense Robert McNamara asked CIA for assessments of the war in Vietnam (including estimates and implicit warning messages) after he became disenchanted with the quality of military intelligence analysis he received, including that from the new DIA, which largely parroted the views of the military command in Saigon.[45] Pessimistic CIA assessments of the situation in Vietnam evidently contributed to McNamara's gradually increasing disenchantment with the war and consequently to Johnson's growing distrust of him. Johnson moved McNamara to the presidency of the World Bank in 1968.

President Richard Nixon had a very different view of intelligence than Johnson had. He particularly disliked the CIA because he regarded it as an institution filled with Ivy League liberals opposed to his agenda, and he believed that US intelligence, especially CIA, had conspired to defeat him in the election of 1960 by alleging a "missile gap" vis-à-vis the Soviet Union, which Senator John Kennedy used against him on the campaign trail.[46] The United States actually then had a better nuclear weapons arsenal than the USSR had. Because Nixon distrusted the CIA and thought its analyses were weak and politically biased, he made many of his own judgments, often in collaboration with National Security Advisor and then Secretary of State Henry Kissinger, who similarly assessed the meaning of world events himself.[47] Both Nixon and Kissinger were extremely well informed about world affairs, making intelligence analysis of all varieties more challenging. In 1969, Nixon asked his *PDB* briefers to give him raw reports because he regarded CIA analysis as virtually worthless.[48] While it is hard to imagine how warning could have altered Nixon's chronically negative view of intelligence, warning officials might have chosen to approach officials who had Nixon's ear.

President Gerald Ford was a US representative for twenty-five years before he became vice president and then president. He was, thus, an experienced leader who understood intelligence well. He did not have Nixon's biases and seems to have been generally receptive to intelligence. His short tenure in office does not contain major warning intelligence events. But Ford did agree in 1976 to a major competition between competing views of the Soviet Union—the so-called Team A / Team B exercise—which had a warning component.[49] A group of outside experts on the Soviet Union and retired senior military officers (Team B) argued that the CIA, and the IC generally, underestimated the Soviet Union's military power and failed to fully appreciate the USSR's hostile intentions. Ford agreed to let the outside team compete against the drafters of the recently completed NIE on Soviet strategic capabilities (Team A). The outcome largely confirmed each group's existing views. The exercise is widely viewed in the IC as having been an unpleasant experience, dampening enthusiasm for the airing of unconventional views. The exercise probably was a net negative for the strategic warning function from an internal IC cultural perspective.

President Jimmy Carter entered office with a dim view of intelligence, especially covert action. He ignored limited (and faulty) intelligence in 1978 about the unfolding revolution in Iran that eventually deposed the shah in early 1979, evidently because for much of 1978 he focused largely on brokering an Egypt-Israel peace deal, which he helped negotiate at Camp David in September 1978.[50] He entered office with high hopes for US-Soviet relations and initially rejected assessments of the Soviet Union that emphasized its dangers to US interests but was shocked when the Soviets invaded Afghanistan in 1979.[51] Thereafter, he reversed his previous aversion to covert action and launched a significant covert action against the Soviet presence in Afghanistan.[52] As noted, Carter also accepted intelligence information suggesting that the Soviets might use force to stop Poland's political liberalization in December 1980 and warned the Kremlin not to intervene. Carter's foreign policy making reflected a mix of his own views, those of influential National Security Advisor Zbigniew Brzezinski, and those of sometimes marginalized Secretary of State Cyrus Vance. Warning officers should have wanted to understand these complex relationships and interact regularly with all three officials.

President Ronald Reagan supported Team B's position in 1976 and supported both a military buildup and increased intelligence capacities that he believed, in the wake of the Vietnam War and Carter's skeptical views of intelligence, had damaged American defenses. As Carter had, Reagan warned Moscow in 1981 about interfering with political reforms in Poland. He named as DCI William Casey, who had served in the OSS during World War II and shared Reagan's views on the USSR. Reagan gave Casey cabinet rank, raising Casey's political profile and making him more of a target for critics of his administration's foreign policies. He was involved in several major controversies, including the Iran-Contra scandal.[53] Casey was a strong supporter of warning, however, enabling NIO/Ws Dave McManus and John Bird fairly direct access to President Reagan—if Casey found their warnings persuasive.

President George H. W. Bush was President Ford's DCI for nearly a year and was Reagan's only vice president. He understood and appreciated intelligence.[54] The Bush years were among the best for intelligence-presidential relations in American history.[55] But even Bush, as we saw in the Yugoslav NIE case study in chapter 2, ignored intelligence at times when other matters carried more weight.

President Bill Clinton cared little for intelligence early in his first term, leading his first DCI, James Woolsey, to resign after two years of frustrating lack of access to the Oval Office.[56] When world events forced Clinton to pay attention to it, he made clear that he wanted only certain messages. In the unpleasant aftermath of the "Black Hawk Down" episode of October 1993 in Mogadishu, Somalia, he told his staff he did not want another military operation in Africa.[57] He therefore discouraged warning of impending genocide in Rwanda in 1994, and subsequent reports of its occurrence, by banning use of the word "genocide" at the White House. Clinton re-emphasized his preference for favorable intelligence by publicly criticizing the IC and NIO for Latin America Brian Latell for intelligence assessments critical of the character of deposed Haitian President Jean-Bertrand Aristide—a favorite of Clinton and his political allies in the Congressional Black Caucus.[58] Once again, a president publicly displayed a lack of receptivity to intelligence and blatantly encouraged intelligence to self-police the content of intelligence messages—a form of politicization the IC finds easy and acceptable, especially in small doses.[59] The IC absorbed Clinton's political use of intelligence but was much less willing to accept policies of Republican Presidents Nixon, Reagan, George W. Bush, and Trump—against whom intelligence professionals leaked and otherwise expressed their unhappiness.[60] This selective self-policing continues to have potentially significant ramifications for the content and timeliness of warning by line units.

President George W. Bush was an enthusiastic consumer of intelligence, evidently at least in part on the advice of his father, and appears generally to have used it well. But Robert Jervis argues that Bush's worldview, including his view of tyrants, predisposed Bush to think of Saddam Hussein as a threat and pushed him toward making war against Saddam's Iraq in 2003.[61] Bush used intelligence on Iraqi weapons of mass destruction for the political purpose of helping rationalize his war to a reluctant public and Congress.[62] The intelligence, as is widely known, was badly flawed by weak collection, analytic methodological errors, and mistaken judgments.[63] Less well known is that much of the IC accurately warned that the war in Iraq would not go smoothly and that post-invasion chaos and an insurgency were likely.[64] Military intelligence, however, thought the war would soon be over without an extended occupation period and with no insurgency. Senior administration officials accepted the military's view, which was consistent with administration hopes but was badly flawed for less understandable reasons than the WMD estimate.[65] Commanding General Tommy Franks retired soon after the "victory," in mid-2003, to write his memoirs.[66]

President Barack Obama was less enthusiastic about intelligence than both Presidents Bush but evidently used it considerably in his decision-making. Obama was the first president to read his *PDB* on an iPad. David Priess reports that DNI Dennis Blair wanted to put more warning intelligence into the *PDB* but Obama asked instead for more current intelligence.[67] Obama made controversial, intelligence-informed foreign policy decisions concerning, for example, significant intervention in Libya in 2011, limited intervention in the Syrian civil war, and negotiations over Iran's nuclear program. As during the Clinton years, these policies did not draw appreciable leaked criticism from the IC.

President Donald Trump is still settling in as we write, but he is off to a controversial start in the intelligence arena. After initially declining daily briefings, by May 2017 he was receiving them from intelligence professionals as well as DNI Dan Coats and D/CIA Mike Pompeo.[68] In late 2017, he called the former agency heads who continued to attack him "political hacks" but expressed satisfaction with the intelligence support he received.[69] Trump, like all presidents, has his own preferences for *PDB* style and content. He reportedly likes short articles with plenty of graphics.[70] His senior advisors attend his briefing and/or get their own—which also is normal.[71]

There is no definitive study on the success rates of leaders as amateur intelligence analysts. But their propensities and analytic skills and biases vary appreciably, presumably helping to account for different records of foreign policy decision-making success.

How Can Intelligence Help Policymakers—and Protect the Producer-Consumer Relationship?

Recognizing these characteristics, a number of intelligence professionals and some decision-makers argue that intelligence officers can take specific measures to help decision-makers make better use of intelligence. These suggestions cover intelligence in general. We believe these points are sometimes applicable to the warning-policy interface as well.

First, warning officers can teach senior consumers about the peculiar aspects of warning analysis. Many intelligence professionals have noted the importance of "educated consumers," and understanding about warning may be more important given, as we have argued repeatedly, the special importance of trust in warning officers' relationships with their primary consumers.[72]

Ambassador Robert Blackwill, who served in senior State Department and NSC staff positions, suggests that intelligence analysts generally, and by extension warning analysts, study government decision-making to identify the "30 or so" key officials in government who influence cabinet-level policymakers and concentrate on understanding their needs.[73] This strategy aims to help inform trusted advisors of the actual senior decision-makers. The positions of these officials may vary from administration to administration.

John McLaughlin argues from personal experience that intelligence can best help policymakers by doing several things. The best way, he argues, is to live and work among them.[74] This means learning how policymakers perceive their problems, avoiding verbose arguments that policymakers have little time or inclination to absorb, avoiding writing irrelevant assessments that make analysts look uninformed or naive, adding to assessments of problems some leverage points or other opportunities for US policy, and educating consumers about the capabilities and limitations of intelligence.[75] Intelligence should flexibly interact with policymakers in ways that make sense to consumers—via written products, briefings, or telephone calls, for example. Intelligence also should help consumers work through the issues and choices they face; this can mean gradually increasing interactions and increasingly specific warnings as events warrant.[76] If intelligence people develop effective relationships with such consumers, they may also learn much from consumers—helping them to do their jobs better.[77]

Policymakers who value their intelligence interlocutors sometimes ask their opinions on complex issues—a sign of the trust that intelligence should strive to earn. Thomas Fingar, for example, recounts how Secretary of State Madeleine Albright once asked his views of a policy issue.[78] After demurring twice on grounds of the intelligence-policy divide, Fingar expressed his assessment after Albright asked again. The secretary then made her own decision. Former NSA and CIA Director General Michael Hayden similarly recounts that he sometimes had "debates" with presidents and vice presidents over the facts and analyses contained in estimates.[79] We believe Fingar and Hayden acted entirely appropriately; indeed, the discussions are evidence of laudable, close, productive relationships with senior intelligence consumers.

In addition to explicitly warning of threats, McLaughlin suggests three conceptual approaches that can help decision-makers work through problems in ways that do not cross the intelligence/policy advocacy divide but help consumers make better decisions. We think these make sense for warning analysts as well:

1. "Test the case." Intelligence can test whether policymakers' beliefs about an issue in fact are accurate. If policymakers are contemplating sanctions against an adversary, intelligence can assess whether the sanctions under consideration are likely to work in the way leaders expect (or hope). If not, the decision-maker can make another choice. The warning analyst can point out mismatches in leaders' perceptions or intentions that may lead to surprise or to opportunities to exploit.
2. "Provide pointers." Intelligence can suggest other arenas in which policy is likely to influence foreign events—as diplomatic tactics or provision of "carrots and sticks." This is the essence of opportunity warning.
3. "Assess underlying forces." Analysts can describe and assess factors affecting the behavior and decision-making of foreign actors, thereby identifying foreign possibilities and constraints useful for consumers. This approach is likely to be useful when complex but potentially important trends are developing. At various stages of this process, warning intelligence can help consumers take preliminary or intermediate steps to defend against, thwart, or exploit unfolding events.[80]

Similarly, Gregory Treverton and Renanah Miles identify four reasons why American policymakers were unreceptive to what was a very accurate NIE 15–90 on the immediate future of Yugoslavia, which we discussed in chapter 2. The nature of the intelligence-policy relationship was an important component of each:

1. Engaging with policymakers and understanding their priorities is critical to ensuring that warning leads to action.
2. Policymakers who are substantive experts may be especially resistant to warning.
3. The likelihood that policymakers will take action based on intelligence warnings increases when such analyses include opportunities.
4. Policymakers read intelligence reports in the context of popular concepts.[81]

Opportunity analyses provide senior decision-makers knowledge and understanding about a current or emerging situation that gives them an opening to make policy decisions that defend or advance national, organizational, or personal interests. It offers ways for decision-makers to exercise initiative, not simply react. Opportunity analyses potentially enable statesmen to use the full spectrum of instruments of national power—including diplomatic, economic, political, and military assets. Such intelligence messages must clearly state situations amenable to external influence and identify prospective ways policymakers can influence persons and situations by specifying potential or likely results—including second-order and tertiary implications—of possible means of influence. Opportunity analysis, or what some call "action" or "implementation" analysis, may enable exploitation of vulnerabilities in targets that damage targets or influence their behavior in ways favorable to them as well as to the exploiting leader.[82] Such analyses can target confirmed enemies, potential adversaries, neutrals, and friends. Targets can be states, NGOs, or individuals. The specific means of effective action implicit or explicit in opportunity warning may range widely, and policymakers always choose which option(s) they take, including a decision to take no action at all. While line analysts can and do provide such analyses, they sometimes do not—leaving the job to warning people who conduct what we call "opportunity warning."

Because such opportunity warning can occur across a wide range of functional areas, there is no single analytic method consistently applicable to opportunity warning that approximates the I&W method's usefulness for threat warning. This is not, however, a problem. It reflects instead the complexity of the world, which requires intelligence officers to be both well connected to policymakers' concerns and imaginative.

And, not least, as Treverton argues in a book on terrorism-related intelligence, analysts who sometimes are quite expert on foreign societies and governments should better study their own government.[83] By so doing, they can learn when and how the government uses intelligence and how intelligence assists decision-making processes. Robert Gates and others have made the same point: there is a need to counter a pernicious side effect of the Kentian doctrine of maintaining a significant producer-consumer divide.

Notes

1. Betts, *Enemies of Intelligence*, 22. See also Roberts and Saldin, "Why Presidents Sometimes Do Not," 779–802.
2. Jervis, "Why Intelligence and Policymakers Clash," 188; Rovner, *Fixing the Facts*.
3. Jervis, "Why Intelligence and Policymakers Clash," 193–95; Treverton, *Intelligence for an Age of Terror*, 170–71.
4. Davis, "Paul Wolfowitz."
5. Ambassador Robert Blackwill, who served in senior policy and intelligence positions, recounts that intelligence analysts sometimes were policy-prescriptive in his presence. See Davis, "Policymaker's Perspective," 12.
6. McLaughlin, "Serving the National Policymaker," 81–84.
7. George, *Presidential Decisionmaking*, 139–48.
8. Neustadt and May, *Thinking in Time*.
9. Khong, *Analogies at War*.
10. Gentry, "Warning Analysis."
11. Jervis, "Why Intelligence and Policymakers Clash," 199.
12. Degaut, "Spies and Policymakers," 509–31.

13. McLaughlin, "Serving the National Policymaker," 82.

14. Wilder, "Educated Consumer," 29–37.

15. Jervis, "Why Intelligence and Policymakers Clash," 191–93.

16. For examples, see Pillar, "Intelligence, Policy"; Miscik, "Intelligence and the Presidency"; Hayden, *Assault on Intelligence*.

17. Davis, "Sherman Kent's Final Thoughts."

18. Gentry, "New Form of Politicization?" For examples of this bias, see Hayden, *Assault on Intelligence*; and Clapper with Brown, *Facts and Fears*.

19. Jervis, "Why Intelligence and Policymakers Clash," 199–200. The authors' impression of the political leaning of US intelligence analysts is consistent with Jervis's view. See Gentry, "New Form of Politicization?"

20. For example, Hayden, *Assault on Intelligence*, 36–37.

21. Jervis, "Why Intelligence and Policymakers Clash," 199–200; Hastedt, "Politics of Intelligence."

22. Gentry, *Lost Promise*, 33.

23. Betts, *Enemies of Intelligence*, 45.

24. Gentry, "Intelligence of Fear," 15.

25. Davis, "Kent-Kendall Debate," 91–103.

26. For example, Gates, "Opportunity Unfulfilled," 17–26.

27. George, *Presidential Decisionmaking*, 149–50.

28. Andrew, *For the President's Eyes Only*, 76–77, 126, 139.

29. George, *Presidential Decisionmaking*, 150–52.

30. Andrew, *For the President's Eyes Only*, 165–66.

31. Kuhns, "Intelligence Failures," 95; Andrew, *For the President's Eyes Only*, 165–66.

32. Hilsman, *Strategic Intelligence and National Decisions*, 46, 49–50.

33. Ibid., 199–256.

34. George, *Presidential Decisionmaking*, 152–54.

35. Andrew, *For the President's Eyes Only*, 258, 262–66.

36. George, *Presidential Decisionmaking*, 157–66.

37. Ibid., 257–306.

38. Priess, *President's Book of Secrets*, 17, 21–22, 32–34.

39. Allen, *None So Blind*, 77, 166–68.

40. Andrew, *For the President's Eyes Only*, 307–49.

41. Ibid., 309, 321, 323, 328.

42. Priess, *President's Book of Secrets*, 42.

43. Rovner, *Fixing the Facts*, 83–86; Andrew, *For the President's Eyes Only*, 321, 324.

44. As quoted in Andrew, *For the President's Eyes Only*, 323.

45. Allen, *None So Blind*, 167–69.

46. Kissinger, *White House Years*, 11, 36.

47. Andrew, *For the President's Eyes Only*, 350–51, 356, 365.

48. Priess, *President's Book of Secrets*, 67.

49. Reich, "Re-examining the Team A–Team B Exercise," 387–403.

50. Jervis, "Why Intelligence and Policymakers Clash," 196.

51. Andrew, *For the President's Eyes Only*, 447–48; Yarhi-Milo, *Knowing the Adversary*, 114–57.

52. Andrew, *For the President's Eyes Only*, 447–48.

53. Persico, *Casey*.

54. Andrew, *For the President's Eyes Only*, 503–36.

55. Priess, *President's Book of Secrets*, 165–90.

56. Ibid., 193–94, 201–4.

57. Power, *"A Problem from Hell,"* 358–64.

58. Jervis, "Why Intelligence and Policymakers Clash," 190; Steven Holmes, "Administration at Odds over Haiti," *New York Times*, October 23, 1993, http://articles.sun-sentinel.com/1993–10–23/news /9310230048_1_aristide-s-return-jean-bertrand-aristide-president-aristide.

59. Gentry, "New Form of Politicization?"

60. Ibid.

61. Jervis, "Why Intelligence and Policymakers Clash," 198.

62. Rovner, *Fixing the Facts*.

63. Jervis, *Why Intelligence Fails*, 123–55.

64. Jervis, "Why Intelligence and Policymakers Clash," 189–90.

65. Senate Select Committee on Intelligence, *Prewar Assessments on Iraq*; Bensahel, "Mission Not Accomplished," 453–74.

66. Franks, *American Soldier*.

67. Priess, *President's Book of Secrets*, 280.

68. Philip Rucker and Ashley Parker, "Serving Intelligence to Trump in Small Bites," *Washington Post*, May 30, 2017.

69. "Russia at Center of Asia Trip," *Express* (Washington), November 13, 2017.

70. Ibid.

71. Ibid.; Priess, *President's Book of Secrets*.

72. Wilder, "Educated Consumer."

73. Davis, "Policymaker's Perspective," 13.

74. McLaughlin, "Serving the National Policymaker," 84.

75. Ibid., 84–85.

76. Ibid., 85–86. See also Wilder, "Educated Consumer."

77. Steinberg, "Policymaker's Perspective," 98.

78. Fingar, *Reducing Uncertainty*, 45–46.

79. Michael V. Hayden, "Trump's Most Important New Partner: The Intelligence Community," *Washington Post*, November 14, 2016.

80. McLaughlin, "Serving the National Policymaker," 86–87.

81. Treverton and Miles, "Unheeded Warning of War," 514–18.

82. Davis, "Strategic Warning: Intelligence Support," 184; Davis, "Kent-Kendall Debate," 100.

83. Treverton, *Intelligence for an Age of Terror*, 170.

CHAPTER 11

Institutional Issues

Over the years, as we discussed in chapter 3, several organizational forms have arisen to perform warning functions. All of them have advantages and limitations or disadvantages due largely to organizational characteristics—how they fit, or not, into the broader institutional contexts, including culture and incentives, of intelligence services. In this chapter, we assess the influence of institutional characteristics on the performance of strategic warning, focusing mainly on the US experience in recent years.

As readers recall, the five basic organizational types we identify are: (1) leaders are their own warning analysts; (2) no distinct warning organization, and every analyst is also a warning analyst, or what we call the EAAWA model; (3) a dedicated organization has exclusive or primary responsibility for warning; (4) a hybrid system in which a small, dedicated warning office led by a senior analyst monitors warning activities of line analytic units and provides warning messages to senior decision-makers; and (5) a whole-of-government approach. As no major country now uses the leader-as-analyst model, we discuss in this chapter institutional characteristics of intelligence services that affect the performance of the last four types—and of strategic warning generally.

Dysfunctional Organizational Cultures and Warning Priorities

Thomas Mahnken argues that the capacity of intelligence agencies to identify emerging weapons and doctrine in foreign military services is influenced appreciably by their own military services, including internal priorities and lessons of internal research efforts, which become part of the organizational cultures of military and intelligence services.[1] He thinks this reflects a form of mirror imaging. We similarly think organizational cultures influence the concept and conduct of strategic warning in intelligence services.[2] Organizational priorities influence the issues that warning entities examine because warning analysts learn from, and to some extent reflect the thinking of, their colleagues in line analytic outfits even if warning analysts are relatively imaginative and independent-minded. Types of leadership, the politicization of intelligence or its absence, and the degree to which consumer interests guide intelligence research programs and/or priorities for current intelligence also potentially affect whether, and if so how, intelligence analysts examine enduring and emerging warning issues.

Two aspects of contemporary US intelligence organizational culture significantly and negatively affect warning: increased intellectual conservatism and the dominant focus on current intelligence. First, intelligence officers have become more intellectually—not politically—conservative in recent decades, especially since the broad attacks on intelligence that accompanied the tactical warning failure of September 2001 and the NIE on Iraqi WMD of 2002. Intelligence people tend to fear controversies that may cause bureaucratic or political problems for agencies and their own careers, especially by angering senior national political leaders or senior intelligence officials wary of angering policymakers.[3] The many manifestations include unwillingness of IC leaders to defend themselves against clearly unjustified criticism.[4]

Perhaps the most blatant example of fear is operations officers' continuing practice of buying insurance to protect themselves against the legal costs of defense should the US government charge that they broke laws by doing work their own government told them to do.[5] This practice started in the 1990s, when the Clinton administration considered charges against CIA officers who dealt with "bad" people, including personnel of foreign governments who allegedly committed human rights violations. For a time, it led to rules that meant, in essence, that it was acceptable to recruit "good" people such as Mother Teresa but not Osama bin Laden's personal aide. In recent years, operations officers have worried that President Barack Obama and his Justice Department, prodded by members of Congress, might charge them over "enhanced interrogation techniques" that the George W. Bush administration ordered and were approved by Justice Department lawyers. For example, Obama in 2009 rejected renewed calls from Senator Patrick Leahy for a "truth commission" to investigate charges that CIA officers tortured prisoners.[6] Intelligence officers would be foolish to think congressional critics will not try again if a new president seems receptive to the idea. Long memories of the partisan politics and ideological battles of Washington on the implications for self-preservation are bureaucratic assets.

While analysts generally do not have to worry about prosecution, they were scrutinized to a historically great extent in the wake of 9/11 and the 2002 Iraqi WMD NIE fiasco. Fear of yet more criticism helps keep analytic messages intellectually conservative because it leads analysts and their managers to wait until situations clarify before they "make the call," to be less definitive about messages, and to add caveats to reduce chances of being wrong, simultaneously reducing chances of being presciently "right" and thereby useful to policymakers.[7] These characteristics inhibit the kind of "leaning forward" that is necessary to give timely warning. The special significance of such fear for warning is that it generates distrust, which damages the mutual understanding, respect, and confidence between intelligence producers and consumers that is essential for effective warning.[8]

The desire to please consumers has led agencies to mainly produce current intelligence. This focus damages the warning function in several ways. It enables managers to avoid warning by claiming (accurately) that senior leaders say they want current intelligence on issues of immediate concern. It emphasizes reporting on the new and recent, shortening time horizons to below that useful for most strategic warning given the need for effective warning to account for time for both decision-making and policy implementation.[9] The bureaucratic incentive structure associated with current intelligence emphasizes "production" numbers, especially articles published in the *PDB*. Built into the personnel management system, this is a powerful incentive. Said Carl Ford, a former CIA analyst and chief of INR:

> If I had to point to one specific problem that explains why we are doing such a bad job on intelligence, it is the almost single minded focus on current reporting. Analysts today are looking at intelligence coming in and then writing what they think about it, but they have no depth of knowledge to determine whether the current intelligence is correct. There are very few people left in the intelligence community who even remember how to do basic research.[10]

Ford estimates that in the thirty-five years before 9/11, the CIA switched from 70 to 80 percent of the analytical workforce conducting long-term research to 90 percent of analysts focused on current reporting.[11] If anything, the 90 percent figure seems to have grown since 2001.

Recent history shows how institutional incentives that primarily value current intelligence damage even excellent organizations with missions other than the production of current intelligence. The CIA's Strategic Assessment Group (SAG) in 2006 was a component of the Office of Transnational Issues (OTI) that had a long-term research focus, developed innovative analytic techniques, interacted widely within the IC and outside government, and by many accounts produced high-quality work.[12] But it produced small numbers of reports. In 2006, the director of OTI abolished the office because it failed to produce enough current intelligence.[13] Given CIA's institutional incentives, the move made good bureaucratic sense; the SAG reduced the OTI's aggregate production, hurting the office director in the ongoing competition with other office directors.

Analysts Cannot All Be Warning Analysts

The "production"-focused incentive structure of most line analytic units means that analysts devote most of their creative energies to what their offices want covered and what is best for their own careers. Therefore, they typically do not display the curious and skeptical outlooks that seasoned warning analysts have.[14] According to Richard Betts, line units mainly employ variants of "normal theory" because it usually meets analytic needs of current intelligence production, while warning requires use of different analytic approaches and "exceptional thinking."[15] Hence, line analysts typically are ill prepared to identify a need to think "exceptionally" or pick effective alternative analytic methods in the rare cases in which they approach a new problem in an unconventional manner. Because it is not required for current intelligence production, they usually do not do what NIO/W Ken Knight required of his staff: prepare indicator lists and collection and communication strategies in advance of crises.[16] This kind of work is not necessary for routine current intelligence production. Because it does not generate "production," incentive structures discourage such work.

An overwhelming focus on current intelligence virtually precludes a healthy strategic warning function unless intelligence leaders establish niches with distinctive incentive systems and performance criteria in which research and warning functions can coexist with current intelligence and analysts can move without personal bureaucratic cost between the functional areas. The IC's leaders show no sign of interest in doing so, however. Indeed, the leaders of IC agencies, including defense agencies, misunderstand the warning function so badly that since the 1950s they periodically have weakened warning organizations by pushing them to become redundant current intelligence units and sometimes abolished them. The DWN, now under similar pressure, may not escape the fate of the Watch Committee in 1973 and the position of the NIO/W in 2011.[17] Evidently in part for similar reasons, the IC's foreign D&D activities also are in substantial decline with no reversal in sight.[18]

Analysts and managers working current intelligence virtually by definition have short time horizons, meaning they are prone to fall victim to the phenomenon of "creeping normalcy"—the slow, evolutionary movement of events, possibly toward a crisis that should be warned about but may escape analyst observation because each individual change is small and does not alone produce a crisis. The colloquial metaphor for this phenomenon is the "boiling frog" fable: a frog in a pot ignores the water's slowly rising temperature until it is too late—it boils to death. Douglas MacEachin calls this phenomenon the "current intelligence trap."[19] Egypt exploited this phenomenon in 1973 by conducting a series of mobilization exercises designed to desensitize Israeli analysts (and political leaders) to the mobilization that preceded the attack of October 1973.[20] Current intelligence analysts also are likely to miss slowly developing issues of warning significance.

The growth in size of the US IC in recent years has added layers of management, increasing the bureaucratic "distance" between analysts and senior consumers and exacerbating the challenge of building and maintaining consumers' trust in warning messages.[21] Managers in recent years are well aware that their people are younger and less experienced than the analyst corps of earlier decades, and managers increasingly have taken roles as intermediaries because, simply put, they do not trust their analysts' judgment in dealing with senior leaders. But senior consumers' confidence in intelligence agencies' middle managers is likely to only partially fill the gap; leaders, like all people, want to know and trust people who ask them to make tough decisions.[22] The IC in the past told the senior analysts of the O/NE, the Watch Committee, NIOs, and now the national intelligence managers (NIMs) to stay in close touch with senior consumers for exactly this reason.[23] Independent of the abilities of analysts, the EAAWA model implicitly rejects this wisdom because line managers retain the role of intermediary between analysts and senior consumers.

We discussed in chapter 8 why virtually all experts on warning believe there are requirements unique to warning that merit specialization and that only certain types of people are good at warning and deception. Most of the US IC rejects these insights, however, and DNI James Clapper consciously wrecked warning structures and damaged the counterdeception elements of the IC. Conscientious line analysts once could grow into decent warning analysts of the moderate EAAWA sort consistent with a hybrid structure because they were able to interact with warning specialists who could mentor them. But Clapper's decision to terminate the position of NIO/W and not replace it with another central warning office means all IC analytic organizations effectively operate strong versions of the EAAWA model, making it much less likely that analysts will become good warning analysts—especially when incentive structures so severely discourage such growth.

Moreover, Clapper's policy has the EAAWA warning structure performing warning analysis in conjunction with the vague concept of "anticipatory intelligence."[24] While the word "warning" appears in IC policy documents defining AI, warning methods as they have been practiced historically are not associated with AI and arguably are discredited. The AI concept is so confused that it muddles the practical meaning of warning. We accept that Clapper did not want senior officials to be surprised, but his system is far better at satisfying officials' desires to avoid surprise by breaking news than by a strategic warning failure.

Michael Handel argues that the practice of deception is a "creative art," not a science or a craft; for that reason, it is hard to teach deception to someone who does not have "an instinct" for it.[25] Handel also says there probably is no way to become good at deception except through experience.[26] Given our belief that deception and warning are similar skills, we take Handel's argument to similarly mean that effective warning requires practice. NIO/W John Bird allowed analysts on his staff some room for error for precisely this reason. The lack of practice that is a core feature of the EAAWA model hampers development of individual and collective warning analytic skills.

The notion that warning can work through normal review and coordination processes similarly is flawed. While observant analysts who mainly work current intelligence sometimes have brought anomalous and noteworthy developments to the attention of their managers as warning (vice current intelligence) issues, line analytic units do not consistently warn persuasively. For example, CIA analyst Joseph Hovey, working in Saigon in late 1967, accurately forecast the purpose and consequences of what we now call the Tet Offensive of January and February 1968.[27] His CIA colleagues and managers found his analysis interesting but unconvincing. He failed to overcome the then general CIA perspective of the situation in Vietnam. Similarly, the Research Department of Israel's AMAN, which had no formal warning element and collectively reviewed assessments in 1973 in a variant of the EAAWA model, quashed minority views of an impending Egyptian attack because the majority held to the Conception. Brigadier General Aryeh Shalev, who headed the Research Department in 1973, later recognized that his procedures should have required reporting of minority judgments, not just the perspective of the majority.[28]

We think the EAAWA system can work if analytic organizations are small, analysts are experts and well respected, managers are insightful and unconstrained by short time horizons, and coordination requirements are modest—none of which consistently exists in today's IC. Richard Betts similarly suggests that a cause of intelligence failure is the "submergence" of critical data "in a viscous bureaucracy."[29]

As recalled, John Gannon as chairman of the NIC sometimes asked NIO/W Robert Vickers to prod line units from their collective comfort zones by asking difficult questions. Not infrequently, Gannon thought, line units needed to be challenged because normal analysis, review, and coordination mechanisms did not always enable organizations to identify or accept important but unconventional insights. For this and other reasons, Gannon told us simply that line analysts "do not perform warning functions."[30]

Thomas Patton in 1959, when the Watch Committee was a dedicated strategic warning office but the IC also asked line analysts to be alert for the emergence of issues of warning significance, suggested some ways to help keep line analysts alert to warning issues. He was, however, plainly skeptical that his proposed methods would work. He suggested that intelligence services could wage a "relentless educational campaign among the body of intelligence personnel. This method faces some of the obstacles of a highway safety campaign or a campaign against sin; and it is possible that in laying extensive general stress on the warning problem that we might overdo it and give rise to unbalanced or unduly alarmist intelligence reporting and estimates."[31]

Because of these concerns, Patton favored the use of an organization specializing in warning. Patton's concerns remain valid, although we see no signs that IC managers now "overdo" such a campaign.

Weak Training of "Warning" Analysts

Having rejected the hybrid model and its implicit judgment that warning requires special skills as well as character traits, the ODNI as lead element of an intelligence confederation leaves the type and quantity of training on warning intelligence to the agencies. If they accepted Michael Handel's arguments about the importance of practicing deception skills, IC agencies could partly offset the lack of analysts' operational practice by offering them more practice in training courses. Jack Davis in 2006 argued similarly for rigorous training in warning "tradecraft," including training on ways to handle uncertainty through complexity theory.[32] But the ODNI and the agencies are moving in the opposite direction: downplaying training in conjunction with their general de-emphasis on the warning and D&D functions. Most agencies provide modest amounts of training on warning to employees generally, with only somewhat more training in specialized warning courses that small numbers of analysts take. Some courses have been abolished, while the duration of most remaining courses has shrunk in recent years.

Most contemporary IC analyst training programs convey basic insights about warning. As of late 2016, the new analyst programs of CIA and DIA—the CIA's Career Analyst Program (CAP) and DIA's similar Professional Analyst Career Education (PACE) program—contain a few hours of instruction on warning.[33] The CAP warning segment lasts one day; it consists of instruction on the I&W method and discussion of case studies of warning failure including the Cuban Missile Crisis, the Yom Kippur War, the Rwandan genocide of 1994, and the Indian nuclear test of 1998, followed by a practical exercise.[34] The CAP's warning segment was three days until 2001, was two days during 2001–11, and has been a single day since 2011.[35] The course tells analysts to be alert for opportunities to conduct opportunity warning but to avoid crossing the line into policy advocacy. Another segment addresses D&D issues.

The DIA has a four-and-a-half-day warning course designed mainly for relatively junior military and civilian DoD analysts. This course, also taught in a mobile mode at bases in the United States and abroad, is the main training course for warning analysts at the combatant commands and some other military commands. Few national-level strategic analysts take it. The course was two weeks long in the late 1980s; the second week, now eliminated, consisted of field trips to watch centers in the Washington area.[36]

The FBI's three-day course is called Effective Warning Intelligence Analysis.[37] It outlines the difference between warning and other types of intelligence analysis, emphasizes the effective communication of warning intelligence analysis from producers to consumers, and covers theories of surprise attack. Combining lectures, discussion, and case studies, the course critiques warning intelligence successes and failures. It is typically conducted twice per fiscal year at the Intelligence and Investigative Training Center at the FBI Academy in Quantico, Virginia, and is taught by personnel of the center's Advanced Intelligence Training Unit. This course is an elective in the Intelligence Community Advanced Analyst Program.

From 2006 to 2013, the NIC sponsored a three-day course on warning, open to analysts throughout the IC, which was called Warning Tools, Tradecraft, and Practice.[38] It no longer exists.

Predecessor organizations of the current National Intelligence University (NIU), such as the Joint Military Intelligence College (JMIC), for many years had warning courses of various sorts in their masters and undergraduate programs. These changed focus and names over the years, but warning often was a core, required course. This requirement ended in 2006. Cynthia Grabo's *Anticipating Surprise* still is assigned reading in general analysis courses at NIU.

The CIA and the Foreign Denial and Deception Center played a prominent role in encouraging training and education on D&D and counter-deception techniques throughout the IC.[39] The CIA in 1983 sponsored a course called Deception Analysis that was developed and for several years taught by Richards Heuer.[40] The course was a week long and was offered four times per year. Heuer recounts that he focused on two topics: (1) the

"Analysis of Competing Hypotheses" (ACH) analytic approach, which he later made into a prominent SAT, and (2) what he called the "Deception Hypothesis."[41] Heuer taught that ACH, by evaluating all possible hypotheses to explain phenomena, could identify the presence of deception. His "deception checklist," derived from the Deception Hypothesis, could then help analysts identify details of deception.[42]

Later, the FDDC sponsored the Denial and Deception Advanced Studies Program (DDASP), which was embedded in the academic program of NIU from 2002 to 2015. At its peak, the DDASP offered an extensive certificate program at night and during the day with a throughput of sixty-five students per year.[43] It graduated over 750 students from IC and other US government agencies during its run. FDDC personnel also taught one of the courses of NIU's warning certificate program in 2013–15. Since 2015, NIU taught D&D courses with newly hired personnel who were initially inexperienced with D&D issues.[44]

Even more troublesome is the limited exposure analysts get to the different kind of thinking important for warning versus current intelligence.[45] The IC as a whole, with the exception of State/INR, has a recruiting and training philosophy that focuses on recruiting primarily young, relatively inexperienced, and moderately educated people whom they train in agency ways to make them proficient in the types of analysis currently in vogue— mainly current intelligence. Partly to respond to the mandate of the Intelligence Reform and Terrorism Prevention Act of 2004 to improve analytic tradecraft, training relies heavily on SATs that have not been systematically demonstrated to improve analysis in general— let alone warning analysis.[46] This amounts to IC doctrinal imposition of a form of normal theory, per Betts, that even strong proponents recognize is but an aid to the real work of analysis: thinking. Indeed, this training does not reach the level of theory; it teaches acceptable analytic processes. Moreover, Welton Chang and Philip Tetlock argue that IC training programs ignore analyst overconfidence and do not emphasize generating good judgment.[47] Tetlock and his colleagues also argue that SATs encourage ideological bias.[48] These are huge deficiencies for any intelligence analyst but are especially debilitating for a strategic warning analyst.

One result unsurprisingly is continuing, widely recognized problems with analysis in general, which DoD is trying to redress by developing accreditation programs of the sort common in technical professions and some blue-collar vocations.[49] This "professionalization" effort, too, seems certain to fail in its primary purpose and cannot possibly produce good warning analysts—a different and harder job.

Despite the generally weak state of warning in the IC, DIA in 2012 reconfirmed the DIA training course noted above and directed the NIU to establish a strategic warning certificate program. The program began in August 2013. A sequence of four courses, the program is designed to provide graduate-level education on warning-related subjects, including many discussed in this book, to line analysts who would inject expertise into warning processes.[50] The four courses span nearly a year and cover, in sequence, aspects of the *history of strategic warning* in the United States and elsewhere; *challenges in strategic warning*, including globalization, cyber threats, terrorism, proliferation of weapons of mass destruction, intelligence collection in support of warning analysis, and intelligence collaboration, both international and interagency; *warning theory and analytic methods*; and *D&D*, including counter-deception techniques. The second and third courses feature expert guest speakers from within the IC and outside of government. The program is open to personnel from all IC agencies, some other parts of the US government, and some closely allied governments. The DWN grants graduates of this program certification as "warning advocates" within the DWN. We believe the NIU program is the only substantial educational (as opposed to training) program on strategic warning anywhere in the world.

The Denigration of Expertise

Warning is damaged by the IC's denigration of expertise, which directly reflects its emphasis on current intelligence.[51] While deep and broad skills are characteristic of good strategic warning specialists, effective strategic warning needs all analysts to have excellent educations and extensive experience because dedicated warning analysts cannot know everything and must rely on the expertise of specialists in line analytic units. Warning needs IC agencies to conduct the long-term research that builds the intellectual capital of individuals and the collective knowledge, insight, and wisdom of organizations. But "current intelligence" as now constituted requires comparatively little expertise, focuses on glib summaries, and has short time horizons. The personnel-management philosophy of hiring mainly modestly educated, inexperienced people means most IC agencies acquire little genuine expertise from their recruits. The common practice of rotating analysts frequently to new assignments effectively discards whatever expertise they develop. This practice is incompatible with the requirements of all varieties of sound analysis, including strategic warning. It also ignores policy directing agencies to develop substantive expertise.[52]

Substantive expertise is critical to strategic warning analysts. Analysts need expertise to adequately monitor enduring warning problems for important changes, and they need to have enough expertise, experience, and good judgment to identify and assess anomalies that may become warning issues of the future. The historical record suggests strongly that this combination of abilities is best assembled in a specialized warning unit that has both experts on high-priority, enduring warning issues and experienced "generalists" who usually are in fact experts in other areas and who have wide-ranging responsibilities and provide "outside" perspectives that effectively challenge specialists on specific issues by asking relevant questions. The outside perspective, if well-informed, complements the deep expertise that line analysts may have and helps prevent emergence of the "paradox of expertise"—the phenomenon in which genuine experts sometimes become so committed to theories and experiences that have served them well in the past that they do not readily recognize or accept changes in situations. In the IC, this sometimes translates into an organizational perspective on an issue—one that groups of specialists collectively accept. Expertise also is a critical component of the credibility essential to persuading skeptical decision-makers of the efficacy of a painful warning message.[53]

Expertise about warning methods and the derivation and use of lessons of past warning successes and failures depends on the existence of an established, durable warning structure that gives dedicated warning analysts freedom to research and otherwise explore potential warning issues. Warning also needs an appreciable D&D study program that can develop new counter-deception techniques. Watch standers monitoring established indicators of enduring warning problems can be reasonably bright generalists, but they cannot make the important decisions about the meaning of new and concerning but ambiguous information, and they cannot design indicator lists or consistently identify emerging issues.[54]

IC policies therefore are major causes of the serious challenges that confront many aspects of intelligence, including warning: the propensity of intelligence to serve immediate consumer wants, to focus on the short-term and current intelligence, and to denigrate the long-term research that builds the intellectual capital of individuals and the collective knowledge, insight, and wisdom of agencies. This situation is, we think, largely a legacy of the dual traumas of the 9/11 attacks and the 2002 Iraqi WMD NIE fiasco.[55] But it also stems from the de facto reforms that the then DCI Robert Gates initiated in 1991–93 to make intelligence more relevant to consumers, or more "actionable." These efforts made sense at the time but morphed in the mid and late 1990s in counterproductive ways that were obvious in the late 1990s but since have become more entrenched.[56] Retired CIA analyst and chairman of the NIC Fritz Ermarth rued the consequences in 1999 in the context of weakened IC analysis of Russian affairs:

> Intelligence analysis brought its own vulnerabilities to the table, first in the form of a post–Cold War agenda that has become ever more operational (i.e., supportive of daily business) rather than focusing on understanding the big picture; and second, a management code that prizes above all serving—which can easily degenerate into pleasing—the customer. Our policymakers did not much want, and our intelligence analysts had little incentive to provide, a big-picture, long-term assessment of Russian realities. They mainly wanted to get through the next Gore-Chernomyrdin meeting, or the next quarrel about Russian missile dealings with Iran.[57]

Rigid Priority Systems Hamper Warning

The relatively rigid collection-priority identification and tasking system of the IC hinders strategic warning. For many years, the United States relied primarily on its intelligence analysts' close relationships with consumers to identify consumer needs. But in 1995, President Bill Clinton ordered the IC in Presidential Decision Directive 35 to focus on a small number of issues, which the Clinton administration did not update.[58] President George W. Bush established the National Intelligence Priorities Framework (NIPF) process in February 2003 after the weaknesses of Clinton's system became obvious.[59] It remains in effect.

The problem for warning of systems like the NIPF is that most collection and analytic priorities are identified by senior consumers who virtually by definition identify issues that worry them now, while the primary purpose of strategic warning is to identify issues that decision-makers do not yet know will one day concern them greatly.[60] The NIPF and the British National Intelligence Requirement and Priorities Paper update collection requirements quarterly and annually, respectively, which may be too infrequently for rapidly emerging warning issues.[61] The NIPF gives some flexibility to IC agencies to devote some collection assets to low-priority issues that seem to warrant investigation if managers choose to exercise the responsibility, which seems to occur infrequently given leaders' focus on the here-and-now and winning kudos from senior consumers—and the consequent "tyranny of current intelligence." British collectors have it worse; the United Kingdom's collection agencies collect only what they are told to collect. These practices mean that collection invariably has gaps that impede warning analysts' research and monitoring activities. Warning could effectively use the NIPF's limited flexibility if it had bureaucratic clout to influence collection requirements, but the EAAWA model gives warning no institutional home and no distinct bureaucratic power.

Organizational Ownership of Warning Problems

Intelligence services are bureaucracies that have bureaucratic needs—including possession of responsibilities that rationalize their existence. Especially but not exclusively in the DoD, sub-organizations of intelligence services "own" warning problems. In DWN member organizations, this sometimes works well, especially because organizations with a direct interest in an issue—for example, US European Command (EUCOM) regarding instability in Ukraine—are vigilant and knowledgeable on the subject. Should there be heightened (reduced) tensions, EUCOM may raise (lower) its alert status(es). Warning issues also are discussed in "community of interest" meetings, which help sensitize IC agencies to emerging issues that may also affect their equities.

But there are serious drawbacks to this system. First, "ownership" creates a potential for parochialism and politicization. The "possessing" organization or analyst may be under considerable pressure from a military commander or manager to see a situation in a specific way, which may reflect good judgment but can also reflect the personal wishes of senior officers or help to justify the perceived needs of organizations.[62] A heightened threat status, for example, may be useful for helping justify a request for a larger budget. This recurrent practice has led some observers to suggest that consumers should distrust intelligence from organizations with parochial interests in the implications of their analyses—opposite the demonstrated need for mutual trust between warning intelligence people and the decision-makers they serve.[63]

Second, possessing organizations may be concerned with only part of a problem—the piece defined by its own organizational responsibilities, not the big picture as the White

House or intelligence target sees their situations. Hypothetically, for example, EUCOM's worries about Ukraine may have a Russian angle. If so, EUCOM would tend to see Russian actions from a European perspective. But Russia is a large country with global interests, and Russian actions in Ukraine may be influenced by policy concerns elsewhere—such as vis-à-vis China or the United States. Hence, EUCOM analysts may see European trees but miss the global forest, while other regionally focused military organizations see other parts of the whole. While published examples of this phenomenon are rare, one does appear in the literature on the Cuban Missile Crisis. This US-Soviet crisis actually was about several things at once, including Cuba's defense against the attacks President John Kennedy directed against the country and Fidel Castro personally, the Soviet-American nuclear balance, Nikita Khrushchev's views of the new, young American president as a leader, and ongoing great-power tensions over Berlin. Yet in the US IC, analysts tended to specialize in one of these aspects only and surely did not examine the weaknesses of their own president, meaning that even the Board of National Estimates, which wrote four national estimates on tensions over Cuba in 1962, did not fully integrate the pieces into an assessment of the whole package of reasons why the Soviets took the risk of employing nuclear-tipped missiles in Cuba.[64] Under the EAAWA model, analysts with narrow analytic responsibilities "own" slivers of a warning problem, making the problem worse. The fact that the IC consists of seventeen major independent organizations with sometimes clear jurisdictional boundaries exacerbates this problem.

Third, warning issues normally are addressed within the standard bureaucratic processes, which impose "coordination" or "collaboration" requirements within and among intelligence units.[65] Even though agencies sometimes ignore opposing views of other agencies, these requirements frequently lead to compromises in language that damage the clarity of messages, producing the "lowest common denominator syndrome." This issue long has afflicted national intelligence estimates, but it is especially troublesome in the warning arena because of the need for sharp and persuasive messages to convince policymakers to make difficult decisions under conditions of considerable uncertainty. The complex mechanisms of coordination processes inherently damage the timeliness of warning messages even if there are no substantive disagreements among agencies.

Coordination requirements grew in the post-9/11 period because Congress demanded, and successive DNIs have tried to produce, intelligence that is "integrated" across the IC. This means, in American bureaucratese, that while single agencies often draft reports and can publish them on their own, IC-wide coordination (or "collaboration") is required to get major papers, especially *PDB* articles, to publication. As Roger George and others note, "feeding the beast" of the *PDB* has become an enormous drain on IC resources given the new coordination rules.[66] Normal IC coordination processes, exacerbated by post-9/11 "reforms," thereby contribute significantly to warning failures.[67]

Fourth, military commands can simply ignore warning if they want to do so, leaving gaps in coverage. Two major military combatant commands periodically in the past have done exactly that.[68] Commands cannot appropriate issues other commands refuse to address.

Fifth, the ownership model means that analysts from outside the "owning" organization have no formal access to debates about the warning problem. This means that the pool of minds that potentially can address any issue is limited for bureaucratic reasons. If there is any lesson in the history of warning, it is that normally one analyst (or a minority of analysts) accurately assesses an emerging issue but is over-ruled by the majority or by senior officials. The ownership model dramatically increases risks that this phenomenon will recur.

Warning Is about Threats *and* Opportunities

Effective warning cannot be about just military threats. Warning must address a broad range of threats and offer policy opportunities to senior decision-makers if it is to survive as a distinct intelligence function. Given the precarious institutional status of warning, kudos from happy senior officials are essential to the bureaucratic health of the warning function.

Opportunities come in many varieties and are, as James Steinberg notes, important to policymakers.[69] Understanding this, former NIO for Latin America Randy Pherson tried to convey to his consumers a balanced mix of threat and opportunity warning messages.[70] He saw opportunity messages as an antidote to negative policymaker reactions to warning personnel who only dropped "cow pies" on decision-makers. This 1:1 ratio reflects an unusually strong focus on opportunities, but even an occasional identification of opportunities helps keep analysts "in the room" when national policies are made. Moreover, threats and opportunities are sometimes related. By identifying early an impending threat, decision-makers can act preemptively in potentially many ways. We believe a primary reason why strategic warning repeatedly has been downgraded during periods of apparent international calm is that military intelligence organizations, especially, have been unwilling to provide opportunity warning, making them seem unhelpful and therefore superfluous.

Major threats occur infrequently, especially during periods of relative calm in international relations, such as the early 1970s détente era and immediately after the collapse of the Soviet Union. Bureaucracies do not typically have the luxury of claiming that they will one day again be useful and deserve preservation for that possible occurrence. In contrast, opportunity-related analysis is always relevant, helping to support decision-makers and earning a clientele who can help protect the warning function. We hesitate to argue in small-minded bureaucratic terms, but the warning function lives in a world in which small-minded bureaucratic concerns sometimes are powerful. Bureaucratic enemies of warning have recurrently used periods of global calm to gut the function, requiring rebuilding thereafter—a problem because some organizational continuity is important to maintain proficiency in specialized warning skills. Even a residual warning office can serve as "seed corn" to expand a capable warning function as changing times may require. While the British JIC may have to rely on amateur "experts" as crises arise, the much larger US IC can, if it wants, easily dedicate a modest number of people to specialty research and writing on strategic warning issues. Jack Davis proposed as much in 2003, without effect.[71]

The IC should regard the warning function as a kind of insurance policy. Insurance offers protection against catastrophe. But insured people do not mind if they have no need to make a claim; their premium payment is not wasted. The return on this kind of insurance "investment" includes the positive returns from opportunity warning and the cost savings derived from effective threat warning.

Defense Organizations Cannot Adequately Address Nonthreat Warning Issues

Warning organizations exist mainly in military and defense ministerial organizations for the obvious reason that warning has long been a security threat–focused activity. But the expanding scope and complexity of warning issues in recent decades increasingly include nonmilitary threats and opportunity warning. This is true even though the US military has conducted a larger range of missions in recent years, including disaster relief and other humanitarian assistance missions, and has long had noncombat missions such as training and noncombatant evacuation responsibilities. Given the nature of defense organizations, it is unreasonable for several reasons to expect defense agencies alone to address the broadening scope of warning effectively.

First, military organizations focus on military threats for reasons of national mission statements, of defense budgets, of popular expectations, and of internal organizational cultures that focus on fighting conventional wars.[72] National leaders direct them to focus primarily on military aspects of national defense. Even national militaries that embrace broader national goals—such as the Canadian and Swedish emphasis in recent years on peacekeeping missions—see themselves as users of intelligence in military-related roles. Most military intelligence personnel and institutions therefore are close to hard-wired to think in military terms. As we have seen, the DWN focuses primarily on defense issues, even though it recognizes nonmilitary threat and opportunity warning as parts of its mission and does it to some extent. More narrowly, the Australian Defence Warning System lists its consumers as consisting only of Defence Ministry decision-makers.[73]

People join armed forces as uniformed members and defense ministries as civilians because they tend to think in defense-related ways, and their organizations generate policy and incentive systems that foster such thinking. Even if the military chooses to expand the scope of the warning issues it covers to include, for example, infectious diseases after the US military supported international health organizations in West Africa in 2014–15 after the outbreak of Ebola there, such priorities are unlikely to last, and military intelligence people understand that such work is peripheral to core organizational missions. Specialization in such areas therefore is unlikely to be career enhancing for themselves personally. Hence, the cultures of military- and civilian-run defense intelligence organizations discourage the broader warning mission.

Moreover, military organizations as a general rule are not equipped intellectually to address nondefense issues such as financial panics and emerging epidemics. Military organizations do not inherently have the expertise needed to perform the detailed studies of economic, medical, or domestic security–related warning issues. This work is best left to organizations such as the Treasury Department for financial issues, to the Centers for Disease Control and Prevention for epidemics, and to the FBI for domestic security, for example. Lack of expertise notwithstanding, military organizations tend to be aggressive bureaucratic infighters, meaning they may claim bureaucratic ownership of issues that affect their people or resources even if they are not best equipped to handle the issues.

The IC cannot count on even the relatively robust DoD effort to conduct warning on all issues of importance to the country. Civilian agencies must contribute too.

The Learning Capacity of Intelligence Services

Intelligence cannot improve if it does not learn from its mistakes and successes.[74] Internal IC studies of both are rare, however. Failures attract far more attention because they often are obvious. Sometimes, too, alleged failures actually are not failures at all.[75] Successes get less attention because they are less obvious, do not attract external criticism, are expected, and in fact do often occur and therefore do not seem to be worth studying. When success occurs fortuitously despite collection gaps and analytic mistakes, there are few incentives to air shortcomings. IC agencies regularly reorganize, but they rarely reexamine core processes.

As we have discussed in many ways, the general causes of failures, if not their specifics, recur. Intelligence services know this, yet they do not publicly or internally discuss much why failures occurred.[76] Broad warning-focused assessments have been few and far between. The 1978 HPSCI study recommending creation of the NIO/W position did in fact lead to reforms, but DCI Gates's 1992 study,[77] a CIA inspector general's assessment in 2002,[78] and DNI Clapper's 2014 study seem to have made little difference. Clapper's "system" of distributing warning responsibilities among the NIMs and enabling agencies to adopt variants of the EAAWA model as they see fit remains in effect. At the same time, readers will recall, Clapper also gutted the D&D function. For the many reasons we note above, we regard these decisions as mistakes.

Among American intelligence agencies, CIA does the most such self-assessment.[79] The CIA's Center for the Study of Intelligence long has conducted some such studies and publishes them internally for US government people with security clearances. The Kent School also does some such work. And the CIA's journal *Studies in Intelligence* publishes insights from current intelligence (mainly CIA) people and retirees, as well as some outsiders.

Other parts of the CIA also assess themselves periodically. Perhaps the two best public such assessments are in Robert Jervis's *Why Intelligence Fails*.[80] Jervis has become one of the most insightful academic students of intelligence, due in part to his long association with the CIA as a consultant. In 1978, the leader of CIA's analysis directorate commissioned him to study the analytic component of the agency's failure to forecast the Iranian

Revolution of 1978–79. Later he reviewed the CIA's work on the 2002 Iraqi WMD NIE. Declassified versions of his reports on those two analytical failures, the first a warning failure, make up the bulk of *Why Intelligence Fails*; the rest contains his contemporary observations and lessons learned.

Other IC elements conduct such assessments much less frequently. Despite the long-standing DoD concern about warning, we do not know of any significant DoD study of the strategic warning function. One additional clear reason for the dearth of study of the warning function is the decline in interest about warning after the demise of the Soviet Union and evaporation of Warsaw Pact military threat that was the focus of so much of the warning effort in the West for four decades. There seems to some to be little reason to study a nearly defunct analytic specialty.

Politically mandated failure investigations are by definition political processes, and they sometimes serve political purposes more than learning processes. For example, the 9/11 Commission in the United States was a politically motivated commission whose report has drawn sharp criticism for its biases and factual errors.[81]

A primary reason the IC does so little self-assessment is that its findings can be, and have been, used against it by its enemies within government. While the most powerful such enemies are on the congressional intelligence oversight committees, there have been executive branch enemies on occasion too. One of the most promising exercises in self-assessment, a series of studies conducted in 1973–75 by the Product Review Division of Intelligence Community Staff—the DCI's office in charge of IC-wide issues—ended in 1975 after finishing postmortem assessments of seven failures when the committee of the House of Representatives established to investigate perceived CIA misdeeds, chaired by Rep. Otis Pike, became belligerently critical and used the IC's work against it.[82] Completed reports assessed the IC's performance concerning then-recent perceived failures: (1) the Arab-Israeli war of 1973, (2) the 1973 coup against Chilean President Salvador Allende, (3) the 1974 Indian nuclear explosion, (4) Israeli operations on the West Bank in October 1973, (5) the Cyprus crisis of 1974, (6) Egyptian military capabilities in 1975, the subject of an NIE, and (7) the *Mayaguez* incident of May 1975, in which Cambodian troops captured an American merchant ship, and the US military effort to free the ship and crew led to many American deaths. Of these topics 1, 3, and 5 had aspects of warning failures. Richard Shryock, a CIA official involved in these reviews, believes that even the truncated IC effort helped improve communication between IC agencies' operations centers.[83] Shryock reports that the Product Review Division conducted only one study of an intelligence "success," which he did not identify but said was the only study of a success any senior policymaker ever requested.[84]

Amy Zegart attributes the 9/11 failure to US intelligence agencies' operational learning failures caused largely by organizational cultural dysfunctions.[85] We agree that organizational cultures specialized to protect bureaucracies can produce chronic operational failures—and inhibit learning and adaptation. The IC's failure to establish a coherent strategic warning complex is another such problem.

But while criticism sometimes hurts egos and careers, the IC has few institutional incentives to improve. It is relatively easy to absorb modest criticisms, and mediocre performance has the virtue of inducing Congress to throw more money at the agencies. The dysfunctions that congressionally mandated "reforms" generate take time to materialize, and both reduce immediate congressional pressure and enable new reforms—and spending—in the future. For these and other reasons Mark Lowenthal articulated in 2008, senior IC management has good reasons to continue to be "spineless."[86] It has failed to learn—or address—the primary reasons for its continuing problems with analysis. We therefore are not surprised that IC leaders have also failed to effectively learn lessons from the decades-long, on-and-off performance of the strategic warning function.

Notes

Portions of this chapter previously appeared in John A. Gentry and Joseph S. Gordon, "U.S. Strategic Warning Intelligence: History and Challenges," *International Journal of Intelligence and CounterIntelligence* 31, no. 1 (Spring 2018): 19–53, reprinted by permission of Taylor & Francis.

1. Mahnken, *Uncovering Ways of War*, 9–11, 17, 179–80.

2. Zegart, "'CNN with Secrets,'" 18–49.

3. Gentry, "Intelligence of Fear."

4. Mark M. Lowenthal, "The Real Intelligence Failure? Spineless Spies," *Washington Post*, May 25, 2008.

5. R. Jeffrey Smith, "Worried CIA Officers Buy Legal Insurance," *Washington Post*, September 11, 2006, http://www.washingtonpost.com/wp-dyn/content/article/2006/09/10/AR2006091001286.html; Shane Scott, "In Legal Cases, C.I.A. Officers Turn to Insurer," *New York Times*, January 20, 2008, http://www.nytimes.com/2008/01/20/washington/20lawyers.html?_r=0; Guy Dinmore, "CIA Agents 'Refused to Operate' at Secret Jails," *Financial Times*, September 21, 2006.

6. Timothy Rutten, "A Truth Commission on Torture Is Needed," *Los Angeles Times*, April 18, 2009, http://articles.latimes.com/2009/apr/18/opinion/oe-rutten18.

7. Gentry, "Intelligence of Fear."

8. See, for example, the prominent role personal relationships played in the success of the *President's Daily Brief*, as demonstrated in Priess, *President's Book of Secrets*, 42, 45, 62, 66, 74, 87, 193–94, 201, 225–26, 271, 281, 289.

9. Gentry, "Intelligence Failure Reframed."

10. Hart and Simon, "Thinking Straight and Talking Straight," 45.

11. Ibid.

12. George, "Reflections on CIA Analysis," 75.

13. Treverton, *Intelligence for an Age of Terror*, 94.

14. Priess, *President's Book of Secrets*, 285.

15. Betts, *Enemies of Intelligence*, 55–62.

16. Authors' discussion with Ken Knight, November 30, 2016.

17. For revised DoD policy regarding the DWN, see DoD Directive 3115.16, *The Defense Warning Network*, December 5, 2013, as revised April 18, 2018, at https://fas.org/irp/doddir/dod/d3115_16.pdf.

18. Bruce, "Countering Denial and Deception."

19. MacEachin, *U.S. Intelligence*, 239.

20. Asher, *Egyptian Strategy*, 10; Shazly, *Crossing of the Suez*, 206–7.

21. George and Wirtz, "Warning in Age of Uncertainty," 216.

22. Davis, "Policymaker's Perspective."

23. For example, see Ford, *Estimative Intelligence*, 83–84.

24. Davis, "Strategic Warning: Intelligence Support," 174–75, 179. See also the editor's note to Davis, "Strategic Warning: If Surprise Is Inevitable," 1.

25. Handel, *Perception, Deception and Surprise*, 27–28.

26. Ibid.

27. Wirtz, *Tet Offensive*, 172–79.

28. Shalev, *Israel's Intelligence Assessment*, 4, 10.

29. Betts, *Enemies of Intelligence*, 26.

30. Authors' discussion with John Gannon, March 16, 2017.

31. Patton, "Monitoring of War Indicators," 60.

32. Davis, "Strategic Warning: Intelligence Support," 173, 180, 183–84.

33. Marrin, "Training and Educating," 131–46.

34. Authors' discussion with a CAP instructor, January 2017.

35. Ibid.

36. Gordon telephone conversation with Ron Woodward, June 7, 2017.

37. Source of the information in this paragraph: an FBI official.

38. Source: Randy Pherson, who taught part of the course.

39. Tiernan, "Hiding in Plain Sight," 71–76.

40. Heuer, *Rethinking Intelligence*, 31–36.

41. Ibid., 33.

42. Ibid., 34.

43. Information from an IC officer, July 2017.

44. Bruce, "Countering Denial and Deception," 23.

45. Grabo, *Handbook of Warning Intelligence*, 111–12.

46. Tetlock and Gardner, *Superforecasting*, 86; Baruch Fischoff and Cherie Chauvin, eds., *Intelligence Analysis: Behavioral and Social Scientific Foundations* (Washington, DC: National Research Council, 2011), and its companion volume, *Intelligence Analysis for Tomorrow: Advances from the Behavioral and Social Sciences* (Washington, DC: National Research Council, 2011), 35–36, http://www.nap.edu/catalog/13040/intelligence-analysis-for-tomorrow-advances-from-the-behavioral-and-social.

47. Chang and Tetlock, "Rethinking Training of Intelligence Analysts."

48. Chang et al., "Restructuring Structured Analytic Techniques," 344.

49. Gentry, "'Professionalization' of Intelligence Analysis," 643–76.

50. Defense Intelligence Agency, "Instruction: Defense Warning," July 16, 2012; Gordon, "National Intelligence University," 128–30.

51. Russell, *Sharpening Strategic Intelligence*, 119–48.

52. Intelligence Community Directive (ICD) 610, "Competence Directories for the Intelligence Community Workforce," lists technical competencies the IC wants its people to have. A subdirective, Intelligence Community Standards 610–7, "Competency Directory for Analysis and Production," lists desirable generic analyst skills, including "subject matter expertise." For the importance of expertise to warning, see George and Wirtz, "Warning in Age of Uncertainty," 217; Gentry, "'Professionalization' of Intelligence Analysis," 649; Gentry, "Has the ODNI Improved."

53. Davis, "Policymaker's Perspective."

54. Gregory Treverton argues that warning specialists should be mainly analytic generalists. We respectfully disagree. See Treverton, *Intelligence for an Age of Terror*, 157.

55. Lowenthal, "Real Intelligence Failure?"

56. Gentry, "'Professionalization' of Intelligence Analysis."

57. Ermarth, "Seeing Russia Plain," 12.

58. Gentry, "Intelligence Failure Reframed," 265.

59. Intelligence Community Directive 204, "National Intelligence Priorities Framework," January 2, 2015, https://www.dni.gov/files/documents/ICD/ICD%20204%20National%20Intelligence%20Prior ities%20Framework.pdf.

60. Fingar, *Reducing Uncertainty*, 51–52.

61. Lowenthal, *Intelligence*, 4th ed., 8–62, 231; Clark, *Technical Collection of Intelligence*, 265–67; FBI website, http://www.fbi.gov/about-us/nsb/faqs, accessed April 20, 2014.

62. For a major allegation along these lines, see US House of Representatives, *(U) Initial Findings of the U.S. House of Representatives Joint Task Force on U.S. Central Command Intelligence Analysis*, August 10, 2016, http://intelligence.house.gov/uploadedfiles/house_jtf_on_centcom_intelligence_initial _report.pdf.

63. Betts, "Analysis, War, and Decision," 65.

64. Grabo, *Anticipating Surprise*, 11.

65. Betts, *Enemies of Intelligence*, 22.

66. George, "Reflections on CIA Analysis," 72–81; Treverton, *Intelligence for Age of Terror*, 145; Priess, *President's Book of Secrets*, 285.

67. Miller, "U.S. Strategic Intelligence Forecasting," 699.

68. Authors' discussions with DoD warning specialists who experienced this behavior.

69. Steinberg, "Policymaker's Perspective." See also Fingar, *Reducing Uncertainty*, 50–51.

70. Personal communication with authors, 2015; Pherson and Pherson, *Critical Thinking for Strategic Intelligence*, 9–11, 190.

71. Davis, "Strategic Warning: If Surprise Is Inevitable."

72. Betts, *Enemies of Intelligence*, 72.

73. Australian Ministry of Defence pamphlet, *Australian Defence Warning System: Providing Strategic Warning*.

74. Bar-Joseph and McDermott, *Intelligence Success and Failure*; Wirtz, "Art of Intelligence Autopsy," 1–18.

75. Berkowitz, "U.S. Intelligence Estimates," 237–50; MacEachin, "CIA Assessments," 57–65.

76. Gentry, "Intelligence Learning and Adaptation," 50–75.

77. Director of Central Intelligence, "DCI Task Force Report."

78. CIA Inspector General, *Inspection of the Warning Function at CIA*, IG 2001–0010-N, April 2002.

79. Hedley, "Learning from Intelligence Failures," 435–50.

80. Jervis, *Why Intelligence Fails*.

81. Zelikow, "Evolution of Intelligence Reform," 1–20; Pillar, "Good Literature and Bad History."

82. Shryock, "Intelligence Community Post-Mortem," 27.

83. Ibid., 26.

84. Ibid., 16n3.

85. Zegart, "September 11 and Adaptation Failure."

86. Lowenthal, "Real Intelligence Failure?"

The Future of Strategic Warning Intelligence

The previous eleven chapters contain a history of warning successes and failures, our assessment of what makes warning hard, and explanations of the periodic shifts in intelligence bureaucracies' priorities for, and concerns about, the strategic warning function. They recount a wide variety of intellectual, personal, and organizational challenges associated with strategic warning intelligence in several countries. We are confident that strategic warning has not reached anything close to a defined role in the intelligence services of the world and that its evolution will continue. The non-security parts of national governments and the private sector seem likely to use warning analytic techniques productively more often and in different ways. The adoption of warning by a broad swath of government agencies and private intelligence entities, including business, think tanks, and academia, as well as the expanded scope of warning analyses and new analytic methods such as horizon scanning and futures analysis indicate progress for the warning function. The embrace of warning-like methods in CT organizations such as those of the Netherlands is also encouraging. But the role of warning in established national intelligence agencies is less clear.[1]

The expanded scope of warning has one troublesome feature, however. Disintegration of the distinction between strategic and tactical warning, especially in the CT arena, poses problems of definition and virtually ensures that there will be more "strategic" warning failures. The extensive focus on CT-related intelligence may push warning toward more tactical concerns at the expense of the broader strategic warning function, including coverage of nonviolent threats and opportunities.

More positively, in the United States and some other countries, police and homeland security–focused organizations, not armed forces or foreign intelligence services, have primary domestic CT responsibilities. An expanded list of acceptable warning topics would improve the institutional security of the warning function and the few distinct warning organizations that exist by making them more visible, more helpful, and more appreciated by senior intelligence consumers and thus by senior intelligence officials. As we have seen, temporary periods of perceptions that conventional military threats had receded repeatedly led agencies to diminish or terminate warning organizations. Significant CT concerns and non-defense-warning issues seem likely to remain significant intelligence issues for the foreseeable future.

The cyclical ups and downs in emphasis on strategic warning intelligence in the United States continue, with warning now deep in one of its periodic troughs. The three major components of strategic warning—dedicated warning organizations, D&D activities, and training and education—are in unhealthy conditions for reasons that reflect unwise leadership choices. Steps backward reflect ignorance of the strategic warning function, denial of its importance, myopia, and an excessive desire to provide immediate gratification to consumers (and thence to the agencies) by providing current intelligence at the expense of future surprises and the long-term performance of intelligence as a whole. This negative assessment leads us to ponder ways the IC could protect and improve the performance of its warning function—if it wants to do so.

Thomas Patton in 1959 described four aspects of "indications intelligence" the Watch Committee of his day used to assess threats from the Soviet Union, which later warning organizations used and which we believe continue to reflect individual and organizational characteristics essential to good strategic warning outcomes. We update Patton's insights for contemporary use. Modern warning entities and analysts should have the following:

1. A "mental *attitude*" (of analysts), which facilitates early understanding of adversary intentions. The warning officer must have assumptions, or working hypotheses subject to evaluation, about the goals and plans of potential adversaries (and sometimes "friends"). Skepticism and a degree of controlled paranoia in warning personnel are good things!

2. A body of *doctrine* that guides the collection, handling, and analysis of relevant information. In other words, warning personnel should develop formal processes for doing at least some of their work, particularly for monitoring enduring warning problems.

3. Means for "developing *new techniques* and methods for collection, processing, evaluation, and analysis significant principally or solely for purposes of strategic early warning." That is, analysts should develop mechanisms for improving their work in many important areas as they develop; the I&W method is the best historical example of such innovation. Warning analysts must address methodological issues as well as learn a lot about countries and issues of possible warning concern, thereby also generating substantive expertise.

4. *Organizations* within an intelligence community that help foster continuous processes of collection, analysis, and communication to senior consumers about the intelligence community's insights about possible strategic threats and opportunities.[2]

None of these characteristics is in good condition in the US IC now. The dominant and conventional *attitude* toward warning is that it is an easy and mundane task that any analyst can accomplish as an additional duty—the EAAWA perspective. As we have argued, this view fundamentally misunderstands warning. Warning *doctrine* is ignored because standard "tradecraft" techniques appear adequate to do EAAWA. This view is partly an internal development from the 1990s, but it also reflects misguided directives from Congress after 9/11 and IC leaders' lack of leadership in declining to resist dysfunctional "reforms."[3] The DoD's *Defense Warning Network* document is a creditworthy move in the right direction, but it is only one step, and, as noted, the organizational practices of the DoD as a whole give Defense warning some problematic characteristics. While the IC invests in *new techniques* related to analysis generally, such as SATs, these are designed primarily to provide elementary methodological rigor and avoid easily avoidable mistakes, not to help solve complex mysteries. Work on specialist techniques such as IARPA's work on crowdsourcing has limited direct applicability to strategic warning analysis, including countering adversary deception efforts. And adoption of the EAAWA perspective has destroyed distinctive warning *organizations*, which are institutional foundations of the first three functions noted above and help enable effective warning relationships with senior decision-makers.

The causes of these challenges in the IC lead us to conclude that a major structural reconstitution of the strategic warning function is necessary. Very different senior-level policies and organizational incentives are essential if warning is to escape the institutional challenges and obstacles it has faced chronically for decades. We favor re-creation of the hybrid institutional model with a small but bureaucratically strong warning office that provides direction, guidance, advocacy, and support to the warning mission, either within the NIO or NIM structures or in some new one.[4] Alternative possibilities are a separate organization that owns strategic warning or a pure EAAWA model that much of the IC now uses—neither of which have worked well. Moreover, we think neither can work well in the current institutional context of the IC.

History indicates that strategic warning needs an institutional home that is moderately, but not excessively, independent. Warning needs independence from normal coordination processes to ensure rapid development of sometimes controversial warning messages while at the same time being an integral part of national intelligence communities; an independent power base should also give it some clout in setting collection priorities. Warning professionals would guide, prod, and help the line analysts who would do much of the analysis that goes into warning messages, but senior warning officials would develop the trust that warning needs to be credible to senior consumers. The 1950s-vintage Watch Committee and the NIO/Ws at times operated similarly; senior warning officers had authority to issue warning messages on their own and were credible enough to have influence. When layers of review or wide coordination requirements affected warning, as happened to the Watch Committee in the 1960s, the quality of strategic warning suffered immediately and drastically. The watch system of Defence Intelligence in the United Kingdom has the advantage of being deeply institutionalized, and we have the impression that it has at least modest authority to release controversial warning messages within the MoD. For warning messages aimed at national audiences, as noted in chapter 4, the JIC must approve its draft assessments.

John Gannon suggests that the key to successful strategic warning is *integrating* it with line analytic units' current, research, and estimative analyses.[5] He argues that strategic warning has developed analytic methods that can help mitigate personal and institutional biases that line units sometimes develop and that close working relationships between warning specialists and line units can help both. As a former senior manager of analysts, Gannon sees this integration as especially useful to senior managers; warning can protect them from criticism by helping to reduce the number and severity of intelligence failures. In Richard Betts's terms, this means figuring a way to integrate people who concentrate on the "normal theory" that is useful most of the time with warning specialists whose "exceptional thinking" usefully complements normal theory in abnormal situations. In this scheme, warning specialists would work to improve warning-related analytic techniques. Gannon also suggests that warning specialists, like outside experts and analytic methodologists, should be parts of teams addressing particularly difficult or contentious issues. Warning analysts could add methodological rigor and specialized insights and challenge conventional wisdom. In this way, he suggests, warning analysts could have helped during discussions in support of the drafting in September 2002 of the flawed NIE on Iraq's WMD programs.

In essence, we think, Gannon suggests a new role for warning: provision of specialized thought processes in support of line units. The hybrid model would evolve and might strengthen if the warning function were widely perceived to contribute appreciably to analytic successes in general. This point suggests a need for additional research on techniques and technologies to facilitate effective methodological support, including techniques useful for analysis of traditional warning problems—enduring and emerging threats and opportunities—and counter-deception techniques. Warning organizations might sponsor such work, perhaps working with IARPA. We agree that such a relationship could be mutually valuable, but the support of senior leaders is critical to the acceptance warning needs to become better integrated with line units, and IC leaders never have collectively embraced warning this way.

Jack Davis in 2003 made Gannon's point in more popular contemporary terms. He suggested that warning be viewed as a kind of "alternative analysis"—a term embraced by the IC under congressional pressure after the failures of 9/11 and the Iraq WMD NIE.[6] This would help warning analysts better work with line analysts, who Davis thought should retain some warning responsibilities.

The DoD and some observers favor a different way of embedding warning attributes in line units: creation of "warning advocates" in analytic units whose job is to prod line analysts to think more creatively using warning techniques. Former NIO/W Ken Knight, for example, thinks such warning advocates should be broadly disbursed within analytic units. Jack Davis in 2006 similarly proposed increasing the time that analysts devote to performing strategic warning—as opposed to the tactical nature of warning in current intelligence work.[7] Proponents do not explain how warning advocates should work in practice or how they should be selected or managed, however. Warning advocates now perform the function on part-time bases and remain subject to incentive structures that reward current intelligence. Graduates of NIU's warning certificate program become, under current DoD policy, certified warning advocates, but NIU produces a small number each year.

While warning-related education that now confers "advocate" status in DoD is good for the IC, we are skeptical that variants of the warning advocate institution will alone improve strategic warning even in DoD. The continuing antipathy of many senior managers to the notion that strategic warning is a distinctive analytic function suggests that warning advocates will not have appreciable roles. Gannon is more doubtful, arguing that managers are unlikely to allow analysts they regard highly to become warning advocates and suggesting that such advocates may exacerbate some of the problems of past years, when warning and line analysts performed separate and often conflicting functions.[8] Instead, Gannon argues, warning personnel will be useful if they help line analysts with methodological or other suggestions that help make their analyses better. Gannon's skepticism has merit; the concepts of devil's advocates and red teaming, while receiving some support in the IC and sometimes being used as SATs in support of complicated analyses, repeatedly have generated animosity between "devils" and those they try to help and led line analysts to ignore the techniques.

The new senior warning official or office should influence warning-related training and education. This includes the warning part of basic analyst training courses and specialized courses. Any fruits of warning- and D&D-related research also should find their way to classrooms.

Whatever the nature of the strategic warning effort in line units is, the dedicated warning staff should be small but senior for several reasons. First, small size would make it a less appealing target for bureaucratic enemies, including budget monitors. Andrew Marshall's Office of Net Assessment is a good example of this virtue.[9] Raiding a small warning function will not be lucrative. Second, good warning personnel are rare, for reasons Philip Tetlock and others have explained and the Twenty Committee demonstrated during World War II. The complexity of strategic warning and the constant, dynamically interactive battle with deceivers mean strategic warning should employ only very good people—for reasons Admiral John Godfrey noted. In warning more than in other areas of strategic intelligence analysis, quality is far more important than quantity. Third, small organizations are inherently more flexible than larger ones, and warning needs to be able and willing to listen to novel and insightful, if controversial and unwelcome, views from all of its people—and act quickly when an unusual perspective seems to have merit. Fourth, the staff must be senior to generate the credibility, trust, and access to senior consumers that effective warning requires. Senior consumers include policymakers and the DNI. Fifth, the staff must be sufficiently senior to have enough bureaucratic clout to be able to shift some collection resources as events of potential significance unfold, enabling effective monitoring of situations and prescient and timely revisions of warning messages. Its performance measurement and incentive systems must be different than the production-quantity focus driven by the tyranny of current intelligence.

We do not, however, expect such reforms in the near term. All of these proposals depend on acceptance by the IC's senior leadership, which we do not see coming soon. Indeed, we see no hint of receptivity to this idea anywhere in the IC.

If the IC does not address its challenges with analysis generally, senior national decision-makers or the Congress may be forced to consider more drastic steps. Prominent former CIA analysts unhappy with the state of analysis generally at CIA and the IC broadly have proposed, some two decades apart, the creation of new analytic organizations as remedies for chronic perceived analytic deficiencies similar to those we see now.

Harold Ford in the early 1990s suggested creation of an independent, national-level "think tank" to do national estimates based on the Research and Analysis arm of the wartime OSS—which included some of the best minds in the country and which Ford considered the best intelligence analytic outfit the United States has ever had.[10] Ford said the think tank should dive deeply into important issues and reach useful conclusions that the current intelligence-focused IC of his day did not do as well as he thought desirable.[11] Ford suggested that the head of the organization be a person of national reputation. It should be staffed by the IC's best analysts and excellent outsiders—a small group of senior "elite" intelligence officers who have direct access to senior decision-makers; the purpose of this institution would be to ensure that excellent insights and advice reach decision-makers without interference by the normal processes of the intelligence bureaucracy.[12] The warning element should similarly be composed of talented and well-connected people. Such an organization could remedy most of the recurrent institutional problems of strategic warning as well as estimative intelligence.

Roger George suggests that, to escape the tyranny of current intelligence, the United States might need to shift its main intelligence analytic effort, now at the CIA, to a new, private-sector organization.[13] In principle, George's new analytic organization could feature either an EAAWA feature or a separate warning unit within it. But a competent such organization surely would not feature "anticipatory intelligence."

Two other possibilities are also likely to be opposed by established IC bureaucratic interests. First, the ODNI could create a small organization that would be dedicated to providing warning to the NSC staff and be composed of senior, well-regarded intelligence officers whose functions would include warning-related communication between the White House and IC components. The office should be accessible, as a matter of policy, to all IC personnel, who could bypass normal hierarchies when they think issues merit senior-level attention but are *not* being adequately worked by normal processes.[14] The closest analogy to this office is the analytic group that has at times supported the NIC. This group has usually contained fairly senior, very good analysts, but it has worked for the NIC only.

Second, the IC could designate a small number of elite, senior intelligence officers within line analytic units of IC agencies who have warning responsibilities and are given unfettered access to senior decision-makers.[15] These people, too, should be formally accessible directly by all IC employees who see a major warning issue *not* being worked adequately in normal ways. These people might be seen as a variant of "warning advocate." The main difference between these people and existing DoD warning advocates is that they would be more senior than the generally midcareer people who complete NIU's warning certificate program and thus would have greater institutional clout.

Finally, despite and because of the changing world, we see strategic warning remaining a critical intelligence function. Given the powerful inertia of bureaucratic rest, we suspect that another major intelligence failure may be needed to make the IC again appreciate strategic warning and to begin again an upswing in the cycle of caring about the function.[16] Mary McCarthy warned in 1998 that "disaster looms" because the IC did not have adequate warning-specific skills—a situation that has worsened considerably since she wrote.[17]

Notes

1. Scott, "Reflections on Age of Intelligence," 617–24; Agrell, "Next 100 Years?," 118–32.
2. Patton, "Monitoring of War Indicators," 55–68.
3. Lowenthal, "Real Intelligence Failure?"
4. Robert Vickers makes a similar argument in "State of Warning Today," 12–15.
5. Authors' discussion with John Gannon, March 16, 2017. The term "integrating" appears repeatedly in DCI Robert Gates's inquiry into the state of strategic warning in 1992. See Director of Central Intelligence, "DCI Task Force Report." The proposal was not acted on then.
6. Davis, "Strategic Warning: If Surprise Is Inevitable," 8–9.
7. Authors' discussion with Ken Knight, November 30, 2016; Davis, "Strategic Warning: Intelligence Support," 182.
8. Authors' discussion with John Gannon, March 16, 2017.
9. Krepinevich and Watts, *Last Warrior*, 248.
10. Ford, *Estimative Intelligence*, 210–11.
11. Ibid., 201.
12. Ibid., 204, 208.
13. George, "Reflections on CIA Analysis," 80–81.
14. For similar thoughts, see Ford, *Estimative Intelligence*, 202.
15. For a similar suggestion focused on communicating the messages of national estimates, see ibid., 208.
16. Travers, "Waking Up on Another September 12th," 46–761; Pappas and Simon, "Intelligence Community," 39–47; Travers, "Coming Intelligence Failure," 35–43.
17. McCarthy, "Mission to Warn," 18–19.

Bibliography

Abels, P. H. M. "Dreigingsbeeld terrorisme Nederland: nut en noodzaak van een 'all-source threat assessment' bij terrorismebestrijding." In *Terrorisme. Studies over terrorisme en terrorismebestrijding.* Edited by E. R. Muller, U. Rosenthal, and R. de Wijk, 535–44. Kluwer, Netherlands: Deventer, 2008.

Adamsky, Dima, and Uri Bar-Joseph. "'The Russians Are Not Coming': Israel's Intelligence Failure and Soviet Military Intervention in the 'War of Attrition.'" *Intelligence and National Security* 21, no. 1 (2006): 1–25.

Adamsky, Dmitry (Dima). "The 1983 Nuclear Crisis: Lessons for Deterrence Theory and Practice." *Journal of Strategic Studies* 36, no. 1 (2013): 4–41.

Agranat Commission. "What Went Wrong on October 6? The Partial Report of the Israeli Commission of Inquiry into the October War." *Journal of Palestine Studies* 3, no. 4 (Summer 1974): 189–207.

Agrell, Wilhelm. "The Next 100 Years? Reflections on the Future of Intelligence." *Intelligence and National Security* 27, no. 1 (February 2012): 118–32.

———. "Sweden: Intelligence in the Middle Way." In *Intelligence Elsewhere: Spies and Espionage outside the Anglosphere.* Edited by Philip H. J. Davies and Kristian C. Gustafson, 239–63. Washington, DC: Georgetown University Press, 2013.

Aid, Matthew M. "All Glory Is Fleeting: Sigint and the Fight against International Terrorism." *Intelligence and National Security* 18, no. 4 (2003): 72–120.

Akerlof, George A., and Robert J. Shiller. *Animal Spirits: How Human Psychology Drives the Economy, and Why It Matters for Global Capitalism.* Princeton, NJ: Princeton University Press, 2009.

Albright, Madeleine K., and William S. Cohen, *Preventing Genocide: A Blueprint for U.S. Policymakers.* Washington, DC: United States Holocaust Memorial Museum, 2008.

Aldrich, Richard J. "British Intelligence during the Cold War." In *Secret Intelligence in the European States System, 1918–1989.* Edited by Jonathan Haslam and Karina Urbach, 149–69. Stanford, CA: Stanford University Press, 2014.

Aldrich, Richard J., Rory Cormac, and Michael S. Goodman. *Spying on the World: The Declassified Documents of the Joint Intelligence Committee, 1936–2013.* Edinburgh: Edinburgh University Press, 2014.

Alexseev, Mikhail A. "Early Warning, Ethnopolitical Conflicts, and the United Nations: Assessing the Violence in Georgia/Abkhazia." *Nationalities Papers* 26, no. 2 (1998): 191–213.

Allen, Charles E. "Warning and Iraq's Invasion of Kuwait: A Retrospective Look." *Defense Intelligence Journal* 7, no. 2 (Fall 1998): 33–44.

Allen, George W. *None So Blind: A Personal Account of the Intelligence Failure in Vietnam.* Chicago: Ivan R. Dee, 2001.

Andrew, Christopher. *For the President's Eyes Only: Secret Intelligence and the American Presidency from Washington to Bush.* New York: Harper Perennial, 1995.

Andrew, Christopher, and Oleg Gordievsky. *KGB: The Inside Story.* New York: HarperCollins, 1990.

Andrew, Christopher, and Vasili Mitrokhin. *The Sword and the Shield: The Mitrokhin Archive and the Secret History of the KGB*. New York: Basic, 1999.

Andriole, Stephen J., and Robert A. Young. "Toward the Development of an Integrated Crisis Warning System." *International Studies Quarterly* 21, no. 1 (1977): 107–50.

Anonymous. "National Warning Intelligence: The Alert Memorandum (U)." *Cryptologic Spectrum* 11, no. 1 (Winter 1981): 13–15. https://www.nsa.gov/news-features/declassified-documents/cryptologic -spectrum/assets/files/national_intell_warning.pdf.

Arcos, Rubén, and José-Miguel Palacios. "The Impact of Intelligence on Decision-Making: The EU and the Arab Spring." *Intelligence and National Security* 33, no. 5 (2018): 737–54.

Asher, Dani. *The Egyptian Strategy for the Yom Kippur War*. Jefferson, NC: McFarland, 2009.

Axelrod, Robert. *The Complexity of Cooperation: Agent-Based Models of Competition and Collaboration*. Princeton, NJ: Princeton University Press, 1997.

Badri, Hassan el-, Taha el-Magdoub, and Mohammed Dia el-Din Zohdy. *The Ramadan War, 1973*. Dunn Loring, VA: T. N. Dupuy Associates, 1978.

Ballast, Jan. "Trust (in) NATO: The Future of Intelligence Sharing within the Alliance." Research Paper No. 140. NATO Defense College, Rome, September 2016.

Bangham, George, and Sarang Shah. *The National Security Council and the Prime Minister.* Cambridge, UK: University of Cambridge, 2012.

Bar-Joseph, Uri. *The Angel: The Egyptian Spy Who Saved Israel*. New York: HarperCollins, 2016.

———. "Forecasting a Hurricane: Israeli and American Estimations of the Khomeini Revolution." *Journal of Strategic Studies* 36, no. 5 (2013): 718–42.

———. "Israel Caught Unaware: Egypt's Sinai Surprise of 1960." *International Journal of Intelligence and CounterIntelligence* 8, no. 2 (1995): 203–19.

———. "Israel's 1973 Intelligence Failure." *Israel Affairs* 6, no. 1 (1999): 11–35.

———. "Lessons Not Learned: Israel in the Post–Yom Kippur War Era." *Israel Affairs* 14, no. 1 (2008): 70–83.

———. "A Question of Loyalty: Ashraf Marwan and Israel's Intelligence Fiasco in the Yom Kippur War." *Intelligence and National Security* 30, no. 5 (2015): 667–85.

———. "The 'Special Means of Collection': The Missing Link in the Surprise of the Yom Kippur War." *Middle East Journal* 67, no. 4 (Autumn 2013): 531–46.

———. *The Watchman Fell Asleep: The Surprise of Yom Kippur and Its Sources*. Albany: State University of New York Press, 2005.

Bar-Joseph, Uri, and Jack S. Levy. "Conscious Action and Intelligence Failure." *Political Science Quarterly* 124, no. 3 (2009): 461–88.

Bar-Joseph, Uri, and Rose McDermott. *Intelligence Success and Failure: The Human Factor*. New York: Oxford University Press, 2017.

———. "Personal Functioning under Stress: Accountability and Social Support of Israeli Leaders in the Yom Kippur War." *Journal of Conflict Resolution* 52, no. 1 (February 2008): 144–70.

Bar-Joseph, Uri, and Zachary Sheaffer. "Surprise and Its Causes in Business Administration and Strategic Studies." *International Journal of Intelligence and CounterIntelligence* 11, no. 3 (1998): 331–49.

Barnes, Alan. "Making Intelligence Analysis More Intelligent: Using Numeric Probabilities." *Intelligence and National Security* 31, no. 3 (2016): 327–44.

Barrass, Gordon. "Able Archer 83: What Were the Soviets Thinking?" *Survival* 58, no. 6 (2016): 7–30.

Barros, James, and Richard Gregor. *Double Deception: Stalin, Hitler, and the Invasion of Russia*. DeKalb: Northern Illinois University Press, 1995.

Belden, Thomas. "Indications, Warning, and Crisis Options." *International Studies Quarterly* 21, no. 1 (March 1977): 181–98.

Bell, Falko. "'Die deutsche Spionage ist auf Zack': German Soldiers Speak about Intelligence Services (1939–1945)." *Journal of Intelligence History* 12, no. 1 (2013): 49–59.

Bell, J. Bowyer. "Toward a Theory of Deception." *International Journal of Intelligence and CounterIntelligence* 16, no. 2 (2003): 244–79.

Bennett, Michael, and Edward Waltz. *Counterdeception Principles and Applications for National Security*. Boston: Artech House, 2007.

———. "Toward a Counterdeception Tradecraft." *American Intelligence Journal* 32, no. 2 (2015): 77–86.

Bensahel, Nora. "Mission Not Accomplished: What Went Wrong with Iraqi Reconstruction." *Journal of Strategic Studies* 29, no. 3 (June 2006): 453–73.

Ben-Zvi, Abraham. "Between Warning and Response: The Case of the Yom Kippur War." *International Journal of Intelligence and CounterIntelligence* 4, no. 2 (1990): 227–42.

———. "Hindsight and Foresight: A Conceptual Framework for the Analysis of Surprise Attacks." *World Politics* 28, no. 3 (April 1976): 381–95.

Berge, Travis, Nitish Sinha, and Michael Smolyansky. "Which Market Indicators Best Forecast Recessions?" Board of Governors of the Federal Reserve System. *Fed Notes*, August 2, 2016. https://www.federalreserve.gov/econresdata/notes/feds-notes/2016/which-market-indicators-best-forecast-recessions-20160802.html.

Berkowitz, Bruce D. "U.S. Intelligence Estimates of the Soviet Collapse: Reality and Perception." *Intelligence and National Security* 21, no. 2 (2008): 237–50.

Betts, Richard. "Strategic Surprise for War Termination: Inchon, Dien Bien Phu, and Tet." In Knorr and Morgan, *Strategic Military Surprise*, 147–71.

Betts, Richard K. "Analysis, War, and Decision: Why Intelligence Failures Are Inevitable." *World Politics* 31, no. 1 (October 1978): 61–89.

———. *Enemies of Intelligence: Knowledge and Power in American National Security*. New York: Columbia University Press, 2007.

———. "Fixing Intelligence." *Foreign Affairs* 81, no. 1 (January/February 2002): 43–59.

———. "Intelligence Warning: Old Problems, New Agendas." *Parameters* 28, no. 1 (Spring 1998): 26–35.

———. "Surprise, Scholasticism, and Strategy: A Review of Ariel Levite's Intelligence and Strategic Surprises (New York: Columbia University Press, 1987)." *International Studies Quarterly* 33, no. 3 (September 1989): 329–43.

———. *Surprise Attack: Lessons for Defense Planning*. Washington, DC: Brookings Institution, 1982.

———. "Surprise Despite Warning: Why Sudden Attack Succeeds." *Political Science Quarterly* 95, no. 4 (Winter 1980–81): 551–72.

———. "Warning Dilemmas: Normal Theory vs. Exceptional Theory." *Orbis* 26, no. 4 (Winter 1983): 828–33.

Betts, Richard K., and Thomas G. Mahnken, eds. *Paradoxes of Strategic Intelligence: Essays in Honor of Michael I. Handel*. London: Frank Cass, 2003.

Bhardwaj, Rakhi, Mukat Lal Sharma, and Ashok Kumar. "Multiparameter Algorithm for Earthquake Early Warning." *Geomatics, Natural Hazards and Risk* 7, no. 4 (2016): 1242–64.

Biddle, Stephen. "Victory Misunderstood: What the Gulf War Tells Us about the Future of Conflict." *International Security* 21, no. 2 (Autumn 1996): 139–79.

Blainey, Geoffrey. *The Causes of War*. 3rd ed. New York: Free Press, 1988.

Bodnar, John W. *Warning Analysis for the Information Age: Rethinking the Intelligence Process*. Washington, DC: National Defense Intelligence College, 2003.

Boutros-Ghali, Boutros. "An Agenda for Peace: Preventive Diplomacy, Peacemaking and Peacekeeping; Report of the Secretary-General." United Nations document A/47/277. New York, June 17, 1992.

Bracken, Paul. "Net Assessment: A Practical Guide." *Parameters* 31, no. 1 (Spring 2006): 90–100.

Breakspear, Alan. "A New Definition of Intelligence." *Intelligence and National Security* 28, no. 5 (2013): 678–93.

Bruce, James B. "Countering Denial and Deception in the Early 21st Century: An Adaptation Strategy When All Else Fails." *American Intelligence Journal* 32, no. 2 (2015): 17–28.

Bruce, James B., and Michael Bennett. "Foreign Denial and Deception: Analytic Imperatives." In George and Bruce, *Analyzing Intelligence*, 197–214.

Budiansky, Stephen. *Code Warriors: NSA's Codebreakers and the Secret Intelligence War against the Soviet Union*. New York: Alfred A. Knopf, 2016.

Byman, Daniel. "The Intelligence War on Terrorism." *Intelligence and National Security* 29, no. 6 (2014): 837–63.

———. "Strategic Surprise and the September 11 Attacks." *Annual Review of Political Science* 8, no. 1 (2005): 145–70.

Calhoun, Ricky-Dale. "The Musketeer's Cloak: Strategic Deception during the Suez Crisis of 1956." *Studies in Intelligence* 51, no. 2 (2007): 47–58.

Carpenter, R. Charli. "Vetting the Advocacy Agenda: Network Centrality and the Paradox of Weapons Norms." *International Organization* 65, no. 1 (2011): 69–102.

Cavelty, Myriam Dunn, and Victor Mauer. "Postmodern Intelligence: Strategic Warning in an Age of Reflexive Intelligence." *Security Dialogue* 40, no. 2 (April 2009): 123–44.

Central Intelligence Agency. *The CIA and Strategic Warning: The 1968 Soviet-Led Invasion of Czechoslovakia*. Washington, DC: Center for the Study of Intelligence, 2009.

Cha, Victor D. "Hawk Engagement and Preventive Defense on the Korean Peninsula." *International Security* 27, no. 1 (Summer 2002): 40–78.

Chairman of the Joint Chief of Staff. *Joint Vision 2020*. Washington, DC: Government Printing Office, 2000.

Chan, Steve. "The Intelligence of Stupidity: Understanding Failures in Strategic Warning." *American Political Science Review* 73, no. 1 (March 1979): 171–80.

Chang, Welton, Elissabeth Berdini, David R. Mandel, and Philip E. Tetlock, "Restructuring Structured Analytic Techniques in Intelligence." *Intelligence and National Security* 33, no. 3 (2018): 337–56.

Chang, Welton, and Philip E. Tetlock. "Rethinking the Training of Intelligence Analysts." *Intelligence and National Security* 31, no. 6 (October 2016): 903–20.

Chesterman, Simon. "Does the UN Have Intelligence?" *Survival* 48, no. 3 (2006): 149–64.

Chong, Tan Kwan, et al. "Risk Assessment and Horizon Scanning Experimentation Centre." Unpublished paper. Government of Singapore. https://www.dsta.gov.sg/docs/publications-documents /risk-assessment-and-horizon-scanning-experimentation-centre.pdf?sfvrsn=0.

Cincotta, Richard. "Will Tunisia's Democracy Survive? A View from Political Demography." Wilson Center, *NewSecurityBeat* blog, May 12, 2015. https://www.newsecuritybeat.org/2015/05/tunisias -democracy-survive-view-political-demography/.

Cincotta, Richard P. "Half a Chance: Youth Bulges and Transition to Liberal Democracy." Wilson Center. *ECSP Report* no. 13 (2008–9): 10–18. https://www.wilsoncenter.org/sites/default/files/ECSP Report13_Cincotta.pdf.

Claasen, Adam. "The German Invasion of Norway, 1940: The Operational Intelligence Dimension." *Journal of Strategic Studies* 27, no. 1 (2004): 114–35.

Clapper, James R., with Trey Brown. *Facts and Fears: Hard Truths from a Life in Intelligence*. New York: Viking, 2018.

Clark, Keith. "On Warning." *Studies in Intelligence* 9, no. 1 (1965): 15–21.

Clark, Robert M. *Intelligence Analysis: A Target-Centric Approach*. Washington, DC: CQ Press, 2010.

———. *The Technical Collection of Intelligence*. Washington, DC: CQ Press, 2010.

Clarke, John N. "Early Warning Analysis for Humanitarian Preparedness and Conflict Prevention." *Civil Wars* 7, no. 1 (2005): 71–97.

Clarke, Richard A., and R. P. Eddy. *Warnings: Finding Cassandras to Stop Catastrophes*. New York: HarperCollins, 2017.

Cohen, Eliot A. *Supreme Command: Soldiers, Statesmen, and Leadership in Wartime*. New York: Anchor, 2003.

Cohen, Eliot, and John Gooch. *Military Misfortunes: The Anatomy of Failure in War*. New York: Free Press, 2006.

Cooper, Jeffrey R. *Curing Analytical Pathologies: Pathways to Improved Intelligence Analysis*. Washington, DC: Center for the Study of Intelligence, 2005.

Cormac, Rory. "Secret Intelligence and Economic Security: The Exploitation of a Critical Asset in an Increasingly Prominent Sphere." *Intelligence and National Security* 29, no. 1 (2014): 99–121.

Cozad, Mark, and John Parachini. "(U) Strategic Warning: Organizing and Managing the Mission for the Current Era." CIA Lessons Learned Program. Washington, DC: Center for the Study of Intelligence / RAND Corp., March 2017.

Crawford, Neta C. "The Passion of World Politics: Propositions on Emotion and Emotional Relationships." *International Security* 24, no. 4 (Spring 2000): 116–56.

Cubbage, T. L., II. "The German Misapprehensions Regarding Overlord: Understanding Failure in the Estimative Process." *Intelligence and National Security* 2, no. 3 (1987): 114–74.

Cukier, Kenneth Neil, and Viktor Mayer-Schoenberger. "The Rise of Big Data: How It's Changing the Way We Think about the World." *Foreign Affairs* 92, no. 3 (May/June 2013): 28–40.

Dahl, Erik. J. *Intelligence and Surprise Attack: Failure and Success from Pearl Harbor to 9/11 and Beyond*. Washington, DC: Georgetown University Press, 2013.

———. "The Plots That Failed: Intelligence Lessons Learned from Unsuccessful Terrorist Attacks against the United States." *Studies in Conflict and Terrorism* 34, no. 8 (2011): 621–48.

———. "Warning of Terror: Explaining the Failure of Intelligence against Terrorism." *Journal of Strategic Studies* 28, no. 1 (2005): 31–55.

———. "Why Won't They Listen? Comparing Receptivity toward Intelligence at Pearl Harbor and Midway." *Intelligence and National Security* 28, no. 1 (2013): 68–90.

Dailey, Brian D., and Patrick J. Parker, eds. *Soviet Strategic Deception*. Lexington, MA: Lexington, 1987.

Daniel, Donald C., and Katherine L. Herbig, eds. *Strategic Military Deception*. Oxford, UK: Pergamon, 1982.

Davies, Pete. "Estimating Soviet Power: The Creation of Britain's Defence Intelligence Staff 1960–65." *Intelligence and National Security* 26, no. 6 (2011): 818–41.

Davies, Philip H. J. *Intelligence and Government in Britain and the United States: Volume 1; Evolution of the U.S. Intelligence Community*. Santa Barbara, CA: Praeger Security International, 2012.

———. *Intelligence and Government in Britain and the United States: Volume 2; Evolution of the U.K. Intelligence Community*. Santa Barbara, CA: Praeger Security International, 2012.

———. "The Problem of Defence Intelligence." *Intelligence and National Security* 31, no. 6 (2016): 797–809.

———. "Twilight of Britain's Joint Intelligence Committee?" *International Journal of Intelligence and CounterIntelligence* 24, no. 3 (2011): 427–46.

Davis, Euan G. "A Watchman for All Seasons." *Studies in Intelligence* 13, no. 2 (Spring 1969): 37–43.

Davis, Euan G., and Cynthia M. Grabo. "Strategic Warning and Deception." *Studies in Intelligence* 17 (Spring 1973): 32–38.

Davis, Jack. "Intelligence Analysts and Policymakers: Benefits and Dangers of Tensions in the Relationship." *Intelligence and National Security* 21, no. 6 (December 2006): 999–1021.

———. "The Kent-Kendall Debate of 1949." *Studies in Intelligence* 35, no. 2 (Summer 1991): 37–50.

———. "Paul Wolfowitz on Intelligence Policy-Relations." *Studies in Intelligence* 39, no. 5 (1996): 35–42.

———. "A Policymaker's Perspective on Intelligence Analysis." *Studies in Intelligence* 38, no. 5 (1995): 7–15.

———. "Sherman Kent's Final Thoughts on Analyst-Policymaker Relations." Kent Center Occasional Papers, vol. 2, no. 3. Central Intelligence Agency, Washington, DC, 2003.

———. "Strategic Warning: If Surprise Is Inevitable, What Role for Analysis?" Kent Center Occasional Papers, vol. 2, no. 1. Central Intelligence Agency, Washington, DC, 2003.

———. "Strategic Warning: Intelligence Support in a World of Uncertainty and Surprise." In *Handbook of Intelligence Studies*. Edited by Loch K. Johnson, 173–88. London: Routledge, 2007.

Degaut, Marcos. "Spies and Policymakers: Intelligence in the Information Age." *Intelligence and National Security* 31, no. 4 (2016): 509–31.

De Graaff, Bob. "Terrorist Threat Levels in the Netherlands and Risk Communication to the Public." Unpublished memorandum.

———. "Terrorist Threat Levels in the Netherlands and Risk Communication to the Public." Unpublished PowerPoint slides, June 7, 2016.

Deibert, Ronald J. "Deep Probe: The Evolution of Network Intelligence." *Intelligence and National Security* 18, no. 4 (2003): 175–93.

DeMattei, Lou Anne. "Developing a Strategic Warning Capability for Information Defense." *Defense Intelligence Journal* 7, no. 2 (Fall 1998): 81–121.

Devanney, Joe, and Josh Harris. *The National Security Council: National Security at the Centre of Government.* London: King's College London, 2014.

Diamond, Jared. *Collapse: How Societies Choose to Fail or Succeed.* New York: Penguin, 2011.

Dippel, John V. H. "Jumping to the Right Conclusion: The State Department Warning on Operation 'Barbarossa.'" *International Journal of Intelligence and CounterIntelligence* 6, no. 2 (1993): 213–27.

Director of Central Intelligence. "DCI Task Force Report: Improving Intelligence Warning; 29 May 1992." Declassified. https://documentcloud.org/documents/368903–1992–05–29-dci-task-force -report-improving.html.

———. "Directive 3/16P: Foreign Denial and Deception Analysis; Effective 1 June 1992." https://fas .org/irp/offdocs/dcid3–16.pdf.

———. "Intelligence Warning of the Tet Offensive in Vietnam." http://www.foia.cia.gov/sites/default /files/document_conversions/89801/DOC_0000097712.pdf.

———. "The Soviet Invasion of Afghanistan: Implications for Warning." Interagency intelligence memorandum, October 1980. http://www.foia.cia.gov/sites/default/files/document_conversions/89801 /DOC_0000278538.pdf.

———. "The Watch Committee and the National Indications Center." January 5, 1955. https://www.cia .gov/library/readingroom/docs/CIA-RDP80B01676R001100020013–6.pdf.

———. *Yugoslavia Transformed.* National Intelligence Estimate 15–90, October 18, 1990. Declassified. http://www.foia.cia.gov/sites/default/files/document_conversions/1817859/1990–10–01.pdf.

Director of National Intelligence. Intelligence Community Directive 203, *Analytic Standards*, January 2, 2015, at https://www.dni.gov/files/documents/ICD/ICD%20203%20Analytic%20Standards.pdf.

———. *The National Intelligence Strategy of the United States of America, 2005.* https://fas.org/irp/off docs/nis.pdf.

———. *The National Intelligence Strategy of the United States of America, 2014.* https://www.dni.gov /files/documents/2014_NIS_Publication.pdf.

Donovan, G. Murphy. "Escaping the New Wilderness of Mirrors." *International Journal of Intelligence and CounterIntelligence* 22, no. 4 (2009): 730–38.

Dorn, A. Walter. "Intelligence at UN Headquarters? The Information and Research Unit and the Intervention in Eastern Zaire 1996." *Intelligence and National Security* 20, no. 3 (2005): 440–65.

———. "Intelligence-Led Peacekeeping: The United Nations Stabilization Mission in Haiti (MINUSTAH), 2006–07." *Intelligence and National Security* 24, no. 6 (2009): 805–35.

Doron, Gideon. "Israeli Intelligence: Tactics, Strategy, and Prediction." *International Journal of Intelligence and CounterIntelligence* 2, no. 3 (1988): 305–19.

Dupont, Alan. "The Strategic Implications of Climate Change." *Survival* 50, no. 3 (September 2008): 29–54.

Dvoinykh, L., and N. Tarkhova. "What Military Intelligence Reported: Historians Have a Chance to Analyze Soviet Intelligence Dispatches on the Eve of the War." *Russian Studies in History* 36, no. 3 (1997): 76–93.

Dylan, Huw. *Defence Intelligence and the Cold War: Britain's Joint Intelligence Bureau, 1945–1964.* Oxford: Oxford University Press, 2014.

Dyson, Stephen Benedict, and Matthew J. Parent. "The Operational Code Approach to Profiling Political Leaders: Understanding Vladimir Putin." *Intelligence and National Security* 33, no. 1 (2018): 84–100.

Easter, David. "Soviet Intelligence and the 1957 Syrian Crisis." *Intelligence and National Security* 33, no. 2 (2018): 227–40.

Eiran, Ehud. "The Three Tensions of Investigating Intelligence Failures." *Intelligence and National Security* 31, no. 4 (2016): 598–618.

Ekpe, Bassey. "The Intelligence Assets of the United Nations: Sources, Methods, and Implications." *International Journal of Intelligence and CounterIntelligence* 20, no. 3 (2007): 377–400.

Ermarth, Fritz W. "Seeing Russia Plain: The Russian Crisis and American Intelligence." *National Interest* 55 (Spring 1999): 5–14.

Feaver, Peter D., and Eric B. Lorber. *Diminishing Returns? The Future of Economic Coercion.* Washington, DC: Center for a New American Security, 2015.

Festinger, Leon. *A Theory of Cognitive Dissonance.* Evanston, IL: Row, Peterson, 1957.

Fingar, Thomas. "Intelligence and Grand Strategy." *Orbis* 56, no. 1 (Winter 2012): 118–34.

———. *Reducing Uncertainty: Intelligence Analysis and National Security.* Stanford, CA: Stanford University Press, 2011.

Fischer, Benjamin B. "Anglo-American Intelligence and the Soviet War Scare: The Untold Story." *Intelligence and National Security* 27, no. 1 (February 2012): 75–92.

———. "The 1980s Soviet War Scare: New Evidence from East German Documents." *Intelligence and National Security* 14, no. 3 (Autumn 1999): 186–97.

———. "Scolding Intelligence: The PFIAB Report on the Soviet War Scare." *International Journal of Intelligence and CounterIntelligence* 31, no. 1 (2018): 102–15.

Fisk, Charles E. "The Sino-Soviet Border Dispute: A Comparison of the Conventional and Bayesian Methods for Intelligence Warning." *Studies in Intelligence* 16, no. 2 (Spring 1972): 53–62.

Ford, Harold P. *CIA and the Vietnam Policymakers: Three Episodes, 1962–1968.* Washington, DC: Center for the Study of Intelligence, 1998.

———. *Estimative Intelligence: The Purposes and Problems of National Estimating.* Rev. ed. Lanham, MD: University Press of America, 1993.

———. "The US Government's Experience with Intelligence Analysis: Pluses and Minuses." *Intelligence and National Security* 10, no. 4 (1995): 34–53.

Franks, Tommy. *American Soldier.* New York: Regan Books, 2004.

Freedman, Sir Lawrence. *The Official History of the Falklands Campaign: The Origins of the Falklands War,* vol. 1. Abingdon, UK: Routledge, 2005.

———. "The Politics of Warning: Terrorism and Risk Communication." *Intelligence and National Security* 20, no. 3 (2005): 379–418.

Friedman, Jeffrey A., and Richard Zeckhauser. "Assessing Uncertainty in Intelligence." *Intelligence and National Security* 27, no. 6 (2012): 824–47.

———. "Why Assessing Estimative Accuracy Is Feasible and Desirable." *Intelligence and National Security* 31, no. 2 (February 2016): 178–200.

Garrett, Laurie. "Biology's Brave New World: The Promise and Perils of the Synbio Revolution." *Foreign Affairs* 92, no. 6 (November/December 2013): 42–46.

Garthoff, Raymond L. "Estimating Soviet Military Intentions and Capabilities." In *Watching the Bear: Essays on CIA's Analysis of the Soviet Union*. Edited by Gerald K. Haines and Robert E. Leggett, 135–86. Washington, DC: Center for the Study of Intelligence, 2009.

———. "On Estimating and Imputing Intentions." *International Security* 2, no. 3 (Winter 1978): 22–32.

———. *Soviet Leaders and Intelligence: Assessing the American Adversary during the Cold War*. Washington, DC: Georgetown University Press, 2015.

Gates, Robert M. "An Opportunity Unfulfilled: The Use and Perceptions of Intelligence Analysis at the White House." *Studies in Intelligence* 24 (Winter 1980): 17–26.

———. "The Prediction of Soviet Intentions." *Studies in Intelligence* 17, no. 1 (Spring 1973): 39–46.

Gazit, Shlomo. "Estimates and Fortune-Telling in Intelligence Work." *International Security* 4, no. 4 (Spring 1980): 36–56.

Gelber, Yoav. "The Collapse of the Israeli Intelligence's Conception: Apologetics, Memory and History of the Israeli Response to Egypt's Alleged Intention to Open War in May 1973." *Intelligence and National Security* 28, no. 4 (2013): 520–46.

Gentry, John A. "Assessing Intelligence Performance." In *The Oxford Handbook of National Security Intelligence*. Edited by Loch K. Johnson, 87–103. New York: Oxford University Press, 2010.

———. "Has the ODNI Improved U.S. Intelligence Analysis?" *International Journal of Intelligence and CounterIntelligence* 28, no. 4 (2015): 637–61.

———. *How Wars Are Won and Lost: Vulnerability and Military Power*. Santa Barbara, CA: Praeger Security International, 2012.

———. "The Instrumental Use of Norms in War: Impact on Strategies and Strategic Outcomes." *Comparative Strategy* 37, no. 1 (2018): 35–48.

———. "Intelligence Failure Reframed." *Political Science Quarterly* 123, no. 2 (2008): 247–70.

———. "Intelligence Learning and Adaptation: Lessons from Counterinsurgency Wars." *Intelligence and National Security* 25, no. 1 (2010): 50–75.

———. "The Intelligence of Fear." *Intelligence and National Security* 32, no. 1 (January 2017): 9–25.

———. *Lost Promise: How CIA Analysis Misserves the Nation*. Lanham, MD: University Press of America, 1993.

———. "A New Form of Politicization? Has the CIA Become Institutionally Biased?" *International Journal of Intelligence and CounterIntelligence* 31, no. 4 (Winter 2018, forthcoming).

———. "Norms as Weapons of War." *Defense and Security Analysis* 26, no. 1 (2010): 11–30.

———. "The 'Professionalization' of Intelligence Analysis: A Skeptical Perspective." *International Journal of Intelligence and CounterIntelligence* 29, no. 4 (Winter 2016): 643–76.

———. "Toward a Theory of Non-State Actors' Intelligence." *Intelligence and National Security* 31, no. 4 (May 2016): 465–89.

———. "Warning Analysis: Focusing on Perceptions of Vulnerability." *International Journal of Intelligence and CounterIntelligence* 28, no. 1 (January 2015): 64–88.

Gentry, John A., and Joseph S. Gordon. "U.S. Strategic Warning Intelligence: History and Challenges." *International Journal of Intelligence and CounterIntelligence* 31, no. 1 (2018): 19–53.

George, Alexander L. *Bridging the Gap: Theory and Practice in Foreign Policy*. Washington, DC: United States Institute of Peace Press, 1993.

———. "The Case for Multiple Advocacy in Making Foreign Policy." *American Political Science Review* 66, no. 3 (September 1972): 751–85.

———. "The Operational Code: A Neglected Approach to the Study of Political Leaders and Decision Making." *International Studies Quarterly* 13, no. 2 (1969): 191–222.

———. *Presidential Decisionmaking in Foreign Policy: The Effective Use of Information and Advice*. Boulder, CO: Westview, 1980.

George, Roger Z. "Reflections on CIA Analysis: Is It Finished?" *Intelligence and National Security* 26, no. 1 (February 2011): 72–81.

George, Roger Z., and James B. Bruce. "Intelligence Analysis: What It Is—and What Does It Take?" In George and Bruce, *Analyzing Intelligence*, 1–19.

———, eds. *Analyzing Intelligence: National Security Practitioners' Perspectives*. 2nd ed. Washington, DC: Georgetown University Press, 2014.

George, Roger Z., and James J. Wirtz, "Warning in an Age of Uncertainty." In George and Bruce, *Analyzing Intelligence*, 215–28.

Geyer, Michael. "National Socialist Germany: The Politics of Information." In May, *Knowing One's Enemies*, 310–46.

Gilad, Ben. *Early Warning: Using Competitive Intelligence to Anticipate Market Shifts, Control Risk, and Create Powerful Strategies*. New York: American Management Association, 2004.

Gladwell, Malcolm. "Connecting the Dots: The Paradoxes of Intelligence Reform." *New Yorker*, March 10, 2003, 83–89.

Glantz, David M. "Soviet Operational Intelligence in the Kursk Operation, July 1943." *Intelligence and National Security* 5, no. 1 (1990): 5–49.

Godson, Roy, and James J. Wirtz. "Strategic Denial and Deception." *International Journal of Intelligence and CounterIntelligence* 13, no. 4 (2000): 424–37.

Goldman, Jan. "Warning and the Policy Process: Problem Definition and Chaos Theory." *Defense Intelligence Journal* 7, no. 2 (Fall 1998): 65–80.

Gooch, John, and Amos Perlmutter, eds. *Military Deception and Strategic Surprise*. Abingdon, UK: Routledge, 1982. Originally published as a special issue of the *Journal of Strategic Studies* 5, no. 1 (1982).

Goodman, Allan E., and Bruce D. Berkowitz. "Intelligence without the Cold War." *Intelligence and National Security* 9, no. 2 (1994): 301–19.

Goodman, Michael S. "Avoiding Surprise: The Nicoll Report and Intelligence Analysis." In *Learning from the Secret Past: Cases in British Intelligence History*. Edited by Robert Dover and Michael S. Goodman, 265–92. Washington, DC: Georgetown University Press, 2011.

———. "Creating the Machinery for Joint Intelligence: The Formative Years of the Joint Intelligence Committee, 1936–1956." *International Journal of Intelligence and CounterIntelligence* 30, no. 1 (Spring 2017): 66–84.

———. "Learning to Walk: The Origins of the UK's Joint Intelligence Committee." *International Journal of Intelligence and CounterIntelligence* 21, no. 1 (2007): 40–56.

Gordon, Joseph S. "National Intelligence University: Certificate of Strategic Warning." *Journal of Strategic Security* 6, no. 3 suppl. (2013): 128–30.

———. "NATO Intelligence Fusion Centre (NIFC)." In *Encyclopedia of U.S. Intelligence*. Edited by Greg Moore, 645–50. New York: Taylor & Francis, 2015.

Grabo, Cynthia. *Handbook of Warning Intelligence: Assessing the Threat to National Security*. Lanham, MD: Scarecrow, 2010.

Grabo, Cynthia M. *Anticipating Surprise: Analysis for Strategic Warning*. Lanham, MD: University Press of America, 2004.

———. "Soviet Deception in the Czechoslovak Crisis." *Studies in Intelligence* 14, no. 1 (Spring 1970): 19–34.

———. "Strategic Warning: The Problem of Timing." *Studies in Intelligence* 16, no. 2 (Spring 1972): 79–92.

———. "The Watch Committee and the National Indications Center: The Evolution of U.S. Strategic Warning 1950–1975." *International Journal of Intelligence and CounterIntelligence* 3, no. 3 (1989): 363–85.

Grabo, Cynthia, with Jan Goldman. *Handbook of Warning Intelligence*. Lanham, MD: Rowman & Littlefield, 2015.

Greenspan, Alan. "Never Saw It Coming: Why the Economic Crisis Took Economists by Surprise." *Foreign Affairs* 92, no. 6 (November/December 2013): 88–96.

Groth, Alexander J., and John D. Froeliger. "Unheeded Warnings: Some Intelligence Lessons of the 1930s and 1940s." *Comparative Strategy* 10, no. 4 (October–December 1991): 331–46.

Guerron-Quintanay, Pablo, and Molin Zhong. *Macroeconomic Forecasting in Times of Crises*. Finance and Economics Discussion Series. Washington, DC: Federal Reserve Board, January 31, 2017. https://www.federalreserve.gov/econresdata/feds/2017/files/2017018pap.pdf.

Gustafson, Kristian. "Strategic Horizons: Futures Forecasting and the British Intelligence Community." *Intelligence and National Security* 25, no. 5 (October 2010): 589–610.

Haass, Richard N. "Supporting US Foreign Policy in the Post-9/11 World." *Studies in Intelligence* 46, no. 3 (2002): 1–13.

———. *War of Necessity, War of Choice: A Memoir of Two Iraq Wars*. New York: Simon & Schuster, 2009.

Habbeger, Beat. *Horizon Scanning in Government: Concept, Country Experiences, and Models for Switzerland.* Zurich: Center for Security Studies, 2009. http://www.css.ethz.ch/content/dam/ethz /special-interest/gess/cis/center-for-securities-studies/pdfs/Horizon-Scanning-in-Government.pdf.

Hall, Wayne Michael, and Gary Citrenbaum. *Intelligence Analysis: How to Think in Complex Environments*. Santa Barbara, CA: Praeger Security International, 2010.

Hammond, Thomas H. "Intelligence Organizations and the Organization of Intelligence." *Intelligence and National Security* 23, no. 4 (2010): 680–724.

Handel, Michael I. "Intelligence and Deception." *Journal of Strategic Studies* 5, no. 1 (1982): 122–54.

———. "Intelligence and the Problem of Strategic Surprise." *Journal of Strategic Studies* 7, no. 3 (1984): 229–81.

———. *Military Deception in Peace and War*. Jerusalem Papers on Peace Problems No. 38. Jerusalem: Hebrew University, 1985.

———. *Perception, Deception and Surprise: The Case of the Yom Kippur War*. Jerusalem Papers on Peace Problems No. 16. Jerusalem: Hebrew University, 1976.

Hare, Nick, and Peter Coghill. "The Future of the Intelligence Analysis Task." *Intelligence and National Security* 31, no. 6 (2016): 858–70.

Harff, Barbara. "No Lessons Learned from the Holocaust? Assessing Risks of Genocide and Political Mass Murder since 1955." *American Political Science Review* 97, no. 1 (February 2003): 57–73.

Hart, Douglas, and Steven Simon. "Thinking Straight and Talking Straight: Problems of Intelligence Analysis." *Survival* 48, no. 1 (2006): 35–60.

Haslam, Jonathan. *Near and Distant Neighbors: A New History of Soviet Intelligence*. New York: Farrar, Straus and Giroux, 2015.

Hastedt, Glenn. "The Politics of Intelligence and the Politicization of Intelligence: The American Experience." *Intelligence and National Security* 28, no. 1 (January 2013): 5–31.

Hayden, Michael V. *The Assault on Intelligence: American National Security in an Age of Lies*. New York: Penguin, 2018.

Hedley, John Hollister. "Learning from Intelligence Failures." *International Journal of Intelligence and CounterIntelligence* 18, no. 3 (Fall 2005): 435–50.

Heikal, Mohamed. *The Road to Ramadan*. New York: Ballantine, 1975.

Herman, Michael. "Intelligence and the Assessment of Military Capabilities: Reasonable Sufficiency or the Worst Case?" *Intelligence and National Security* 4, no. 4 (1989): 765–99.

Hermann, Margaret G. "Explaining Foreign Policy Behavior Using the Personal Characteristics of Political Leaders." *International Studies Quarterly* 24, no. 1 (March 1980): 7–46.

———. "How Decision Units Shape Foreign Policy: A Theoretical Framework." *International Studies Review* 3, no. 2 (June 2001): 47–81.

Herring, Jan P. *Measuring the Effectiveness of Competitive Intelligence: Assessing and Communicating CI's Value to Your Organization.* San Antonio, TX: Society of Competitive Intelligence Professionals, 1996.

Hersh, Seymour M. "On the Nuclear Edge." *New Yorker*, March 29, 1993. http://www.newyorker.com/magazine/1993/03/29/on-the-nuclear-edge.

Hershkovitz, Shay. "'A Three-Story Building': A Critical Analysis of Israeli Early Warning Discourse." *International Journal of Intelligence and CounterIntelligence* 30, no. 4 (2017): 765–84.

Hesketh, Roger. *Fortitude: The D-Day Deception Plan.* Woodstock, NY: Overview, 2000.

Heuer, Richards J., Jr. "Limits of Intelligence Analysis." *Orbis* 49, no. 1 (Winter 2005): 75–94.

———. *Psychology of Intelligence Analysis.* Washington, DC: Center for the Study of Intelligence, 1999.

———. *Rethinking Intelligence: Richards J. Heuer Jr.'s Life of Public Service.* Reston, VA: Pherson Associates, 2018.

———. "Soviet Organization and Doctrine for Strategic Deception." In Dailey and Parker, *Soviet Strategic Deception*, 21–53.

———. "Strategic Deception and Counterdeception: A Cognitive Process Approach." *International Studies Quarterly* 25, no. 2 (June 1981): 294–327.

Hilsman, Roger, Jr. "Intelligence and Policy-Making in Foreign Affairs." *World Politics* 5, no. 1 (October 1952): 1–45.

———. *Strategic Intelligence and National Decisions.* Glencoe, IL: Free Press, 1956.

Hoffman, Steven A. "Anticipation, Disaster, and Victory: India 1962–71." *Asian Survey* 12, no. 11 (November 1972): 960–79.

Holbrooke, Richard. *To End a War.* New York: Modern Library, 1999.

Holt, Thaddeus. *The Deceivers: Allied Military Deception in the Second World War.* New York: Skyhorse, 2007.

Honig, Or. "Surprise Attacks—Are They Inevitable? Moving beyond the Orthodox-Revisionist Dichotomy." *Security Studies* 17, no. 1 (2008): 72–106.

Honig, Or Arthur. "A New Direction for Theory-Building in Intelligence Studies." *International Journal of Intelligence and CounterIntelligence* 20, no. 4 (2007): 699–716.

Hopple, Gerald W. "Intelligence and Warning: Implications and Lessons of the Falkland Islands War." *World Politics* 36, no. 3 (April 1984): 339–61.

Horelick, Arnold L. "The Cuban Missile Crisis: An Analysis of Soviet Calculations and Behavior." *World Politics* 16, no. 3 (April 1964): 363–89.

Horowitz, Michael C., Allan C. Stam, and Cali M. Ellis. *Why Leaders Fight.* New York: Cambridge University Press, 2015.

Hughes-Wilson, John. *Military Intelligence Blunders and Cover-Ups.* New York: Carroll & Graf, 2004.

Hulnick, Arthur S. "Indications and Warning for Homeland Security: Seeking a New Paradigm." *International Journal of Intelligence and CounterIntelligence* 18, no. 4 (2005): 593–608.

———. "The Intelligence Producer–Policy Consumer Linkage: A Theoretical Approach." *Intelligence and National Security* 1, no. 2 (1996): 212–33.

Janis, Irving L. *Victims of Groupthink: A Psychological Study of Foreign-Policy Decisions and Fiascoes.* Boston: Houghton Mifflin, 1972.

Janis, Irving L., and Leon Mann. *Decision Making: A Psychological Analysis of Conflict, Choice, and Commitment.* New York: Free Press, 1979.

Jensen, Mark A. "Intelligence Failures: What Are They Really and What Do We Do about Them?" *Intelligence and National Security* 27, no. 2 (April 2012): 261–82.

Jervis, Robert. "Cooperation under the Security Dilemma." *World Politics* 30, no. 2 (January 1978): 167–214.

———. "Do Leaders Matter and How Would We Know?" *Security Studies* 22, no. 2 (2013): 153–79.

———. *How Statesmen Think: The Psychology of International Politics*. Princeton, NJ: Princeton University Press, 2017.

———. "Hypotheses on Misperception." *World Politics* 20, no. 3 (April 1968): 454–79.

———. *Perception and Misperception in International Politics*. Princeton, NJ: Princeton University Press, 1976.

———. "Political Implications of Loss Aversion." *Political Psychology* 13, no. 2 (June 1992): 187–204.

———. "Reports, Politics, and Intelligence Failures: The Case of Iraq." *Journal of Strategic Studies* 29, no. 1 (February 2006): 3–52.

———. *System Effects: Complexity in Political and Social Life*. Princeton, NJ: Princeton University Press, 1997.

———. "What's Wrong with the Intelligence Process?" *International Journal of Intelligence and CounterIntelligence* 1, no. 1 (1986): 28–41.

———. "Why Intelligence and Policymakers Clash." *Political Science Quarterly* 125, no. 2 (2010): 185–204.

———. *Why Intelligence Fails: Lessons from the Iranian Revolution and the Iraq War*. Ithaca, NY: Cornell University Press, 2010.

Johnson, Loch K. "Glimpses into the Gems of American Intelligence: The President's Daily Brief and the National Intelligence Estimate." *Intelligence and National Security* 23, no. 3 (June 2008): 333–70.

Johnston, Paul. "No Cloak and Dagger Required: Intelligence Support to UN Peacekeeping." *Intelligence and National Security* 12, no. 4 (1997): 102–12.

Joint Chiefs of Staff, Joint Staff J2, Defense Warning Staff, J2 Warning. *(U) Defense Warning Network Handbook*. 3rd ed. Washington, DC: Joint Chiefs of Staff, May 2014.

Jones, Chris. "Secrecy Reigns at the EU's Intelligence Analysis Centre." *Statewatch* 22, no. 3 (January 2013). http://www.statewatch.org/analyses/no-223-eu-intcen.pdf.

Jones, Clive. "'One Size Fits All': Israel, Intelligence, and the al-Aqsa Intifada." *Studies in Conflict and Terrorism* 26, no. 4 (2003): 273–88.

Jones, Milo, and Philippe Silberzahn. *Constructing Cassandra: Reframing Intelligence Failure at the CIA, 1947–2001*. Stanford, CA: Stanford University Press, 2013.

Jones, R. V. *The Wizard War: British Scientific Intelligence, 1939–1945*. New York: Coward, McCann & Geoghegan, 1978.

Kahana, Ephraim. "Analyzing Israel's Intelligence Failures." *International Journal of Intelligence and CounterIntelligence* 18, no. 2 (2005): 262–79.

———. "Early Warning versus Concept: The Case of the Yom Kippur War 1973." *Intelligence and National Security* 17, no. 2 (2002): 81–104.

Kahana, Ephraim, and Sagit Stivi-Kerbis. "The Assassination of Anwar al-Sadat: An Intelligence Failure." *Intelligence and National Security* 27, no. 1 (2014): 178–92.

Kahn, David. *Hitler's Spies: German Military Intelligence in World War II*. New York: Macmillan, 1978.

———. "The Intelligence Failure at Pearl Harbor." *Foreign Affairs* 70, no. 5 (Winter 1991–92): 138–52.

Kahneman, Daniel. *Judgment under Uncertainty: Heuristics and Biases*. New York: Cambridge University Press, 1982.

Kahneman, Daniel, and Amos Tversky. "Prospect Theory: An Analysis of Decision under Risk." *Econometrica* 47, no. 2 (March 1979): 263–91.

Kam, Ephraim. *Surprise Attack: The Victim's Perspective*. Cambridge, MA: Harvard University Press, 1988.

Kass, Lani, and J. Phillip "Jack" London. "Surprise, Deception, Denial and Warning: Strategic Imperatives." *Orbis* 57, no. 1 (Winter 2013): 59–82.

Katz, Jonathan I. "Deception and Denial in Iraq: The Intelligent Adversary Corollary." *International Journal of Intelligence and CounterIntelligence* 19, no. 4 (Winter 2006–7): 577–85.

Kaufman, Stuart J. *Modern Hatreds: The Symbolic Politics of Ethnic War*. Ithaca, NY: Cornell University Press, 2001.

Kent, Sherman. "A Crucial Estimate Relived." *Studies in Intelligence* 35, no. 5 (Spring 1964): 111–19.

———. "Estimates and Influence." *Studies in Intelligence* 12, no. 3 (Summer 1968): 11–21.

———. *Strategic Intelligence for American World Policy*. Princeton, NJ: Princeton University Press, 1949.

———. "Words of Estimative Probability." *Studies in Intelligence* 8, no. 4 (Fall 1964): 49–65.

Kerbel, Josh. "Thinking Straight: Cognitive Bias in the US Debate about China." *Studies in Intelligence* 48, no. 3 (2004): 27–35.

Kerbel, Josh, and Anthony Alcott. "Synthesizing with Clients, Not Analyzing for Customers." *Studies in Intelligence* 54, no. 4 Extracts (December 2010): 11–27.

Khong, Yuen Foong. *Analogies at War*. Princeton, NJ: Princeton University Press, 1992.

Kissinger, Henry. *White House Years*. Boston: Little, Brown, 1979.

Knight, Frank H. *Risk, Uncertainty, and Profit*. Eastford, CT: Martino Fine Books, 2014 (1921).

Knorr, Klaus. "Failures in National Intelligence Estimates: The Case of the Cuban Missiles." *World Politics* 16, no. 3 (April 1964): 455–67.

———. "Strategic Surprise: The Incentive Structure." In Knorr and Morgan, *Strategic Military Surprise*, 173–93.

Knorr, Klaus, and Patrick Morgan, eds. *Strategic Military Surprise: Incentives and Opportunities*. New Brunswick, NJ: Transaction, 1983.

Kobayashi, Yoshiki. "Assessing Reform of the Japanese Intelligence Community." *International Journal of Intelligence and CounterIntelligence* 28, no. 4 (2015): 717–33.

Koblentz, Gregory D. "Biosecurity Reconsidered: Calibrating Biological Threats and Responses." *International Security* 34, no. 4 (Spring 2010): 96–132.

Krepinevich, Andrew, and Barry Watts. *The Last Warrior: Andrew Marshall and the Shaping of Modern American Defense Strategy*. New York: Basic, 2015.

Kriendler, John. "Anticipating Crises." *NATO Review* (Winter 2002). www.nato.int/docu/review/2002/Managing-Crisis/Anticipating-crises/EN/index.htm.

———. "NATO Intelligence and Early Warning." Conflict Studies Research Centre, Special Series. March 2006. https://www.files.ethz.ch/isn/39988/06_Apr.pdf.

Kringen, John. "Serving the Senior Military Consumer: A National Agency Perspective." In George and Bruce, *Analyzing Intelligence*, 103–17.

Kuhns, Woodrow J. "Intelligence Failures: Forecasting and the Lessons of Epistemology." In Betts and Mahnken, *Paradoxes of Strategic Intelligence*, 80–100.

Kuperman, Alan J. "A Model Humanitarian Intervention? Reassessing NATO's Libya Campaign." *International Security* 38, no. 1 (2013): 105–36.

———. "The Moral Hazard of Humanitarian Intervention: Lessons from the Balkans." *International Studies Quarterly* 52, no. 1 (March 2008): 49–80.

Kuran, Timur. "Now Out of Never: The Element of Surprise in the East European Revolution of 1989." *World Politics* 44, no. 1 (October 1991): 7–48.

Lahneman, William J. "IC Data Mining in the Post-Snowden Era." *International Journal of Intelligence and CounterIntelligence* 29, no. 4 (2016): 700–723.

Landers, Daniel F. "The Defense Warning System." *Defense Intelligence Journal* 3, no. 1 (Summer 1994): 21–31.

Larson, Deborah Welch. "The Role of Belief Systems and Schemas in Foreign Policy Decision-Making." *Political Psychology* 15, no. 1 (March 1994): 17–33.

Lasoen, Kenneth L. "Indications and Warning in Belgium: Brussels Is Not Delphi." *Journal of Strategic Studies* 40, no. 7 (2017): 927–62.

Latimer, Jon. *Deception in War*. Woodstock, NY: Overlook, 2001.

Lefebvre, Stéphane. "'The Belgians Just Aren't Up to It': Belgian Intelligence and Contemporary Terrorism." *International Journal of Intelligence and CounterIntelligence* 30, no. 1 (Spring 2017): 1–29.

———. "Poland's Attempts to Develop a Democratic and Effective Intelligence System, Phase 1: 1989–1999." *International Journal of Intelligence and CounterIntelligence* 29, no. 3 (Summer 2016): 470–502.

Leites, Nathan. *A Study of Bolshevism*. Glencoe, IL: Free Press, 1953.

Levite, Ariel. *Intelligence and Strategic Surprise*. New York: Columbia University Press, 1987.

Libbey, James K. "CoCom, Comecon, and the Economic Cold War." *Russian History* 37, no. 2 (2010): 133–52.

Lim, Kevjn. "Big Data and Strategic Intelligence." *Intelligence and National Security* 31, no. 4 (May 2016): 619–35.

Lowenthal, Mark M. *Intelligence: From Secrets to Policy*. 4th ed. Washington, DC: CQ Press, 2009.

———. *Intelligence: From Secrets to Policy*. 6th ed. Los Angeles: SAGE, 2015.

———. "The Intelligence Time Event Horizon." *International Journal of Intelligence and CounterIntelligence* 22, no. 3 (2009): 369–81.

———. "The Real Intelligence Failure? Spineless Spies." *Washington Post*, May 28, 2008.

———. "Strategic Early Warning: Where Are We Now?" *Journal of Intelligence and Analysis* 22, no. 2 (April 2015): 1–10.

———. "Towards a Reasonable Standard for Analysis: How Right, How Often on Which Issues?" *Intelligence and National Security* 23, no. 3 (2008): 303–15.

Luikart, Kenneth A., and Georgia Ang. "Transforming Homeland Security: Intelligence Indications and Warning." *Air and Space Power Journal* 17, no. 2 (Summer 2003): 69–77.

Lynch, Marc, Deen Freelon, and Sean Aday. *Syria's Socially Mediated Civil War*. Washington, DC: United States Institute of Peace Press, 2014.

MacEachin, Douglas. "Predicting the Soviet Invasion of Afghanistan: The Intelligence Community's Record." Washington, DC: Center for the Study of Intelligence, 2007. https://www.cia.gov/library /center-for-the-study-of-intelligence/csi-publications/books-and-monographs/predicting-the -soviet-invasion-of-afghanistan-the-intelligence-communitys-record/predicting-the-soviet -invasion-of-afghanistan-the-intelligence-communitys-record.html.

MacEachin, Douglas J. "CIA Assessments of the Soviet Union: The Record versus the Charges." *Studies in Intelligence*, semiannual ed. no. 1 (1997): 57–65.

———. *U.S. Intelligence and the Confrontation in Poland, 1980–1981*. University Park: Pennsylvania State University Press, 2002.

Mahnken, Thomas G. *Uncovering Ways of War: U.S. Intelligence and Foreign Military Innovation, 1918–1941*. Ithaca, NY: Cornell University Press, 2002.

Mandel, David R., and Alan Barnes. "Accuracy of Forecasts in Strategic Intelligence." *Proceedings of the National Academy of Sciences* 111, no. 3 (July 29, 2014): 10984–89.

Mandel, Robert. "On Estimating Post–Cold War Enemy Intentions." *Intelligence and National Security* 24, no. 2 (2009): 194–215.

Marrin, Stephen. "Evaluating the Quality of Intelligence Analysis: By What (Mis)Measure?" *Intelligence and National Security* 27, no. 6 (2012): 896–912.

———. "The 9/11 Terrorist Attacks: A Failure of Policy Not Strategic Intelligence Analysis." *Intelligence and National Security* 26, nos. 2–3 (2011): 182–202.

———. "Preventing Intelligence Failures by Learning from the Past." *International Journal of Intelligence and CounterIntelligence* 17, no. 4 (2004): 655–72.

———. "Training and Educating U.S. Intelligence Analysts." *International Journal of Intelligence and CounterIntelligence* 22, no. 1 (2008): 131–46.

———. "Why Strategic Intelligence Has Limited Influence on American Foreign Policy." *Intelligence and National Security* 32, no. 6 (2017): 725–42.

Marten, Kimberly. "Putin's Choices: Explaining Russian Foreign Policy and Intervention in Ukraine." *Washington Quarterly* 38, no. 2 (Summer 2015): 189–204.

Martin, Wayne R. "The Measurement of International Military Commitments for Crisis Early Warning." *International Studies Quarterly* 21, no. 1 (March 1977): 151–80.

Masterman, J. C. *The Double-Cross System in the War of 1939 to 1945*. New Haven, CT: Yale University Press, 1972.

May, Ernest R. *Strange Victory: Hitler's Conquest of France*. New York: Hill & Wang, 2000.

———, ed. *Knowing One's Enemies: Intelligence Assessment before the Two World Wars*. Princeton, NJ: Princeton University Press, 1984.

McCarthy, Mary O. "The Mission to Warn: Disaster Looms." *Defense Intelligence Journal* 7, no. 2 (Fall 1998): 17–31.

———. "The National Warning System: Striving for an Elusive Goal." *Defense Intelligence Journal* 3, no. 1 (Spring 1994): 5–19.

McCormick, Gordon H. "Terrorist Decision Making." *Annual Review of Political Science* 6 (2003): 473–507.

McCreary, John F. "Warning Cycles." *Studies in Intelligence* 27, no. 3 (Fall 1983): 71–79.

McDermott, Rose. "Experimental Intelligence." *Intelligence and National Security* 26, no. 1 (2011): 82–98.

———. "The Use and Abuse of Medical Intelligence." *Intelligence and National Security* 22, no. 4 (2007): 491–520.

McDermott, Rose, and Uri Bar–Joseph. "Pearl Harbor and Midway: The Decisive Influence of Two Men on the Outcomes." *Intelligence and National Security* 31, no. 7 (December 2016): 949–62.

McIntyre, Ben. *Double Cross: The True Story of the D-Day Spies*. New York: Crown, 2012.

———. *Operation Mincemeat: How a Dead Man and a Bizarre Plan Fooled the Nazis and Assured an Allied Victory*. New York: Harmony, 2010.

McLaughlin, John. "Serving the National Policymaker." In George and Bruce, *Analyzing Intelligence*, 81–92.

Mellers, Barbara, Eric Stone, Pavel Atanasov, Nick Rohrbaugh, S. Emlen Metz, Lyle Ungar, Michael M. Bishop, Michael Horowitz, Ed Merkle, and Philip Tetlock. "The Psychology of Intelligence Analysis: Drivers of Prediction Accuracy in World Politics." *Journal of Experimental Psychology: Applied* 21, no. 1 (March 2015): 1–12.

Mercer, Jonathan. "Prospect Theory and Political Science." *Annual Review of Political Science* 8, no. 1 (2005): 1–21.

Miller, Bowman H. "U.S. Strategic Intelligence Forecasting and the Perils of Prediction." *International Journal of Intelligence and CounterIntelligence* 27, no. 4 (2014): 687–701.

Miller, Paul D. "Graveyard of Analogies: The Use and Abuse of History for the War in Afghanistan." *Journal of Strategic Studies* 39, no. 3 (2016): 446–76.

Miscik, Jami. "Intelligence and the Presidency: How to Get It Right." *Foreign Affairs* 96, no. 3 (May/June 2017): 57–64.

Mitzen, Jennifer, and Randall L. Schweller. "Knowing the Unknown Unknowns: Misplaced Certainty and the Onset of War." *Security Studies* 20, no. 1 (2011): 2–35.

Mobley, Richard A. "Gauging the Iraqi Threat to Kuwait in the 1960s." *Studies in Intelligence* 11 (Fall/Winter 2001): 19–31.

———. "North Korea's Surprise Attack: Weak U.S. Analysis?" *International Journal of Intelligence and CounterIntelligence* 13, no. 4 (2000): 490–514.

Montagu, Ewen. *Beyond Top Secret U.* London: Corgi, 1979.

Moore, David T. "Critical Thinking and Intelligence Analysis." Occasional Paper No. 14. Joint Military Intelligence College, Washington, DC, May 2006.

Morgan, Patrick. "Examples of Strategic Surprise in the Far East." In Knorr and Morgan, *Strategic Military Surprise*, 43–76.

———. "Opportunity for a Strategic Surprise." In Knorr and Morgan, *Strategic Military Surprise*, 195–245.

Moyar, Mark. "Hanoi's Strategic Surprise, 1964–65." *Intelligence and National Security* 18, no. 1 (2003): 155–70.

Muller, David G., Jr. "Improving Futures Intelligence." *International Journal of Intelligence and CounterIntelligence* 22, no. 3 (2009): 382–95.

Murphy, David E. *What Stalin Knew: The Enigma of Barbarossa.* New Haven, CT: Yale University Press, 2005.

National Commission on Terrorist Attacks upon the United States. *Final Report of the National Commission on Terrorist Attacks upon the United States* (aka *The 9/11 Commission Report*). New York: W. W. Norton, 2004.

Neustadt, Richard E., and Ernest R. May. *Thinking in Time: The Uses of History for Decision Makers.* New York: Free Press, 1986.

Nguyen, Lien-Hang T. *Hanoi's War: An International History of the War for Peace in Vietnam.* Chapel Hill: University of North Carolina Press, 2012.

Nye, Joseph S., Jr. "Peering into the Future." *Foreign Affairs* 73, no. 4 (July/August 1994): 82–93.

Omand, Sir David, Jamie Bartlett, and Carl Miller. "Introducing Social Media Intelligence (SOCMINT)." *Intelligence and National Security* 27, no. 6 (2012): 801–23.

Organisation for Economic Co-operation and Development. *Preventing Violence, War and State Collapse: The Future of Conflict Early Warning and Response.* OECD, 2009, https://www.oecd.org/dac/conflict-fragility-resilience/docs/preventing%20violence%20war%20and%20state%20collapse.pdf.

Oros, Andrew. "Japanese Foreign Intelligence-Related Activities." *Intelligence and National Security* 14, no. 3 (1999): 235–43.

Pappas, Aris A., and James M. Simon Jr. "The Intelligence Community: 2001–2015." *Studies in Intelligence* 46, no. 1 (2002): 39–47.

Paris, Roland. "Kosovo and the Metaphor War." *Political Science Quarterly* 117, no. 3 (Fall 2002): 423–50.

Parker, Charles F., and Eric K. Stern. "Bolt from the Blue or Avoidable Failure? Revisiting September 11 and the Origins of Strategic Surprise." *Foreign Policy Analysis* 1, no. 3 (November 2005): 301–31.

Patton, Thomas J. "The Monitoring of War Indicators." *Studies in Intelligence* 3, no. 1 (Winter 1959): 55–68.

Persico, Joseph E. *Casey: The Lives and Secrets of William J. Casey: From the OSS to the CIA.* New York: Penguin, 1990.

Petersen, Martin. "What I Learned in 40 Years of Doing Intelligence Analysis for US Foreign Policymakers." *Studies in Intelligence* 55, no. 1 (extracts, March 2011): 13–20.

Pherson, Katherine Hibbs, and Randolph H. Pherson. *Critical Thinking for Strategic Intelligence.* Los Angeles: CQ Press, 2013.

Phythian, Mark. "Policing Uncertainty: Intelligence, Security and Risk." *Intelligence and National Security* 27, no. 2 (2012): 187–205.

Pillar, Paul. "Intelligence, Policy, and the War in Iraq." *Foreign Affairs* 85, no. 2 (March/April 2006): 15–27.

Pillar, Paul R. "Good Literature and Bad History: The 9/11 Commission's Tale of Strategic Intelligence." *Intelligence and National Security* 21, no. 6 (December 2006): 1022–44.

———. *Intelligence and U.S. Foreign Policy: Iraq, 9/11, and Misguided Reform.* New York: Columbia University Press, 2011.

———. "Predictive Intelligence: Policy Support or Spectator Sport." *SAIS Review of International Affairs* 28, no. 1 (Winter/Spring 2008): 25–35.

Posner, Richard A. "Thinking about Catastrophe." In *Blindside: How to Anticipate Forcing Events and Wild Cards in Global Politics.* Edited by Francis Fukuyama, 7–19. Washington, DC: Brookings Institution Press, 2007.

Post, Jerrold M., ed. *The Psychological Assessment of Political Leaders.* Ann Arbor: University of Michigan Press, 2005.

Power, Samantha. *"A Problem from Hell": America and the Age of Genocide.* New York: Harper Perennial, 2002.

Prescott, E. M. "SARS: A Warning." *Survival* 45, no. 3 (2003): 207–26.

Priess, David. *The President's Book of Secrets: The Untold Story of Intelligence Briefings of America's Presidents from Kennedy to Obama.* New York: PublicAffairs, 2016.

Pry, Peter Vincent. "Ideology as a Factor in Deterrence." *Comparative Strategy* 31, no. 2 (2012): 111–46.

Quiggin, Thomas. *Seeing the Invisible: National Security Intelligence in an Uncertain Age.* Singapore: World Scientific Publishing, 2007.

Ramsey, Diane M., and Mark S. Boerner. "A Study in Indications Methodology." *Studies in Intelligence* 7, no. 3 (Summer 1963): 75–94.

Rapport, Aaron. "The Long and the Short of It: Cognitive Constraints on Leaders' Assessments of 'Postwar' Iraq." *International Security* 37, no. 3 (Winter 2012–13): 133–71.

Reich, Robert C. "Re-examining the Team A–Team B Exercise." *International Journal of Intelligence and CounterIntelligence* 3, no. 3 (1989): 387–403.

Rice, Condoleezza. "Rethinking the National Interest: American Realism for a New World." *Foreign Affairs* 87, no. 4 (July/August 2008): 2–26.

Richelson, Jeffrey T. *The US Intelligence Community.* 7th ed. Boulder, CO: Westview, 2016.

Rietjens, Sebastiaan, and Erik de Waard. "UN Peacekeeping Intelligence: The ASIFU Experiment." *International Journal of Intelligence and CounterIntelligence* 30, no. 3 (Fall 2017): 532–56.

Riley, William S. "Deceived to Intervene: Non-State Actors' Use of Deception to Elicit Western Intervention in Libya in 2011." *American Intelligence Journal* 32, no. 2 (2015): 35–46.

Roberts, Patrick S., and Robert P. Saldin. "Why Presidents Sometimes Do Not Use Intelligence Information." *Political Science Quarterly* 131, no. 4 (2016–17): 779–802.

Rolington, Alfred. *Strategic Intelligence for the 21st Century: The Mosaic Method.* Oxford, UK: Oxford University Press, 2013.

Rovner, Joshua. *Fixing the Facts: National Security and the Politics of Intelligence.* Ithaca, NY: Cornell University Press, 2011.

———. "Intelligence in the Twitter Age." *International Journal of Intelligence and CounterIntelligence* 26, no. 2 (2013): 260–71.

Russell, Richard L. "CIA's Strategic Intelligence in Iraq." *Political Science Quarterly* 117, no. 2 (Summer 2002): 191–207.

———. *Sharpening Strategic Intelligence: Why the CIA Gets It Wrong and What Needs to Be Done to Get It Right.* New York: Cambridge University Press, 2007.

Sadat, Anwar el-. *In Search of Identity: An Autobiography.* New York: Harper & Row, 1978.

Saffo, Paul. "Six Rules for Effective Forecasting." *Harvard Business Review* 85, nos. 7–8 (July/August 2007): 122–31.

Schelling, Thomas. *The Strategy of Conflict.* Cambridge, MA: Harvard University Press, 1960.

Schwartz, Peter. *The Art of the Long View: Planning for the Future in an Uncertain World.* New York: Currency Doubleday, 1996.

Scott, Len. "Intelligence and the Risk of Nuclear War: Able Archer-83 Revisited." *Intelligence and National Security* 26, no. 6 (2011): 759–77.

———. "Reflections on the Age of Intelligence." *Intelligence and National Security* 27, no. 5 (2012): 617–24.

Senate Select Committee on Intelligence. *Postwar Findings about Iraq's WMD Programs and Links to Terrorism and How They Compare with Prewar Assessments*. S. Report 109–331. 109th Congress, 2d Session, September 8, 2006.

———. *Report of the Select Committee on Intelligence on the U.S. Intelligence Community's Prewar Assessments on Iraq together with Additional Views*. S. Report 108-301, 108th Congress, 2d Session, July 9, 2004.

Shalev, Aryeh. *Israel's Intelligence Assessment before the Yom Kippur War: Disentangling Deception and Distraction*. Brighton, UK: Sussex Academic Press, 2010.

Sharma, S. "Asia's Economic Crisis and the IMF." *Survival* 40, no. 2 (1998): 27–52.

Shazly, Saad el-. *The Crossing of the Suez*. San Francisco: American Mideast Research, 2003.

Sheffy, Yigal. "Early Warning of Intentions or of Capabilities? Revisiting the Israeli-Egyptian Rotem Affair, 1960." *Intelligence and National Security* 28, no. 3 (2013): 420–37.

———. "Overcoming Strategic Weakness: The Egyptian Deception and the Yom Kippur War." *Intelligence and National Security* 21, no. 5 (2006): 809–28.

Shelton, Christina. "The Roots of Analytic Failures in the U.S. Intelligence Community." *International Journal of Intelligence and CounterIntelligence* 24, no. 4 (2011): 637–55.

Shlaim, Avi. "Failures in National Intelligence Estimates: The Case of the Yom Kippur War." *World Politics* 28, no. 3 (April 1976): 348–80.

Shryock, Richard W. "The Intelligence Community Post-Mortem Program, 1973–1975." *Studies in Intelligence* 21, no. 1 (Fall 1977): 15–28.

Sindawi, Khalid, and Ephraim Kahana. "The Yom Kippur War: The Successes of Israeli Intelligence." *International Journal of Intelligence and CounterIntelligence* 28, no. 4 (2015): 762–74.

Sirseloudi, Matenia P. "How to Predict the Unpredictable: On the Early Detection of Terrorist Campaigns." *Defense and Security Analysis* 21, no. 4 (December 2005): 369–85.

Skowronek, Stephen. *Presidential Leadership in Political Time: Reprise and Reappraisal*. Lawrence: University Press of Kansas, 2009.

Smith, Michael Douglas. "A Good Intelligence Analyst." *International Journal of Intelligence and CounterIntelligence* 30, no. 1 (2017): 181–85.

Smith, Timothy J. "*Overlord/Bodyguard*: Intelligence Failure through Adversary Deception." *International Journal of Intelligence and CounterIntelligence* 27, no. 3 (2014): 550–68.

Snider, L. Britt. *The Agency and the Hill: CIA's Relationship with Congress, 1946–2004*. Washington, DC: Center for the Study of Intelligence, 2008.

Sorley, Lewis. A *Better War: The Unexamined Victories and Final Tragedy of America's Last Years in Vietnam*. New York: Harcourt, 2007.

Spielmann, Karl. "I Got Algorithm: Can There Be a Nate Silver in Intelligence?" *International Journal of Intelligence and CounterIntelligence* 29, no. 3 (2016): 525–44.

———. "Strengthening Intelligence Threat Analysis." *International Journal of Intelligence and CounterIntelligence* 25, no. 1 (2012): 19–43.

———. "Using Enhanced Analytic Techniques for Threat Analysis: A Case Study Illustration." *International Journal of Intelligence and CounterIntelligence* 27, no. 1 (2014): 132–55.

Stack, Kevin P. "Competitive Intelligence." *Intelligence and National Security* 13, no. 4 (Winter 1998): 194–202.

Stanton, Gregory H. "The Rwandan Genocide: Why Early Warning Failed." *Journal of African Conflicts and Peace Studies* 1, no. 2 (September 2009): 6–25.

Stein, Janice Gross. "'Intelligence' and 'Stupidity' Reconsidered: Estimation and Decision in Israel, 1973." *Journal of Strategic Studies* 3, no. 2 (September 1980): 147–77.

———. "Military Deception, Strategic Surprise, and Conventional Deterrence: A Political Analysis of Egypt and Israel, 1971–73." In Gooch and Perlmutter, *Military Deception and Strategic Surprise*, 94–122.

———. *Psychology and Deterrence*. Baltimore: Johns Hopkins University Press, 1985.

Steinberg, James B. "The Policymaker's Perspective: Transparency and Partnership." In George and Bruce, *Analyzing Intelligence*, 93–101.

Steinbruner, John. *The Cybernetic Theory of Decision*. Princeton, NJ: Princeton University Press, 1974.

Stolfi, Russel H. S. "Barbarossa: German Grand Deception and the Achievement of Strategic and Tactical Surprise against the Soviet Union, 1940–1941." In Daniel and Herbig, *Strategic Military Deception*, 195–223.

Stottlemyre, Steven A. "HUMINT, OSINT, or Something New? Defining Crowdsourced Intelligence." *International Journal of Intelligence and CounterIntelligence* 28, no. 3 (2015): 578–89.

Strachan-Morris, David. "Threat and Risk: What Is the Difference and Why Does It Matter?" *Intelligence and National Security* 27, no. 2 (2012): 172–86.

Sullivan, John P., and James J. Wirtz. "Terrorism Early Warning and Counterterrorism Intelligence." *International Journal of Intelligence and CounterIntelligence* 21, no. 1 (2007): 13–25.

Sun Tzu. *The Art of War*. Translated by Samuel B. Griffith. New York: Oxford University Press, 1973.

Suskind, Ron. *The One Percent Doctrine: Deep Inside America's Pursuit of Its Enemies since 9/11*. New York: Simon & Schuster, 2006.

Svendsen, Adam D. M. "The Federal Bureau of Investigation and Change: Addressing US Domestic Counter-Terrorism Intelligence." *Intelligence and National Security* 27, no. 3 (June 2012): 371–97.

Taleb, Nassim Nicholas. *The Black Swan: The Impact of the Highly Improbable*. New York: Random House, 2007.

Tetlock, Philip E. *Expert Political Judgment: How Good Is It? How Can We Know?* Princeton, NJ: Princeton University Press, 2005.

Tetlock, Philip E., and Dan Gardner. *Superforecasting: The Art and Science of Prediction*. New York: Crown, 2015.

Tiernan, R. Kent. "Hiding in Plain Sight." *American Intelligence Journal* 32, no. 2 (2015): 71–76.

Travers, Russ. "The Coming Intelligence Failure." *Studies in Intelligence* 40, no. 2 (1996): 35–43.

Travers, Russell E. "Waking Up on Another September 12th: Implications for Intelligence Reform." *Intelligence and National Security* 31, no. 5 (June 2016): 746–61.

Treverton, Gregory F. *Intelligence for an Age of Terror*. New York: Cambridge University Press, 2009.

Treverton, Gregory F., and Renanah Miles. "Unheeded Warning of War: Why Policymakers Ignored the 1990 Yugoslavia Estimate." *Intelligence and National Security* 32, no. 4 (June 2017): 506–22.

Tromblay, Darren E. "The Threat Review and Prioritization Trap: How the FBI's New Threat Review and Prioritization Process Compounds the Bureau's Oldest Problems." *Intelligence and National Security* 31, no. 5 (2016): 762–70.

United Kingdom Government. *National Intelligence Machinery*, at https://assets.publishing.service.gov .uk/government/uploads/system/uploads/attachment_data/file/61808/nim-november2010.pdf.

United Kingdom Ministry of Defence. *Global Strategic Trends: Out to 2040*. 4th ed. Development, Concepts and Doctrine Centre. January 2010. https://www.gov.uk/government/uploads/system/uploads /attachment_data/file/33717/GST4_v9_Feb10.pdf.

Unsinger, Peter C. "Three Intelligence Blunders in Korea." *International Journal of Intelligence and CounterIntelligence* 3, no. 4 (1989): 549–61.

Urquhart, Brian. *A Life in Peace and War*. New York: Harper & Row, 1987.

Valenta, Jiri. *Soviet Intervention in Czechoslovakia, 1968: Anatomy of a Decision*. Baltimore: Johns Hopkins University Press, 1979.

Vickers, Robert D., Jr. "The State of Warning Today." *Defense Intelligence Journal* 7, no. 2 (Fall 1998): 9–15.

Volkogonov, Dmitri. *Stalin: Triumph and Tragedy*. Edited and translated by Harold Shukman. New York: Grove Weidenfeld, 1988.

Voros, Joseph. "A Generic Foresight Process Framework." *Foresight* 5, no. 3 (2003): 10–21.

Voskian, Walter, and Randolph H. Pherson. *Analytic Production Guide for Managers of Intelligence and Business Analysts*. Reston, VA: Pherson Association, 2015.

Walsh, Patrick F. "Managing Emerging Health Security Threats since 9/11: The Role of Intelligence." *International Journal of Intelligence and CounterIntelligence* 29, no. 2 (2016): 341–67.

Warner, Michael. "Intelligence as Risk Sharing'" In *Intelligence Theory: Key Questions and Debates*. Edited by Peter Gill, Stephen Marrin, and Mark Phythian, 16–32. London: Routledge, 2009.

Watt, Donald Cameron. "British Intelligence and the Coming of the Second World War in Europe." In May, *Knowing One's Enemies*, 237–70.

Weiser, Benjamin. *A Secret Life: The Polish Officer, His Covert Mission, and the Price He Paid to Save His Country*. New York: PublicAffairs, 2004.

Whaley, Bart, and Jeffrey Busby. "Detecting Deception: Practice, Practitioners, and Theory." In *Strategic Denial and Deception: The Twenty-First Century Challenge*. Edited by Roy Godson and James J. Wirtz, 181–221. New Brunswick, NJ: Transaction, 2002.

Whaley, Barton. *Codeword Barbarossa*. Cambridge, MA: MIT Press, 1973.

———. "Covert Rearmament in Germany 1919–1939: Deception and Misperception." In Gooch and Perlmutter, *Military Deception and Strategic Surprise*, 3–39.

———. *Practise to Deceive: Learning Curves of Military Deception Planners*. Annapolis, MD: Naval Institute Press, 2016.

———. *Stratagem: Deception and Surprise in War*. Cambridge, MA: MIT Center for International Studies, 1969.

———. *Textbook of Political-Military Counterdeception*. Washington, DC: Foreign Denial and Deception Committee, National Intelligence Council, 2008.

———. "Toward a General Theory of Deception." In Gooch and Perlmutter, *Military Deception and Strategic Surprise*, 178–92.

———. *Turnabout and Deception: Crafting the Double Cross and the Theory of Outs*. Annapolis, MD: Naval Institute Press, 2016.

Wilder, Dennis C. "An Educated Consumer Is Our Best Customer." *Studies in Intelligence* 55, no. 2 (2011): 29–37.

Wilson, James M. V. "Signal Recognition during the Emergence of Pandemic Influenza Type A/H1N1: A Commercial Disease Intelligence Unit's Perspective." *Intelligence and National Security* 32, no. 2 (2017): 222–30.

Wirtz, James J. "The Art of Intelligence Autopsy." *Intelligence and National Security* 29, no. 1 (2014): 1–18.

———. "The Cyber Pearl Harbor." *Intelligence and National Security* 32, no. 6 (2017): 758–67.

———. "Indications and Warning in an Age of Uncertainty." *International Journal of Intelligence and CounterIntelligence* 26, no. 3 (2013): 550–62.

———. "Miscalculation, Surprise and American Intelligence after the Cold War." *International Journal of Intelligence and CounterIntelligence* 5, no. 1 (1991): 1–16.

———. *The Tet Offensive: Intelligence Failure in War*. Ithaca, NY: Cornell University Press, 1991.

———. "Theory of Surprise." In Betts and Mahnken, *Paradoxes of Strategic Intelligence*, 101–16.

Wohlstetter, Roberta. "Cuba and Pearl Harbor: Hindsight and Foresight." Memorandum RM-4328-ISA. RAND Corp., April 1965.

————. *Pearl Harbor: Warning and Decision.* Stanford, CA: Stanford University Press, 1962.

Yarhi-Milo, Keren. *Knowing the Adversary: Leaders, Intelligence, and Assessments of Intentions in International Relations.* Princeton, NJ: Princeton University Press, 2014.

Yeh, Puong Fei. "Using Prediction Markets to Enhance US Intelligence Capabilities: A 'Standard & Poors 500 Index' for Intelligence." *Studies in Intelligence* 50, no. 4 (2006): 137–49.

Zegart, Amy B. "'CNN with Secrets': 9/11, the CIA, and the Organizational Roots of Failure." *International Journal of Intelligence and CounterIntelligence* 20, no. 1 (March 2007): 18–49.

————. "September 11 and the Adaptation Failure of US Intelligence Agencies." *International Security* 29, no. 1 (Spring 2005): 78–111.

————. *Spying Blind: The CIA, the FBI, and the Origins of 9/11.* Princeton, NJ: Princeton University Press, 2009.

Zelikow, Philip. "American Economic Intelligence: Past Practice and Future Principles." *Intelligence and National Security* 12, no. 1 (1997): 164–77.

————. "The Evolution of Intelligence Reform, 2002–2004." *Studies in Intelligence* 56, no. 3 (September 2012): 1–20.

Zenko, Micah. *Red Team: How to Succeed by Thinking like the Enemy.* New York: Basic, 2015.

Zenko, Micah, and Rebecca R. Friedman. "UN Early Warning for Preventing Conflict." *International Peacekeeping* 18, no. 1 (2011): 21–37.

Ziegler, Charles A. "Intelligence Assessments of Soviet Atomic Capability, 1945–1949: Myths, Monopolies and Maskirovka." *Intelligence and National Security* 12, no. 4 (1997): 1–24.

Index

About the Authors

John A. Gentry is adjunct professor with the Center for Security Studies of Georgetown University's Walsh School of Foreign Service and adjunct associate professor with the School of International and Public Affairs, Columbia University. He was for twelve years an intelligence analyst at the Central Intelligence Agency, where he worked mainly economic issues associated with the Soviet Union and Warsaw Pact countries; during 1987–89 he was senior analyst on the staff of National Intelligence Officers for Warning John Bird and Charles Allen. He is a retired US Army Reserve officer, with most assignments in special operations and intelligence arenas. He was mobilized in 1996 and spent much of that year as a civil affairs officer in Bosnia. He formerly taught at the College of International Security Affairs, a part of the National Defense University, and at the National Intelligence University, where he taught parts of Strategic Warning Analysis Certificate Program. He has been an adjunct professor at George Mason University. His research interests primarily are in intelligence and security studies. His most recent book is *How Wars Are Won and Lost: Vulnerability and Military Power*. He received his PhD in political science from the George Washington University.

Joseph S. Gordon is professor and Colin Powell Chair for Intelligence Analysis at the National Intelligence University, where he began teaching in 1981. In 1986 he became director of European studies, establishing a seven-course concentration in European studies. In 1991 he became chair of the military history and strategy department. In 1993, he became an analyst at the Defense Intelligence Agency, where he worked technology transfer and European analytic issues. He served as a Senior Intelligence Officer in the Yugoslav Task Force in the Pentagon (deploying twice to the Balkans), as chief of the Diplomatic Intelligence Support Cell at the US embassy in Sarajevo, and as the DIA representative at NATO Headquarters in Kosovo. From 2003 to 2005, he was the DIA Senior Command Representative at NATO Headquarters in Brussels before returning to NIU. He established the Strategic Warning Analysis Certificate Program at NIU in 2012 as part of the restoration of Defense Department Warning, which had been abolished in 2008. He was president of the International Association for Intelligence Education from 2011 to 2015. He is a retired

US Army Reserve intelligence officer, having served three years in Germany on active duty, commanded reserve intelligence organizations at three levels, and taught at the Army Command and General Staff College and the Army War College. He has published on psychological operations, European history, and security issues. He received a PhD in European history from Duke University.

CPSIA information can be obtained
at www.ICGtesting.com
Printed in the USA
LVHW062109130421
684404LV00026B/298